OAT

SECRETS

Study Guide
Your Key to Exam Success

OAT Exam Review for the
Optometry Admission Test

Published by
Mometrix Test Preparation
OAT Exam Secrets Test Prep Staff

Written and edited by the OAT Exam Secrets Test Prep Team

Printed in the United States of America

This paper meets the requirements of ANSI/NISO Z39.48-1992 (Permanence of Paper).

Mometrix offers volume discount pricing to institutions. For more information or a price quote, please contact our sales department at sales@mometrix.com or 888-248-1219.

Mometrix Test Preparation is not affiliated with or endorsed by any official testing organization. All organizational and test names are trademarks of their respective owners.

ISBN 13: 978-1-61072-386-2
ISBN 10: 1-61072-386-4

Dear Future Exam Success Story:

Congratulations on your purchase of our study guide. Our goal in writing our study guide was to cover the content on the test, as well as provide insight into typical test taking mistakes and how to overcome them.

Standardized tests are a key component of being successful, which only increases the importance of doing well in the high-pressure high-stakes environment of test day. How well you do on this test will have a significant impact on your future- and we have the research and practical advice to help you execute on test day.

The product you're reading now is designed to exploit weaknesses in the test itself, and help you avoid the most common errors test takers frequently make.

How to use this study guide

We don't want to waste your time. Our study guide is fast-paced and fluff-free. We suggest going through it a number of times, as repetition is an important part of learning new information and concepts.

First, read through the study guide completely to get a feel for the content and organization. Read the general success strategies first, and then proceed to the content sections. Each tip has been carefully selected for its effectiveness.

Second, read through the study guide again, and take notes in the margins and highlight those sections where you may have a particular weakness.

Finally, bring the manual with you on test day and study it before the exam begins.

Your success is our success

We would be delighted to hear about your success. Send us an email and tell us your story. Thanks for your business and we wish you continued success-

Sincerely,

Mometrix Test Preparation Team

Need more help? Check out our flashcards at: http://MometrixFlashcards.com/OAT

TABLE OF CONTENTS

Top 20 Test Taking Tips

1. Carefully follow all the test registration procedures
2. Know the test directions, duration, topics, question types, how many questions
3. Setup a flexible study schedule at least 3-4 weeks before test day
4. Study during the time of day you are most alert, relaxed, and stress free
5. Maximize your learning style; visual learner use visual study aids, auditory learner use auditory study aids
6. Focus on your weakest knowledge base
7. Find a study partner to review with and help clarify questions
8. Practice, practice, practice
9. Get a good night's sleep; don't try to cram the night before the test
10. Eat a well balanced meal
11. Know the exact physical location of the testing site; drive the route to the site prior to test day
12. Bring a set of ear plugs; the testing center could be noisy
13. Wear comfortable, loose fitting, layered clothing to the testing center; prepare for it to be either cold or hot during the test
14. Bring at least 2 current forms of ID to the testing center
15. Arrive to the test early; be prepared to wait and be patient
16. Eliminate the obviously wrong answer choices, then guess the first remaining choice
17. Pace yourself; don't rush, but keep working and move on if you get stuck
18. Maintain a positive attitude even if the test is going poorly
19. Keep your first answer unless you are positive it is wrong
20. Check your work, don't make a careless mistake

The Reading Comprehension Test

Comprehension Skills

One of the most important skills in reading comprehension is the identification of **topics** and **main ideas.** There is a subtle difference between these two features. The topic is the subject of a text, or what the text is about. The main idea, on the other hand, is the most important point being made by the author. The topic is usually expressed in a few words at the most, while the main idea often needs a full sentence to be completely defined. As an example, a short passage might have the topic of penguins and the main idea *Penguins are different from other birds in many ways.* In most nonfiction writing, the topic and the main idea will be stated directly, often in a sentence at the very beginning or end of the text. When being tested on an understanding of the author's topic, the reader can quickly *skim* the passage for the general idea, stopping to read only the first sentence of each paragraph. A paragraph's first sentence is often (but not always) the main topic sentence, and it gives you a summary of the content of the paragraph. However, there are cases in which the reader must figure out an unstated topic or main idea. In these instances, the student must read every sentence of the text, and try to come up with an overarching idea that is supported by each of those sentences.

> ➤ **Review Video: Topic and Main Idea**
> *Visit mometrix.com/academy and enter Code:* **407801**

While the main idea is the overall premise of a story, **supporting details** provide evidence and backing for the main point. In order to show that a main idea is correct, or valid, the author needs to add details that prove their point. All texts contain details, but they are only classified as supporting details when they serve to reinforce some larger point. Supporting details are most commonly found in informative and persuasive texts. In some cases, they will be clearly indicated with words like *for example* or *for instance*, or they will be enumerated with words like *first*, *second*, and *last*. However, they may not be indicated with special words. As a reader, it is important to consider whether the author's supporting details really back up his or her main point. Supporting details can be factual and correct but still not relevant to the author's point. Conversely, supporting details can seem pertinent but be ineffective because they are based on opinion or assertions that cannot be proven.

> ➤ **Review Video: Supporting Details**
> *Visit mometrix.com/academy and enter Code:* **396297**

An example of a main idea is: "Giraffes live in the Serengeti of Africa." A supporting detail about giraffes could be: "A giraffe uses its long neck to reach twigs and leaves on trees." The main idea gives the general idea that the text is about giraffes. The supporting detail gives a specific fact about how the giraffes eat.

As opposed to a main idea, themes are seldom expressed directly in a text, so they can be difficult to identify. A **theme** is an issue, an idea, or a question raised by the text. For instance, a theme of William Shakespeare's *Hamlet* is indecision, as the title character explores his own psyche and the results of his failure to make bold choices. A great work of literature may have many themes, and the reader is justified in identifying any for which he or she can find support. One common characteristic of themes is that they raise more questions than they answer. In a good piece of fiction, the author is not always trying to convince the reader, but is instead trying to elevate the reader's perspective and encourage him to consider the themes more deeply. When reading, one can identify themes by constantly asking what general issues the text is addressing. A good way to evaluate an author's approach to a theme is to begin reading with a question in mind (for example, how does this text approach the theme of love?) and then look for evidence in the text that addresses that question.

> **Review Video: <u>Theme</u>**
*Visit **mometrix.com/academy** and enter **Code: 732074***

Purposes for Writing

In order to be an effective reader, one must pay attention to the author's **position** and purpose. Even those texts that seem objective and impartial, like textbooks, have some sort of position and bias. Readers need to take these positions into account when considering the author's message. When an author uses emotional language or clearly favors one side of an argument, his position is clear. However, the author's position may be evident not only in what he writes, but in what he doesn't write. For this reason, it is sometimes necessary to review some other texts on the same topic in order to develop a view of the author's position. If this is not possible, then it may be useful to acquire a little background personal information about the author. When the only source of information is the text, however, the reader should look for language and argumentation that seems to indicate a particular stance on the subject.

Identifying the **purpose** of an author is usually easier than identifying her position. In most cases, the author has no interest in hiding his or her purpose. A text that is meant to entertain, for instance, should be obviously written to please the reader. Most narratives, or stories, are written to entertain, though they may also inform or persuade. Informative texts are easy to identify as well. The most difficult purpose of a text to identify is persuasion, because the author has an interest in making this purpose hard to detect. When a person knows that the author is trying to convince him, he is automatically more wary and skeptical of the argument. For this reason persuasive texts often try to establish an entertaining tone, hoping to amuse the reader into agreement, or an informative tone, hoping to create an appearance of authority and objectivity.

An author's purpose is often evident in the organization of the text. For instance, if the text has headings and subheadings, if key terms are in bold, and if the author makes his main idea clear from the beginning, then the likely purpose of the text is to inform. If the author begins by making a claim and then makes various arguments to support that claim, the purpose is probably to persuade. If the author is telling a story, or is more interested in holding the attention of the reader than in making a particular point or delivering information, then his purpose is most likely to entertain. As a reader, it is best to judge an author on how well he accomplishes his purpose. In other words, it is not entirely fair to complain that a textbook is boring: if the text is clear and easy to understand, then the author has done his job. Similarly, a storyteller should not be judged too harshly for getting some facts wrong, so long as he is able to give pleasure to the reader.

> **Review Video: <u>Purpose</u>**
*Visit **mometrix.com/academy** and enter **Code: 511819***

The author's purpose for writing will affect his writing style and the response of the reader. In a **persuasive essay**, the author is attempting to change the reader's mind or convince him of something he did not believe previously. There are several identifying characteristics of persuasive writing. One is opinion presented as fact. When an author attempts to persuade the reader, he often presents his or her opinions as if they were fact. A reader must be on guard for statements that sound factual but which cannot be subjected to research, observation, or experiment. Another characteristic of persuasive writing is emotional language. An author will often try to play on the reader's emotion by appealing to his sympathy or sense of morality. When an author uses colorful or evocative language with the intent of arousing the reader's passions, it is likely that he is attempting to persuade. Finally, in many cases a persuasive text will give an unfair explanation of opposing positions, if these positions are mentioned at all.

An **informative text** is written to educate and enlighten the reader. Informative texts are almost always nonfiction, and are rarely structured as a story. The intention of an informative text is to deliver information in the most comprehensible way possible, so the structure of the text is likely to be very clear. In an informative text, the thesis statement is often in the first sentence. The author may use some colorful language, but is likely to put more emphasis on clarity and precision. Informative essays do not typically appeal to the emotions. They often contain facts and figures, and rarely include the opinion of the author. Sometimes a persuasive essay can resemble an informative essay, especially if the author maintains an even tone and presents his or her views as if they were established fact.

The success or failure of an author's intent to **entertain** is determined by those who read the author's work. Entertaining texts may be either fiction or nonfiction, and they may describe real or imagined people, places, and events. Entertaining texts are often narratives, or stories. A text that is written to entertain is likely to contain colorful language that engages the imagination and the emotions. Such writing often features a great deal of figurative language, which typically enlivens its subject matter with images and analogies. Though an entertaining text is not usually written to persuade or inform, it may accomplish both of these tasks. An entertaining text may appeal to the reader's emotions and cause him or her to think differently about a particular subject. In any case, entertaining texts tend to showcase the personality of the author more so than do other types of writing.

When an author intends to **express feelings,** she may use colorful and evocative language. An author may write emotionally for any number of reasons. Sometimes, the author will do so because she is describing a personal situation of great pain or happiness. Sometimes an author is attempting to persuade the reader, and so will use emotion to stir up the passions. It can be easy to identify this kind of expression when the writer uses phrases like *I felt* and *I sense*. However, sometimes the author will simply describe feelings without introducing them. As a reader, it is important to recognize when an author is expressing emotion, and not to become overwhelmed by sympathy or passion. A reader should maintain some detachment so that he or she can still evaluate the strength of the author's argument or the quality of the writing.

In a sense, almost all writing is descriptive, insofar as it seeks to describe events, ideas, or people to the reader. Some texts, however, are primarily concerned with **description**. A descriptive text focuses on a particular subject, and attempts to depict it in a way that will be clear to the reader. Descriptive texts contain many adjectives and adverbs, words that give shades of meaning and create a more detailed mental picture for the reader. A descriptive text fails when it is unclear or vague to the reader. On the other hand, however, a descriptive text that compiles too much detail can be boring and overwhelming to the reader. A descriptive text will certainly be informative, and it may be persuasive and entertaining as well. Descriptive writing is a challenge for the author, but when it is done well, it can be fun to read.

Writing Devices

Authors will use different stylistic and writing devices to make their meaning more clearly understood. One of those devices is comparison and contrast. When an author describes the ways in which two things are alike, he or she is **comparing** them. When the author describes the ways in which two things are different, he or she is **contrasting** them. The "compare and contrast" essay is one of the most common forms in nonfiction. It is often signaled with certain words: a comparison may be indicated with such words as *both, same, like, too,* and *as well*; while a contrast may be indicated by words like *but, however, on the other hand, instead,* and *yet*. Of course, comparisons and contrasts may be implicit without using any such signaling language. A single sentence may both compare and contrast. Consider the sentence *Brian and Sheila love ice cream, but Brian prefers vanilla and Sheila prefers strawberry*. In one sentence, the author has described both a similarity (love of ice cream) and a difference (favorite flavor).

> ➤ **Review Video: <u>Compare and Contrast</u>**
> Visit *mometrix.com/academy* and enter *Code:* **798319**

One of the most common text structures is **cause and effect**. A cause is an act or event that makes something happen, and an effect is the thing that happens as a result of that cause. A cause-and-effect relationship is not always explicit, but there are some words in English that signal causality, such as *since, because,* and *as a result*. As an example, consider the sentence *Because the sky was clear, Ron did not bring an umbrella*. The cause is the clear sky, and the effect is that Ron did not bring an umbrella. However, sometimes the cause-and-effect relationship will not be clearly noted. For instance, the sentence *He was late and missed the meeting* does not contain any signaling words, but it still contains a cause (he was late) and an effect (he missed the meeting). It is possible for a single cause to have multiple effects, or for a single effect to have multiple causes. Also, an effect can in turn be the cause of another effect, in what is known as a cause-and-effect chain.

Authors often use analogies to add meaning to the text. An **analogy** is a comparison of two things. The words in the analogy are connected by a certain, often undetermined relationship. Look at this analogy: moo is to cow as quack is to duck. This analogy compares the sound that a cow makes with the sound that a duck makes. Even if the word 'quack' was not given, one could figure out it is the correct word to complete the analogy based on the relationship between the words 'moo' and 'cow'. Some common relationships for analogies include synonyms, antonyms, part to whole, definition, and actor to action.

Another element that impacts a text is the author's point of view. The **point of view** of a text is the perspective from which it is told. The author will always have a point of view about a story before he draws up a plot line. The author will know what events they want to take place, how they want the characters to interact, and how the story will resolve. An author will also have an opinion on the topic, or series of events, which is presented in the story, based on their own prior experience and beliefs.

The two main points of view that authors use are first person and third person. If the narrator of the story is also the main character, or *protagonist*, the text is written in first-person point of view. In first person, the author writes with the word *I*. Third-person point of view is probably the most common point of view that authors use. Using third person, authors refer to each character using the words *he* or *she*. In third-person omniscient, the narrator is not a character in the story and tells the story of all of the characters at the same time.

> ➤ **Review Video: Point of View**
> *Visit **mometrix.com/academy** and enter Code:* **383336**

A good writer will use **transitional words** and phrases to guide the reader through the text. You are no doubt familiar with the common transitions, though you may never have considered how they operate. Some transitional phrases (*after, before, during, in the middle of*) give information about time. Some indicate that an example is about to be given (*for example, in fact, for instance*). Writers use them to compare (*also, likewise*) and contrast (*however, but, yet*). Transitional words and phrases can suggest addition (*and, also, furthermore, moreover*) and logical relationships (*if, then, therefore, as a result, since*). Finally, transitional words and phrases can demarcate the steps in a process (*first, second, last*). You should incorporate transitional words and phrases where they will orient your reader and illuminate the structure of your composition.

> ➤ **Review Video: Transitional Words and Phrases**
> *Visit **mometrix.com/academy** and enter Code:* **197796**

Types of Passages

A **narrative** passage is a story. Narratives can be fiction or nonfiction. However, there are a few elements that a text must have in order to be classified as a narrative. To begin with, the text must have a plot. That is, it must describe a series of events. If it is a good narrative, these events will be interesting and emotionally engaging to the reader. A narrative also has characters. These could be people, animals, or even inanimate objects, so long as they participate in the plot. A narrative passage often contains figurative language, which is meant to stimulate the imagination of the reader by making comparisons and observations. A metaphor, which is a description of one thing in terms of another, is a common piece of figurative language. *The moon was a frosty snowball* is an example of a metaphor: it is obviously untrue in the literal sense, but it suggests a certain mood for the reader. Narratives often proceed in a clear sequence, but they do not need to do so.

An **expository** passage aims to inform and enlighten the reader. It is nonfiction and usually centers around a simple, easily defined topic. Since the goal of exposition is to teach, such a passage should be as clear as possible. It is common for an expository passage to contain helpful organizing words, like *first, next, for example*, and *therefore*. These words keep the reader oriented in the text. Although expository passages do not need to feature colorful language and artful writing, they are often more effective when they do. For a reader, the challenge of expository passages is to maintain steady attention. Expository passages are not always about subjects in which a reader will naturally be interested, and the writer is often more concerned with clarity and comprehensibility than with engaging the reader. For this reason, many expository passages are dull. Making notes is a good way to maintain focus when reading an expository passage.

A **technical** passage is written to describe a complex object or process. Technical writing is common in medical and technological fields, in which complicated mathematical, scientific, and engineering ideas need to be explained simply and clearly. To ease comprehension, a technical passage usually proceeds in a very logical order. Technical passages often have clear headings and subheadings, which are used to keep the reader oriented in the text. It is also common for these passages to break sections up with numbers or letters. Many technical passages look more like an outline than a piece of prose. The amount of jargon or difficult vocabulary will vary in a technical passage depending on the intended audience. As much as possible, technical passages try to avoid language that the reader will have to research in order to understand the message. Of course, it is not always possible to avoid jargon.

A **persuasive** passage is meant to change the reader's mind or lead her into agreement with the author. The persuasive intent may be obvious, or it may be quite difficult to discern. In some cases, a persuasive passage will be indistinguishable from an informative passage: it will make an assertion and offer supporting details. However, a persuasive passage is more likely to make claims based on opinion and to appeal to the reader's emotions. Persuasive passages may not describe alternate positions and, when they do, they often display significant bias. It may be clear that a persuasive passage is giving the author's viewpoint, or the passage may adopt a seemingly objective tone. A persuasive passage is successful if it can make a convincing argument and win the trust of the reader.

A persuasive essay will likely focus on one central argument, but it may make many smaller claims along the way. These are subordinate arguments with which the reader must agree if he or she is going to agree with the central argument. The central argument will only be as strong as the subordinate claims. These claims should be rooted in fact and observation, rather than subjective judgment. The best persuasive essays provide enough supporting detail to justify claims without overwhelming the reader. Remember that a fact must be susceptible to independent verification: that is, it must be something the reader could confirm. Also, statistics are only effective when they take into account possible objections. For instance, a statistic on the number of foreclosed houses would only be useful if it was taken over a defined interval and in a defined area. Most readers are wary of statistics, because they are so often misleading. If possible, a persuasive essay should always include references so that the reader can obtain more information. Of course, this means that the writer's accuracy and fairness may be judged by the inquiring reader.

Opinions are formed by emotion as well as reason, and persuasive writers often appeal to the feelings of the reader. Although readers should always be skeptical of this technique, it is often used in a proper and ethical manner. For instance, there are many subjects that have an obvious emotional component, and therefore cannot be completely treated without an appeal to the emotions. Consider an article on drunk driving: it makes sense to include some specific examples that will alarm or sadden the reader. After all, drunk driving often has serious and tragic consequences. Emotional appeals are not appropriate, however, when they attempt to mislead the reader. For instance, in political advertisements it is common to emphasize the patriotism of the preferred candidate, because this will encourage the audience to link their own positive feelings about the country with their opinion of the candidate. However, these ads often imply that the other candidate is unpatriotic, which in most cases is far from the truth. Another common and improper emotional appeal is the use of loaded language, as for instance referring to an avidly religious person as a "fanatic" or a passionate environmentalist as a "tree hugger." These terms introduce an emotional component that detracts from the argument.

Critical Thinking Skills

Opinions, Facts, & Fallacies

Critical thinking skills are mastered through understanding various types of writing and the different purposes that authors have for writing the way they do. Every author writes for a purpose. Understanding that purpose, and how they accomplish their goal, will allow you to critique the writing and determine whether or not you agree with their conclusions.

Readers must always be conscious of the distinction between fact and opinion. A **fact** can be subjected to analysis and can be either proved or disproved. An **opinion**, on the other hand, is the author's personal feeling, which may not be alterable by research, evidence, or argument. If the author writes that the distance from New York to Boston is about two hundred miles, he is stating a fact. But if he writes that New York is too crowded, then he is giving an opinion, because there is no objective standard for overpopulation. An opinion may be indicated by words like *believe*, *think*, or *feel*. Also, an opinion may be supported by facts: for instance, the author might give the population density of New York as a reason for why it is overcrowded. An opinion supported by fact tends to be more convincing. When authors support their opinions with other opinions, the reader is unlikely to be moved.

Facts should be presented to the reader from reliable sources. An opinion is what the author thinks about a given topic. An opinion is not common knowledge or proven by expert sources, but it is information that the author believes and wants the reader to consider. To distinguish between fact and opinion, a reader needs to look at the type of source that is presenting information, what information backs-up a claim, and whether or not the author may be motivated to have a certain point of view on a given topic. For example, if a panel of scientists has conducted multiple studies on the effectiveness of taking a certain vitamin, the results are more likely to be factual than if a company selling a vitamin claims that taking the vitamin can produce positive effects. The company is motivated to sell its product, while the scientists are using the scientific method to prove a theory. If the author uses words such as "I think...", the statement is an opinion.

> ➤ **Review Video: Fact or Opinion**
> *Visit **mometrix.com/academy** and enter **Code: 870899***

In their attempt to persuade, writers often make mistakes in their thinking patterns and writing choices. It's important to understand these so you can make an informed decision. Every author has a point of view, but when an author ignores reasonable counterarguments or distorts opposing viewpoints, she is demonstrating a **bias**. A bias is evident whenever the author is unfair or inaccurate in his or her presentation. Bias may be intentional or unintentional, but it should always alert the reader to be skeptical of the argument being made. It should be noted that a biased author may still be correct. However, the author will be correct in spite of her bias, not because of it. A **stereotype** is like a bias, except that it is specifically applied to a group or place. Stereotyping is considered to be particularly abhorrent because it promotes negative generalizations about people. Many people are familiar with some of the hateful stereotypes of certain ethnic, religious, and cultural groups. Readers should be very wary of authors who stereotype. These faulty assumptions typically reveal the author's ignorance and lack of curiosity.

> ➤ **Review Video: Bias and Stereotype**
> *Visit **mometrix.com/academy** and enter **Code: 644829***

Sometimes, authors will **appeal to the reader's emotion** in an attempt to persuade or to distract the reader from the weakness of the argument. For instance, the author may try to inspire the pity of the reader by delivering a heart-rending story. An author also might use the bandwagon approach, in which he suggests that his opinion is correct because it is held by the majority. Some authors resort to name-calling, in which insults and harsh words are delivered to the opponent in an attempt to distract. In advertising, a common appeal is the testimonial, in which a famous person endorses a product. Of course, the fact that a celebrity likes something should not really mean anything to the reader. These and other emotional appeals are usually evidence of poor reasoning and a weak argument.

> ➤ **Review Video: <u>Appeal to Emotions</u>**
> *Visit **mometrix.com/academy** and enter **Code: 163442***

Certain *logical fallacies* are frequent in writing. A logical fallacy is a failure of reasoning. As a reader, it is important to recognize logical fallacies, because they diminish the value of the author's message. The four most common logical fallacies in writing are the false analogy, circular reasoning, false dichotomy, and overgeneralization. In a **false analogy**, the author suggests that two things are similar, when in fact they are different. This fallacy is often committed when the author is attempting to convince the reader that something unknown is like something relatively familiar. The author takes advantage of the reader's ignorance to make this false comparison. One example might be the following statement: *Failing to tip a waitress is like stealing money out of somebody's wallet.* Of course, failing to tip is very rude, especially when the service has been good, but people are not arrested for failing to tip as they would for stealing money from a wallet. To compare stingy diners with thieves is a false analogy.

> ➤ **Review Video: <u>False Analogy</u>**
> *Visit **mometrix.com/academy** and enter **Code: 865045***

Circular reasoning is one of the more difficult logical fallacies to identify, because it is typically hidden behind dense language and complicated sentences. Reasoning is described as circular when it offers no support for assertions other than restating them in different words. Put another way, a circular argument refers to itself as evidence of truth. A simple example of circular argument is when a person uses a word to define itself, such as saying *Niceness is the state of being nice*. If the reader does not know what *nice* means, then this definition will not be very useful. In a text, circular reasoning is usually more complex. For instance, an author might say *Poverty is a problem for society because it creates trouble for people throughout the community*. It is redundant to say that poverty is a problem because it creates trouble. When an author engages in circular reasoning, it is often because he or she has not fully thought out the argument, or cannot come up with any legitimate justifications.

> ➤ **Review Video: <u>Circular Reasoning</u>**
> *Visit **mometrix.com/academy** and enter **Code: 398925***

One of the most common logical fallacies is the **false dichotomy**, in which the author creates an artificial sense that there are only two possible alternatives in a situation. This fallacy is common when the author has an agenda and wants to give the impression that his view is the only sensible one. A false dichotomy has the effect of limiting the reader's options and imagination. An example of a false dichotomy is the statement *You need to go to the party with me, otherwise you'll just be bored* *at home*. The speaker suggests that the only other possibility besides being at the party is being bored at home. But this is not true, as it is perfectly possible to be entertained at home, or even to go somewhere other than the party. Readers should always be wary of the false dichotomy: when an author limits alternatives, it is always wise to ask whether he is being valid.

> ➤ **Review Video: <u>False Dichotomy</u>**
> *Visit **mometrix.com/academy** and enter **Code: 484397***

Overgeneralization is a logical fallacy in which the author makes a claim that is so broad it cannot be proved or disproved. In most cases, overgeneralization occurs when the author wants to create an illusion of authority, or when he is using sensational language to sway the opinion of the reader. For instance, in the sentence *Everybody knows that she is a terrible teacher*, the author makes an assumption that cannot really be believed. This kind of statement is made when the author wants to create the illusion of consensus when none actually exists: it may be that most people have a negative view of the teacher, but to say that *everybody* feels that way is an exaggeration. When a reader spots overgeneralization, she should become skeptical about the argument that is being made, because an author will often try to hide a weak or unsupported assertion behind authoritative language.

> ➤ **Review Video: <u>Overgeneralization</u>**
> *Visit **mometrix.com/academy** and enter **Code: 367357***

Two other types of logical fallacies are **slippery slope** arguments and **hasty generalizations**. In a slippery slope argument, the author says that if something happens, it automatically means that something else will happen as a result, even though this may not be true. (i.e., just because you study hard does not mean you are going to ace the test). "Hasty generalization" is drawing a conclusion too early, without finishing analyzing the details of the argument. Writers of persuasive texts often use these techniques because they are very effective. In order to **identify logical fallacies**, readers need to read carefully and ask questions as they read. Thinking critically means not taking everything at face value. Readers need to critically evaluate an author's argument to make sure that the logic used is sound.

Organization of the Text

The way a text is organized can help the reader to understand more clearly the author's intent and his conclusions. There are various ways to organize a text, and each one has its own purposes and uses.

Some nonfiction texts are organized to **present a problem** followed by a solution. In this type of text, it is common for the problem to be explained before the solution is offered. In some cases, as when the problem is well known, the solution may be briefly introduced at the beginning. The entire passage may focus on the solution, and the problem will be referenced only occasionally. Some texts will outline multiple solutions to a problem, leaving the reader to choose among them. If the author has an interest or an allegiance to one solution, he may fail to mention or may describe inaccurately some of the other solutions. Readers should be careful of the author's agenda when reading a problem-solution text. Only by understanding the author's point of view and interests can one develop a proper judgment of the proposed solution.

Authors need to organize information logically so the reader can follow it and locate information within the text. Two common organizational structures are cause and effect and chronological order. When using **chronological order**, the author presents information in the order that it happened. For example, biographies are written in chronological order; the subject's birth and childhood are presented first, followed by their adult life, and lastly by the events leading up to the person's death.

In **cause and effect**, an author presents one thing that makes something else happen. For example, if one were to go to bed very late, they would be tired. The cause is going to bed late, with the effect of being tired the next day.

It can be tricky to identify the cause-and-effect relationships in a text, but there are a few ways to approach this task. To begin with, these relationships are often signaled with certain terms. When an author uses words like *because*, *since*, *in order*, and *so*, she is likely describing a cause-and-effect relationship. Consider the sentence, "He called her because he needed the homework." This is a simple causal relationship, in which the cause was his need for the homework and the effect was his phone call. Not all cause-and-effect relationships are marked in this way, however. Consider the sentences, "He called her. He needed the homework." When the cause-and-effect relationship is not indicated with a keyword, it can be discovered by asking why something happened. He called her: why? The answer is in the next sentence: He needed the homework.

Persuasive essays, in which an author tries to make a convincing argument and change the reader's mind, usually include cause-and-effect relationships. However, these relationships should not always be taken at face value. An author frequently will assume a cause or take an effect for granted. To read a persuasive essay effectively, one needs to judge the cause-and-effect relationships the author is presenting. For instance, imagine an author wrote the following: "The parking deck has been unprofitable because people would prefer to ride their bikes." The relationship is clear: the cause is that people prefer to ride their bikes, and the effect is that the parking deck has been unprofitable. However, a reader should consider whether this argument is conclusive. Perhaps there are other reasons for the failure of the parking deck: a down economy, excessive fees, etc. Too often, authors present causal relationships as if they are fact rather than opinion. Readers should be on the alert for these dubious claims.

Thinking critically about ideas and conclusions can seem like a daunting task. One way to make it easier is to understand the basic elements of ideas and writing techniques. Looking at the way different ideas relate to each other can be a good way for the reader to begin his analysis. For instance, sometimes writers will write about two different ideas that are in opposition to each other. The analysis of these opposing ideas is known as **contrast**. Contrast is often marred by the author's obvious partiality to one of the ideas. A discerning reader will be put off by an author who does not engage in a fair fight. In an analysis of opposing ideas, both ideas should be presented in their clearest and most reasonable terms. If the author does prefer a side, he should avoid indicating this preference with pejorative language. An analysis of opposing ideas should proceed through the major differences point by point, with a full explanation of each side's view. For instance, in an analysis of capitalism and communism, it would be important to outline each side's view on labor, markets, prices, personal responsibility, etc. It would be less effective to describe the theory of communism and then explain how capitalism has thrived in the West. An analysis of opposing views should present each side in the same manner.

Many texts follow the **compare-and-contrast** model, in which the similarities and differences between two ideas or things are explored. Analysis of the similarities between ideas is called comparison. In order for a comparison to work, the author must place the ideas or things in an equivalent structure. That is, the author must present the ideas in the same way. Imagine an author wanted to show the similarities between cricket and baseball. The correct way to do so would be to summarize the equipment and rules for each game. It would be incorrect to summarize the equipment of cricket and then lay out the history of baseball, since this would make it impossible for the reader to see the similarities. It is perhaps too obvious to say that an analysis of similar ideas should emphasize the similarities. Of course, the author should take care to include any differences that must be mentioned. Often, these small differences will only reinforce the more general similarity.

Drawing Conclusions

Authors should have a clear purpose in mind while writing. Especially when reading informational texts, it is important to understand the logical conclusion of the author's ideas. **Identifying this logical conclusion** can help the reader understand whether he agrees with the writer or not. Identifying a logical conclusion is much like making an inference: it requires the reader to combine the information given by the text with what he already knows to make a supportable assertion. If a passage is written well, then the conclusion should be obvious even when it is unstated. If the author intends the reader to draw a certain conclusion, then all of his argumentation and detail should be leading toward it. One way to approach the task of drawing conclusions is to make brief notes of all the points made by the author. When these are arranged on paper, they may clarify the logical conclusion. Another way to approach conclusions is to consider whether the reasoning of the author raises any pertinent questions. Sometimes it will be possible to draw several conclusions from a passage, and on occasion these will be conclusions that were never imagined by the author. It is essential, however, that these conclusions be supported directly by the text.

The term **text evidence** refers to information that supports a main point or points in a story, and can help lead the reader to a conclusion. Information used as *text evidence* is precise, descriptive, and factual. A main point is often followed by supporting details that provide evidence to back-up a claim. For example, a story may include the claim that winter occurs during opposite months in the Northern and Southern hemispheres. *Text evidence* based on this claim may include countries where winter occurs in opposite months, along with reasons that winter occurs at different times of the year in separate hemispheres (due to the tilt of the Earth as it rotates around the sun).

Readers interpret text and respond to it in a number of ways. Using textual support helps defend your response or interpretation because it roots your thinking in the text. You are interpreting based on information in the text and not simply your own ideas. When crafting a response, look for important quotes and details from the text to help bolster your argument. If you are writing about a character's personality trait, for example, use details from the text to show that the character acted in such a way. You can also include statistics and facts from a nonfiction text to strengthen your response. For example, instead of writing, "A lot of people use cell phones," use statistics to provide the exact number. This strengthens your argument because it is more precise.

The text used to support an argument can be the argument's downfall if it is not credible. A text is **credible**, or believable, when the author is knowledgeable and objective, or unbiased. The author's motivations for writing the text play a critical role in determining the credibility of the text and must be evaluated when assessing that credibility. The author's motives should be for the dissemination of information. The purpose of the text should be to inform or describe, not to persuade. When an author writes a persuasive text, he has the motivation that the reader will do what they want. The extent of the author's knowledge of the topic and their motivation must be evaluated when assessing the credibility of a text. Reports written about the Ozone layer by an environmental scientist and a hairdresser will have a different level of credibility.

After determining your own opinion and evaluating the credibility of your supporting text, it is sometimes necessary to communicate your ideas and findings to others. When **writing a response to a text**, it is important to use elements of the text to support your assertion or defend your position. Using supporting evidence from the text strengthens the argument because the reader can see how in depth the writer read the original piece and based their response on the details and facts within that text. Elements of text that can be used in a response include: facts, details, statistics, and direct quotations from the text. When writing a response, one must make sure they indicate which information comes from the original text and then base their discussion, argument, or defense around this information.

A reader should always be drawing conclusions from the text. Sometimes conclusions are implied from written information, and other times the information is **stated directly** within the passage. It is always more comfortable to draw conclusions from information stated within a passage, rather than to draw them from mere implications. At times an author may provide some information and then describe a counterargument. The reader should be alert for direct statements that are subsequently rejected or weakened by the author. The reader should always read the entire passage before drawing conclusions. Many readers are trained to expect the author's conclusions at either the beginning or the end of the passage, but many texts do not adhere to this format.

Drawing conclusions from information implied within a passage requires confidence on the part of the reader. **Implications** are things the author does not state directly, but which can be assumed based on what the author does say. For instance, consider the following simple passage: "I stepped outside and opened my umbrella. By the time I got to work, the cuffs of my pants were soaked." The author never states that it is raining, but this fact is clearly implied. Conclusions based on implication must be well supported by the text. In order to draw a solid conclusion, a reader should have multiple pieces of evidence, or, if he only has one, must be assured that there is no other possible explanation than his conclusion. A good reader will be able to draw many conclusions from information implied by the text, which enriches the reading experience considerably.

As an aid to drawing conclusions, the reader should be adept at **outlining** the information contained in the passage; an effective outline will reveal the structure of the passage, and will lead to solid conclusions. An effective outline will have a title that refers to the basic subject of the text, though it need not recapitulate the main idea. In most outlines, the main idea will be the first major section. It will have each major idea of the passage established as the head of a category. For instance, the most common outline format calls for the main ideas of the passage to be indicated with Roman numerals. In an effective outline of this kind, each of the main ideas will be represented by a Roman numeral and none of the Roman numerals will designate minor details or secondary ideas. Moreover, all supporting ideas and details should be placed in the appropriate place on the outline. An outline does not need to include every detail listed in the text, but it should feature all of those that are central to the argument or message. Each of these details should be listed under the appropriate main idea.

It is also helpful to **summarize** the information you have read in a paragraph or passage format. This process is similar to creating an effective outline. To begin with, a summary should accurately define the main idea of the passage, though it does not need to explain this main idea in exhaustive detail. It should continue by laying out the most important supporting details or arguments from the passage. All of the significant supporting details should be included, and none of the details included should be irrelevant or insignificant. Also, the summary should accurately report all of these details. Too often, the desire for brevity in a summary leads to the sacrifice of clarity or veracity. Summaries are often difficult to read, because they omit all of graceful language, digressions, and asides that distinguish great writing. However, if the summary is effective, it should contain much the same message as the original text.

Paraphrasing is another method the reader can use to aid in comprehension. When paraphrasing, one puts what they have read into their own words, rephrasing what the author has written to make it their own, to "translate" all of what the author says to their own words, including as many details as they can.

Testing Tips

Skimming

Your first task when you begin reading is to answer the question "What is the topic of the selection?" This can best be answered by quickly skimming the passage for the general idea, stopping to read only the first sentence of each paragraph. A paragraph's first sentence is usually the main topic sentence, and it gives you a summary of the content of the paragraph.

Once you've skimmed the passage, stopping to read only the first sentences, you will have a general idea about what it is about, as well as what is the expected topic in each paragraph.

Each question will contain clues as to where to find the answer in the passage. Do not just randomly search through the passage for the correct answer to each question. Search scientifically. Find key word(s) or ideas in the question that are going to either contain or be near the correct answer. These are typically nouns, verbs, numbers, or phrases in the question that will probably be duplicated in the passage. Once you have identified those key word(s) or idea, skim the passage quickly to find where those key word(s) or idea appears. The correct answer choice will be nearby.

Example: What caused Martin to suddenly return to Paris?
The key word is Paris. Skim the passage quickly to find where this word appears. The answer will be close by that word.

However, sometimes key words in the question are not repeated in the passage. In those cases, search for the general idea of the question.

Example: Which of the following was the psychological impact of the author's childhood upon the remainder of his life?
Key words are "childhood" or "psychology". While searching for those words, be alert for other words or phrases that have similar meaning, such as "emotional effect" or "mentally" which could be used in the passage, rather than the exact word "psychology".

Numbers or years can be particularly good key words to skim for, as they stand out from the rest of the text.

Example: Which of the following best describes the influence of Monet's work in the 20th century?
20th contains numbers and will easily stand out from the rest of the text. Use 20th as the key word to skim for in the passage.

Other good key word(s) may be in quotation marks. These identify a word or phrase that is copied directly from the passage. In those cases, the word(s) in quotation marks are exactly duplicated in the passage.

Example: In her college years, what was meant by Margaret's "drive for excellence"?
"Drive for excellence" is a direct quote from the passage and should be easy to find.

Once you've quickly found the correct section of the passage to find the answer, focus upon the answer choices. Sometimes a choice will repeat word for word a portion of the passage near the answer. However, beware of such duplication – it may be a trap! More than likely, the correct choice will paraphrase or summarize the related portion of the passage, rather than being exactly the same wording.

For the answers that you think are correct, read them carefully and make sure that they answer the question. An answer can be factually correct, but it MUST answer the question asked. Additionally, two answers can both be seemingly correct, so be sure to read all of the answer choices, and make sure that you get the one that BEST answers the question.

Some questions will not have a key word.

Example: Which of the following would the author of this passage likely agree with?

In these cases, look for key words in the answer choices. Then skim the passage to find where the answer choice occurs. By skimming to find where to look, you can minimize the time required.

Sometimes it may be difficult to identify a good key word in the question to skim for in the passage. In those cases, look for a key word in one of the answer choices to skim for. Often the answer choices can all be found in the same paragraph, which can quickly narrow your search.

Paragraph Focus

Focus upon the first sentence of each paragraph, which is the most important. The main topic of the paragraph is usually there.

Once you've read the first sentence in the paragraph, you have a general idea about what each paragraph will be about. As you read the questions, try to determine which paragraph will have the answer. Paragraphs have a concise topic. The answer should either obviously be there or obviously not. It will save time if you can jump straight to the paragraph, so try to remember what you learned from the first sentences.

Example: The first paragraph is about poets; the second is about poetry. If a question asks about poetry, where will the answer be? *The second paragraph.*

The main idea of a passage is typically spread across all or most of its paragraphs. Whereas the main idea of a paragraph may be completely different than the main idea of the very next paragraph, a main idea for a passage affects all of the paragraphs in one form or another. Example: What is the main idea of the passage?

For each answer choice, try to see how many paragraphs are related. It can help to count how many sentences are affected by each choice, but it is best to see how many paragraphs are affected by the choice. Typically the answer choices will include incorrect choices that are main ideas of individual paragraphs, but not the entire passage. That is why it is crucial to choose ideas that are supported by the most paragraphs possible.

Eliminate Choices

Some choices can quickly be eliminated. "Andy Warhol lived there." Is Andy Warhol even mentioned in the article? If not, quickly eliminate it.

When trying to answer a question such as "the passage indicates all of the following EXCEPT" quickly skim the paragraph searching for references to each choice. If the reference exists, scratch it off as a choice. Similar choices may be crossed off simultaneously if they are close enough.

In choices that ask you to choose "which answer choice does NOT describe?" or "all of the following answer choices are identifiable characteristics, EXCEPT which?" look for answers that are similarly worded. Since only one answer can be correct, if there are two answers that appear to mean the same thing, they must BOTH be incorrect, and can be eliminated.
Example:
  A. changing values and attitudes
  B. a large population of mobile or uprooted people

These answer choices are similar; they both describe a fluid culture. Because of their similarity, they can be linked together. Since the answer can have only one choice, they can also be eliminated together.

Contextual Clues

Look for contextual clues. An answer can be right but not correct. The contextual clues will help you find the answer that is most right and is correct. Understand the context in which a phrase is stated.

When asked for the implied meaning of a statement made in the passage, immediately go find the statement and read the context it was made in. Also, look for an answer choice that has a similar phrase to the statement in question.
Example: In the passage, what is implied by the phrase "Churches have become more or less part of the furniture"?

Find an answer choice that is similar or describes the phrase "part of the furniture" as that is the key phrase in the question. "Part of the furniture" is a saying that means something is fixed, immovable, or set in their ways. Those are all similar ways of saying "part of the furniture." As such, the correct answer choice will probably include a similar rewording of the expression.
Example: Why was John described as "morally desperate"?

The answer will probably have some sort of definition of morals in it. "Morals" refers to a code of right and wrong behavior, so the correct answer choice will likely have words that mean something like that.

Fact/Opinion

When asked about which statement is a fact or opinion, remember that answer choices that are facts will typically have no ambiguous words. For example, how long is a long time? What defines an ordinary person? These ambiguous words of "long" and "ordinary" should not be in a factual statement. However, if all of the choices have ambiguous words, go to the context of the passage. Often a factual statement may be set out as a research finding.
Example: "The scientist found that the eye reacts quickly to change in light."

Opinions may be set out in the context of words like thought, believed, understood, or wished.
Example: "He thought the Yankees should win the World Series."

Opposites

Answer choices that are direct opposites are usually correct. The paragraph will often contain established relationships (when this goes up, that goes down). The question may ask you to draw conclusions for this and will give two similar answer choices that are opposites.
Example:
  A. a decrease in housing starts
  B. an increase in housing starts

Make Predictions

As you read and understand the passage and then the question, try to guess what the answer will be. Remember that three of the four answer choices are wrong, and once you being reading them, your mind will immediately become cluttered with answer choices designed to throw you off. Your mind is typically the most focused immediately after you have read the passage and question and digested its contents. If you can, try to predict what the correct answer will be. You may be surprised at what you can predict.

Quickly scan the choices and see if your prediction is in the listed answer choices. If it is, then you can be quite confident that you have the right answer. It still won't hurt to check the other answer choices, but most of the time, you've got it!

Answer the Question

It may seem obvious to only pick answer choices that answer the question, but the test can contain some excellent answer choices that are wrong. Don't pick an answer just because it sounds right, or you believe it to be true. It MUST answer the question. Once you've made your selection, always go back and check it against the question and make sure that you didn't misread the question, and the answer choice does answer the question posed.

Benchmark

After you read the first answer choice, decide if you think it sounds correct or not. If it doesn't, move on to the next answer choice. If it does, make a mental note about that choice. This doesn't mean that you've definitely selected it as your answer choice, it just means that it's the best you've seen thus far. Go ahead and read the next choice. If the next choice is worse than the one you've already selected, keep going to the next answer choice. If the next choice is better than the choice you've already selected, then make a mental note about that answer choice.

As you read through the list, you are mentally noting the choice you think is right. That is your new standard. Every other answer choice must be benchmarked against that standard. That choice is correct until proven otherwise by another answer choice beating it out. Once you've decided that no other answer choice seems as good, do one final check to ensure that it answers the question posed.

New Information

Correct answers will usually contain the information listed in the paragraph and question. Rarely will completely new information be inserted into a correct answer choice. Occasionally the new information may be related in a manner that the test is asking for you to interpret, but seldom. Example:
The argument above is dependent upon which of the following assumptions?
    A. Charles's Law was used

If Charles's Law is not mentioned at all in the referenced paragraph and argument, then it is unlikely that this choice is correct. All of the information needed to answer the question is provided for you, and so you should not have to make guesses that are unsupported or choose answer choices that have unknown information that cannot be reasoned.

Valid Information

Don't discount any of the information provided in the passage, particularly shorter ones. Every piece of information may be necessary to determine the correct answer. None of the information in the paragraph is there to throw you off (while the answer choices will certainly have information to throw you off). If two seemingly unrelated topics are discussed, don't ignore either. You can be confident there is a relationship, or it wouldn't be included in the paragraph, and you are probably going to have to determine what that relationship is for the answer.

Time Management

In technical passages, do not get lost on the technical terms. Skip them and move on. You want a general understanding of what is going on, not a mastery of the passage.

When you encounter material in the selection that seems difficult to understand, it often may not be necessary and can be skipped. Only spend time trying to understand it if it is going to be relevant for a question. Understand difficult phrases only as a last resort.

Answer general questions before detail questions. A reader with a good understanding of the whole passage can often answer general questions without rereading a word. Get the easier questions out of the way before tackling the more time consuming ones.

Identify each question by type. Usually the wording of a question will tell you whether you can find the answer by referring directly to the passage or by using your reasoning powers. You alone know which question types you customarily handle with ease and which give you trouble and will require more time. Save the difficult questions for last.

Final Warnings

Word Usage Questions

When asked how a word is used in the passage, don't use your existing knowledge of the word. The question is being asked precisely because there is some strange or unusual usage of the word in the passage. Go to the passage and use contextual clues to determine the answer. Don't simply use the popular definition you already know.

Switchback Words

Stay alert for "switchbacks". These are the words and phrases frequently used to alert you to shifts in thought. The most common switchback word is "but". Others include although, however, nevertheless, on the other hand, even though, while, in spite of, despite, regardless of.

Avoid "Fact Traps"

Once you know which paragraph the answer will be in, focus on that paragraph. However, don't get distracted by a choice that is factually true about the paragraph. Your search is for the answer that answers the question, which may be about a tiny aspect in the paragraph. Stay focused and don't fall for an answer that describes the larger picture of the paragraph. Always go back to the question and make sure you're choosing an answer that actually answers the question and is not just a true statement.

The Quantitative Reasoning Test

Numerical Calculations

Numbers and their Classifications

Numbers are the basic building blocks of mathematics. Specific features of numbers are identified by the following terms:

Integers – The set of whole positive and negative numbers, including zero. Integers do not include fractions $\left(\frac{1}{3}\right)$, decimals (0.56), or mixed numbers $\left(7\frac{3}{4}\right)$.

Prime number – A whole number greater than 1 that has only two factors, itself and 1; that is, a number that can be divided evenly only by 1 and itself.

Composite number – A whole number greater than 1 that has more than two different factors; in other words, any whole number that is not a prime number. For example: The composite number 8 has the factors of 1, 2, 4, and 8.

Even number – Any integer that can be divided by 2 without leaving a remainder. For example: 2, 4, 6, 8, and so on.

Odd number – Any integer that cannot be divided evenly by 2. For example: 3, 5, 7, 9, and so on.
Decimal number – a number that uses a decimal point to show the part of the number that is less than one. Example: 1.234.

Decimal point – a symbol used to separate the ones place from the tenths place in decimals or dollars from cents in currency.

Decimal place – the position of a number to the right of the decimal point. In the decimal 0.123, the 1 is in the first place to the right of the decimal point, indicating tenths; the 2 is in the second place, indicating hundredths; and the 3 is in the third place, indicating thousandths.

The decimal, or base 10, system is a number system that uses ten different digits (0, 1, 2, 3, 4, 5, 6, 7, 8, 9). An example of a number system that uses something other than ten digits is the binary, or base 2, number system, used by computers, which uses only the numbers 0 and 1. It is thought that the decimal system originated because people had only their 10 fingers for counting.

Rational, irrational, and real numbers can be described as follows:
Rational numbers include all integers, decimals, and fractions. Any terminating or repeating decimal number is a rational number.

Irrational numbers cannot be written as fractions or decimals because the number of decimal places is infinite and there is no recurring pattern of digits within the number. For example, pi (π) begins with 3.141592 and continues without terminating or repeating, so pi is an irrational number.

Real numbers are the set of all rational and irrational numbers.

> ➤ **Review Video: <u>Numbers and their Classifications</u>**
> *Visit **mometrix.com/academy** and enter **Code: 461071***

Operations

There are four basic mathematical operations:
Addition increases the value of one quantity by the value of another quantity. Example:
$2 + 4 = 6; 8 + 9 = 17$. The result is called the sum. With addition, the order does not matter.
$4 + 2 = 2 + 4$.

Subtraction is the opposite operation to addition; it decreases the value of one quantity by the value of another quantity. Example: $6 - 4 = 2; 17 - 8 = 9$. The result is called the difference. Note that with subtraction, the order does matter. $6 - 4 \neq 4 - 6$.

Multiplication can be thought of as repeated addition. One number tells how many times to add the other number to itself. Example: 3×2 (three times two) $= 2 + 2 + 2 = 6$. With multiplication, the order does not matter. $2 \times 3 = 3 \times 2$ or $3 + 3 = 2 + 2 + 2$.

Division is the opposite operation to multiplication; one number tells us how many parts to divide the other number into. Example: $20 \div 4 = 5$; if 20 is split into 4 equal parts, each part is 5. With division, the order of the numbers does matter. $20 \div 4 \neq 4 \div 20$.

An exponent is a superscript number placed next to another number at the top right. It indicates how many times the base number is to be multiplied by itself. Exponents provide a shorthand way to write what would be a longer mathematical expression. Example: $a^2 = a \times a; 2^4 = 2 \times 2 \times 2 \times 2$. A number with an exponent of 2 is said to be "squared," while a number with an exponent of 3 is said to be "cubed." The value of a number raised to an exponent is called its power. So, 8^4 is read as "8 to the 4th power," or "8 raised to the power of 4." A negative exponent is the same as the reciprocal of a positive exponent. Example: $a^{-2} = \frac{1}{a^2}$.

Parentheses are used to designate which operations should be done first when there are multiple operations. Example: $4 - (2 + 1) = 1$; the parentheses tell us that we must add 2 and 1, and then subtract the sum from 4, rather than subtracting 2 from 4 and then adding 1 (this would give us an answer of 3).

Order of Operations is a set of rules that dictates the order in which we must perform each operation in an expression so that we will evaluate at accurately. If we have an expression that includes multiple different operations, Order of Operations tells us which operations to do first. The most common mnemonic for Order of Operations is PEMDAS, or "Please Excuse My Dear Aunt Sally." PEMDAS stands for Parentheses, Exponents, Multiplication, Division, Addition, Subtraction. It is important to understand that multiplication and division have equal precedence, as do addition and subtraction, so those pairs of operations are simply worked from left to right in order.
Example: Evaluate the expression $5 + 20 \div 4 \times (2 + 3)^2 - 6$ using the correct order of operations.
P: Perform the operations inside the parentheses, $(2 + 3) = 5$.
E: Simplify the exponents, $(5)^2 = 25$.
The equation now looks like this: $5 + 20 \div 4 \times 25 - 6$.
MD: Perform multiplication and division from left to right, $20 \div 4 = 5$; then $5 \times 25 = 125$.
The equation now looks like this: $5 + 125 - 6$.
AS: Perform addition and subtraction from left to right, $5 + 125 = 130$; then $130 - 6 = 124$.

> ➤ **Review Video: <u>Order of Operations</u>**
> *Visit **mometrix.com/academy** and enter **Code: 259675***

The laws of exponents are as follows:
1)   Any number to the power of 1 is equal to itself: $a^1 = a$.
2)   The number 1 raised to any power is equal to 1: $1^n = 1$.
3)   Any number raised to the power of 0 is equal to 1: $a^0 = 1$.
4)   Add exponents to multiply powers of the same base number: $a^n \times a^m = a^{n+m}$.
5)   Subtract exponents to divide powers of the same number; that is $a^n \div a^m = a^{n-m}$.
6)   Multiply exponents to raise a power to a power: $(a^n)^m = a^{n \times m}$.
7)   If multiplied or divided numbers inside parentheses are collectively raised to a power, this is the same as each individual term being raised to that power: $(a \times b)^n = a^n \times b^n$; $(a \div b)^n = a^n \div b^n$.

Note: Exponents do not have to be integers. Fractional or decimal exponents follow all the rules above as well. Example: $5^{\frac{1}{4}} \times 5^{\frac{3}{4}} = 5^{\frac{1}{4}+\frac{3}{4}} = 5^1 = 5$.

> ➤ **Review Video: <u>Law of Exponents</u>**
> *Visit **mometrix.com/academy** and enter **Code: 532558***

A root, such as a square root, is another way of writing a fractional exponent. Instead of using a superscript, roots use the radical symbol ($\sqrt{}$) to indicate the operation. A radical will have a number underneath the bar, and may sometimes have a number in the upper left: $\sqrt[n]{a}$, read as "the nth root of a." The relationship between radical notation and exponent notation can be described by this equation: $\sqrt[n]{a} = a^{\frac{1}{n}}$. The two special cases of $n = 2$ and $n = 3$ are called square roots and cube roots. If there is no number to the upper left, it is understood to be a square root ($n = 2$). Nearly all of the roots you encounter will be square roots. A square root is the same as a number raised to the one-half power. When we say that a is the square root of b ($a = \sqrt{b}$), we mean that a multiplied by itself equals b: ($a \times a = b$).

A perfect square is a number that has an integer for its square root. There are 10 perfect squares from 1 to 100: 1, 4, 9, 16, 25, 36, 49, 64, 81, 100 (the squares of integers 1 through 10).

Scientific notation is a way of writing large numbers in a shorter form. The form $a \times 10^n$ is used in scientific notation, where a is greater than or equal to 1, but less than 10, and n is the number of places the decimal must move to get from the original number to a. Example: The number 230,400,000 is cumbersome to write. To write the value in scientific notation, place a decimal point between the first and second numbers, and include all digits through the last non-zero digit ($a = 2.304$). To find the appropriate power of 10, count the number of places the decimal point had to move ($n = 8$). The number is positive if the decimal moved to the left, and negative if it moved to the right. We can then write 230,400,000 as 2.304×10^8. If we look instead at the number 0.00002304, we have the same value for a, but this time the decimal moved 5 places to the right ($n = -5$). Thus, 0.00002304 can be written as 2.304×10^{-5}. Using this notation makes it simple to compare very large or very small numbers. By comparing exponents, it is easy to see that 3.28×10^4 is smaller than 1.51×10^5, because 4 is less than 5.

Positive & Negative Numbers

A precursor to working with negative numbers is understanding what absolute values are. A number's *Absolute Value* is simply the distance away from zero a number is on the number line. The absolute value of a number is always positive and is written $|x|$.

When adding signed numbers, if the signs are the same simply add the absolute values of the addends and apply the original sign to the sum. For example, $(+4) + (+8) = +12$ and $(-4) + (-8) = -12$. When the original signs are different, take the absolute values of the addends and subtract the smaller value from the larger value, then apply the original sign of the larger value to the difference. For instance, $(+4) + (-8) = -4$ and $(-4) + (+8) = +4$.

For subtracting signed numbers, change the sign of the number after the minus symbol and then follow the same rules used for addition. For example, $(+4) - (+8) = (+4) + (-8) = -4$.

If the signs are the same the product is positive when multiplying signed numbers. For example, $(+4) \times (+8) = +32$ and $(-4) \times (-8) = +32$. If the signs are opposite, the product is negative. For example, $(+4) \times (-8) = -32$ and $(-4) \times (+8) = -32$. When more than two factors are multiplied together, the sign of the product is determined by how many negative factors are present. If there are an odd number of negative factors then the product is negative, whereas an even number of negative factors indicates a positive product. For instance, $(+4) \times (-8) \times (-2) = +64$ and $(-4) \times (-8) \times (-2) = -64$.

The rules for dividing signed numbers are similar to multiplying signed numbers. If the dividend and divisor have the same sign, the quotient is positive. If the dividend and divisor have opposite signs, the quotient is negative. For example, $(-4) \div (+8) = -0.5$.

Factors and Multiples

Factors are numbers that are multiplied together to obtain a product. For example, in the equation $2 \times 3 = 6$, the numbers 2 and 3 are factors. A prime number has only two factors (1 and itself), but other numbers can have many factors.

A common factor is a number that divides exactly into two or more other numbers. For example, the factors of 12 are 1, 2, 3, 4, 6, and 12, while the factors of 15 are 1, 3, 5, and 15. The common factors of 12 and 15 are 1 and 3.

A prime factor is also a prime number. Therefore, the prime factors of 12 are 1, 2, and 3. For 15, the prime factors are 1, 3, and 5.

The greatest common factor (GCF) is the largest number that is a factor of two or more numbers. For example, the factors of 15 are 1, 3, 5, and 15; the factors of 35 are 1, 5, 7, and 35. Therefore, the greatest common factor of 15 and 35 is 5.

> ➢ **Review Video: Factors**
> Visit ***mometrix.com/academy*** *and enter* ***Code: 920086***

The least common multiple (LCM) is the smallest number that is a multiple of two or more numbers. For example, the multiples of 3 include 3, 6, 9, 12, 15, etc.; the multiples of 5 include 5, 10, 15, 20, etc. Therefore, the least common multiple of 3 and 5 is 15.

> ➢ **Review Video: Multiples**
> Visit ***mometrix.com/academy*** *and enter* ***Code: 626738***

Fractions, Percentages, and Related Concepts

A fraction is a number that is expressed as one integer written above another integer, with a dividing line between them ($\frac{x}{y}$). It represents the quotient of the two numbers "x divided by y." It can also be thought of as x out of y equal parts.

The top number of a fraction is called the numerator, and it represents the number of parts under consideration. The 1 in $\frac{1}{4}$ means that 1 part out of the whole is being considered in the calculation. The bottom number of a fraction is called the denominator, and it represents the total number of equal parts. The 4 in $\frac{1}{4}$ means that the whole consists of 4 equal parts. A fraction cannot have a denominator of zero; this is referred to as "undefined."

Fractions can be manipulated, without changing the value of the fraction, by multiplying or dividing (but not adding or subtracting) both the numerator and denominator by the same number. If you divide both numbers by a common factor, you are reducing or simplifying the fraction. Two fractions that have the same value, but are expressed differently are known as equivalent fractions. For example, $\frac{2}{10}, \frac{3}{15}, \frac{4}{20}$, and $\frac{5}{25}$ are all equivalent fractions. They can also all be reduced or simplified to $\frac{1}{5}$.

When two fractions are manipulated so that they have the same denominator, this is known as finding a common denominator. The number chosen to be that common denominator should be the least common multiple of the two original denominators. Example: $\frac{3}{4}$ and $\frac{5}{6}$; the least common multiple of 4 and 6 is 12. Manipulating to achieve the common denominator: $\frac{3}{4} = \frac{9}{12}; \frac{5}{6} = \frac{10}{12}$.

If two fractions have a common denominator, they can be added or subtracted simply by adding or subtracting the two numerators and retaining the same denominator. Example: $\frac{1}{2} + \frac{1}{4} = \frac{2}{4} + \frac{1}{4} = \frac{3}{4}$. If the two fractions do not already have the same denominator, one or both of them must be manipulated to achieve a common denominator before they can be added or subtracted.

Two fractions can be multiplied by multiplying the two numerators to find the new numerator and the two denominators to find the new denominator. Example: $\frac{1}{3} \times \frac{2}{3} = \frac{1 \times 2}{3 \times 3} = \frac{2}{9}$.

Two fractions can be divided flipping the numerator and denominator of the second fraction and then proceeding as though it were a multiplication. Example: $\frac{2}{3} \div \frac{3}{4} = \frac{2}{3} \times \frac{4}{3} = \frac{8}{9}$.

A fraction whose denominator is greater than its numerator is known as a proper fraction, while a fraction whose numerator is greater than its denominator is known as an improper fraction. Proper fractions have values less than one and improper fractions have values greater than one.

A mixed number is a number that contains both an integer and a fraction. Any improper fraction can be rewritten as a mixed number. Example: $\frac{8}{3} = \frac{6}{3} + \frac{2}{3} = 2 + \frac{2}{3} = 2\frac{2}{3}$. Similarly, any mixed number can be rewritten as an improper fraction. Example: $1\frac{3}{5} = 1 + \frac{3}{5} = \frac{5}{5} + \frac{3}{5} = \frac{8}{5}$.

Percentages can be thought of as fractions that are based on a whole of 100; that is, one whole is equal to 100%. The word percent means "per hundred." Fractions can be expressed as percents by finding equivalent fractions with a denomination of 100. Example: $\frac{7}{10} = \frac{70}{100} = 70\%$; $\frac{1}{4} = \frac{25}{100} = 25\%$.

To express a percentage as a fraction, divide the percentage number by 100 and reduce the fraction to its simplest possible terms. Example: $60\% = \frac{60}{100} = \frac{3}{5}$; $96\% = \frac{96}{100} = \frac{24}{25}$.

Converting decimals to percentages and percentages to decimals is as simple as moving the decimal point. To convert from a decimal to a percent, move the decimal point two places to the right. To convert from a percent to a decimal, move it two places to the left. Example: 0.23 = 23%; 5.34 = 534%; 0.007 = 0.7%; 700% = 7.00; 86% = 0.86; 0.15% = 0.0015. It may be helpful to remember that the percentage number will always be larger than the equivalent decimal number.

A percentage problem can be presented three main ways: (1) Find what percentage of some number another number is. Example: What percentage of 40 is 8? (2) Find what number is some percentage of a given number. Example: What number is 20% of 40? (3) Find what number another number is a given percentage of. Example: What number is 8 20% of? The three components in all of these cases are the same: a whole (W), a part (P), and a percentage (%). These are related by the equation: $P = W \times \%$. This is the form of the equation you would use to solve problems of type (2). To solve types (1) and (3), you would use these two forms: $\% = \frac{P}{W}$ and $W = \frac{P}{\%}$.

The thing that frequently makes percentage problems difficult is that they are most often also word problems, so a large part of solving them is figuring out which quantities are what. Example: In a school cafeteria, 7 students choose pizza, 9 choose hamburgers, and 4 choose tacos. Find the percentage that chooses tacos. To find the whole, you must first add all of the parts: 7 + 9 + 4 = 20. The percentage can then be found by dividing the part by the whole ($\% = \frac{P}{W}$): $\frac{4}{20} = \frac{20}{100} = 20\%$.

> **Review Video: <u>Fractions, Decimals, and Percentages</u>**
> *Visit **mometrix.com/academy** and enter **Code: 350606***

A ratio is a comparison of two quantities in a particular order. Example: If there are 14 computers in a lab, and the class has 20 students, there is a student to computer ratio of 20 to 14, commonly written as 20:14. Ratios are normally reduced to their smallest whole number representation, so 20:14 would be reduced to 10:7 by dividing both sides by 2.

A proportion is a relationship between two quantities that dictates how one changes when the other changes. A direct proportion describes a relationship in which a quantity increases by a set amount for every increase in the other quantity, or decreases by that same amount for every decrease in the other quantity. Example: Assuming a constant driving speed, the time required for a car trip increases as the distance of the trip increases. The distance to be traveled and the time required to travel are directly proportional.

Inverse proportion is a relationship in which an increase in one quantity is accompanied by a decrease in the other, or vice versa. Example: the time required for a car trip decreases as the speed increases, and increases as the speed decreases, so the time required is inversely proportional to the speed of the car.

Algebra

Equations and Graphing

When algebraic functions and equations are shown graphically, they are usually shown on a *Cartesian Coordinate Plane*. The Cartesian coordinate plane consists of two number lines placed perpendicular to each other, and intersecting at the zero point, also known as the origin. The horizontal number line is known as the *x*-axis, with positive values to the right of the origin, and negative values to the left of the origin. The vertical number line is known as the *y*-axis, with positive values above the origin, and negative values below the origin. Any point on the plane can be identified by an ordered pair in the form (*x,y*), called coordinates. The *x*-value of the coordinate is called the abscissa, and the *y*-value of the coordinate is called the ordinate. The two number lines divide the plane into four quadrants: I, II, III, and IV.

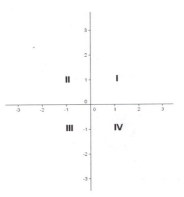

Before learning the different forms equations can be written in, it is important to understand some terminology. A ratio of the change in the vertical distance to the change in horizontal distance is called the *Slope*. On a graph with two points, (x_1, y_1) and (x_2, y_2), the slope is represented by the formula $= \frac{y_2 - y_1}{x_2 - x_1}$; $x_1 \neq x_2$. If the value of the slope is positive, the line slopes upward from left to right. If the value of the slope is negative, the line slopes downward from left to right. If the *y*-coordinates are the same for both points, the slope is 0 and the line is a *Horizontal Line*. If the *x*-coordinates are the same for both points, there is no slope and the line is a *Vertical Line*. Two or more lines that have equal slopes are *Parallel Lines*. *Perpendicular Lines* have slopes that are negative reciprocals of each other, such as $\frac{a}{b}$ and $\frac{-b}{a}$.

Equations are made up of monomials and polynomials. A *Monomial* is a single variable or product of constants and variables, such as x, $2x$, or $\frac{2}{x}$. There will never be addition or subtraction symbols in a monomial. Like monomials have like variables, but they may have different coefficients. *Polynomials* are algebraic expressions which use addition and subtraction to combine two or more monomials. Two terms make a binomial; three terms make a trinomial; etc.. The *Degree of a Monomial* is the sum of the exponents of the variables. The *Degree of a Polynomial* is the highest degree of any individual term.

As mentioned previously, equations can be written many ways. Below is a list of the many forms equations can take.

- *Standard Form*: $Ax + By = C$; the slope is $\frac{-A}{B}$ and the y-intercept is $\frac{C}{B}$
- *Slope Intercept Form*: $y = mx + b$, where m is the slope and b is the y-intercept
- *Point-Slope Form*: $y - y_1 = m(x - x_1)$, where m is the slope and (x_1, y_1) is a point on the line
- *Two-Point Form*: $\frac{y-y_1}{x-x_1} = \frac{y_2-y_1}{x_2-x_1}$, where (x_1, y_1) and (x_2, y_2) are two points on the given line
- *Intercept Form*: $\frac{x}{x_1} + \frac{y}{y_1} = 1$, where $(x_1, 0)$ is the point at which a line intersects the x-axis, and $(0, y_1)$ is the point at which the same line intersects the y-axis

Equations can also be written as $ax + b = 0$, where $a \neq 0$. These are referred to as *One Variable Linear Equations*. A solution to such an equation is called a *Root*. In the case where we have the equation $5x + 10 = 0$, if we solve for x we get a solution of $x = -2$. In other words, the root of the equation is -2. This is found by first subtracting 10 from both sides, which gives $5x = -10$. Next, simply divide both sides by the coefficient of the variable, in this case 5, to get $x = -2$. This can be checked by plugging -2 back into the original equation $(5)(-2) + 10 = -10 + 10 = 0$.

The *Solution Set* is the set of all solutions of an equation. In our example, the solution set would simply be -2. If there were more solutions (there usually are in multivariable equations) then they would also be included in the solution set. When an equation has no true solutions, this is referred to as an *Empty Set*. Equations with identical solution sets are *Equivalent Equations*. An *Identity* is a term whose value or determinant is equal to 1.

Other Important Concepts

Commonly in algebra and other upper-level fields of math you find yourself working with mathematical expressions that do not equal each other. The statement comparing such expressions with symbols such as < (less than) or > (greater than) is called an *Inequality*. An example of an inequality is $7x > 5$. To solve for x, simply divide both sides by 7 and the solution is shown to be $x > \frac{5}{7}$. Graphs of the solution set of inequalities are represented on a number line. Open circles are used to show that an expression approaches a number but is never quite equal to that number.

Conditional Inequalities are those with certain values for the variable that will make the condition true and other values for the variable where the condition will be false. *Absolute Inequalities* can have any real number as the value for the variable to make the condition true, while there is no real number value for the variable that will make the condition false. Solving inequalities is done by following the same rules as for solving equations with the exception that when multiplying or dividing by a negative number the direction of the inequality sign must be flipped or reversed. *Double Inequalities* are situations where two inequality statements apply to the same variable expression. An example of this is $-c < ax + b < c$.

A *Weighted Mean*, or weighted average, is a mean that uses "weighted" values. The formula is weighted mean $= \frac{w_1 x_1 + w_2 x_2 + w_3 x_3 \ldots + w_n x_n}{w_1 + w_2 + w_3 + \cdots + w_n}$. Weighted values, such as $w_1, w_2, w_3, \ldots w_n$ are assigned to each member of the set $x_1, x_2, x_3, \ldots x_n$. If calculating weighted mean, make sure a weight value for each member of the set is used.

Calculations Using Points

Sometimes you need to perform calculations using only points on a graph as input data. Using points, you can determine what the midpoint and distance are. If you know the equation for a line you can calculate the distance between the line and the point.

To find the *Midpoint* of two points (x_1, y_1) and (x_2, y_2), average the x-coordinates to get the x-coordinate of the midpoint, and average the y-coordinates to get the y-coordinate of the midpoint. The formula is midpoint $= \left(\frac{x_1+x_2}{2}, \frac{y_1+y_2}{2}\right)$.

The *Distance* between two points is the same as the length of the hypotenuse of a right triangle with the two given points as endpoints, and the two sides of the right triangle parallel to the x-axis and y-axis, respectively. The length of the segment parallel to the x-axis is the difference between the x-coordinates of the two points. The length of the segment parallel to the y-axis is the difference between the y-coordinates of the two points. Use the Pythagorean Theorem $a^2 + b^2 = c^2$ or $c = \sqrt{a^2 + b^2}$ to find the distance. The formula is: distance $= \sqrt{(x_2 - x_1)^2 + (y_2 - y_1)^2}$.

When a line is in the format $Ax + By + C = 0$, where A, B, and C are coefficients, you can use a point (x_1, y_1) not on the line and apply the formula $d = \frac{|Ax_1+By_1+C|}{\sqrt{A^2+B^2}}$ to find the distance between the line and the point (x_1, y_1).

Systems of Equations

Systems of Equations are a set of simultaneous equations that all use the same variables. A solution to a system of equations must be true for each equation in the system. *Consistent Systems* are those with at least one solution. *Inconsistent Systems* are systems of equations that have no solution.

To solve a system of linear equations by *substitution*, start with the easier equation and solve for one of the variables. Express this variable in terms of the other variable. Substitute this expression in the other equation, and solve for the other variable. The solution should be expressed in the form (x, y). Substitute the values into both of the original equations to check your answer. Consider the following problem.

Solve the system using substitution:
$x + 6y = 15$
$3x - 12y = 18$

Solve the first equation for x:
$x = 15 - 6y$

Substitute this value in place of x in the second equation, and solve for y:
$$3(15 - 6y) - 12y = 18$$
$$45 - 18y - 12y = 18$$
$$30y = 27$$
$$y = \frac{27}{30} = \frac{9}{10} = 0.9$$

Plug this value for y back into the first equation to solve for x:
$$x = 15 - 6(0.9) = 15 - 5.4 = 9.6$$

Check both equations if you have time:
$$9.6 + 6(0.9) = 9.6 + 5.4 = 15$$
$$3(9.6) - 12(0.9) = 28.8 - 10.8 = 18$$
Therefore, the solution is $(9.6, 0.9)$.

To solve a system of equations using *elimination*, begin by rewriting both equations in standard form $Ax + By = C$. Check to see if the coefficients of one pair of like variables add to zero. If not, multiply one or both of the equations by a non-zero number to make one set of like variables add to zero. Add the two equations to solve for one of the variables. Substitute this value into one of the original equations to solve for the other variable. Check your work by substituting into the other equation. Next we will solve the same problem as above, but using the addition method.

Solve the system using elimination:
$$x + 6y = 15$$
$$3x - 12y = 18$$

If we multiply the first equation by 2, we can eliminate the y terms:
$$2x + 12y = 30$$
$$3x - 12y = 18$$

Add the equations together and solve for x:
$$5x = 48$$
$$x = \frac{48}{5} = 9.6$$

Plug the value for x back into either of the original equations and solve for y:
$$9.6 + 6y = 15$$
$$y = \frac{15 - 9.6}{6} = 0.9$$

Check both equations if you have time:
$$9.6 + 6(0.9) = 9.6 + 5.4 = 15$$
$$3(9.6) - 12(0.9) = 28.8 - 10.8 = 18$$
Therefore, the solution is $(9.6, 0.9)$.

Polynomial Algebra

To multiply two binomials, follow the *FOIL* method. FOIL stands for:
- First: Multiply the first term of each binomial
- Outer: Multiply the outer terms of each binomial
- Inner: Multiply the inner terms of each binomial
- Last: Multiply the last term of each binomial

Using FOIL, $(Ax + By)(Cx + Dy) = ACx^2 + ADxy + BCxy + BDy^2$.

To divide polynomials, begin by arranging the terms of each polynomial in order of one variable. You may arrange in ascending or descending order, but be consistent with both polynomials. To get the first term of the quotient, divide the first term of the dividend by the first term of the divisor. Multiply the first term of the quotient by the entire divisor and subtract that product from the dividend. Repeat for the second and successive terms until you either get a remainder of zero or a remainder whose degree is less than the degree of the divisor. If the quotient has a remainder, write the answer as a mixed expression in the form: quotient $+ \frac{\text{remainder}}{\text{divisor}}$.

Rational Expressions are fractions with polynomials in both the numerator and the denominator; the value of the polynomial in the denominator cannot be equal to zero. To add or subtract rational expressions, first find the common denominator, then rewrite each fraction as an equivalent fraction with the common denominator. Finally, add or subtract the numerators to get the numerator of the answer, and keep the common denominator as the denominator of the answer. When multiplying rational expressions factor each polynomial and cancel like factors (a factor which appears in both the numerator and the denominator). Then, multiply all remaining factors in the numerator to get the numerator of the product, and multiply the remaining factors in the denominator to get the denominator of the product. Remember – cancel entire factors, not individual terms. To divide rational expressions, take the reciprocal of the divisor (the rational expression you are dividing by) and multiply by the dividend.

Below are patterns of some special products to remember: *perfect trinomial squares*, the *difference between two squares*, the *sum and difference of two cubes*, and *perfect cubes*.

- Perfect Trinomial Squares: $x^2 + 2xy + y^2 = (x + y)^2$ or $x^2 - 2xy + y^2 = (x - y)^2$
- Difference between Two Squares: $x^2 - y^2 = (x + y)(x - y)$
- Sum of Two Cubes: $x^3 + y^3 = (x + y)(x^2 - xy + y^2)$
  Note: the second factor is NOT the same as a perfect trinomial square, so do not try to factor it further.
- Difference between Two Cubes: $x^3 - y^3 = (x - y)(x^2 + xy + y^2)$
  Again, the second factor is NOT the same as a perfect trinomial square.
- Perfect Cubes: $x^3 + 3x^2y + 3xy^2 + y^3 = (x + y)^3$ and $x^3 - 3x^2y + 3xy^2 - y^3 = (x - y)^3$

In order to *factor* a polynomial, first check for a common monomial factor. When the greatest common monomial factor has been factored out, look for patterns of special products: differences of two squares, the sum or difference of two cubes for binomial factors, or perfect trinomial squares for trinomial factors. If the factor is a trinomial but not a perfect trinomial square, look for a factorable form, such as $x^2 + (a + b)x + ab = (x + a)(x + b)$ or $(ac)x^2 + (ad + bc)x + bd = (ax + b)(cx + d)$. For factors with four terms, look for groups to factor. Once you have found the factors, write the original polynomial as the product of all the factors. Make sure all of the polynomial factors are prime. Monomial factors may be prime or composite. Check your work by multiplying the factors to make sure you get the original polynomial.

Solving Quadratic Equations

The *Quadratic Formula* is used to solve quadratic equations when other methods are more difficult. To use the quadratic formula to solve a quadratic equation, begin by rewriting the equation in standard form $ax^2 + bx + c = 0$, where a, b, and c are coefficients. Once you have identified the values of the coefficients, substitute those values into the quadratic formula $x = \frac{-b \pm \sqrt{b^2 - 4ac}}{2a}$. Evaluate the equation and simplify the expression. Again, check each root by substituting into the original equation. In the quadratic formula, the portion of the formula under the radical $(b^2 - 4ac)$

- 31 -

is called the *Discriminant*. If the discriminant is zero, there is only one root: zero. If the discriminant is positive, there are two different real roots. If the discriminant is negative, there are no real roots.

To solve a quadratic equation by *Factoring*, begin by rewriting the equation in standard form, if necessary. Factor the side with the variable then set each of the factors equal to zero and solve the resulting linear equations. Check your answers by substituting the roots you found into the original equation. If, when writing the equation in standard form, you have an equation in the form $x^2 + c = 0$ or $x^2 - c = 0$, set $x^2 = -c$ or $x^2 = c$ and take the square root of c. If $c = 0$, the only real root is zero. If c is positive, there are two real roots—the positive and negative square root values. If c is negative, there are no real roots because you cannot take the square root of a negative number.

To solve a quadratic equation by *Completing the Square*, rewrite the equation so that all terms containing the variable are on the left side of the equal sign, and all the constants are on the right side of the equal sign. Make sure the coefficient of the squared term is 1. If there is a coefficient with the squared term, divide each term on both sides of the equal side by that number. Next, work with the coefficient of the single-variable term. Square half of this coefficient, and add that value to both sides. Now you can factor the left side (the side containing the variable) as the square of a binomial. $x^2 + 2ax + a^2 = C \Rightarrow (x + a)^2 = C$, where x is the variable, and a and C are constants. Take the square root of both sides and solve for the variable. Substitute the value of the variable in the original problem to check your work.

Probability and Statistics

Probability is a branch of statistics that deals with the likelihood of something taking place. One classic example is a coin toss. There are only two possible results: heads or tails. The likelihood, or probability, that the coin will land as heads is 1 out of 2 (1/2, 0.5, 50%). Tails has the same probability. Another common example is a 6-sided die roll. There are six possible results from rolling a single die, each with an equal chance of happening, so the probability of any given number coming up is 1 out of 6.

Terms frequently used in probability:
Event – a situation that produces results of some sort (a coin toss)
Compound event – event that involves two or more independent events (rolling a pair of dice; taking the sum)
Outcome – a possible result in an experiment or event (heads, tails)
Desired outcome (or success) – an outcome that meets a particular set of criteria (a roll of 1 or 2 if we are looking for numbers less than 3)
Independent events – two or more events whose outcomes do not affect one another (two coins tossed at the same time)
Dependent events – two or more events whose outcomes affect one another (two cards drawn consecutively from the same deck)
Certain outcome – probability of outcome is 100% or 1
Impossible outcome – probability of outcome is 0% or 0
Mutually exclusive outcomes – two or more outcomes whose criteria cannot all be satisfied in a single event (a coin coming up heads and tails on the same toss)

> ➤ **Review Video: Simple Probability**
> *Visit mometrix.com/academy and enter Code:* **212374**

Probability is the likelihood of a certain outcome occurring for a given event. The **theoretical probability** can usually be determined without actually performing the event. The likelihood of a outcome occurring, or the probability of an outcome occurring, is given by the formula

$$P(A) = \frac{\text{Number of acceptable outcomes}}{\text{Number of possible outcomes}}$$

where $P(A)$ is the probability of an outcome A occurring, and each outcome is just as likely to occur as any other outcome. If each outcome has the same probability of occurring as every other possible outcome, the outcomes are said to be equally likely to occur. The total number of acceptable outcomes must be less than or equal to the total number of possible outcomes. If the two are equal, then the outcome is certain to occur and the probability is 1. If the number of acceptable outcomes is zero, then the outcome is impossible and the probability is 0.
Example: There are 20 marbles in a bag and 5 are red. The theoretical probability of randomly selecting a red marble is 5 out of 20, (5/20 = 1/4, 0.25, or 25%).

When trying to calculate the probability of an event using the $\frac{desired\ outcomes}{total\ outcomes}$ formula, you may frequently find that there are too many outcomes to individually count them. Permutation and combination formulas offer a shortcut to counting outcomes. A permutation is an arrangement of a specific number of a set of objects in a specific order. The number of **permutations** of r items given a set of n items can be calculated as $_nP_r = \frac{n!}{(n-r)!}$. Combinations are similar to permutations, except

- 33 -

there are no restrictions regarding the order of the elements. While ABC is considered a different permutation than BCA, ABC and BCA are considered the same combination. The number of **combinations** of r items given a set of n items can be calculated as $_nC_r = \dfrac{n!}{r!(n-r)!}$ or $_nC_r = \dfrac{_nP_r}{r!}$.

Example: Suppose you want to calculate how many different 5-card hands can be drawn from a deck of 52 cards. This is a combination since the order of the cards in a hand does not matter. There are 52 cards available, and 5 to be selected. Thus, the number of different hands is $_{52}C_5 = \dfrac{52!}{5! \times 47!} = 2{,}598{,}960$.

Sometimes it may be easier to calculate the possibility of something not happening, or the **complement of an event**. Represented by the symbol $\bar{A}$, the complement of A is the probability that event A does not happen. When you know the probability of event A occurring, you can use the formula $P(\bar{A}) = 1 - P(A)$, where $P(\bar{A})$ is the probability of event A not occurring, and $P(A)$ is the probability of event A occurring.

The **addition rule** for probability is used for finding the probability of a compound event. Use the formula $P(A \text{ or } B) = P(A) + P(B) - P(A \text{ and } B)$, where $P(A \text{ and } B)$ is the probability of both events occurring to find the probability of a compound event. The probability of both events occurring at the same time must be subtracted to eliminate any overlap in the first two probabilities.

Conditional probability is the probability of an event occurring once another event has already occurred. Given event A and dependent event B, the probability of event B occurring when event A has already occurred is represented by the notation $P(A|B)$. To find the probability of event B occurring, take into account the fact that event A has already occurred and adjust the total number of possible outcomes. For example, suppose you have ten balls numbered 1–10 and you want ball number 7 to be pulled in two pulls. On the first pull, the probability of getting the 7 is $\dfrac{1}{10}$ because there is one ball with a 7 on it and 10 balls to choose from. Assuming the first pull did not yield a 7, the probability of pulling a 7 on the second pull is now $\dfrac{1}{9}$ because there are only 9 balls remaining for the second pull.

The **multiplication rule** can be used to find the probability of two independent events occurring using the formula $P(A \text{ and } B) = P(A) \times P(B)$, where $P(A \text{ and } B)$ is the probability of two independent events occurring, $P(A)$ is the probability of the first event occurring, and $P(B)$ is the probability of the second event occurring.

The multiplication rule can also be used to find the probability of two dependent events occurring using the formula $P(A \text{ and } B) = P(A) \times P(B|A)$, where $P(A \text{ and } B)$ is the probability of two dependent events occurring and $P(B|A)$ is the probability of the second event occurring after the first event has already occurred.

Before using the multiplication rule, you MUST first determine whether the two events are dependent or independent.

Use a combination of the multiplication rule and the rule of complements to find the probability that at least one outcome of the element will occur. This given by the general formula $P(\text{at least one event occurring}) = 1 - P(\text{no outcomes occurring})$. For example, to find the probability that at least one even number will show when a pair of dice is rolled, find the probability that two odd numbers will be rolled (no even numbers) and subtract from one. You can always use a tree diagram or make a chart to list the possible outcomes when the sample space is

- 34 -

small, such as in the dice-rolling example, but in most cases it will be much faster to use the multiplication and complement formulas.

Expected value is a method of determining expected outcome in a random situation. It is really a sum of the weighted probabilities of the possible outcomes. Multiply the probability of an event occurring by the weight assigned to that probability (such as the amount of money won or lost). A practical application of the expected value is to determine whether a game of chance is really fair. If the sum of the weighted probabilities is equal to zero, the game is generally considered fair because the player has a fair chance to at least to break even. If the expected value is less than zero, then players lose more than they win. For example, a lottery drawing might allow the player to choose any three-digit number, 000–999. The probability of choosing the winning number is 1:1000. If it costs $1 to play, and a winning number receives $500, the expected value is $\left(-\$1 \cdot \frac{999}{1,000}\right) +$ $\left(\$500 \cdot \frac{1}{1,000}\right) = -0.499$ or $-\$0.50$. You can expect to lose on average 50 cents for every dollar you spend.

Most of the time, when we talk about probability, we mean theoretical probability. **Empirical probability**, or experimental probability or relative frequency, is the number of times an outcome occurs in a particular experiment or a certain number of observed events. While theoretical probability is based on what *should* happen, experimental probability is based on what *has* happened. Experimental probability is calculated in the same way as theoretical, except that actual outcomes are used instead of possible outcomes.

Theoretical and experimental probability do not always line up with one another. Theoretical probability says that out of 20 coin tosses, 10 should be heads. However, if we were actually to toss 20 coins, we might record just 5 heads. This doesn't mean that our theoretical probability is incorrect; it just means that this particular experiment had results that were different from what was predicted. A practical application of empirical probability is the insurance industry. There are no set functions that define life span, health, or safety. Insurance companies look at factors from hundreds of thousands of individuals to find patterns that they then use to set the formulas for insurance premiums.

Objective probability is based on mathematical formulas and documented evidence. Examples of objective probability include raffles or lottery drawings where there is a pre-determined number of possible outcomes and a predetermined number of outcomes that correspond to an event. Other cases of objective probability include probabilities of rolling dice, flipping coins, or drawing cards. Most gambling games are based on objective probability.

Subjective probability is based on personal or professional feelings and judgments. Often, there is a lot of guesswork following extensive research. Areas where subjective probability is applicable include sales trends and business expenses. Attractions set admission prices based on subjective probabilities of attendance based on varying admission rates in an effort to maximize their profit.

The total set of all possible results of a test or experiment is called a **sample space**, or sometimes a universal sample space. The sample space, represented by one of the variables S, Ω, or U (for universal sample space) has individual elements called outcomes. Other terms for outcome that may be used interchangeably include elementary outcome, simple event, or sample point. The number of outcomes in a given sample space could be infinite or finite, and some tests may yield multiple unique sample sets. For example, tests conducted by drawing playing cards from a standard deck would have one sample space of the card values, another sample space of the card suits, and a third sample space of suit-denomination combinations. For most tests, the sample spaces considered will be finite.

An event, represented by the variable E, is a portion of a sample space. It may be one outcome or a group of outcomes from the same sample space. If an event occurs, then the test or experiment will generate an outcome that satisfies the requirement of that event. For example, given a standard deck of 52 playing cards as the sample space, and defining the event as the collection of face cards, then the event will occur if the card drawn is a J, Q, or K. If any other card is drawn, the event is said to have not occurred.

For every sample space, each possible outcome has a specific likelihood, or probability, that it will occur. The probability measure, also called the distribution, is a function that assigns a real number probability, from zero to one, to each outcome. For a probability measure to be accurate, every outcome must have a real number probability measure that is greater than or equal to zero and less than or equal to one. Also, the probability measure of the sample space must equal one, and the probability measure of the union of multiple outcomes must equal the sum of the individual probability measures.

Probabilities of events are expressed as real numbers from zero to one. They give a numerical value to the chance that a particular event will occur. The probability of an event occurring is the sum of the probabilities of the individual elements of that event. For example, in a standard deck of 52 playing cards as the sample space and the collection of face cards as the event, the probability of drawing a specific face card is $\frac{1}{52} = 0.019$, but the probability of drawing any one of the twelve face cards is $12(0.019) = 0.228$. Note that rounding of numbers can generate different results. If you multiplied 12 by the fraction $\frac{1}{52}$ before converting to a decimal, you would get the answer $\frac{12}{52} = 0.231$.

For a simple sample space, possible outcomes may be determined by using a **tree diagram** or an organized chart. In either case, you can easily draw or list out the possible outcomes. For example, to determine all the possible ways three objects can be ordered, you can draw a tree diagram:

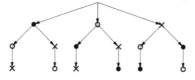

You can also make a chart to list all the possibilities:

First object	Second object	Third object
●	X	O
●	O	X
O	●	X
O	X	●
X	●	O
X	O	●

Either way, you can easily see there are six possible ways the three objects can be ordered.

If two events have no outcomes in common, they are said to be mutually exclusive. For example, in a standard deck of 52 playing cards, the event of all card suits is mutually exclusive to the event of all card values. If two events have no bearing on each other so that one event occurring has no influence on the probability of another event occurring, the two events are said to be independent. For example, rolling a standard six-sided die multiple times does not change that probability that a particular number will be rolled from one roll to the next. If the outcome of one event does affect the probability of the second event, the two events are said to be dependent. For example, if cards are drawn from a deck, the probability of drawing an ace after an ace has been drawn is different than the probability of drawing an ace if no ace (or no other card, for that matter) has been drawn.

In probability, the odds in favor of an event are the number of times the event will occur compared to the number of times the event will not occur. To calculate the odds in favor of an event, use the formula $\frac{P(A)}{1-P(A)}$, where $P(A)$ is the probability that the event will occur. Many times, odds in favor is given as a ratio in the form $\frac{a}{b}$ or $a:b$, where a is the probability of the event occurring and b is the complement of the event, the probability of the event not occurring. If the odds in favor are given as 2:5, that means that you can expect the event to occur two times for every 5 times that it does not occur. In other words, the probability that the event will occur is $\frac{2}{2+5} = \frac{2}{7}$.

In probability, the odds against an event are the number of times the event will not occur compared to the number of times the event will occur. To calculate the odds against an event, use the formula $\frac{1-P(A)}{P(A)}$, where $P(A)$ is the probability that the event will occur. Many times, odds against is given as a ratio in the form $\frac{b}{a}$ or $b:a$, where b is the probability the event will not occur (the complement of the event) and a is the probability the event will occur. If the odds against an event are given as 3:1, that means that you can expect the event to not occur 3 times for every one time it does occur. In other words, 3 out of every 4 trials will fail.

Statistics

In statistics, the *Population* is the entire collection of people, plants, etc., that data can be collected from. For example, a study to determine how well students in the area schools perform on a standardized test would have a population of all the students enrolled in those schools, although a study may include just a small sample of students from each school. A *Parameter* is a numerical value that gives information about the population, such as the mean, median, mode, or standard deviation. Remember that the symbol for the mean of a population is μ and the symbol for the standard deviation of a population is σ.

A *Sample* is a portion of the entire population. Where as a parameter helped describe the population, a *Statistic* is a numerical value that gives information about the sample, such as mean, median, mode, or standard deviation. Keep in mind that the symbols for mean and standard deviation are different when they are referring to a sample rather than the entire population. For a sample, the symbol for mean is $\bar{x}$ and the symbol for standard deviation is s. The mean and standard deviation of a sample may or may not be identical to that of the entire population due to a sample only being a subset of the population. However, if the sample is random and large enough, statistically significant values can be attained. Samples are generally used when the population is too large to justify including every element or when acquiring data for the entire population is impossible.

Inferential Statistics is the branch of statistics that uses samples to make predictions about an entire population. This type of statistics is often seen in political polls, where a sample of the population is questioned about a particular topic or politician to gain an understanding about the attitudes of the entire population of the country. Often, exit polls are conducted on election days using this method. Inferential statistics can have a large margin of error if you do not have a valid sample.

Statistical values calculated from various samples of the same size make up the sampling distribution. For example, if several samples of identical size are randomly selected from a large population and then the mean of each sample is calculated, the distribution of values of the means would be a *Sampling Distribution*.

The *Sampling Distribution of the Mean* is the distribution of the sample mean, $\bar{x}$, derived from random samples of a given size. It has three important characteristics. First, the mean of the sampling distribution of the mean is equal to the mean of the population that was sampled. Second, assuming the standard deviation is non-zero, the standard deviation of the sampling distribution of the mean equals the standard deviation of the sampled population divided by the square root of the sample size. This is sometimes called the standard error. Finally, as the sample size gets larger, the sampling distribution of the mean gets closer to a normal distribution via the Central Limit Theorem.

A *Survey Study* is a method of gathering information from a small group in an attempt to gain enough information to make accurate general assumptions about the population. Once a survey study is completed, the results are then put into a summary report. Survey studies are generally in the format of surveys, interviews, or questionnaires as part of an effort to find opinions of a particular group or to find facts about a group. It is important to note that the findings from a survey study are only as accurate as the sample chosen from the population.

Correlational Studies seek to determine how much one variable is affected by changes in a second variable. For example, correlational studies may look for a relationship between the amount of time a student spends studying for a test and the grade that student earned on the test or between student scores on college admissions tests and student grades in college. It is important to note that correlational studies cannot show a cause and effect, but rather can show only that two variables are or are not potentially correlated.

Experimental Studies take correlational studies one step farther, in that they attempt to prove or disprove a cause-and-effect relationship. These studies are performed by conducting a series of experiments to test the hypothesis. For a study to be scientifically accurate, it must have both an experimental group that receives the specified treatment and a control group that does not get the treatment. This is the type of study pharmaceutical companies do as part of drug trials for new medications. Experimental studies are only valid when proper scientific method has been followed. In other words, the experiment must be well-planned and executed without bias in the testing process, all subjects must be selected at random, and the process of determining which subject is in which of the two groups must also be completely random.

Observational Studies are the opposite of experimental studies. In observational studies, the tester cannot change or in any way control all of the variables in the test. For example, a study to determine which gender does better in math classes in school is strictly observational. You cannot change a person's gender, and you cannot change the subject being studied. The big downfall of observational studies is that you have no way of proving a cause-and-effect relationship because you cannot control outside influences. Events outside of school can influence a student's performance in school, and observational studies cannot take that into consideration.

For most studies, a *Random Sample* is necessary to produce valid results. Random samples should not have any particular influence to cause sampled subjects to behave one way or another. The goal is for the random sample to be a *Representative Sample*, or a sample whose characteristics give an accurate picture of the characteristics of the entire population. To accomplish this, you must make sure you have a proper *Sample Size*, or an appropriate number of elements in the sample.

In statistical studies, biases must be avoided. *Bias* is an error that causes the study to favor one set of results over another. For example, if a survey to determine how the country views the president's job performance only speaks to registered voters in the president's party, the results will be skewed because a disproportionately large number of responders would tend to show approval, while a disproportionately large number of people in the opposite party would tend to express disapproval.

Extraneous Variables are, as the name implies, outside influences that can affect the outcome of a study. They are not always avoidable, but could trigger bias in the result.

Data Analysis

The *Measure of Central Tendency* is a statistical value that gives a general tendency for the center of a group of data. There are several different ways of describing the measure of central tendency. Each one has a unique way it is calculated, and each one gives a slightly different perspective on the data set. Whenever you give a measure of central tendency, always make sure the units are the same. If the data has different units, such as hours, minutes, and seconds, convert all the data to the same unit, and use the same unit in the measure of central tendency. If no units are given in the data, do not give units for the measure of central tendency.

The statistical *Mean* of a group of data is the same as the arithmetic average of that group. To find the mean of a set of data, first convert each value to the same units, if necessary. Then find the sum of all the values, and count the total number of data values, making sure you take into consideration each individual value. If a value appears more than once, count it more than once. Divide the sum of the values by the total number of values and apply the units, if any. Note that the mean does not have to be one of the data values in the set, and may not divide evenly.

$$\text{mean} = \frac{\text{sum of the data values}}{\text{quantity of data values}}$$

While the mean is relatively easy to calculate and averages are understood by most people, the mean can be very misleading if used as the sole measure of central tendency. If the data set has outliers (data values that are unusually high or unusually low compared to the rest of the data values), the mean can be very distorted, especially if the data set has a small number of values. If unusually high values are countered with unusually low values, the mean is not affected as much. For example, if five of twenty students in a class get a 100 on a test, but the other 15 students have an average of 60 on the same test, the class average would appear as 70. Whenever the mean is skewed by outliers, it is always a good idea to include the median as an alternate measure of central tendency.

The statistical *Median* is the value in the middle of the set of data. To find the median, list all data values in order from smallest to largest or from largest to smallest. Any value that is repeated in the set must be listed the number of times it appears. If there are an odd number of data values, the median is the value in the middle of the list. If there is an even number of data values, the median is the arithmetic mean of the two middle values.

The statistical *Mode* is the data value that occurs the most number of times in the data set. It is possible to have exactly one mode, more than one mode, or no mode. To find the mode of a set of data, arrange the data like you do to find the median (all values in order, listing all multiples of data values). Count the number of times each value appears in the data set. If all values appear an equal number of times, there is no mode. If one value appears more than any other value, that value is the mode. If two or more values appear the same number of times, but there are other values that appear fewer times and no values that appear more times, all of those values are the modes.

The big disadvantage of using the median as a measure of central tendency is that is relies solely on a value's relative size as compared to the other values in the set. When the individual values in a set of data are evenly dispersed, the median can be an accurate tool. However, if there is a group of rather large values or a group of rather small values that are not offset by a different group of values, the information that can be inferred from the median may not be accurate because the distribution of values is skewed.

The main disadvantage of the mode is that the values of the other data in the set have no bearing on the mode. The mode may be the largest value, the smallest value, or a value anywhere in between in the set. The mode only tells which value or values, if any, occurred the most number of times. It does not give any suggestions about the remaining values in the set.

The *Measure of Dispersion* is a single value that helps to "interpret" the measure of central tendency by providing more information about how the data values in the set are distributed about the measure of central tendency. The measure of dispersion helps to eliminate or reduce the disadvantages of using the mean, median, or mode as a single measure of central tendency, and give a more accurate picture of the data set as a whole. To have a measure of dispersion, you must know or calculate the range, standard deviation, or variance of the data set.

The *Range* of a set of data is the difference between the greatest and lowest values of the data in the set. To calculate the range, you must first make sure the units for all data values are the same, and then identify the greatest and lowest values. Use the formula range = highest value – lowest value. If there are multiple data values that are equal for the highest or lowest, just use one of the values in the formula. Write the answer with the same units as the data values you used to do the calculations.

Standard Deviation is a measure of dispersion that compares all the data values in the set to the mean of the set to give a more accurate picture. To find the standard deviation of a population, use the formula

$$\sigma = \sqrt{\frac{\sum_{i=1}^{n}(x_i - \bar{x})^2}{n}}$$

where σ is the standard deviation of a population, x represents the individual values in the data set, $\bar{x}$ is the mean of the data values in the set, and n is the number of data values in the set. The higher the value of the standard deviation is, the greater the variance of the data values from the mean. If a constant is added to every value in the population, the mean will increase by that constant, but the standard deviation will remain the same. If every value in the population is multiplied by a constant factor, both the mean and standard deviation will increase by that factor.

The *Variance* of a population, or just variance, is the square of the standard deviation of that population. While the mean of a set of data gives the average of the set and gives information about where a specific data value lies in relation to the average, the variance of the population gives information about the degree to which the data values are spread out and tell you how close an individual value is to the average compared to the other values. The units associated with variance are the same as the units of the data values.

Percentiles and Quartiles are other methods of describing data within a set. *Percentiles* tell what percentage of the data in the set fall below a specific point. For example, achievement test scores are often given in percentiles. A score at the 80th percentile is one which is equal to or higher than 80 percent of the scores in the set. In other words, 80 percent of the scores were lower than that score.

Quartiles are percentile groups that make up quarter sections of the data set. The first quartile is the 25th percentile. The second quartile is the 50th percentile; this is also the median of the data set. The third quartile is the 75th percentile.

Skewness is a way to describe the symmetry or asymmetry of the distribution of values in a data set. If the distribution of values is symmetrical, there is no skew. In general the closer the mean of a data set is to the median of the data set, the less skew there is. Generally, if the mean is to the right of the median, the data set is *Positively Skewed*, or right-skewed, and if the mean is to the left of the median, the data set is *negatively skewed*, or left-skewed. However, this rule of thumb is not infallible. When the data values are graphed on a curve, a set with no skew will be a perfect bell curve. To estimate skew, use the formula

$$\text{skew} = \frac{\sqrt{n(n-1)}}{n-2}\left(\frac{\frac{1}{n}\sum_{i=1}^{n}(x_i - \bar{x})^3}{\left(\frac{1}{n}\sum_{i=1}^{n}(x_i - \bar{x})^2\right)^{\frac{3}{2}}}\right)$$

where n is the number of values is the set, x_i is the ith value in the set, and $\bar{x}$ is the mean of the set.

In statistics, *Simple Regression* is using an equation to represent a relation between an independent and dependent variables. The independent variable is also referred to as the explanatory variable or the predictor, and is generally represented by the variable x in the equation. The dependent variable, usually represented by the variable y, is also referred to as the response variable. The equation may be any type of function – linear, quadratic, exponential, etc. The best way to handle this task is to use the regression feature of your graphing calculator. This will easily give you the curve of best fit and provide you with the coefficients and other information you need to derive an equation.

In a scatter plot, the *Line of Best Fit* is the line that best shows the trends of the data. The line of best fit is given by the equation $\hat{y} = ax + b$, where a and b are the regression coefficients. The regression coefficient a is also the slope of the line of best fit, and b is also the y-coordinate of the point at which the line of best fit crosses the x-axis. Not every point on the scatter plot will be on the line of best fit. The differences between the y-values of the points in the scatter plot and the corresponding y-values according to the equation of the line of best fit are the residuals. The line of best fit is also called the least-squares regression line because it is also the line that has the lowest sum of the squares of the residuals.

The *Correlation Coefficient* is the numerical value that indicates how strong the relationship is between the two variables of a linear regression equation. A correlation coefficient of –1 is a perfect negative correlation. A correlation coefficient of +1 is a perfect positive correlation. Correlation coefficients close to –1 or +1 are very strong correlations. A correlation coefficient equal to zero indicates there is no correlation between the two variables. This test is a good indicator of whether or not the equation for the line of best fit is accurate. The formula for the correlation coefficient is

$$r = \frac{\sum_{i=1}^{n}(x_i - \bar{x})(y_i - \bar{y})}{\sqrt{\sum_{i=1}^{n}(x_i - \bar{x})^2}\sqrt{\sum_{i=1}^{n}(y_i - \bar{y})^2}}$$

where r is the correlation coefficient, n is the number of data values in the set, (x_i, y_i) is a point in the set, and $\bar{x}$ and $\bar{y}$ are the means.

A *Z-score* is an indication of how many standard deviations a given value falls from the mean. To calculate a z-score, use the formula $= \frac{x-\mu}{\sigma}$, where x is the data value, μ is the mean of the data set, and σ is the standard deviation of the population. If the z-score is positive, the data value lies above the mean. If the z-score is negative, the data value falls below the mean. These scores are useful in interpreting data such as standardized test scores, where every piece of data in the set has been counted, rather than just a small random sample. In cases where standard deviations are calculated from a random sample of the set, the z-scores will not be as accurate.

According to the *Central Limit Theorem*, regardless of what the original distribution of a sample is, the distribution of the means tends to get closer and closer to a normal distribution as the sample size gets larger and larger (this is necessary because the sample is becoming more all-encompassing of the elements of the population). As the sample size gets larger, the distribution of the sample mean will approach a normal distribution with a mean of the population mean and a variance of the population variance divided by the sample size.

Displaying Information

Charts and *Tables* are ways of organizing information into separate rows and columns that are labeled to identify and explain the data contained in them. Some charts and tables are organized horizontally, with row lengths giving the details about the labeled information. Other charts and tables are organized vertically, with column heights giving the details about the labeled information.

Frequency Tables show how frequently each unique value appears in the set. A *Relative Frequency Table* is one that shows the proportions of each unique value compared to the entire set. Relative frequencies are given as percents; however, the total percent for a relative frequency table will not necessarily equal 100 percent due to rounding. An example of a frequency table with relative frequencies is below.

Favorite Color	Frequency	Relative Frequency
Blue	4	13%
Red	7	22%
Purple	3	9%
Green	6	19%
Cyan	12	38%

A *Pictograph* is a graph, generally in the horizontal orientation, that uses pictures or symbols to represent the data. Each pictograph must have a key that defines the picture or symbol and gives the quantity each picture or symbol represents. Pictures or symbols on a pictograph are not always shown as whole elements. In this case, the fraction of the picture or symbol shown represents the same fraction of the quantity a whole picture or symbol stands for. For example, a row with $3\frac{1}{2}$ ears of corn, where each ear of corn represents 100 stalks of corn in a field, would equal $3\frac{1}{2} \cdot 100 = 350$ stalks of corn in the field.

Circle Graphs, also known as *Pie Charts*, provide a visual depiction of the relationship of each type of data compared to the whole set of data. The circle graph is divided into sections by drawing radii to create central angles whose percentage of the circle is equal to the individual data's percentage of the whole set. Each 1% of data is equal to 3.6º in the circle graph. Therefore, data represented by a 90º section of the circle graph makes up 25% of the whole. When complete, a circle graph often looks like a pie cut into uneven wedges. The pie chart below shows the data from the frequency table referenced earlier where people were asked their favorite color.

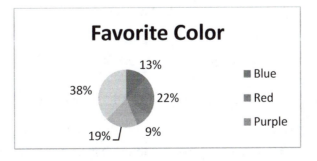

Line Graphs have one or more lines of varying styles (solid or broken) to show the different values for a set of data. The individual data are represented as ordered pairs, much like on a Cartesian plane. In this case, the *x*- and *y*- axes are defined in terms of their units, such as dollars or time. The individual plotted points are joined by line segments to show whether the value of the data is increasing (line sloping upward), decreasing (line sloping downward) or staying the same (horizontal line). Multiple sets of data can be graphed on the same line graph to give an easy visual comparison. An example of this would be graphing achievement test scores for different groups of students over the same time period to see which group had the greatest increase or decrease in performance from year-to-year (as shown below).

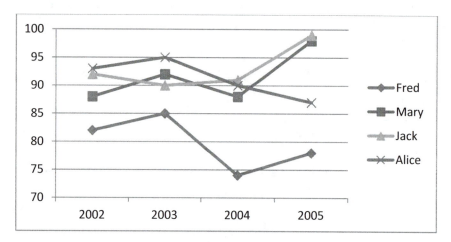

A *Line Plot*, also known as a *Dot Plot*, has plotted points that are NOT connected by line segments. In this graph, the horizontal axis lists the different possible values for the data, and the vertical axis lists the number of times the individual value occurs. A single dot is graphed for each value to show the number of times it occurs. This graph is more closely related to a bar graph than a line graph. Do not connect the dots in a line plot or it will misrepresent the data.

A *Stem and Leaf Plot* is useful for depicting groups of data that fall into a range of values. Each piece of data is separated into two parts: the first, or left, part is called the stem; the second, or right, part is called the leaf. Each stem is listed in a column from smallest to largest. Each leaf that has the common stem is listed in that stem's row from smallest to largest. For example, in a set of two-digit numbers, the digit in the tens place is the stem, and the digit in the ones place is the leaf. With a stem and leaf plot, you can easily see which subset of numbers (10s, 20s, 30s, etc.) is the largest. This information is also readily available by looking at a histogram, but a stem and leaf plot also allows you to look closer and see exactly which values fall in that range. Using all of the test scores from above, we can assemble a stem and leaf plot like the one below.

Test Scores								
7	4	8						
8	2	5	7	8	8			
9	0	0	1	2	2	3	5	8	9

A *Bar Graph* is one of the few graphs that can be drawn correctly in two different configurations – both horizontally and vertically. A bar graph is similar to a line plot in the way the data is organized on the graph. Both axes must have their categories defined for the graph to be useful. Rather than placing a single dot to mark the point of the data's value, a bar, or thick line, is drawn from zero to the exact value of the data, whether it is a number, percentage, or other numerical value. Longer bar lengths correspond to greater data values. To read a bar graph, read the labels for the axes to find the units being reported. Then look where the bars end in relation to the scale given on the corresponding axis and determine the associated value. The bar chart below represents the responses from our favorite color survey.

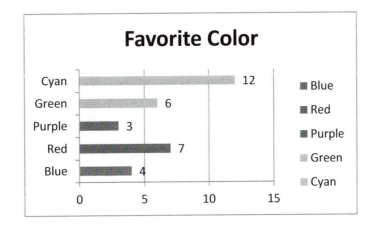

At first glance, a *Histogram* looks like a vertical bar graph. The difference is that a bar graph has a separate bar for each piece of data and a histogram has one continuous bar for each *Range* of data. For example, a histogram may have one bar for the range 0–9, one bar for 10–19, etc. While a bar graph has numerical values on one axis, a histogram has numerical values on both axes. Each range is of equal size, and they are ordered left to right from lowest to highest. The height of each column on a histogram represents the number of data values within that range. Like a stem and leaf plot, a histogram makes it easy to glance at the graph and quickly determine which range has the greatest quantity of values. A simple example of a histogram is below.

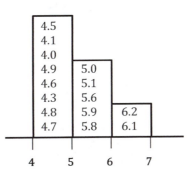

Bivariate Data is simply data from two different variables. (The prefix *bi-* means *two*.) In a *Scatter Plot*, each value in the set of data is plotted on a grid similar to a Cartesian plane, where each axis represents one of the two variables. By looking at the pattern formed by the points on the grid, you can often determine whether or not there is a relationship between the two variables, and what that relationship is, if it exists. The variables may be directly proportionate, inversely proportionate, or show no proportion at all. It may also be possible to determine if the data is linear, and if so, to find an equation to relate the two variables. The following scatter plot shows the relationship between preference for brand "A" and the age of the consumers surveyed.

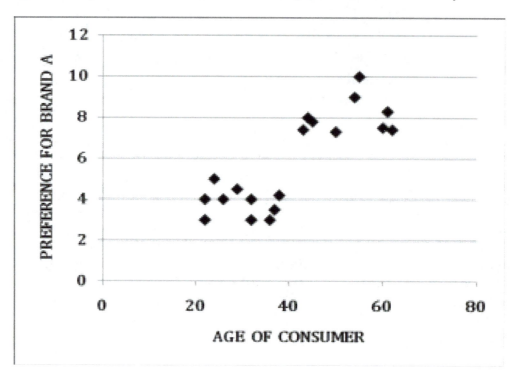

Scatter Plots are also useful in determining the type of function represented by the data and finding the simple regression. Linear scatter plots may be positive or negative. Nonlinear scatter plots are generally exponential or quadratic. Below are some common types of scatter plots:

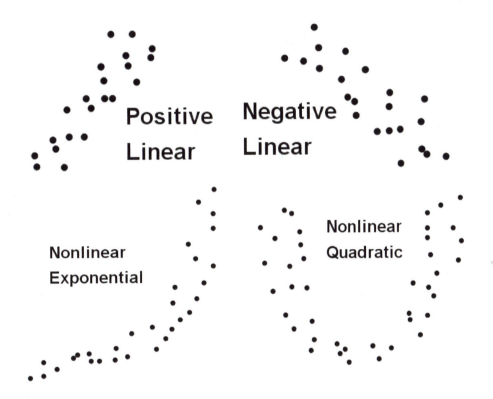

The *5-Number Summary* of a set of data gives a very informative picture of the set. The five numbers in the summary include the minimum value, maximum value, and the three quartiles. This information gives the reader the range and median of the set, as well as an indication of how the data is spread about the median.

A *Box-and-Whiskers Plot* is a graphical representation of the 5-number summary. To draw a box-and-whiskers plot, plot the points of the 5-number summary on a number line. Draw a box whose ends are through the points for the first and third quartiles. Draw a vertical line in the box through the median to divide the box in half. Draw a line segment from the first quartile point to the minimum value, and from the third quartile point to the maximum value.

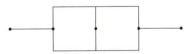

The *68–95–99.7 Rule* describes how a normal distribution of data should appear when compared to the mean. This is also a description of a normal bell curve. According to this rule, 68 percent of the data values in a normally distributed set should fall within one standard deviation of the mean (34 percent above and 34 percent below the mean), 95 percent of the data values should fall within two standard deviations of the mean (47.5 percent above and 47.5 percent below the mean), and 99.7 percent of the data values should fall within three standard deviations of the mean, again, equally distributed on either side of the mean. This means that only 0.3 percent of all data values should fall more than three standard deviations from the mean. On the graph below, the normal curve is centered on the y-axis. The x-axis labels are how many standard deviations away from the center you are. Therefore, it is easy to see how the 68-95-99.7 rule can apply.

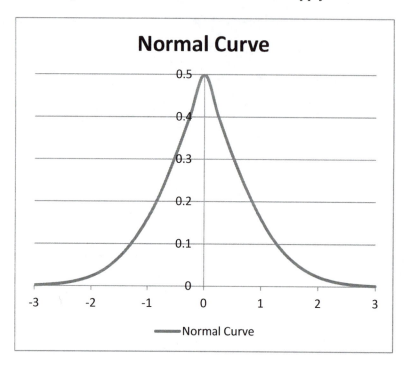

The five general shapes of frequency curves are *Symmetrical, U-shaped, Skewed, J-shaped,* and *Multimodal.* Symmetrical curves are also known as bell curves or normal curves. Values equidistant from the median have equal frequencies. U-shaped curves have two maxima – one at each end. Skewed curves have the maximum point off-center. Curves that are negative skewed, or left skewed, have the maximum on the right side of the graph so there is longer tail and lower slope on the left side. The opposite is true for curves that are positive skewed, or right skewed. J-shaped curves have a maximum at one end and a minimum at the other end. Multimodal curves have multiple maxima. For example, if the curve has exactly two maxima, it is called a bimodal curve.

Geometry

Lines and Planes

A point is a fixed location in space; has no size or dimensions; commonly represented by a dot.

A line is a set of points that extends infinitely in two opposite directions. It has length, but no width or depth. A line can be defined by any two distinct points that it contains. A line segment is a portion of a line that has definite endpoints. A ray is a portion of a line that extends from a single point on that line in one direction along the line. It has a definite beginning, but no ending.

> ➤ **Review Video: Geometric Symbols: Segments, Lines, Rays, and Vectors**
> *Visit **mometrix.com/academy** and enter **Code: 122404***

A plane is a two-dimensional flat surface defined by three non-collinear points. A plane extends an infinite distance in all directions in those two dimensions. It contains an infinite number of points, parallel lines and segments, intersecting lines and segments, as well as parallel or intersecting rays. A plane will never contain a three-dimensional figure or skew lines. Two given planes will either be parallel or they will intersect to form a line. A plane may intersect a circular conic surface, such as a cone, to form conic sections, such as the parabola, hyperbola, circle or ellipse.

Perpendicular lines are lines that intersect at right angles. They are represented by the symbol ⊥. The shortest distance from a line to a point not on the line is a perpendicular segment from the point to the line.

Parallel lines are lines in the same plane that have no points in common and never meet. It is possible for lines to be in different planes, have no points in common, and never meet, but they are not parallel because they are in different planes.

> ➤ **Review Video: Parallel and Perpendicular Lines**
> *Visit **mometrix.com/academy** and enter **Code: 815923***

A bisector is a line or line segment that divides another line segment into two equal lengths. A perpendicular bisector of a line segment is composed of points that are equidistant from the endpoints of the segment it is dividing.

Intersecting lines are lines that have exactly one point in common. Concurrent lines are multiple lines that intersect at a single point.

A transversal is a line that intersects at least two other lines, which may or may not be parallel to one another. A transversal that intersects parallel lines is a common occurrence in geometry.

Angles

An angle is formed when two lines or line segments meet at a common point. It may be a common starting point for a pair of segments or rays, or it may be the intersection of lines. Angles are represented by the symbol ∠.

The vertex is the point at which two segments or rays meet to form an angle. If the angle is formed by intersecting rays, lines, and/or line segments, the vertex is the point at which four angles are formed. The pairs of angles opposite one another are called vertical angles, and their measures are equal.

An acute angle is an angle with a degree measure less than 90°.
A right angle is an angle with a degree measure of exactly 90°.
An obtuse angle is an angle with a degree measure greater than 90° but less than 180°.
A straight angle is an angle with a degree measure of exactly 180°. This is also a semicircle.
A reflex angle is an angle with a degree measure greater than 180° but less than 360°.
A full angle is an angle with a degree measure of exactly 360°.

Two angles whose sum is exactly 90° are said to be complementary. The two angles may or may not be adjacent. In a right triangle, the two acute angles are complementary.

Two angles whose sum is exactly 180° are said to be supplementary. The two angles may or may not be adjacent. Two intersecting lines always form two pairs of supplementary angles. Adjacent supplementary angles will always form a straight line.

Two angles that have the same vertex and share a side are said to be adjacent. Vertical angles are not adjacent because they share a vertex but no common side.

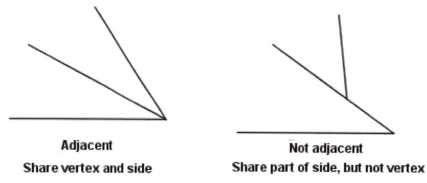

Adjacent
Share vertex and side

Not adjacent
Share part of side, but not vertex

When two parallel lines are cut by a transversal, the angles that are between the two parallel lines are interior angles. In the diagram below, angles 3, 4, 5, and 6 are interior angles.

When two parallel lines are cut by a transversal, the angles that are outside the parallel lines are exterior angles. In the diagram below, angles 1, 2, 7, and 8 are exterior angles.

When two parallel lines are cut by a transversal, the angles that are in the same position relative to the transversal and a parallel line are corresponding angles. The diagram below has four pairs of corresponding angles: angles 1 and 5; angles 2 and 6; angles 3 and 7; and angles 4 and 8. Corresponding angles formed by parallel lines are congruent.

When two parallel lines are cut by a transversal, the two interior angles that are on opposite sides of the transversal are called alternate interior angles. In the diagram below, there are two pairs of alternate interior angles: angles 3 and 6, and angles 4 and 5. Alternate interior angles formed by parallel lines are congruent.

When two parallel lines are cut by a transversal, the two exterior angles that are on opposite sides of the transversal are called alternate exterior angles. In the diagram below, there are two pairs of alternate exterior angles: angles 1 and 8, and angles 2 and 7. Alternate exterior angles formed by parallel lines are congruent.

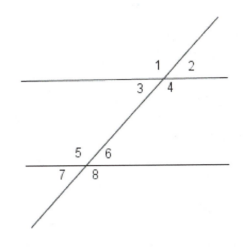

When two lines intersect, four angles are formed. The non-adjacent angles at this vertex are called vertical angles. Vertical angles are congruent. In the diagram, $\angle ABD \cong \angle CBE$ and $\angle ABC \cong \angle DBE$.

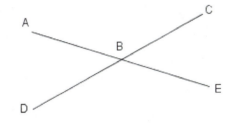

> ➢ **Review Video: Angles**
> Visit *mometrix.com/academy* and enter **Code: 264624**

Triangles

An equilateral triangle is a triangle with three congruent sides. An equilateral triangle will also have three congruent angles, each 60°. All equilateral triangles are also acute triangles.

An isosceles triangle is a triangle with two congruent sides. An isosceles triangle will also have two congruent angles opposite the two congruent sides.

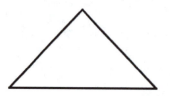

A scalene triangle is a triangle with no congruent sides. A scalene triangle will also have three angles of different measures. The angle with the largest measure is opposite the longest side, and the angle with the smallest measure is opposite the shortest side.

An acute triangle is a triangle whose three angles are all less than 90°. If two of the angles are equal, the acute triangle is also an isosceles triangle. If the three angles are all equal, the acute triangle is also an equilateral triangle.

A right triangle is a triangle with exactly one angle equal to 90°. All right triangles follow the Pythagorean Theorem. A right triangle can never be acute or obtuse.

An obtuse triangle is a triangle with exactly one angle greater than 90°. The other two angles may or may not be equal. If the two remaining angles are equal, the obtuse triangle is also an isosceles triangle.

Terminology

Altitude of a Triangle: A line segment drawn from one vertex perpendicular to the opposite side. In the diagram below, $\overline{BE}$, $\overline{AD}$, and $\overline{CF}$ are altitudes. The three altitudes in a triangle are always concurrent.

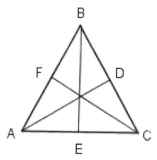

Height of a Triangle: The length of the altitude, although the two terms are often used interchangeably.

Orthocenter of a Triangle: The point of concurrency of the altitudes of a triangle. Note that in an obtuse triangle, the orthocenter will be outside the circle, and in a right triangle, the orthocenter is the vertex of the right angle.

Median of a Triangle: A line segment drawn from one vertex to the midpoint of the opposite side. This is not the same as the altitude, except the altitude to the base of an isosceles triangle and all three altitudes of an equilateral triangle.

Centroid of a Triangle: The point of concurrency of the medians of a triangle. This is the same point as the orthocenter only in an equilateral triangle. Unlike the orthocenter, the centroid is always inside the triangle. The centroid can also be considered the exact center of the triangle. Any shape triangle can be perfectly balanced on a tip placed at the centroid. The centroid is also the point that is two-thirds the distance from the vertex to the opposite side.

Pythagorean Theorem

The side of a triangle opposite the right angle is called the hypotenuse. The other two sides are called the legs. The Pythagorean Theorem states a relationship among the legs and hypotenuse of a right triangle: $a^2 + b^2 = c^2$, where a and b are the lengths of the legs of a right triangle, and c is the length of the hypotenuse. Note that this formula will only work with right triangles.

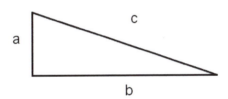

> ➤ **Review Video: Pythagorean Theorem**
> *Visit **mometrix.com/academy** and enter **Code: 906576***

General rules

The Triangle Inequality Theorem states that the sum of the measures of any two sides of a triangle is always greater than the measure of the third side. If the sum of the measures of two sides were equal to the third side, a triangle would be impossible because the two sides would lie flat across the third side and there would be no vertex. If the sum of the measures of two of the sides was less than the third side, a closed figure would be impossible because the two shortest sides would never meet.

The sum of the measures of the interior angles of a triangle is always 180°. Therefore, a triangle can never have more than one angle greater than or equal to 90°.

In any triangle, the angles opposite congruent sides are congruent, and the sides opposite congruent angles are congruent. The largest angle is always opposite the longest side, and the smallest angle is always opposite the shortest side.

The line segment that joins the midpoints of any two sides of a triangle is always parallel to the third side and exactly half the length of the third side.

Similarity and congruence rules

Similar triangles are triangles whose corresponding angles are equal and whose corresponding sides are proportional. Represented by AA. Similar triangles whose corresponding sides are congruent are also congruent triangles.

Three sides of one triangle are congruent to the three corresponding sides of the second triangle. Represented as SSS.

Two sides and the included angle (the angle formed by those two sides) of one triangle are congruent to the corresponding two sides and included angle of the second triangle. Represented by SAS.

Two angles and the included side (the side that joins the two angles) of one triangle are congruent to the corresponding two angles and included side of the second triangle. Represented by ASA.

Two angles and a non-included side of one triangle are congruent to the corresponding two angles and non-included side of the second triangle. Represented by AAS.

Note that AAA is not a form for congruent triangles. This would say that the three angles are congruent, but says nothing about the sides. This meets the requirements for similar triangles, but not congruent triangles.

Area and perimeter formulas

The perimeter of any triangle is found by summing the three side lengths; $P = a + b + c$. For an equilateral triangle, this is the same as $P = 3s$, where s is any side length, since all three sides are the same length.

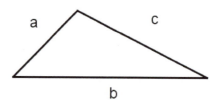

The area of any triangle can be found by taking half the product of one side length (base or b) and the perpendicular distance from that side to the opposite vertex (height or h). In equation form, $A = \frac{1}{2}bh$. For many triangles, it may be difficult to calculate h, so using one of the other formulas given here may be easier.

Another formula that works for any triangle is $A = \sqrt{s(s - a)(s - b)(s - c)}$, where A is the area, s is the semiperimeter $s = \frac{a+b+c}{2}$, and a, b, and c are the lengths of the three sides.

The area of an equilateral triangle can found by the formula $A = \frac{\sqrt{3}}{4}s^2$, where A is the area and s is the length of a side. You could use the $30° - 60° - 90°$ ratios to find the height of the triangle and then use the standard triangle area formula, but this is faster.

The area of an isosceles triangle can found by the formula, $A = \frac{1}{2}b\sqrt{a^2 - \frac{b^2}{4}}$, where A is the area, b is the base (the unique side), and a is the length of one of the two congruent sides. If you do not remember this formula, you can use the Pythagorean Theorem to find the height so you can use the standard formula for the area of a triangle.

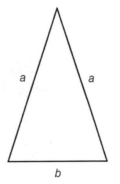

Trigonometric formulas

In the diagram below, angle C is the right angle, and side c is the hypotenuse. Side a is the side adjacent to angle B and side b is the side adjacent to angle A. These formulas will work for any acute angle in a right triangle. They will NOT work for any triangle that is not a right triangle. Also, they will not work for the right angle in a right triangle, since there are not distinct adjacent and opposite sides to differentiate from the hypotenuse.

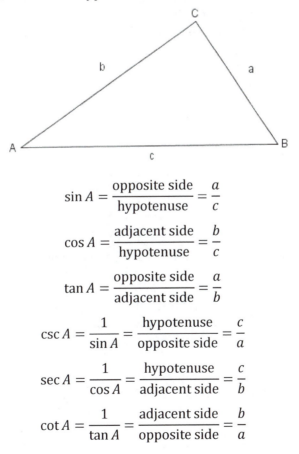

$$\sin A = \frac{\text{opposite side}}{\text{hypotenuse}} = \frac{a}{c}$$

$$\cos A = \frac{\text{adjacent side}}{\text{hypotenuse}} = \frac{b}{c}$$

$$\tan A = \frac{\text{opposite side}}{\text{adjacent side}} = \frac{a}{b}$$

$$\csc A = \frac{1}{\sin A} = \frac{\text{hypotenuse}}{\text{opposite side}} = \frac{c}{a}$$

$$\sec A = \frac{1}{\cos A} = \frac{\text{hypotenuse}}{\text{adjacent side}} = \frac{c}{b}$$

$$\cot A = \frac{1}{\tan A} = \frac{\text{adjacent side}}{\text{opposite side}} = \frac{b}{a}$$

Laws of Sines and Cosines

The Law of Sines states that $\frac{\sin A}{a} = \frac{\sin B}{b} = \frac{\sin C}{c}$, where A, B, and C are the angles of a triangle, and a, b, and c are the sides opposite their respective angles. This formula will work with all triangles, not just right triangles.

The Law of Cosines is given by the formula $c^2 = a^2 + b^2 - 2ab(\cos C)$, where a, b, and c are the sides of a triangle, and C is the angle opposite side c. This formula is similar to the Pythagorean Theorem, but unlike the Pythagorean Theorem, it can be used on any triangle.

Polygons

Each straight line segment of a polygon is called a side.

The point at which two sides of a polygon intersect is called the vertex. In a polygon, the number of sides is always equal to the number of vertices.

A polygon with all sides congruent and all angles equal is called a regular polygon.

A line segment from the center of a polygon perpendicular to a side of the polygon is called the apothem. In a regular polygon, the apothem can be used to find the area of the polygon using the formula $A = \frac{1}{2}ap$, where a is the apothem and p is the perimeter.

A line segment from the center of a polygon to a vertex of the polygon is called a radius. The radius of a regular polygon is also the radius of a circle that can be circumscribed about the polygon.

Triangle – 3 sides
Quadrilateral – 4 sides
Pentagon – 5 sides
Hexagon – 6 sides
Heptagon – 7 sides
Octagon – 8 sides
Nonagon – 9 sides
Decagon – 10 sides
Dodecagon – 12 sides

More generally, an n-gon is a polygon that has n angles and n sides.

The sum of the interior angles of an n-sided polygon is $(n - 2)180°$. For example, in a triangle n = 3, so the sum of the interior angles is $(3 - 2)180° = 180°$. In a quadrilateral, n = 4, and the sum of the angles is $(4 - 2)180° = 360°$. The sum of the interior angles of a polygon is equal to the sum of the interior angles of any other polygon with the same number of sides.

A diagonal is a line segment that joins two non-adjacent vertices of a polygon.
A convex polygon is a polygon whose diagonals all lie within the interior of the polygon.

A concave polygon is a polygon with a least one diagonal that lies outside the polygon. In the diagram below, quadrilateral *ABCD* is concave because diagonal $\overline{AC}$ lies outside the polygon.

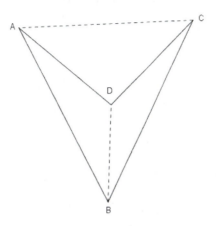

The number of diagonals a polygon has can be found by using the formula: number of diagonals $= \frac{n(n-3)}{2}$, where *n* is the number of sides in the polygon. This formula works for all polygons, not just regular polygons.

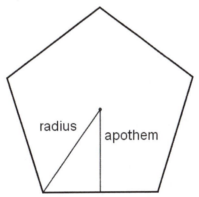

Congruent figures are geometric figures that have the same size and shape. All corresponding angles are equal, and all corresponding sides are equal. It is indicated by the symbol $\cong$.

Congruent polygons

Similar figures are geometric figures that have the same shape, but do not necessarily have the same size. All corresponding angles are equal, and all corresponding sides are proportional, but they do not have to be equal. It is indicated by the symbol ~.

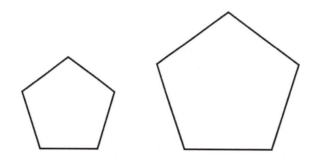

Similar polygons

Note that all congruent figures are also similar, but not all similar figures are congruent.
Line of Symmetry: The line that divides a figure or object into two symmetric parts. Each symmetric half is congruent to the other. An object may have no lines of symmetry, one line of symmetry, or more than one line of symmetry.

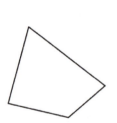 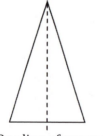 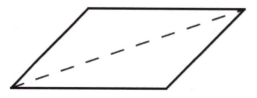

No lines of symmetry   One line of symmetry   Multiple lines of symmetry

Quadrilateral: A closed two-dimensional geometric figure composed of exactly four straight sides. The sum of the interior angles of any quadrilateral is 360°.

Parallelogram: A quadrilateral that has exactly two pairs of opposite parallel sides. The sides that are parallel are also congruent. The opposite interior angles are always congruent, and the consecutive interior angles are supplementary. The diagonals of a parallelogram bisect each other. Each diagonal divides the parallelogram into two congruent triangles.

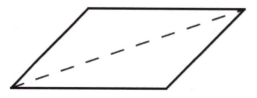

Trapezoid: Traditionally, a quadrilateral that has exactly one pair of parallel sides. Some math texts define trapezoid as a quadrilateral that has at least one pair of parallel sides. Because there are no

rules governing the second pair of sides, there are no rules that apply to the properties of the diagonals of a trapezoid.

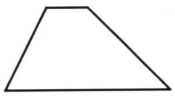

Rectangles, rhombuses, and squares are all special forms of parallelograms.
Rectangle: A parallelogram with four right angles. All rectangles are parallelograms, but not all parallelograms are rectangles. The diagonals of a rectangle are congruent.

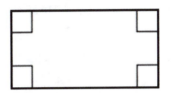

Rhombus: A parallelogram with four congruent sides. All rhombuses are parallelograms, but not all parallelograms are rhombuses. The diagonals of a rhombus are perpendicular to each other.

Square: A parallelogram with four right angles and four congruent sides. All squares are also parallelograms, rhombuses, and rectangles. The diagonals of a square are congruent and perpendicular to each other.

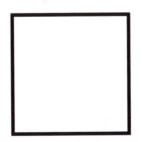

A quadrilateral whose diagonals bisect each other is a parallelogram. A quadrilateral whose opposite sides are parallel (2 pairs of parallel sides) is a parallelogram.

A quadrilateral whose diagonals are perpendicular bisectors of each other is a rhombus. A quadrilateral whose opposite sides (both pairs) are parallel and congruent is a rhombus.

A parallelogram that has a right angle is a rectangle. (Consecutive angles of a parallelogram are supplementary. Therefore if there is one right angle in a parallelogram, there are four right angles in that parallelogram.)

A rhombus with one right angle is a square. Because the rhombus is a special form of a parallelogram, the rules about the angles of a parallelogram also apply to the rhombus.

Area and perimeter formulas

The area of a square is found by using the formula $A = s^2$, where and s is the length of one side.

The perimeter of a square is found by using the formula $P = 4s$, where s is the length of one side. Because all four sides are equal in a square, it is faster to multiply the length of one side by 4 than to add the same number four times. You could use the formulas for rectangles and get the same answer.

The area of a rectangle is found by the formula $A = lw$, where A is the area of the rectangle, l is the length (usually considered to be the longer side) and w is the width (usually considered to be the shorter side). The numbers for l and w are interchangeable.

The perimeter of a rectangle is found by the formula $P = 2l + 2w$ or $P = 2(l + w)$, where l is the length, and w is the width. It may be easier to add the length and width first and then double the result, as in the second formula.

The area of a parallelogram is found by the formula $A = bh$, where b is the length of the base, and h is the height. Note that the base and height correspond to the length and width in a rectangle, so this formula would apply to rectangles as well. Do not confuse the height of a parallelogram with the length of the second side. The two are only the same measure in the case of a rectangle.

The perimeter of a parallelogram is found by the formula $P = 2a + 2b$ or $P = 2(a + b)$, where a and b are the lengths of the two sides.

The area of a trapezoid is found by the formula $A = \frac{1}{2}h(b_1 + b_2)$, where h is the height (segment joining and perpendicular to the parallel bases), and b_1 and b_2 are the two parallel sides (bases). Do not use one of the other two sides as the height unless that side is also perpendicular to the parallel bases.

The perimeter of a trapezoid is found by the formula $P = a + b_1 + c + b_2$, where a, b_1, c, and b_2 are the four sides of the trapezoid.

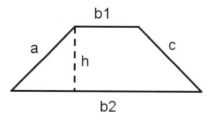

Circles

The center is the single point inside the circle that is equidistant from every point on the circle. (Point O in the diagram below.)

The radius is a line segment that joins the center of the circle and any one point on the circle. All radii of a circle are equal. (Segments OX, OY, and OZ in the diagram below.)

The diameter is a line segment that passes through the center of the circle and has both endpoints on the circle. The length of the diameter is exactly twice the length of the radius. (Segment XZ in the diagram below.)

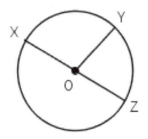

The area of a circle is found by the formula $A = \pi r^2$, where r is the length of the radius. If the diameter of the circle is given, remember to divide it in half to get the length of the radius before proceeding.

The circumference of a circle is found by the formula $C = 2\pi r$, where r is the radius. Again, remember to convert the diameter if you are given that measure rather than the radius.

Concentric circles are circles that have the same center, but not the same length of radii. A bulls-eye target is an example of concentric circles.

An arc is a portion of a circle. Specifically, an arc is the set of points between and including two points on a circle. An arc does not contain any points inside the circle. When a segment is drawn from the endpoints of an arc to the center of the circle, a sector is formed.

A central angle is an angle whose vertex is the center of a circle and whose legs intercept an arc of the circle. Angle XOY in the diagram above is a central angle. A minor arc is an arc that has a measure less than 180°. The measure of a central angle is equal to the measure of the minor arc it intercepts. A major arc is an arc having a measure of at least 180°. The measure of the major arc can be found by subtracting the measure of the central angle from 360°.

A semicircle is an arc whose endpoints are the endpoints of the diameter of a circle. A semicircle is exactly half of a circle.

An inscribed angle is an angle whose vertex lies on a circle and whose legs contain chords of that circle. The portion of the circle intercepted by the legs of the angle is called the intercepted arc. The measure of the intercepted arc is exactly twice the measure of the inscribed angle. In the diagram below, angle ABC is an inscribed angle. $\overset{\frown}{AC} = 2(m\angle ABC)$

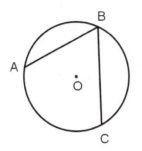

Any angle inscribed in a semicircle is a right angle. The intercepted arc is 180°, making the inscribed angle half that, or 90°. In the diagram below, angle ABC is inscribed in semicircle ABC, making angle ABC equal to 90°.

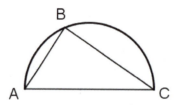

A chord is a line segment that has both endpoints on a circle. In the diagram below, $\overline{EB}$ is a chord.

Secant: A line that passes through a circle and contains a chord of that circle. In the diagram below, $\overleftrightarrow{EB}$ is a secant and contains chord $\overline{EB}$.

A tangent is a line in the same plane as a circle that touches the circle in exactly one point. While a line segment can be tangent to a circle as part of a line that is tangent, it is improper to say a tangent can be simply a line segment that touches the circle in exactly one point. In the diagram below, $\overleftrightarrow{CD}$ is tangent to circle A. Notice that $\overline{FB}$ is not tangent to the circle. $\overline{FB}$ is a line segment that touches the circle in exactly one point, but if the segment were extended, it would touch the circle in a second point. The point at which a tangent touches a circle is called the point of tangency. In the diagram below, point B is the point of tangency.

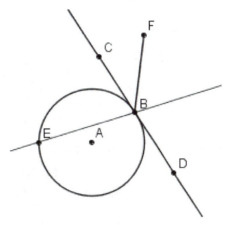

A secant is a line that intersects a circle in two points. Two secants may intersect inside the circle, on the circle, or outside the circle. When the two secants intersect on the circle, an inscribed angle is formed.

When two secants intersect inside a circle, the measure of each of two vertical angles is equal to half the sum of the two intercepted arcs. In the diagram below, $m\angle AEB = \frac{1}{2}(\overset{\frown}{AB} + \overset{\frown}{CD})$ and $m\angle BEC = \frac{1}{2}(\overset{\frown}{BC} + \overset{\frown}{AD})$.

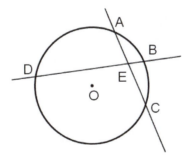

When two secants intersect outside a circle, the measure of the angle formed is equal to half the difference of the two arcs that lie between the two secants. In the diagram below, m∠$E = \frac{1}{2}(\widehat{AB} - \widehat{CD})$.

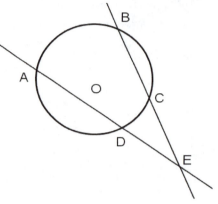

The arc length is the length of that portion of the circumference between two points on the circle. The formula for arc length is $s = \frac{\pi r \theta}{180°}$ where s is the arc length, r is the length of the radius, and θ is the angular measure of the arc in degrees, or $s = r\theta$, where θ is the angular measure of the arc in radians (2π radians = 360 degrees).

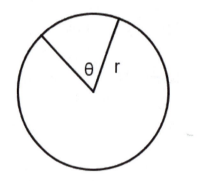

A sector is the portion of a circle formed by two radii and their intercepted arc. While the arc length is exclusively the points that are also on the circumference of the circle, the sector is the entire area bounded by the arc and the two radii.

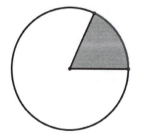

The area of a sector of a circle is found by the formula, $A = \frac{\theta r^2}{2}$, where A is the area, θ is the measure of the central angle in radians, and r is the radius. To find the area when the central angle is in degrees, use the formula, $A = \frac{\theta \pi r^2}{360}$, where θ is the measure of the central angle in degrees and r is the radius.

A circle is inscribed in a polygon if each of the sides of the polygon is tangent to the circle. A polygon is inscribed in a circle if each of the vertices of the polygon lies on the circle.

A circle is circumscribed about a polygon if each of the vertices of the polygon lies on the circle. A polygon is circumscribed about the circle if each of the sides of the polygon is tangent to the circle.

If one figure is inscribed in another, then the other figure is circumscribed about the first figure.

Circle circumscribed about a pentagon
Pentagon inscribed in a circle

Other conic sections

An ellipse is the set of all points in a plane, whose total distance from two fixed points called the foci (singular: focus) is constant, and whose center is the midpoint between the foci.

The standard equation of an ellipse that is taller than it is wide is $\frac{(y-k)^2}{a^2} + \frac{(x-h)^2}{b^2} = 1$, where a and b are coefficients. The center is the point (h, k) and the foci are the points $(h, k + c)$ and $(h, k - c)$, where $c^2 = a^2 - b^2$ and $a^2 > b^2$.

The major axis has length $2a$, and the minor axis has length $2b$.

Eccentricity (e) is a measure of how elongated an ellipse is, and is the ratio of the distance between the foci to the length of the major axis. Eccentricity will have a value between 0 and 1. The closer to 1 the eccentricity is, the closer the ellipse is to being a circle. The formula for eccentricity is $= \frac{c}{a}$.

Parabola: The set of all points in a plane that are equidistant from a fixed line, called the directrix, and a fixed point not on the line, called the focus.

Axis: The line perpendicular to the directrix that passes through the focus.

For parabolas that open up or down, the standard equation is $(x - h)^2 = 4c(y - k)$, where h, c, and k are coefficients. If c is positive, the parabola opens up. If c is negative, the parabola opens down. The vertex is the point (h, k). The directrix is the line having the equation $y = -c + k$, and the focus is the point $(h, c + k)$.

For parabolas that open left or right, the standard equation is $(y - k)^2 = 4c(x - h)$, where k, c, and h are coefficients. If c is positive, the parabola opens to the right. If c is negative, the parabola opens to the left. The vertex is the point (h, k). The directrix is the line having the equation $x = -c + h$, and the focus is the point $(c + h, k)$.

A hyperbola is the set of all points in a plane, whose distance from two fixed points, called foci, has a constant difference.

The standard equation of a horizontal hyperbola is $\frac{(x-h)^2}{a^2} - \frac{(y-k)^2}{b^2} = 1$, where a, b, h, and k are real numbers. The center is the point (h, k), the vertices are the points $(h + a, k)$ and $(h - a, k)$, and the foci are the points that every point on one of the parabolic curves is equidistant from and are found using the formulas $(h + c, k)$ and $(h - c, k)$, where $c^2 = a^2 + b^2$. The asymptotes are two lines the graph of the hyperbola approaches but never reaches, and are given by the equations $y = \left(\frac{b}{a}\right)(x - h) + k$ and $y = -\left(\frac{b}{a}\right)(x - h) + k$.

A vertical hyperbola is formed when a plane makes a vertical cut through two cones that are stacked vertex-to-vertex.

The standard equation of a vertical hyperbola is $\frac{(y-k)^2}{a^2} - \frac{(x-h)^2}{b^2} = 1$, where a, b, k, and h are real numbers. The center is the point (h, k), the vertices are the points $(h, k + a)$ and $(h, k - a)$, and the foci are the points that every point on one of the parabolic curves is equidistant from and are found using the formulas $(h, k + c)$ and $(h, k - c)$, where $c^2 = a^2 + b^2$. The asymptotes are two lines the graph of the hyperbola approaches but never reach, and are given by the equations $y = \left(\frac{a}{b}\right)(x - h) + k$ and $y = -\left(\frac{a}{b}\right)(x - h) + k$.

Solids

The surface area of a solid object is the area of all sides or exterior surfaces. For objects such as prisms and pyramids, a further distinction is made between base surface area (B) and lateral surface area (LA). For a prism, the total surface area (SA) is $SA = LA + 2B$. For a pyramid or cone, the total surface area is $SA = LA + B$.

The surface area of a sphere can be found by the formula $A = 4\pi r^2$, where r is the radius. The volume is given by the formula $V = \frac{4}{3}\pi r^3$, where r is the radius. Both quantities are generally given in terms of π.

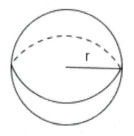

➤ **Review Video: <u>Volume and Surface Area of a Sphere</u>**
*Visit **mometrix.com/academy** and enter **Code: 786928***

The volume of any prism is found by the formula $V = Bh$, where B is the area of the base, and h is the height (perpendicular distance between the bases). The surface area of any prism is the sum of the areas of both bases and all sides. It can be calculated as $SA = 2B + Ph$, where P is the perimeter of the base.

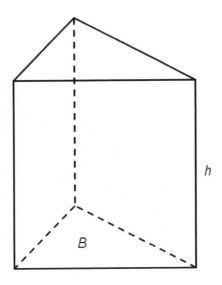

For a rectangular prism, the volume can be found by the formula $V = lwh$, where V is the volume, l is the length, w is the width, and h is the height. The surface area can be calculated as $SA = 2lw + 2hl + 2wh$ or $SA = 2(lw + hl + wh)$.

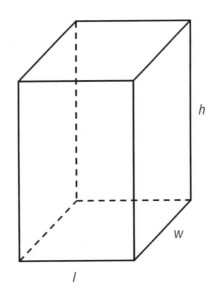

The volume of a cube can be found by the formula $V = s^3$, where s is the length of a side. The surface area of a cube is calculated as $SA = 6s^2$, where SA is the total surface area and s is the length of a side. These formulas are the same as the ones used for the volume and surface area of a rectangular prism, but simplified since all three quantities (length, width, and height) are the same.

> ➤ **Review Video: <u>Volume and Surface Area of a Cube</u>**
> *Visit **mometrix.com/academy** and enter **Code: 664455**

- 67 -

The volume of a cylinder can be calculated by the formula $V = \pi r^2 h$, where r is the radius, and h is the height. The surface area of a cylinder can be found by the formula $SA = 2\pi r^2 + 2\pi r h$. The first term is the base area multiplied by two, and the second term is the perimeter of the base multiplied by the height.

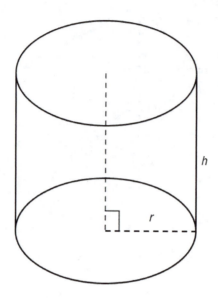

➤ **Review Video: <u>Volume of a Cylinder</u>**
*Visit **mometrix.com/academy** and enter **Code: 439978***

The volume of a pyramid is found by the formula $V = \frac{1}{3}Bh$, where B is the area of the base, and h is the height (perpendicular distance from the vertex to the base). Notice this formula is the same as $\frac{1}{3}$ times the volume of a prism. Like a prism, the base of a pyramid can be any shape. Finding the surface area of a pyramid is not as simple as the other shapes we've looked at thus far. If the pyramid is a right pyramid, meaning the base is a regular polygon and the vertex is directly over the center of that polygon, the surface area can be calculated as $SA = B + \frac{1}{2}Ph_s$, where P is the perimeter of the base, and h_s is the slant height (distance from the vertex to the midpoint of one side of the base). If the pyramid is irregular, the area of each triangle side must be calculated individually and then summed, along with the base.

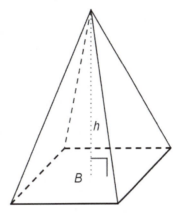

➤ **Review Video:** <u>**Volume and Surface Area of a Pyramid**</u>
*Visit **mometrix.com/academy** and enter **Code: 621932***

The volume of a cone is found by the formula $V = \frac{1}{3}\pi r^2 h$, where r is the radius, and h is the height. Notice this is the same as $\frac{1}{3}$ times the volume of a cylinder. The surface area can be calculated as $SA = \pi r^2 + \pi rs$, where s is the slant height. The slant height can be calculated using the Pythagorean Thereom to be $\sqrt{r^2 + h^2}$, so the surface area formula can also be written as $SA = \pi r^2 + \pi r\sqrt{r^2 + h^2}$.

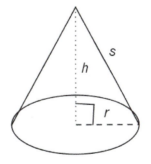

➤ **Review Video:** <u>**Volume and Surface Area of a Right Circular Cone**</u>
*Visit **mometrix.com/academy** and enter **Code: 573574***

Trigonometry

Basic Trigonometric Functions

The three basic trigonometric functions are sine, cosine, and tangent.

Sine

The sine (sin) function has a period of 360° or 2π radians. This means that its graph makes one complete cycle every 360° or 2π. Because $\sin 0 = 0$, the graph of $y = \sin x$ begins at the origin, with the x-axis representing the angle measure, and the y-axis representing the sine of the angle. The graph of the sine function is a smooth curve that begins at the origin, peaks at the point $\left(\frac{\pi}{2}, 1\right)$, crosses the x-axis at $(\pi, 0)$, has its lowest point at $\left(\frac{3\pi}{2}, -1\right)$, and returns to the x-axis to complete one cycle at $(2\pi, 0)$.

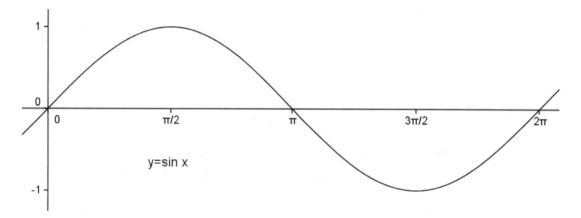

Cosine

The cosine (cos) function also has a period of 360° or 2π radians, which means that its graph also makes one complete cycle every 360° or 2π. Because $\cos 0° = 1$, the graph of $y = \cos x$ begins at the point $(0, 1)$, with the x-axis representing the angle measure, and the y-axis representing the cosine of the angle. The graph of the cosine function is a smooth curve that begins at the point $(0, 1)$, crosses the x-axis at the point $\left(\frac{\pi}{2}, 0\right)$, has its lowest point at $(\pi, -1)$, crosses the x-axis again at the point $\left(\frac{3\pi}{2}, 0\right)$, and returns to a peak at the point $(2\pi, 1)$ to complete one cycle.

> ➤ **Review Video: Cosine**
> *Visit **mometrix.com/academy** and enter **Code: 605566***

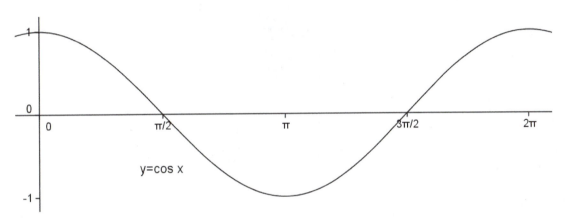

Tangent

The tangent (tan) function has a period of 180° or π radians, which means that its graph makes one complete cycle every 180° or π radians. The x-axis represents the angle measure, and the y-axis represents the tangent of the angle. The graph of the tangent function is a series of smooth curves that cross the x-axis at every 180° or π radians and have an asymptote every $k \cdot 90°$ or $\frac{k\pi}{2}$ radians, where k is an odd integer. This can be explained by the fact that the tangent is calculated by dividing the sine by the cosine, since the cosine equals zero at those asymptote points.

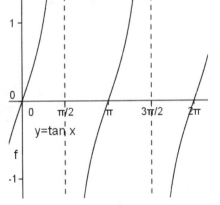

Defined and Reciprocal Functions

The tangent function is defined as the ratio of the sine to the cosine:

Tangent (tan):

$$\tan x = \frac{\sin x}{\cos x}$$

To take the reciprocal of a number means to place that number as the denominator of a fraction with a numerator of 1. The reciprocal functions are thus defined quite simply.

Cosecant (csc):

$$\csc x = \frac{1}{\sin x}$$

Secant (sec):

$$\sec x = \frac{1}{\cos x}$$

Cotangent (cot):

$$\cot x = \frac{1}{\tan x}$$

It is important to know these reciprocal functions, but they are not as commonly used as the three basic functions.

Inverse Functions

Each of the trigonometric functions accepts an angular measure, either degrees or radians, and gives a numerical value as the output. The inverse functions do the opposite; they accept a numerical value and give an angular measure as the output. The inverse sine, or arcsine, commonly written as either $\sin^{-1} x$ or $\arcsin x$, gives the angle whose sine is x. Similarly:

The inverse of $\cos x$ is written as $\cos^{-1} x$ or $\arccos x$ and means the angle whose cosine is x.
The inverse of $\tan x$ is written as $\tan^{-1} x$ or $\arctan x$ and means the angle whose tangent is x.
The inverse of $\csc x$ is written as $\csc^{-1} x$ or $\text{arccsc}\, x$ and means the angle whose cosecant is x.
The inverse of $\sec x$ is written as $\sec^{-1} x$ or $\text{arcsec}\, x$ and means the angle whose secant is x.
The inverse of $\cot x$ is written as $\cot^{-1} x$ or $\text{arccot}\, x$ and means the angle whose cotangent is x.

Important note about solving trigonometric equations
Trigonometric and algebraic equations are solved following the same rules, but while algebraic expressions have one unique solution, trigonometric equations could have multiple solutions, and you must find them all. When solving for an angle with a known trigonometric value, you must consider the sign and include all angles with that value. Your calculator will probably only give one value as an answer, typically in the following ranges:
For the inverse sine function, $\left[-\frac{\pi}{2}, \frac{\pi}{2}\right]$ or [–90°, 90°]
For the inverse cosine function, $[0, \pi]$ or [0°, 180°]
For the inverse tangent function, $\left[-\frac{\pi}{2}, \frac{\pi}{2}\right]$ or [–90°, 90°]

It is important to determine if there is another angle in a different quadrant that also satisfies the problem. To do this, find the other quadrant(s) with the same sign for that trigonometric function and find the angle that has the same reference angle. Then check whether this angle is also a solution.

In the first quadrant, all six trigonometric functions are positive (sin, cos, tan, csc, sec, cot).
In the second quadrant, sin and csc are positive.
In the third quadrant, tan and cot are positive.
In the fourth quadrant, cos and sec are positive.

If you remember the phrase, "ALL Students Take Classes," you will be able to remember the sign of each trigonometric function in each quadrant. ALL represents all the signs in the first quadrant. The "S" in "Students" represents the sine function and its reciprocal in the second quadrant. The "T" in "Take" represents the tangent function and its reciprocal in the third quadrant. The "C" in "Classes" represents the cosine function and its reciprocal.

Trigonometric Identities

Sum and Difference
To find the sine, cosine, or tangent of the sum or difference of two angles, use one of the following formulas:

$$\sin(\alpha \pm \beta) = \sin\alpha\cos\beta \pm \cos\alpha\sin\beta$$
$$\cos(\alpha \pm \beta) = \cos\alpha\cos\beta \mp \sin\alpha\sin\beta$$
$$\tan(\alpha \pm \beta) = \frac{\tan\alpha \pm \tan\beta}{1 \mp \tan\alpha\tan\beta}$$

where α and β are two angles with known sine, cosine, or tangent values as needed.

Half angle
To find the sine or cosine of half of a known angle, use the following formulas:

$$\sin\frac{\theta}{2} = \pm\sqrt{\frac{1-\cos\theta}{2}}$$

$$\cos\frac{\theta}{2} = \pm\sqrt{\frac{1+\cos\theta}{2}}$$

where θ is an angle with a known exact cosine value.
To determine the sign of the answer, you must notice the quadrant the given angle is in and apply the correct sign for the trigonometric function you are using. If you need to find the exact sine or cosine of an angle that you do not know, such as $\sin 22.5°$, you can rewrite the given angle as a half angle, such as $\sin\frac{45°}{2}$, and use the formula above.

To find the tangent or cotangent of half of a known angle, use the following formulas:

$$\tan\frac{\theta}{2} = \frac{\sin\theta}{1+\cos\theta}$$
$$\cot\frac{\theta}{2} = \frac{\sin\theta}{1-\cos\theta}$$

where θ is an angle with known exact sine and cosine values. These formulas will work for finding the tangent or cotangent of half of any angle unless the cosine of θ happens to make the denominator of the identity equal to 0.

Double angles
In each case, use one of the Double Angle Formulas.
To find the sine or cosine of twice a known angle, use one of the following formulas:
$$\sin(2\theta) = 2\sin\theta\cos\theta$$
$$\cos(2\theta) = \cos^2\theta - \sin^2\theta \quad \text{or}$$
$$\cos(2\theta) = 2\cos^2\theta - 1 \quad \text{or}$$
$$\cos(2\theta) = 1 - 2\sin^2\theta$$

To find the tangent or cotangent of twice a known angle, use the formulas:
$$\tan(2\theta) = \frac{2\tan\theta}{1 - \tan^2\theta}$$
$$\cot(2\theta) = \frac{\cot\theta - \tan\theta}{2}$$

In each case, θ is an angle with known exact sine, cosine, tangent, and cotangent values.

Products
To find the product of the sines and cosines of two different angles, use one of the following formulas:
$$\sin\alpha\sin\beta = \frac{1}{2}[\cos(\alpha - \beta) - \cos(\alpha + \beta)]$$
$$\cos\alpha\cos\beta = \frac{1}{2}[\cos(\alpha + \beta) + \cos(\alpha - \beta)]$$
$$\sin\alpha\cos\beta = \frac{1}{2}[\sin(\alpha + \beta) + \sin(\alpha - \beta)]$$
$$\cos\alpha\sin\beta = \frac{1}{2}[\sin(\alpha + \beta) - \sin(\alpha - \beta)]$$
where α and β are two unique angles.

Complementary
The trigonometric cofunction identities use the trigonometric relationships of complementary angles (angles whose sum is 90°). These are:
$$\cos x = \sin(90° - x)$$
$$\csc x = \sec(90° - x)$$
$$\cot x = \tan(90° - x)$$

Pythagorean
The Pythagorean Theorem states that $a^2 + b^2 = c^2$ for all right triangles. The trigonometric identity that derives from this principle is stated in this way:
$$\sin^2\theta + \cos^2\theta = 1$$

Dividing each term by either $\sin^2\theta$ or $\cos^2\theta$ yields two other identities, respectively:
$$1 + \cot^2\theta = \csc^2\theta$$
$$\tan^2\theta + 1 = \sec^2\theta$$

Unit Circle

A unit circle is a circle with a radius of 1 that has its center at the origin. The equation of the unit circle is $x^2 + y^2 = 1$. Notice that this is an abbreviated version of the standard equation of a circle. Because the center is the point $(0, 0)$, the values of h and k in the general equation are equal to zero and the equation simplifies to this form.

Standard Position is the position of an angle of measure θ whose vertex is at the origin, the initial side crosses the unit circle at the point $(1, 0)$, and the terminal side crosses the unit circle at some other point (a, b). In the standard position, $\sin\theta = b$, $\cos\theta = a$, and $\tan\theta = \frac{b}{a}$.

Rectangular coordinates are those that lie on the square grids of the Cartesian plane. They should be quite familiar to you. The polar coordinate system is based on a circular graph, rather than the square grid of the Cartesian system. Points in the polar coordinate system are in the format (r, θ), where r is the distance from the origin (think radius of the circle) and θ is the smallest positive angle (moving counterclockwise around the circle) made with the positive horizontal axis.

To convert a point from rectangular (x, y) format to polar (r, θ) format, use the formula
$$(x, y) \text{ to } (r, \theta) \Rightarrow r = \sqrt{x^2 + y^2}; \theta = \arctan\frac{y}{x} \text{ when } x \neq 0$$

If x is positive, use the positive square root value for r. If x is negative, use the negative square root value for r.
If x = 0, use the following rules:
If x = 0 and y = 0, then $\theta = 0$
If x = 0 and y > 0, then $\theta = \frac{\pi}{2}$
If x = 0 and y < 0, then $\theta = \frac{3\pi}{2}$

To convert a point from polar (r, θ) format to rectangular (x, y) format, use the formula
$$(r, \theta) \text{ to } (x, y) \Rightarrow x = r\cos\theta; y = r\sin\theta$$

> ➤ **Review Video: <u>Unit Circles and Standard Position</u>**
> *Visit **mometrix.com/academy** and enter **Code: 249181***

Table of commonly encountered angles

$0° = 0$ radians, $30° = \frac{\pi}{6}$ radians, $45° = \frac{\pi}{4}$ radians, $60° = \frac{\pi}{3}$ radians, and $90° = \frac{\pi}{2}$ radians

$\sin 0° = 0$	$\cos 0° = 1$	$\tan 0° = 0$
$\sin 30° = \frac{1}{2}$	$\cos 30° = \frac{\sqrt{3}}{2}$	$\tan 30° = \frac{\sqrt{3}}{3}$
$\sin 45° = \frac{\sqrt{2}}{2}$	$\cos 45° = \frac{\sqrt{2}}{2}$	$\tan 45° = 1$
$\sin 60° = \frac{\sqrt{3}}{2}$	$\cos 60° = \frac{1}{2}$	$\tan 60° = \sqrt{3}$
$\sin 90° = 1$	$\cos 90° = 0$	$\tan 90° = $ undefined
$\csc 0° = $ undefined	$\sec 0° = 1$	$\cot 0° = $ undefined
$\csc 30° = 2$	$\sec 30° = \frac{2\sqrt{3}}{3}$	$\cot 30° = \sqrt{3}$
$\csc 45° = \sqrt{2}$	$\sec 45° = \sqrt{2}$	$\cot 45° = 1$
$\csc 60° = \frac{2\sqrt{3}}{3}$	$\sec 60° = 2$	$\cot 60° = \frac{\sqrt{3}}{3}$
$\csc 90° = 1$	$\sec 90° = $ undefined	$\cot 90° = 0$

The values in the upper half of this table are values you should have memorized or be able to find quickly.

Natural Sciences

Biology

Enzymes

Structure and function
Enzymes are biologically active, highly specific protein catalysts that lower the activation energy requirement, and increase the speed, for specific chemical reactions. The delicate and vulnerable living systems depend on the activity of enzymes to run the cells biochemical reactions. Many different enzymes are found in the cells interior, but each enzyme functions in only one kind of reaction. That is, the enzyme interacts with and reorganizes only one specific substrate. Enzymes function to lower the activation energy of a reaction, thus helping the reaction to proceed more quickly.

Characteristics
The following are characteristics of enzymes:
- They are proteins.
- They are highly specific in their reactions.
- They reduce the amount of activation energy that is required for chemical reactions.

This specificity of an enzyme for its substrate is in part determined by the shape of the enzyme. The active sites that are located on the surface of the enzyme have a particular shape, and that shape fits only one type of substrate. Should another type of substrate collide with the active site of the enzyme, there would be no coordinated interaction or enzymatic activity.

Classifications
Currently, enzymes are grouped into 6 functional classes by the International Union of Biochemists (I.U.B.), as follows:
- Oxidoreductases – Act on many chemical groupings to add or remove hydrogen atoms.
- Transferases – Transfer functional groups between donor and acceptor molecules. Kinases are specialized transferases that regulate metabolism by transferring the tertiary phosphate from ATP to other molecules.
- Hydrolases – Add water across a bond, thus hydrolyzing it.
- Lyases – Add water, ammonia, or carbon dioxide across double bonds, or remove these elements to produce double bonds.
- Isomerases – Carry out many kinds of isomerization: L to D isomerizations, mutase reactions (shifts of chemical groups), and others.
- Ligases – Catalyze reactions in which two chemical groups are joined, or ligated, with the use of energy from ATP.

> ➤ **Review Video: Enzymes**
> *Visit* **mometrix.com/academy** *and enter* *Code:* **656995**

Cofactors and coenzymes

Many enzymes require non-protein cofactors in order to become catalytically active. Most cofactors are metallic ions, such as Iron (Fe^{2+}), manganese (Mn^{2+}), or zinc (Zn^+). Other enzymes require more complex organic molecules, called coenzymes, in order to produce their catalytic activity. Many of these coenzymes are derived from vitamins. Although cofactors and coenzymes are found in very low concentrates within cells, they are critical to the functioning of enzymes, and therefore critical to cell metabolism. These cofactors may bind to the enzyme and change its shape sufficiently to produce just the right active site shape that will allow for catalytic activity. Others may supply a needed functional group to the reaction, or a pair of energized electrons (called the "enzymatic teeth"), etc.

Role of coenzymes

The functional role of coenzymes is to act as transporters of chemical groups from one reactant to another. The chemical groups that are carried can be as simple as the hydride ion ($H^+ + 2e^-$) that is carried by NAD^+, or the hydrogen molecule carried by FAD, or they can be even more complex than the amine ($-NH_2$) that is carried by pyridoxal phosphate. Since coenzymes are chemically changed as a consequence of enzymatic activity, it is often useful to consider coenzymes to be a special class of substrates, or second substrates, which are common to many different holoenzymes. In all cases, the coenzymes donate the carried chemical grouping to an acceptor molecule, and are thus regenerated to their original form. This regeneration of coenzyme and holoenzyme fulfills the definition of an enzyme as a chemical catalyst since coenzymes are generally regenerated (unlike the usual substrates, which are used up during the course of a reaction).

Enzyme inhibitors

Competitive inhibitor

The competitive inhibitor functions specifically at the catalytic site, where it competes with substrate for binding in a dynamic equilibrium-like process. Inhibition is reversible by the substrate (S). V_{max} is unchanged, and K_m, as defined by the [S] required for ½ maximal activity, is increased.

Noncompetitive inhibitor

The noncompetitive inhibitor binds the Enzyme (E) or enzyme-substrate (ES) complex at a site other than the catalytic site. Substrate binding is unaltered, but the enzyme-substrate-inhibitor (ESI) complex cannot form products. Inhibition cannot be reversed by the substrate. K_m appears unaltered, and V_{max} is decreased proportionately to the inhibitor concentration.

Uncompetitive inhibitor

The uncompetitive inhibitor binds only to ES complexes at locations other than the catalytic site. Substrate binding modifies the E structure, making the inhibitor binding site available. Inhibition cannot be reversed by substrate. The apparent V_{max} is decreased, and K_m, as defined by the [S] required for 1/2 maximal activity, is decreased.

Digestion of dietary carbohydrates

The first step in the metabolism of digestible carbohydrate is the conversion of the higher polymers into simpler, soluble forms that can be transported across the intestinal wall, and delivered to the tissues. The breakdown of polymeric sugars begins in the mouth. Saliva has a slightly acidic pH of 6.8, and contains lingual amylase, which begins the digestion of carbohydrates. The action of lingual amylase is limited to the area of the mouth and the esophagus, as it is virtually inactivated by the much stronger acid pH of the stomach. Once the food has arrived in the stomach, acid hydrolysis contributes to its degradation, and specific gastric proteases and lipases aid this process for proteins and fats, respectively. Subsequently, the mixture of gastric secretions, saliva, and food, known collectively as chyme, moves to the small intestine. The main polymeric-carbohydrate digesting enzyme of the small intestine is α-amylase. This enzyme is secreted by the pancreas, and has the same activity as salivary amylase, producing disaccharides and trisaccharides. The latter are converted to monosaccharides by intestinal saccharidases, including maltases that hydrolyze di- and trisaccharides, and the more specific disaccharidases (i.e., sucrase, lactase, and trehalase).

Hexokinase reaction

The hexokinase reaction is the first step of glycolysis, and consists of the ATP-dependent phosphorylation of glucose by hexokinase to form glucose-6-phosphate (G6P). The hexokinase reaction accomplishes two goals:
- It converts nonionic glucose into an anion that is trapped in the cell, since cells lack transport systems for phosphorylated sugars.
- The otherwise biologically inert glucose becomes activated into a labile form that is capable of being further metabolized.

Four mammalian isozymes of hexokinase are known (types I-IV), with the type IV isozyme often referred to as glucokinase. Glucokinase is the form of hexokinase that is found in hepatocytes. The high K_m of glucokinase for glucose means that this enzyme can only be saturated at very high concentrations of substrate.

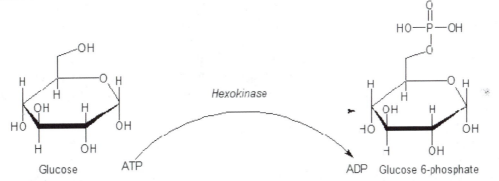

Glycolysis

Glycolysis is the process of converting glucose into pyruvate, nicotinamide adenine dinucleotide (NADH), flavin adenine dinucleotide ($FADH_2$), ATP, and H_2O. The steps of glycolysis are as follows:
1. Glucose is converted into glucose-6-phosphate (G6P) by hexokinase (uses 1 ATP, releases 1 H^+).
2. G6P is converted into fructose-6-phosphate (F6P) by phosphoglucose isomerase.
3. F6P is converted into fructose-1,6-biphosphate (F1,6BP) by phosphofructokinase (uses 1 ATP, releases 1 H^+).
4. F1,6BP is broken down into glyceraldehyde-3-phosphate (G3P) and dihydroxyacetone phosphate (DHAP) by aldolase.
5. DHAP is converted into another molecule of G3P by triosephosphate isomerase.
6. 2 G3P are converted into 2 1,3-biphosphoglycerate (1,3BPG) molecules by glyceraldehyde phosphate dehydrogenase (converts 2 NAD^+ into 2 NADH, releases 2 H^+, uses 2 P_i).

7. 2 1,3BPG are converted into 2 3-phosphoglycerate (3PG) molecules by phosphoglycerate kinase (produces 2 ATP).
8. 2 3PG are converted into 2 2-phosphoglycerate (2PG) molecules by phosphoglycerate mutase.
9. 2 2PG are converted into 2 phosphoenolpyruvate (PEP) molecules by enolase (releases 2 H_2O).
10. 2 PEP are converted into 2 pyruvate molecules by pyruvate kinase (produces 2 ATP, uses 2 H^+).

The net glycolysis reaction is as follows:
1 Glucose + 2 [NAD]$^+$ + 2 [ADP] + 2 [P]$_i$ → 2 Pyruvate + 2 [NADH] + 2 H^+ + 2 [ATP] + 2 H_2O

Anaerobic glycolysis

Under aerobic conditions, pyruvate in most cells is further metabolized via the trichloroacetic acid (TCA) cycle. Under anaerobic conditions, and in erythrocytes under aerobic conditions, pyruvate is converted to lactate by the enzyme lactate dehydrogenase (LDH), and the lactate is transported out of the cell and into the circulation. The conversion of pyruvate to lactate, under anaerobic conditions, provides the cell with a mechanism for the oxidation of NADH (produced during the glyceraldehyde-3-phosphate dehydrogenase (G3PDH) reaction) to NAD$^+$. This reduction is required since NAD$^+$ is a necessary substrate for G3PDH, without which glycolysis will cease. Normally, during aerobic glycolysis the electrons of cytoplasmic NADH are transferred to mitochondrial carriers of the oxidative phosphorylation pathway, generating a continuous pool of cytoplasmic NAD$^+$. Aerobic glycolysis generates substantially more ATP than does anaerobic glycolysis. The utility of anaerobic glycolysis to a muscle cell when it needs large amounts of energy stems from the fact that the rate of ATP production from glycolysis is approximately 100x faster than from oxidative phosphorylation. During exertion, muscle cells do not need to energize anabolic reaction pathways. The requirement is to generate the maximum amount of ATP for muscle contraction in the shortest time frame. This is why muscle cells derive almost all of the ATP consumed during exertion from anaerobic glycolysis.

Cori cycle

The formation of lactic acid buys time, and shifts part of the metabolic burden to the liver. Even though glycolysis alone cannot produce much ATP, it is a significant source of ATP when muscular activity continues for any length of time. The final limiting factor in continued muscular activity is the buildup of lactic acid. The lactic acid eventually produces muscular pain and cramps, which force the discontinuation of muscular activity. Usually, before this happens, and after activity has ceased, lactic acid diffuses out of the muscle cells and into the blood, where it enters the liver. The body is very efficient in that lactic acid is sent through the blood to the liver, which can convert it back to pyruvate, and then to glucose, via gluconeogenesis. The glucose is then able to enter the blood, and travel back to the muscles for immediate use. If, by this time, the muscles have ceased activity, the glucose can be used to rebuild their supplies of glycogen through glycogenesis. This recycling of lactic acid is referred to as the Cori cycle. The Cori cycle also operates more efficiently when muscular activity has stopped. At this time, the oxygen debt can be made up so that the citric acid cycle and electron transport chain also begin to function again. In order for most of the lactic acid to be converted back into glucose, some must be converted to pyruvate, and then to acetyl-CoA. The citric acid cycle and electron transport chain must provide enough ATP to "fuel" the gluconeogenesis to convert the remainder of the lactic acid to glucose.

Pyruvate dehydrogenase complex

The bulk of ATP that is used by cells to maintain homeostasis is produced by the oxidation of pyruvate in the TCA cycle. During this oxidation process, reduced NADH and $FADH_2$ are generated. The enzymatic activities of the TCA cycle, and of oxidative phosphorylation, are located in the mitochondria. When transported into the mitochondria, pyruvate encounters two principal metabolizing enzymes: pyruvate carboxylase (a gluconeogenic enzyme) and pyruvate dehydrogenase (PDH), the first enzyme of the PDH complex. With a high cell-energy charge, coenzyme A (CoA) is highly acylated, principally as acetyl-CoA, and is able to allosterically activate pyruvate carboxylase, directing pyruvate toward gluconeogenesis. When the cell-energy charge is low, CoA is not acylated, pyruvate carboxylase is inactive, and pyruvate is preferentially metabolized via the PDH complex, and the enzymes of the TCA cycle, into CO_2 and H_2O. The activities of the PDH complex are regulated by their state of phosphorylation. This modification is carried out by PDH kinase, and the phosphates are removed by PDH phosphatase. The phosphorylation of PDH by PDH kinase inhibits its activity, and thus leads to decreased oxidation of pyruvate. PDH kinase is activated by NADH and acetyl-CoA, and inhibited by pyruvate, ADP, non-acetylated-CoA (CoASH), Ca^{2+}, and Mg^{2+}. In contrast, the PDH phosphatase is activated by Mg^{2+} and Ca^{2+}. The PDH complex is comprised of multiple copies of 3 separate enzymes: pyruvate dehydrogenase (20-30 copies), dihydrolipoyl transacetylase (60 copies), and dihydrolipoyl dehydrogenase (6 copies).

Trichloroacetic acid cycle

The TCA cycle is also known as the citric acid cycle, or Krebs cycle. The GTP that is generated during the succinate thiokinase (succinyl-CoA synthetase) reaction is equivalent to a mole of ATP by virtue of the presence of nucleoside diphosphokinase. The 3 moles of NADH and 1 mole of $FADH_2$ generated during each round of the cycle feed into the oxidative phosphorylation pathway. Each mole of NADH leads to 3 moles of ATP, while each mole of $FADH_2$ leads to 2 moles of ATP. Therefore, for each mole of pyruvate that enters the trichloroacetic acid (TCA) cycle, 12 moles of ATP can be generated. Regulation of the TCA cycle, like that of glycolysis, occurs at both the level of the entry of substrates into the cycle, as well as at the key reactions of the cycle. Fuel enters the TCA cycle primarily as acetyl-CoA, and the generation of acetyl-CoA from carbohydrates is, thus, a major control point of the cycle. This reaction is catalyzed by the pyruvate dehydrogenase complex.

Control of the TCA cycle:
- The input of acetyl-CoA and availability of oxaloacetate limit how fast the TCA cycle can run.
- Excess NADH (the product of the cycle) inhibits both pyruvate dehydrogenase and ketoglutarate dehydrogenase.
- The arcAB dual-component regulatory system switches off the genes for most enzymes of the TCA cycle in the absence of oxygen.
- Citrate synthase is feedback-inhibited by succinyl-CoA, and succinate dehydrogenase is inhibited by oxaloacetate. This does not affect the overall speed but helps to keep the cycle from getting out of balance.

Mobilization of fat stores

The primary sources of fatty acids for oxidation are from the diet, and from the mobilization of cellular stores. Fatty acids from the diet can are delivered from the gut to cells via transport in the blood. Fatty acids are stored, in the form of triacylglycerols, primarily within adipocytes of adipose tissue. In response to energy demands, the fatty acids of stored triacylglycerols can be mobilized for use by peripheral tissues. The release of metabolic energy, in the form of fatty acids, is controlled by a complex series of interrelated cascades that result in the activation of hormone-sensitive lipase. The stimulus to activate this cascade in adipocytes can be glucagon, epinephrine, or β-corticotropin. These hormones bind cell-surface receptors that are coupled to the activation of adenylate cyclase upon ligand binding. The resultant increase in cAMP leads to activation of PKA, which in turn phosphorylates and activates hormone-sensitive lipase. This enzyme hydrolyzes fatty acids from carbon atoms 1 or 3 of triacylglycerols. The resulting diacylglycerols are substrates for either hormone-sensitive lipase, or for non-inducible diacylglycerol lipase. Finally, the monoacylglycerols are substrates for monoacylglycerol lipase. The net result of the action of these enzymes is three moles of free fatty acid, and one mole of glycerol. The free fatty acids diffuse from adipose cells, combine with albumin in the blood, and are thereby transported to other tissues where they passively diffuse into cells.

Pancreatic lipase

Pancreatic lipase is an enzyme that hydrolyses triglyceride molecules into 2-monoglyceride and two free fatty acids. Triglycerides are the primary form of dietary fats, and cannot be absorbed across the intestinal mucosa without first being broken down by pancreatic lipase. Pancreatic lipase is delivered into the intestinal lumen as a constituent of pancreatic juice. Sufficient quantities of bile salts must also be present in the lumen of the intestine for lipase to efficiently digest dietary triglycerides, and for the resulting fatty acids and monoglycerides to be absorbed. This means that normal digestion and absorption of dietary fat is critically dependent on secretions from both the pancreas and the liver. Recently, pancreatic lipase has been in the limelight as a target for the management of obesity. The drug Orlistat (Xenical) inhibits pancreatic lipase, and thus interferes with the digestion of triglycerides, thereby reducing the absorption of dietary fats. Clinical trials support the contention that inhibiting lipase can lead to significant reductions in the body weight of some patients.

Ketogenesis

The fate of the products of fatty acid metabolism is determined by an individual's physiological status. Ketogenesis takes place primarily in the liver, and may be affected by several factors:
- Control in the release of free fatty acids from adipose tissue directly affects the level of ketogenesis in the liver. This is substrate-level regulation.
- Once fats enter the liver, they have two distinct fates: they may be activated to acyl-CoAs and oxidized, or they may be esterified to glycerol in the production of triacylglycerols. If the liver has sufficient supplies of glycerol-3-phosphate, most of the fats will be turned to the production of triacylglycerols.
- The acetyl-CoA that is generated by the oxidation of fats can be completely oxidized in the TCA cycle. Therefore, if the demand for ATP is high, the fate of acetyl-CoA is likely to be further oxidation into CO_2.
- The level of fat oxidation is regulated hormonally through the phosphorylation of acetyl-CoA carboxylase, which may activate it in response to glucagon, or inhibit it in the presence of insulin.

Fatty acid synthesis

The pathway for fatty acid synthesis occurs in the cytoplasm, whereas oxidation occurs in the mitochondria. The synthesis of fats involves the oxidation of NADPH, while the oxidation of fats involves the reduction of FADH+ and NAD+. However, the essential chemistry of the two processes are reversals of each other. Both the synthesis and oxidation of fats utilize an activated two-carbon intermediate, acetyl-CoA. However, the acetyl-CoA in fat synthesis exists temporarily bound to the enzyme complex as malonyl-CoA. The synthesis of malonyl-CoA is the first committed step of fatty acid synthesis, and the enzyme that catalyzes this reaction, acetyl-CoA carboxylase (ACC), is the major site of regulation of fatty acid synthesis. Like other enzymes that transfer CO_2 to substrates, ACC requires a biotin co-factor. The rate of fatty acid synthesis is controlled by the equilibrium between monomeric and polymeric ACC. The activity of ACC requires polymerization, which is enhanced by citrate, and inhibited by long-chain fatty acids. ACC is also controlled through hormone-mediated phosphorylation.

Biosynthesis of cholesterol

Slightly less than half of the cholesterol in the body derives from *de novo* biosynthesis. Biosynthesis in the liver accounts for approximately 10%, and biosynthesis in the intestine accounts for approximately 15%, of the amount produced each day. Cholesterol synthesis occurs in the cytoplasm and microsomes, and is produced from the two-carbon acetate group of acetyl-CoA. The biosynthesis of cholesterol has five major steps:
- Acetyl-CoA is converted into 3-hydroxy-3-methylglutaryl-CoA (HMG-CoA).
- HMG-CoA is converted into mevalonate.
- Mevalonate is converted into the isoprene-based molecule, isopentenyl pyrophosphate (IPP), with the concomitant loss of CO_2.
- IPP is converted into squalene.
- Squalene is converted into cholesterol.

Regulation of the urea cycle

The urea cycle operates only to eliminate excess nitrogen. With high-protein diets, the carbon skeletons of the amino acids are oxidized for energy or stored as fat and glycogen, but the amine nitrogen must be excreted. To facilitate this process, enzymes of the urea cycle are controlled at the genetic level. With long-term changes in the quantity of dietary protein, changes of 20-fold or greater in the concentration of cycle enzymes are observed. When dietary proteins increase significantly, enzyme concentrations rise. With return to a balanced diet, enzyme levels decline. Under conditions of starvation, enzyme levels rise as proteins are degraded and amino acid carbon skeletons are used to provide energy, thus increasing the quantity of nitrogen that must be excreted. Short-term regulation of the cycle occurs principally at CPS-I, which is relatively inactive in the absence of its allosteric activator, N-acetylglutamate. The steady-state concentration of N-acetyl-glutamate is set by the concentration of its components, acetyl-CoA and glutamate, and by arginine, which is a positive allosteric effector of N-acetylglutamate synthetase.

DNA structure and function

DNA molecules are the largest biological macromolecules known. Within cells, the DNA collectively composes the genome, which encodes the instructions for the development and functioning of all living processes. Structurally, DNA is composed of two antiparallel strands that are bound together through hydrogen bonding, and then coiled together in the form of a double helix. DNA also forms tertiary and quanternary structures, where the DNA is wrapped around histone core proteins to form nucleosomes that are further aggregated to form chromosomes. Such packaging of the DNA allows the enormous quantity of genetic material that comprises the genome to be packaged within the nucleus of cells.

> ➢ **Review Video: <u>DNA</u>**
> Visit *mometrix.com/academy* and enter *Code:* **639552**

Nucleotides, purines, and pyrimidines

The primary building blocks of DNA are the nucleotides: adenine (A), thymine (T), cytosine (C), and guanine (G). Nucleotides are organic molecules that consist of a nitrogenous base (a purine or a pyrimidine), a pentose sugar (i.e., deoxyribose in deoxyribonucleic acid (DNA), or ribose in ribonucleic acid (RNA)), and a mono-, di- or triphosphate group. Nucleosides are similar to nucleotides, except that they contain only the sugar and base without a phosphate group. The nucleotides are divided into two groups, known as purines and pyrimidines. Only two purines and three pyrimidines are typically present in nucleic acids:
- Purines – Adenine and guanine.
- Pyrimidines – Cytosine, thymine, and uracil (used in RNA in the place of thymine).

When the two antiparallel strands of DNA hybridize with one another, the nucleotides interact with each other in a very specific manner in order to maintain a consistent helical diameter that does not strain the molecule: each hydrogen-bonded pair is composed of one purine and one pyrimidine. Specifically, adenine binds to thymine (or uracil), and cytosine binds to guanine. Of these two interactions, the C:G interactions are much stronger than the A:T interactions because cytosine binds to guanine with 3 hydrogen bonds, while adenine binds to thymine with 2 hydrogen bonds.

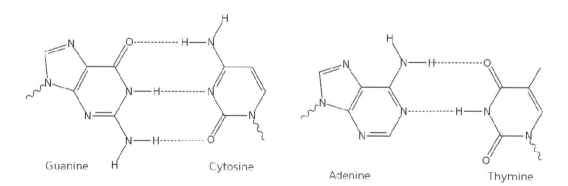

Genes

Genes are segments of DNA that code for proteins or other important biomolecules. Genes that encode proteins are generally composed of exons that code for segments of the protein, and introns that do not code for the protein and are cut out of the template through mRNA splicing. Every gene that encodes a protein begins with the sequence ATG, known as the start codon, which translates into methionine. Upstream of the start codon, the DNA contains various enhancer sequences and many binding sites for transcription factors, polymerases, and cofactors. In addition, adjacent to the start codon is a segment of DNA referred to as the TATA box (because of its sequence), which serves as the binding sight for RNA polymerase in order to initiate transcription.

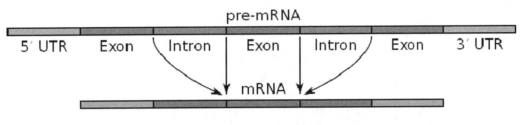

> **Review Video: Genes**
> Visit **mometrix.com/academy** and enter **Code: 363997**

Transcription

Transcription is the process of converting the genetic code into messenger RNA (mRNA) that is used as a template for producing proteins. When transcription begins, the histone proteins that package the segment of the target DNA are acetylated, which results in the unfolding of that section of the genome. Transcription factors and enhancer proteins then bind to promoter elements and the TATA box upstream of the start site. Once the transcription initiation complex is assembled, RNA polymerase is recruited to the complex, binds to the TATA box, and then transcription takes place as follows:

1. RNA polymerase separates the DNA strands to create a transcription bubble, and continues separating the DNA strands by breaking the hydrogen bonding as transcription progresses.
2. RNA polymerase adds matching RNA nucleotides to complementary DNA bases of the template, and synthesizes strands of RNA in the 5' to 3' direction.
3. Once transcription is complete, the temporary hydrogen bonds of the RNA:DNA are broken, and the DNA reassociates.
4. If the cell has a nucleus, the RNA is further processed to add a poly-A tail and a 5' cap, and is transported into the cytoplasm through the nuclear pore.

DNA replication

DNA replication is essential to the propagation of DNA in all cellular organisms. DNA replication occurs similar to transcription, except that it takes place genome wide and the products are DNA rather than RNA. When replication begins, the DNA is separated at many places throughout the genome at what are called origins of replication. At these points, replication initiation proteins bind to the DNA and separate the DNA strands. Then, an enzyme, known as primase, binds to the DNA and creates a short segment of RNA to provide a 3'OH group in order to allow DNA polymerase to function. DNA polymerase then associates with the DNA and continues the production of new strands of DNA in the 5' to 3' direction. As replication proceeds, the DNA is separated by the leading strand at the replication fork, while the lagging strand, produced on the opposing complementary strand, is filled in as the fork progresses, albeit at a slower rate. The leading strands are referred to as semiconservative strands, while the DNA segments of the lagging strand are referred to as Okazaki fragments. Once the replication forks meet, the newly synthesized semiconservative strands and Okazaki fragments are annealed to each other by DNA ligase. The products of DNA replication are two copies of the genome, each composed of one parent and one daughter strand.

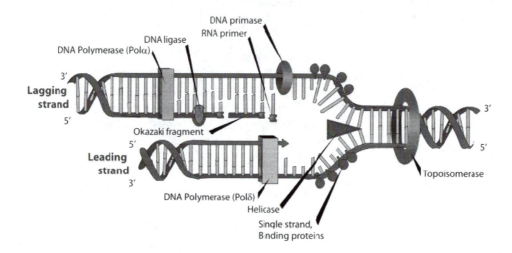

The following enzymes function to promote replication:
- DNA Helicase – Unwinds the DNA at the replication fork.
- DNA Polymerase – Produces new DNA strands in the 5' to 3' direction, and proofreads the fidelity of the newly synthesized DNA as replication proceeds.
- Single-Strand Binding Proteins – Bind to the single-stranded DNA to prevent it from reassociating with its complementary strand.
- DNA Clamp – Prevents the polymerase from dissociating from the DNA.
- Topoisomerase – Cleaves the DNA to relax supercoiling.
- DNA Gyrase – Relieves the strain of unwinding by helicase.
- DNA Ligase – Anneals the semiconservative strands and Okazaki fragments.
- Primase – Produces the initial RNA primer to initiate DNA synthesis.
- Telomerase – Extends the telomeric DNA.

DNA polymerase, DNA ligase, and reverse transcriptase

DNA polymerase is the enzyme responsible for the synthesis of DNA. DNA polymerase is used during most procedures where DNA synthesis is required, including PCR and *in vitro* mutagenesis. DNA ligase is the enzyme that covalently attaches a free 5' phosphate to a 3' hydroxyl of a DNA molecule. DNA ligase is used in all procedures where molecules of DNA need to be covalently attached. Reverse transcriptase is an RNA-dependent DNA polymerase that synthesizes DNA from an RNA template. Reverse transcriptase is used to convert mRNA into complimentary DNA (cDNA) in order to clone genes, or to quantify the expression of a particular gene using quantitative PCR (qPCR).

Polymerase chain reaction

Most DNA polymerases only function at low temperatures. However, at low temperatures, the DNA is tightly coiled, and the polymerases are unable to access most parts of the DNA. In order to open up the DNA, it has to be denatured at 95° Celsius, which will also inactivate the polymerases. Moreover, the procedure for DNA amplification, called the polymerase chain reaction (PCR), requires many cycles (typically > 30 cycles), and would thus require the addition of a lot of polymerase following each denaturation step (expensive and time consuming).
Two key discoveries enabled the streamlining of this process:

- The discovery of a species of bacteria that live in thermal vents, called *Thermus aquaticus* (Taq), which are able to live, thrive, and perform enzymatic reactions between 70 to 80-degrees Celsius. The polymerase that is cloned or purified from these bacteria is able to withstand many rounds of denaturation, thus removing the requirement for the addition of fresh polymerase following each denaturation step.
- The invention of the thermocycler, which is a machine that can be programmed to automatically and rapidly cycle between different temperatures, thus allowing for the automation of the PCR.

Components that are required for a PCR are target DNA, primers, dNTPs, Taq polymerase, polymerase buffer including $MgCl_2$, and a thermocycler.

Southern and Northern blotting

Southern blotting was named after Edward M. Southern, whom developed this procedure at Edinburgh University in the 1970s. Southern blotting was designed to locate a particular sequence of DNA within a complex mixture. For example, Southern blotting can be used to locate a particular gene within a genome. The steps for Southern blotting are as follows:
1. Digest the DNA with an appropriate restriction enzyme.
2. Run the digest on an agarose gel.
3. Denature the DNA (usually while it is still in the gel).
4. Transfer the denatured DNA to the membrane.
5. Probe (hybridize) the membrane with radio-labeled ssDNA.
6. Visualize your radioactively labeled target sequence.

The amount of DNA that is required is dependent on the size and specific activity of the probe. And, shorter probes tend to be more specific. In a tongue-in-cheek fashion, scientists who used a similar method for locating an RNA sequence named it Northern Blotting. Northern blotting is also known as northern hybridization or RNA hybridization. The procedure for, and theory behind, northern blotting is almost identical to Southern blotting, except that it is for RNA instead of DNA.

Transcription and translation

Gene expression occurs in two steps:
- Transcription – Where the information encoded in DNA is converted into a molecule of mRNA.
- Translation – Where the information encoded in mRNA is converted into a defined sequence of amino acids, thus producing a protein.

In eukaryotes, the processes of transcription and translation are separated both spatially and temporally. Transcription of DNA into mRNA occurs in the nucleus, while translation of mRNA into

- 87 -

polypeptides occurs in the endoplasmic reticulum, or on polysomes in the cytoplasm. In prokaryotes, which have no nucleus, both of these steps occur simultaneously: the nascent mRNA molecule begins to be translated even before its transcription from DNA is complete.

RNA classes

The three RNA Classes are as follows:
- Messenger RNAs (mRNAs) – The genetic coding templates that are used by the translational machinery to determine the order of amino acids to be incorporated into an elongating polypeptide during the process of translation.
- Transfer RNAs (tRNAs) – Form covalent bonds to individual amino acids, and recognize the encoded sequences of the mRNAs to allow for correct insertion of amino acids into the elongating polypeptide chain.
- Ribosomal RNAs (rRNAs) – These are assembled together with numerous ribosomal proteins in order to form the ribosomes. Ribosomes engage with the mRNAs and form a catalytic domain into which the tRNAs enter with their attached amino acids. All RNA polymerases are dependent upon a DNA template in order to synthesize RNA. The resultant RNA is, therefore, complimentary to the template strand of the DNA duplex, and identical to the non-template strand. The non-template strand is called the coding strand because its sequences are identical to those of the mRNA. However, in RNA, uridine (U) is substituted for thymidine (T).

> **Review Video: RNA**
> *Visit mometrix.com/academy and enter Code:* **888852**

tRNAs

More than 300 different tRNAs have been identified. tRNAs vary in length from 60-95 nucleotides (18-28 kDa), and the majority contain 76 nucleotides. Evidence has shown that the role of tRNAs in translation is to carry activated amino acids to the elongating polypeptide chain. All tRNAs have the following characteristics:
- Exhibit a cloverleaf-like secondary structure.
- Have a 5'-terminal phosphate.
- Have a 7-bp stem, which includes the 5'-terminal nucleotide, and may contain non-Watson-Crick base pairs (e.g., GU). This portion of the tRNA is called the acceptor, since the amino acid is carried by the tRNA while attached to the 3'-terminal OH group.
- Have a D loop and a TJC loop.
- Have an anti-codon loop, complementary to a codon on mRNA.
- Terminate at the 3'-end with the sequence 5'-CCA-3'.
- Contain 13 invariant positions, and 8 semi-variant positions.
- Contain numerous modified nucleotide bases.

Ribosomes

Ribosomes occur freely in the cytoplasm or may be attached to the membranes of the endoplasmic reticulum, which is then designated as rough endoplasmic reticulum. Ribosomes are the sites of protein synthesis in the cell. If ribosomes appear in clusters (rosettes) in the cytoplasm, they are commonly termed *polyribosomes* or *polysomes*. Ribosomes possess two subunits, a large subunit and a small subunit, composed of proteins and RNA, known as ribosomal RNA (rRNA).

Start and stop codons

The start codon marks the site at which the translation of mRNA into a peptide sequence begins, while the stop codon marks the site at which translation ends. Translation begins with a chain initiation codon (start codon). But, unlike stop codons, the start codons are not sufficient to begin the process on their own. Rather, nearby initiation sequences in the mRNA are also required to induce binding by ribosomes and initiation factors. The most notable start codon is AUG, which also codes for methionine. CUG and UUG, and in prokaryotes GUG and AUU, will also work. Many codons are redundant, where more than one codon will code for the same amino acid. This redundancy is typically confined to the third position (e.g., both GAA and GAG code for the amino acid glutamine), and is partly due to the "wobble" of the transfer RNA (tRNA) molecules, where the structure of the tRNA molecules causes them to bind more strongly to the first two nucleotides than to the third, making the third position more flexible. Only two amino acids are specified by a single codon: one of these is the amino acid, methionine, specified by the codon AUG, and the other is tryptophan, specified by the codon UGG.

Wobble hypothesis

61 of the possible 64 codons might be considered as being recognized by individual tRNAs, while the remaining 3 are recognized as termination codons. Most cells contain isoaccepting tRNAs, which are different tRNAs that are specific for the same amino acid. However, many tRNAs bind to two or three codons that specify their cognate amino acids. For example, in yeast, tRNA^{Phe} has the anticodon 5'-GmAA-3', and can recognize the codons 5'-UUC-3' and 5'-UUU-3'. It is, therefore, possible for non-Watson-Crick base pairing to occur at the third codon position (i.e., the 3' nucleotide of the mRNA codon, and the 5' nucleotide of the tRNA anticodon). This phenomenon has been termed the wobble hypothesis.

Western blotting

Western blotting is an experimental procedure that provides scientists with information about the size and relative quantity of protein present in a given sample. It involves the gel separation of a protein sample using sodium dodecyl sulfate polyacrylamide gel electrophoresis (SDS-PAGE), followed by transfer of the separated sample to a membrane (i.e., nitrocellulose, polyvinylidine fluoride, etc.), and finally the blotting of the membrane with antibodies in order to detect one protein within a mixture of any number of proteins. When combined with radioimmunoprecipitation assays, immunoprecipitation assays, or co-immunoprecipitation assays, western blotting can further be used to more precisely detect the rate of synthesis or degradation of a protein, the quantity of a particular protein, or modified version of a protein, present within a sample (e.g., whether phosphorylated, nitrosylated, ubiquitinated, sumoylated, etc.), or the presence and degree of protein-protein interactions present for particular proteins within a sample, respectively.

Western blotting is one of the most widely utilized techniques in biological research. However, this method is dependent upon the use of a concentrated, highly specific antibody directed against a desired target protein, which are not always available for proteins that have not already been highly characterized. One method for circumventing this problem is to genetically fuse the coding DNA (cDNA) for the protein of interest with a small protein tag (e.g., HA, FLAG, MYC), insert them into an expression vector, overexpress the protein, and then use a well-characterized antibody directed to the small protein tag in order to study the protein of interest.

Radioimmunoprecipitation Assays

Radioimmunoprecipitation assays (RIPAs) are used to concentrate radio-labeled protein samples prior to SDS polyacrylamide gel electrophoresis (SDS PAGE), in order to determine the rate of synthesis or modification states of proteins. When non-radio-labeled samples are used, immuno-precipitation assays can be used to concentrate protein samples prior to western blotting, or co-immunoprecipitation assays can be used to determine protein-protein interactions. Western blotting alone will only indicate how much protein is present, or has accumulated, in a sample. RIPAs and other immunoprecipitation assays add another dimension to western blotting, and increase the amount of information that can be gathered from a protein sample. The following are the steps of RIPAs:

1. Incubate living cells or tissue with radioactive isotopes that can be incorporated into newly synthesized proteins (e.g., ^{14}C or ^{35}S).
2. Treat or stimulate the cells or tissue as desired.
3. Extract the proteins from the sample using RIPA buffer.
4. Incubate the different protein samples with antibodies to the specific protein targets of interest, at 4° Celsius.
5. Add protein A- or protein G-cross-linked agarose beads and further incubate the samples to cross-link the antibodies to the beads.
6. Precipitate the cross-linked complexes, wash, and western blot.

Enzyme-Linked Immunosorbent Assays

Enzyme-linked immunosorbent assays (ELISAs) are a fundamental tool of clinical immunology, and are used as an initial screen for the detection of HIV and other diseases. Based on the principle of antibody-antibody interaction, this test allows for easy visualization of results and can be completed without the additional concern of using radioactive isotopes. The test is performed in a 8 x 12 cm plastic plate, which contains an 8 x 12 matrix of 96-wells, each of which are about 1 cm in height and 0.7 cm in diameter. The method for an HIV ELISA is as follows:

1. Partially purified, inactivated HIV antigens are precoated onto an ELISA plate.
2. Patient serum is incubated within the wells of the plate. If the patient is HIV+, then this serum will contain antibodies to HIV, and those antibodies will bind to the HIV antigens on the plate.
3. Antihuman immunoglobulin, coupled to a fluorescent protein or an enzyme that will perform a chromogenic reaction, is added to the plate. These secondary antibodies will then bind to and detect the primary human antibodies that are bound to the antigens on the plate.
4. The presence of fluorescent secondary antibodies is quantified using a fluorescent plate reader, while the differences in the absorbances of the byproducts of chromogenic reactions are quantified using a plate reader.

Chromatin

Chromatin is the superstructure in which DNA exists within cells. The structure of chromatin is determined by, and stabilized through, the interaction of the DNA with DNA-binding proteins. There are 2 classes of DNA-binding proteins:
- Histones – The major class of DNA-binding proteins that are involved in maintaining the compacted structure of chromatin. There are 5 different histone proteins, called H1, H2A, H2B, H3, and H4.
- Non-Histone Proteins – A diverse class of DNA-binding proteins, including the various transcription factors, polymerases, hormone receptors, and other nuclear enzymes. In any given cell, there are greater than 1000 different types of non-histone proteins bound to the DNA.

The binding of DNA by the histones generates a structure called the nucleosome. The nucleosome core contains an octamer protein structure, which consists of 2 subunits each of H2A, H2B, H3, and H4. The nucleosome cores themselves coil into a solenoid shape, which further coils to compact the DNA. These final coils are compacted further into the characteristic chromatin that can be seen in a karyotyping spread. The protein-DNA structure of chromatin is stabilized by attachment to a non-histone protein scaffold, called the nuclear matrix.

Eukaryotic gene regulation

In eukaryotes, genes for related functions can be found scattered around on different chromosomes, and control of these genes generally occurs through induction rather than inhibition. In addition, there are multiple levels of regulation for eukaryotic gene expression. The eukaryotic gene structure is as follows:
- Promoter – The initial binding site for RNA polymerase.
- Enhancers – The binding sites for regulatory proteins that enhance the binding of RNA polymerase to a promoter.
- Exons – DNA segments that code for sections of proteins.
- Introns – DNA segments that exists between exons, and produce non-coding segments of mRNA that must be spliced out of the coding mRNA (cRNA) prior to the efflux of the cRNA from the nucleus, and prior to the initiation of translation (there are checkpoints that will inhibit progression at both of these steps if the mRNA is not properly spliced).

The levels of eukaryotic gene regulation are:
- Transcriptional
- Post-transcriptional
- Translational
- Post-translational

Cancer as a failure of normal cellular controls

CDK, MPF, and p53 are important proteins in the regulation of the cell cycle, and mutations in the genes coding for these proteins can lead to cancer. Cancer is a disease where the regulation of the cell cycle goes awry, and normal cell growth and behavior is lost. CDK (Cyclin Dependent Kinase) along with the cyclins, are major control switches for the cell cycle, causing the cell to move from G1 to S, or G2 to M. MPF (Maturation Promoting Factor) includes CDK and the cyclins that trigger progression through the cell cycle. p53 is a protein that functions to inhibit progression through the cell cycle if the DNA is damaged. If the DNA damage is severe, p53 may cause apoptosis (cell death). p53 levels are increased in damaged cells. This provides the cell with time to repair its DNA by blocking the cell cycle. A p53 mutation is the most frequent mutation that has been found to lead to cancer. An extreme case of this is Li Fraumeni syndrome, where a genetic defect in p53 leads to a high frequency of cancer in affected individuals. p27 is a protein that binds to cyclin and CDK, blocking cellular entry into S phase. Recent research suggests that breast cancer prognosis is determined by p27 levels. Specifically, reduced levels of p27 predict a poor outcome for breast cancer patients.

Kingdom Fungi

Fungi (singular: fungus) are a major group of living organisms. They were originally considered plants, but are now treated as the separate kingdom Fungi. They occur in all environments on the planet, and include important decomposers and parasites. Parasitic fungi infect animals, including humans, other mammals, birds, and insects, with the consequences varying from mild itching to death. Other parasitic fungi infect plants, causing diseases such as butt rot, and making trees more vulnerable to toppling. The vast majority of vascular plants are associated with mutualistic fungi, called mycorrhizae, which assist their roots in the absorption of nutrients and water.

> ➤ **Review Video: <u>Kingdom Fungi</u>**
> *Visit **mometrix.com/academy** and enter **Code: 315081***

Kingdom Protista

Protists are a heterogeneous group of living things, comprising eukaryotes that are neither animals, plants, nor fungi. They are usually treated as a kingdom Protista or Protoctista, first introduced by Haeckel. The protists are a paraphyletic grade, and – aside from a relatively simple organization – there are not many characteristics common to the group. Protists were traditionally divided based on similarities to the higher kingdoms. The animal-like protozoa are mostly single-celled, motile, and feed through phagocytosis, though there are numerous exceptions. They are usually only 0.01-0.5 mm in size, and are generally too small to be seen without a microscope. They are ubiquitous throughout aqueous environments and the soil, commonly surviving dry periods as cysts, and include several important parasites. The plant-like algae produce energy through photosynthesis. They include many single-celled creatures that are also considered protozoa, such as Euglena. Others are non-motile and colonial, and a few are truly multicellular. Of these, the green and red algae appear to be close relatives of other plants – and thus may be included among the Plantae, but the brown algae developed separately.

RNA viruses

The following are different types of RNA viruses:
- Human Respiratory Virus – Respiratory tract infection.
- Hepatitis A Virus – Hepatitis A.
- Influenza Virus A-C – Influenza.
- Measles Virus – Measles.
- Mumps Virus – Mumps.
- Respiratory Syncytial Virus – Respiratory tract infection in children
- Poliovirus – Poliomyelitis.
- Rhinovirus Types 1-89 – Cold.

- Human Immunodeficiency Virus (HIV) – AIDS.
- Rabies Virus – Rabies.
- Alphavirus – Encephalitis.
- Rubella Virus – Rubella.

DNA viruses

The following are different types of DNA viruses:
- Adenovirus – Eye and respiratory infections.
- Hepatitis B Virus – Hepatitis B infections.
- Cytomegalovirus – Cytomegalic inclusion disease.
- Epstein - Barr virus – Infectious mononucleosis.
- Herpes Virus Types 1 & 2 – Local infections, oral and genital.
- Varicella-Zoster – Chickenpox, herpes zoster.
- Smallpox – Smallpox.

Kingdom Monera

The kingdom Monera was a biological kingdom, which included all living things that have a prokaryotic cell organization. Prior to its creation, these were treated as two separate divisions of plants: the Schizomycetes, or prokaryotes (bacteria, although then considered fungi), and the Cyanophyta, or blue-green algae (now also considered a group of bacteria, typically called the cyanobacteria). Recently, DNA and RNA sequence analyses have demonstrated that there are actually two major groups of prokaryotes, the Bacteria and Archaea, which do not appear to be closer in relationship to each other than they are to the eukaryotes. These may be treated as subkingdoms, but most new schemes tend to abandon the kingdom Monera, and treat these as separate domains or kingdoms. The Monera are the smallest of organisms: they are single-cellular organisms without a nucleus. In fact, the Monera are so small that their entire DNA fits into one circular chromosome.

Bacteria

The properties of bacteria are as follows:
- Prokaryotic (no membrane-enclosed nucleus).
- No mitochondria or chloroplasts.
- A single chromosome.
- A closed circle of double-stranded DNA with no associated histones.
- If flagella are present, they are made up of a single filament of the protein flagellin; they do not have any of the "9+2" tubulin-containing microtubules of the eukaryotes.
- Prokaryotic ribosomes differ in their structure from those of eukaryotes.
- Have a rigid cell wall that is composed of peptidoglycan.
- The plasma membrane is a phospholipid bilayer, but contains no cholesterol or other steroids.
- They do not undergo mitosis.
- They mostly divide by asexual reproduction.

- Any sexual reproduction is very different from that of eukaryotes: they do not undergo meiosis.
- When their food supply runs low, many bacteria form a single spore, where most of the water is removed from the cell and metabolism ceases. Spores are so resistant to adverse conditions of dryness and temperature that they may remain viable even after 50 years of dormancy, and can theoretically survive interplanetary travel.

The following are the structural characteristics of bacteria:
- Plasma membrane – The bacterial plasma membrane is composed primarily of protein and phospholipid (about 3:1). It performs many functions, including transport, biosynthesis, and energy transduction.
- Organelles – The bacterial cytoplasm is densely packed with 70S ribosomes. Other granules represent metabolic reserves (e.g., poly-β-hydroxybutyrate, polysaccharide, polymetaphosphate, and metachromatic granules).
- Endospores – *Bacillus* and *Clostridium* species can produce endospores: heat-resistant, dehydrated, resting cells that are formed intracellularly, and contain a genome and all essential metabolic machinery. The endospore is encased in a complex protective spore coat.
- Flagella – The flagella of motile bacteria differ in structure from eukaryotic flagella. A basal body, anchored in the plasma membrane, and the cell wall give rise to a cylindrical protein filament. The flagellum moves by whirling about on its long axis. The number and arrangement of flagella on the cell are diagnostically useful.
- Pili (Fimbriae) – Pili are slender, hair-like, proteinaceous appendages on the surface of many bacteria (particularly Gram-negative bacteria). They are important in adhesion to host surfaces.
- Capsules – Some bacteria form a thick outer capsule of high-molecular-weight, viscous polysaccharide gel; others have more amorphous slime layers. Capsules confer resistance to phagocytosis.

Gram stain procedure

The Gram stain is named after the 19th century Danish bacteriologist, Hans Christian Gram. The Gram stain procedure is as follows:
1. The bacterial cells are first stained with a purple dye, called crystal violet.
2. Then, the preparation is treated with alcohol or acetone, which washes the stain out of Gram-negative cells.
3. A counterstain of a different color (e.g., the pink of safranin) is added to enable visualization.
4. Bacteria that are not decolorized by the alcohol/acetone wash are Gram positive.

"Murein gets the red out" (allusion to an old eye-wash slogan):
Peptidoglycan (murein) remains purple during Gram staining. Gram-negative bacteria, which are devoid of murein, turn red, while Gram-positive bacteria remain purple because the murein in their cell walls prevents redness.

Anaerobe and obligate anaerobe

- Anaerobe – O_2 is not the final electron acceptor:
  - An anaerobe is a microorganism that need not utilize molecular O_2 as a final electron acceptor (in order to produce ATP).

- o Anaerobes can employ fermentation to generate ATP.
- o Some anaerobes are capable of growth in the presence of O_2, and consequently cannot be described as strict anaerobes.
- o *Clostridium perfringens* and *Treponema pallidum* are examples of organisms that are not facultative anaerobes but are capable of growth in the presence of some O_2 (some isolates of *Treponema pallidum* are instead microaerophiles).
- Obligate anaerobe – Are O_2 intolerant (strict anaerobe):
  - o Many anaerobes not only cannot utilize molecular oxygen but are harmed by it as well.
  - o One usage of the term "obligate anaerobe" is to describe only microorganisms that are unable to grow (or survive) in the presence of O_2.
  - o The other, less strict usage of the term "obligate anaerobe" is simply to distinguish the term "anaerobe" from the term "facultative anaerobe".

Prokaryotic gene regulation

The basics of prokaryotic gene regulation are as follows:
- The prokaryotic gene is directly translated into functional mRNA. No noncoding sequences are present, as occurs in eukaryotes.
- The prokaryote DNA is arranged in operons.
- Regulation is by inhibition of transcription.

The components of the prokaryotic operon are:
- Regulatory Gene – Codes for repressor proteins that bind to operator genes.
- Promoter Region – RNA polymerase binding site to initiate transcription.
- Operator Gene – Controls the binding of RNA polymerase to the promoter region.
- Structural Gene – Codes for a protein.
- Inducer – Substance that binds to a repressor, inhibiting it from binding to the operator.

Operons

In prokaryotic cells (and viruses), genes are often regulated as operons:
- Operons are a form of transcriptional control.
- An operon consists of the structural gene (or genes) that actually codes for specific proteins, and the controlling elements that are associated with the control of those genes. An operon typically contains several genes that are all under the same control mechanism.
- Though rather similar controlling systems have been found for some eukaryotic genes, control mechanisms in eukaryotes are generally more diverse and more complex; and, with the exception of a few examples in simple eukaryotic organisms like yeasts, multiple genes are not found to function under a single control mechanism. In other words, eukaryotic cells do not have operons.

Prokaryotic and eukaryotic cells

The differences between prokaryotic and eukaryotic cells are as follows:
- Eukaryotic cells have a true nucleus bound by a double membrane, while prokaryotic cells have no nucleus (although they do have DNA).
- Eukaryotic DNA is linear, while prokaryotic DNA is circular.

- Eukaryotic DNA is complexed with proteins, called histones, and is organized into chromosomes, while prokaryotic DNA is naked, meaning that it has no associated histones and does not form chromosomes. Although commonly misused, the term chromosome does not technically apply to anything within a prokaryotic cell.
- A eukaryotic cell contains many chromosomes, while a prokaryotic cell contains only one circular DNA molecule and a varied assortment of much smaller circlets of DNA, called plasmids.
- Both cell types have many, many ribosomes, but the ribosomes of the eukaryotic cells are larger and more complex than those of the prokaryotic cell: eukaryotic ribosomes are composed of five kinds of rRNA and about 80 kinds of proteins, while prokaryotic ribosomes are composed of only three kinds of rRNA and about 50 kinds of protein.
- The cytoplasm of eukaryotic cells is filled with a large, complex collection of organelles, many of them enclosed in their own membranes, while the prokaryotic cell contains no membrane-bound organelles that are independent of the plasma membrane.

> ➤ **Review Video: Eukaryotic and Prokaryotic**
> *Visit mometrix.com/academy and enter Code: 231438*

Kingdom Animalia

Animals are a major group of organisms, classified as the kingdom Animalia or Metazoa. In general, they are multicellular, capable of locomotion, responsive to their environment, and feed by consuming other organisms. Their body plan becomes fixed as they develop, usually early on in their development as embryos, although some undergo a process of metamorphosis later on. Biologically, human beings fall under the animal kingdom. With a few exceptions, most notably the sponges (phylum Porifera), animals have bodies that are differentiated into separate tissues. These include muscles, which are able to contract and control locomotion, and a nervous system, which sends and processes signals. There is also typically an internal digestive chamber, with one or two openings. Animals with this sort of organization are called metazoans, or eumetazoans when the former is used for animals in general. All animals have eukaryotic cells, surrounded by a characteristic extracellular matrix composed of collagen and elastic glycoproteins. This may be calcified to form structures, including shells, bones, and spicules. During development, it forms a relatively flexible framework upon which cells can move about and be reorganized, making complex structures possible. In contrast, other multicellular organisms, like plants and fungi, have cells held in place by cell walls, and develop by progressive growth. Also unique to animal cells are the following intercellular junctions: tight junctions, gap junctions, and desmosomes.

> ➤ **Review Video: Kingdom Animalia**
> *Visit mometrix.com/academy and enter Code: 558413*

Chordates

Chordates (phylum Chordata) include the vertebrates, together with several closely related invertebrates. They are united by having at some stage in their life a notochord, a hollow dorsal nerve cord, pharyngeal slits, a dorsal hollow neural tube, and a muscular tail extending past the anus. The phylum Chordata is broken down into three subphyla: Urochordata, Cephalochordata, and Vertebrata. Urochordate larvae have a notochord and a nerve cord, but they are both lost in adulthood. Cephalochordates have a notochord and a nerve cord, but no vertebrae. In vertebrates, the notochord has been replaced by a bony vertebral column.

Human taxonomy

Classification Group		Distinguishing Features
Kingdom	Animalia	Consume food and are mobile.
Phylum	Chordata	Notochord; dorsally positioned hollow nervous system (neural tube); gill slits in pharyngeal wall; heart ventral to digestive system.
Subphylum	Mammalia	Segmental vertebral column.
Class	Vertebrata	Mammary glands for nourishment of young; hair or fur; warm-blooded; diaphragm.
Order	Primates	Large cerebral hemispheres; opposable digits; nails; highly developed sense of sight—eyes directed forward; teeth specialized for different functions.
Family	Hominidae	Walk with two limbs (bipedal locomotion); binocular color vision.
Genus	Homo	Ability to speak; most highly developed and largest brain.
Species	Sapiens	Large skull; high forehead; reduced size of brow (supraorbital) ridges; prominent chin; decreased amount of body hair.

Organization of the human body

Humans are multicellular organisms composed of millions of cells organized into functional units (organs and systems), which are formed by various groups of similar cells (tissues) that work together. These cells are embedded in intercellular substances and tissue fluids. A *tissue* consists of a group of cells that perform a similar function. Four basic tissues compose the human (mammalian) body: muscle, nerve, epithelium, and connective tissues. The four basic tissues may be organized to form functional units known as *organs*. Several organs that function together as a unit for a specified purpose make up an organ *system*.

Organ systems

The human body is composed of the systems listed in the following table:

System	Functions
Muscular	Produces motion of body parts and viscera.
Skeletal	Supports the body, protects organs, and produces blood cells.
Circulatory	Transports nutrients, wastes, gases (oxygen and carbon dioxide), hormones, and blood cells throughout the body; also protects body against foreign organisms.
Nervous	Responds to internal and external stimuli; regulates and coordinates body activities and movements.
Integumentary	Limits and protects the body as a whole; prevents excess loss of water and functions in regulating body temperature.
Digestive	Enzymatically breaks down food materials into usable and absorbable nutrients.
Respiratory	Functions in the exchange of gases (oxygen and carbon dioxide).
Urinary	Removes body wastes from blood stream and helps regulate homeostasis of internal environment.
Reproductive	Perpetuates the living organism by the production of sex cells (gametes) and future offspring.
Endocrine	Regulates body growth and function via hormones.

Tissues

The following are the four basic tissues:
- Muscle tissue – Muscle tissue is contractile in nature and functions to move the skeletal system and the body viscera. The types of muscle tissue are skeletal, smooth, and cardiac.
- Nervous tissue – Nervous tissue is composed of cells (*neurons*) that respond to external and internal stimuli and have the capability to transmit a message (*impulse*) from one area of the body to another. This tissue induces responses in distant muscles or glands, and regulates bodily processes, such as respiration, circulation, and digestion.
- Epithelial tissue – Epithelial tissue covers the external surfaces of the body and lines the internal tubes and cavities. It also forms the glands of the body.
- Connective tissue – Connective tissue is the packing and supporting material of the bodily tissues and organs. All connective tissues consist of three distinct components: ground substance, cells, and fibers.

Nucleus

The nucleus is often the most prominent organelle (little organ) in the cell. The nucleus is bounded by a double membrane, called the nuclear envelope. These two tightly attached membranes are of the same basic structure as the familiar lipid-protein bilayer. Scattered throughout the double membrane nuclear envelope are nuclear pores, which are holes, or passages, through which large molecules can pass. There are two major types of material within the nucleus:

- Nucleoplasm – The jelly-like matrix within the nucleus, in which all other nuclear materials float.
- Chromatin –DNA and its associated histone proteins, which together form the supermolecular DNA-protein complexes, called chromosomes. Chromatin gets its name because it is easily stained (i.e., "chromatic").

Also found within the nucleus are dark-staining parts, called nucleoli (little nuclei), which are rich in the other type of nucleic acid, RNA. The nucleoli have the task of synthesizing a special type of RNA that is used to create ribosomes, called rRNA.

Mitochondria

Mitochondria are the best known of the cellular organelles. They had been described during the 19th century, notably by Kollicker and Fleming. Altman, using Janus green, was able to stain them in 1890. Structurally, the mitochondrion is composed of an outer trilaminar membrane and an inner trilaminar membrane; the inner one forms folds which are known as *cristae*. The space between the two membranes is about 6-10 nm wide. Mitochondria as a whole, and specifically the cristae, vary in size, shape, and number not only in different cells but also in the same cell depending on its functional state. Mitochondria are present in greater numbers in cells exhibiting high levels of activity and having more energy requirements. Muscle and grandular tissues fall in the above category. DNA has been found in the mitochondria of animals and the chloroplasts of plants. Mitochondria are capable of division and are not generated *de novo.* Granules have been observed in the mitochondria matrix. Their identity is in question; however, some believe they might be reservoirs of calcium and other divalent ions. Phosphate is taken up with Ca^{2+} and calcium phosphate deposition may be the end result. Mitochondria are the biochemical power plants of the cell. They recover energy from food stuffs (i.e., via glycolysis, the TCA cycle, and the respiratory chain), and convert it via phosphorylation into adenosine triphosphate (ATP). In this manner, they produce the energy necessary for the metabolic processes.

> ➤ **Review Video: Mitochondria**
> *Visit* **mometrix.com/academy** *and enter* **Code: 444287**

Coenzyme Q_{10}

Coenzyme Q_{10} (CoQ_{10}) is a compound found naturally in the mitochondria. CoQ_{10} is involved in the production of ATP. ATP serves as the cell's major energy source, and drives a number of biological processes, including muscle contraction and the production of protein. CoQ_{10} also enhances the immune system, and works as an antioxidant. Antioxidants are substances that scavenge free radicals, damaging compounds in the body that alter cell membranes, tamper with DNA, and even cause cell death. Free radicals occur naturally in the body, but environmental toxins, including UV light, radiation, cigarette smoking, and air pollution, can also increase the number of these damaging particles. Free radicals are believed to contribute to the aging process, as well as the

- 99 -

development of a number of health problems, including heart disease and cancer. Antioxidants, such as CoQ_{10}, can neutralize free radicals, and may reduce or even prevent the damage they cause.

Lysosomes

Lysosomes are described as containing proteolytic enzymes (hydrolases). Lysosomes contain acid phosphatase and other hydrolytic enzymes. These enzymes are enclosed by a membrane and are released when needed into the cell or into phagocytic vesicles. Lysosomal enzymes have the capacity to hydrolyze all classes of macromolecules. A generalized list of substrates acted upon by their respective enzymes is given below:

- Lipids by lipases and phospholipases.
- Proteins by proteases.
- Polysaccharides by glycosidases.
- Nucleic acids by nucleases.
- Phosphates (organic-linked) by phosphatases.
- Sulphates (organic-linked) by sulfatases.

Peroxisomes

Peroxisomes are found in virtually all mammalian cell types and probably arise from swellings of the endoplasmic reticulum. These structures are often smaller than lysosomes. The enzymes they possess are active in the production of hydrogen peroxide (e.g., urate oxidase, D-amino acid oxidase, and α-hydroxyacid oxidase), and one functions in destroying hydrogen peroxide (catalase). The peroxisomes function in purine catabolism and in the degradation of nucleic acids.

Endoplasmic reticulum

The endoplasmic reticulum is an interconnected network of tubules, vesicles, and sacs. It may serve specialized functions within the cell, including protein synthesis, sequestration of calcium, production of steroids, storage and production of glycogen, and insertion of membrane proteins. The rough endoplasmic reticulum contains ribosomes in its membrane for protein synthesis. Following translation, the newly synthesized proteins are sequestered within sacs, called cisternae. The system then sends these proteins, via small vesicles, to the Golgi complex. Or, in the case of membrane proteins, it inserts them into the membrane. The ribosomes sit on the outer surfaces of the cisternae. They resemble small beads sitting in rosettes, or in a linear pattern. The rough endoplasmic reticulum forms a branched reticulum that expands as the cell becomes more active in protein synthesis. Sometimes, the reticulum branches out; other times, the cisternae dilate and form large sacs that fill the cell.

Insertion of transmembrane proteins

Proteins enter and pass through membranes as follows:
- The endoplasmic reticulum membrane contains a gated pore (also called a channel or translocon) for the growing chain.
- The signal peptidase (SP) forms a loop, and the loop enters the membrane channel (translocon). The SP loop is probably what opens (gates) the channel.
- The growing protein chain passes through channel as the chain is synthesized.
- The protein can go all the way through the membrane and end up as a soluble protein in the lumen, or it can go part way through the membrane and end up as a transmembrane protein, with the final cellular location of its membrane portion being determined by the vesicle sorting of the Golgi apparatus.

Golgi complex

The Golgi complex controls trafficking of different types of proteins. Some are destined for secretion; others are destined for the extracellular matrix. In addition, other proteins, such as lysosomal enzymes, may need to be sorted and sequestered from the remaining constituents because of their potentially destructive effects. The regulated secretory pathway, as its name implies, is a pathway for proteins that requires a stimulus or trigger in order to elicit secretion. Some stimuli regulate the synthesis of a protein, as well as its release. The constitutive pathway allows for the secretion of proteins that are needed outside of the cell, such the extracellular matrix. It does not require stimuli, although growth factors may enhance the process. The most important role of the Golgi complex is to make certain that the plasma membrane proteins reach their destination. Phosphorylation occurs in the cis region. In other regions, different types of carbohydrates are added as glycoproteins pass through the cisternae. The final sorting of proteins is done in the trans Golgi complex. The inner cis region is rich in lipid-bearing membranes, and can be delineated by osmium tetroxide labeling. The middle regions can be labeled for enzymes that add carbohydrates, or other groups, to the protein products. The outer, or trans region, is the area where the lysosomes are sorted. Thus, it is heavily labeled for acid phosphatase.

Cisternal maturation model

The Cisternal maturation model is described below:
- Transport vesicles move retrogradely (towards the cis face).
- Vesicles carry enzymes in order to modify and sort proteins. They do not carry the newly made proteins from the endoplasmic reticulum.
- Sacs of Golgi move, carrying the newly made proteins inside, while new sacs are constantly being formed at the cis face (and lost from the trans face as they age).
- The enzyme composition of each sac changes constantly as it ages, and as it moves from the cis face to the trans face. However, the characteristic enzymes that are found in the sacs at each position of the Golgi (cis, medial, and trans) remain the same. This is because the enzymes are "passed back", meaning that the enzymes from the older sacs are retrieved by the vesicles, and carried back to the newer sacs.

Plasma membranes

The cell membrane, or unit membrane, is usually about 75-100 Å thick, and has a trilaminar structure. As described by Danielli and Davson (1935), these three layers consist of a bimolecular lipid layer sandwiched by two protein layers. Due to the lipid bilayer, the plasma membrane is only semi-permeable to most molecules, dependent upon transmembrane protein channels or transporters that control the passage of materials into and out of the cell. The movement of materials into and out of the cell is called transport. The functions of the plasma membrane are as follows:

- Maintains a relatively watertight barrier.
- Provides a boundary resulting in a controlled environment, which allows for permeability of one type of molecule, and impermeability of another. All biological membranes are selectively permeable.
- Segregate reaction areas that can be distinguished due to their chemical composition, their pH value, and their electric potential. Both the pH and the electrical gradient can be measured.

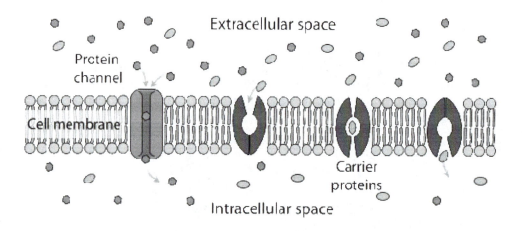

- Some ions or small molecules (substrates) can be transported through the membrane. This transport is energy-consuming, requiring active transport against the concentration gradient of the ion or molecule.
- Different compositions of proteins are found in different regions of the plasma membrane, and this causes individual membrane types to have different functions, as well. Highly specialized membranes, such as the thylakoid membranes of chloroplasts and the inner membranes of mitochondria, are involved in energy turnovers.

> ➤ **Review Video: <u>Plasma Membrane</u>**
> *Visit **mometrix.com/academy** and enter **Code: 943095***

Membrane structure

Electron microscopy suggests that the central region of the membrane consists of two layers of lipid molecules, mainly phospholipids and steroids. Each layer is thought to be one molecule thick. The phospholipids molecules are fairly long and have two functional poles: one exhibits lipid properties (hydrophobic), while the other exhibits polar properties (hydrophilic). The hydrophobic ends of both layers of lipid molecules associate with each other since they have affinity for one another. The hydrophilic portions face toward the protein layers, and parts of the proteins associate readily with water. Electron microscopy substantiates that there is a light central layer surrounded by two denser layers. The two denser layers are thought to represent the proteins and hydrophilic portions of the lipid molecules.

Active and passive transport

Active transport
Active transport occurs when a substance moves against its concentration gradient with the help of a pump protein and the expenditure of energy. There are two types of active transport:
- Primary active transport – Where the energy for transport is supplied by the hydrolysis of adenosine triphosphate (ATP).
- Secondary active transport – Where the energy for transport is supplied by a secondary substance that is running against its own concentration gradient.

Passive transport
Passive transport occurs when a substance moves in the same direction as its concentration gradient. This can be performed by simple diffusion through a channel, or with the help of a carrier protein.

Diffusion and osmosis

Diffusion is the movement of ions or molecules from regions of higher concentration to regions of lower concentration (down a concentration gradient). Osmosis is specifically the diffusion of water from a region of higher to lower water concentration, through a semi-permeable membrane. Molecules that easily pass through the phospholipid bilayer are as follows:
- Hydrophobic (oil soluble) molecules, such as O_2 and N_2.
- Nonpolar benzene.
- Small, uncharged, polar molecules, such as H_2O, urea, glycerol, and CO_2.

Molecules that do not easily pass through the phospholipid bilayer are as follows:
- Large, uncharged molecules, such as glucose.
- Polar molecules, such as sucrose.
- Charged ions, such as H^+, Na^+, HCO_3^-, K^+, Ca^{2+}, Cl^-, and Mg^{2+}.

Gating and channels

Some channels are gated, meaning that the percent of time any particular gate is open is regulated. However, each individual gate is either open all of the way or closed. The different methods of gating are as follows:
- Ligand gated – Opens or shuts in response to ligands (chemicals that bind to the substance under discussion). Typical ligands that open ligand gated channels are hormones, neurotransmitters, etc.
- Voltage gated – Opens or shuts in response to changes in voltage. Allows for the transmission of electrical signals, as occurs in muscle and neurons.
- Mechanically gated – Opens or shuts in response to pressure. Important in touch, hearing and balance.

Conversely, some channels are open all of the time (ungated), such as in the case of K^+-leak channels. These channels allow for a small amount of K^+ to constantly leak out of cells, causing the cells to have a slightly negative charge overall.

Glucose transporters

The glucose transporters (GLUTs) are responsible for carrier-mediated transport of glucose across cell membranes. All facilitated diffusion of glucose across cell membranes depends upon a family of proteins, called GLUT1, GLUT2, etc. All of the proteins of this family are similar, and have a similar overall structure: 12 transmembrane segments, with the carboxyl- and amino-terminal ends on the intracellular side of the plasma membrane. However, they have significant structural and functional differences.

Clathrin

Clathrin is required for the active formation of endocytic and secretory vesicles. Clathrin is specifically a coat protein for vesicles that are formed from the plasma membrane and the trans-Golgi network. The budding of other membranes involves different coat proteins, the best known of these being COPI and COPII, which are involved in endoplasmic reticulum-Golgi transport.

Cell division

Cell division is the process of a biological cell, called a mother cell, dividing into two daughter cells. This leads to growth in multicellular organisms (the growth of tissue), and to procreation (vegetative reproduction) in unicellular organisms. Prokaryotic cells divide by binary fission. Eukaryotic cells usually undergo a process of nuclear division, called mitosis, followed by division of the cell, called cytokinesis. A diploid cell may also undergo meiosis to produce haploid cells (usually four). Haploid cells serve as gametes in multicellular organisms, fusing with gametes from a compatible mate to form new diploid cells, thus conceiving offspring. Multicellular organisms replace worn-out cells through cell division. However, in some animals, cell division eventually halts, and the cell is then referred to as senescent. Senescent cells deteriorate over time and die, causing the body to age. Cells stop dividing because the telomeres, protective segments of DNA on the ends of chromosomes, become shorter with each cell division, and are eventually unable to protect the chromosomes. Cancer cells, on the other hand, are "immortal". An enzyme, called telomerase, allows them to continue dividing indefinitely.

Interphase and cytokinesis

Interphase
The cell is engaged in metabolic activity, and is preparing for mitosis (the next four phases that lead up to, and include, nuclear division). Chromosomes are not clearly visible in the nucleus, although a dark spot, called the nucleolus, may be visible. The cell may contain a pair of centrioles (or microtubule organizing centers in plants), both of which are organizational sites for microtubules.

Cytokinesis
In animal cells, cytokinesis results when a fiber ring (composed of a protein called actin) forms around the center of the cell, and then contracts, pinching the cell into two daughter cells, each with one nucleus.

Mitosis

The stages of mitosis are:

- Prophase – Chromatin in the nucleus begins to condense, and becomes visible as chromosomes under the light microscope. The nucleolus disappears, centrioles begin moving to opposite ends of the cell, and fibers extend from the centromeres.
- Prometaphase – The nuclear membrane dissolves, marking the beginning of prometaphase. Proteins attach to the centromeres, creating the kinetochores, microtubules attach at the kinetochores, and the chromosomes begin to move.
- Metaphase – Spindle fibers align the chromosomes along the middle line of the cell nucleus. This line is referred to as the metaphase plate. This organization helps to ensure that, in the next phase, when the chromosomes are separated, each new nucleus will receive exactly one copy of each chromosome.
- Anaphase – The paired chromosomes separate at the kinetochores, and move to opposite sides of the cell. Motion results from a combination of kinetochore movement along the spindle microtubules, and through the physical interaction of polar microtubules.
- Telophase – Chromatids arrive at the opposite poles of the cell, and new membranes form around the daughter nuclei. The chromosomes disperse, and are no longer visible under the light microscope. The spindle fibers disperse, and cytokinesis (partitioning of the cell) may also begin during this stage.

Prophase	Prometaphase	Metaphase	Anaphase	Telophase

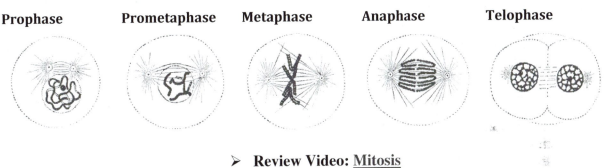

> ➤ **Review Video: Mitosis**
> *Visit **mometrix.com/academy** and enter **Code: 849894***

Cell cycle

The cell cycle is an ordered set of events that culminate in cell growth and the division of a cell into two daughter cells. The stages of the cell cycle are as follows:

- M Phase – The period when cells prepare for, and then undergo, cytokinesis. M phase stands for mitotic phase. During mitosis the chromosomes are paired, and then divided, prior to cell division. The events in this stage are prophase, metaphase, anaphase, and telophase.
- G1 Phase – Corresponds to the gap in the cell cycle that occurs following cytokinesis. During this phase, cells make a decision whether to exit the cell cycle and then become quiescent, terminally differentiated, or to continue dividing. Terminal differentiation is identified as a non-dividing state for a cell. Quiescent and terminally differentiated cells are identified as being in G0 phase. Cells in G0 can remain in this state for extended periods of time. Specific stimuli may induce the G0 cell to re-enter the cell cycle at the G1 phase, or may induce permanent terminal differentiation. During G1, cells begin synthesizing all of the cellular components that are needed to generate two identically complimented daughter cells. As a result, the size of cells begins to increase during G1.

- S Phase – The phase of the cell cycle during which the DNA is replicated. This is the DNA-synthesis phase. Additionally, some specialized proteins are synthesized during S phase, particularly the histones.
- G2 Phase – This phase is reached following completion of DNA replication. During G2, the chromosomes begin condensing, the nucleoli disappear, and two microtubule organizing centers begin polymerizing tubulins for eventual production of the spindle poles.

Neurons

Nervous tissue consists of neurons and supportive elements. The neurons are highly specialized cellular elements that carry out the function of nervous transmission. The supportive elements are the neuroglia in the central nervous system and the Schwann cells in the peripheral nervous system. Neurons consist of a nucleus with an associated nucleolus and a cytoplasm that is rich in organelles. Neurons are polarized with one axon extending from one side of the cell and multiple dendrites extending from the other side of the cell.

Axons

Neurons have only one axon. This process arises from a conical elevation of cytoplasm, which is devoid of rough-surfaced endoplasmic reticulum (i.e., Nissl bodies), and this area is called the axon hillock. It is usually thinner and longer than the dendrites of the same neuron. It may be surrounded by a myelin sheath. At its ending, the axon transmits impulses.

Dendrites

Dendrites are direct extensions of the cytoplasm and are generally multiple. They provide an increased surface area, the dendritic zone, to allow for synaptic intersection.

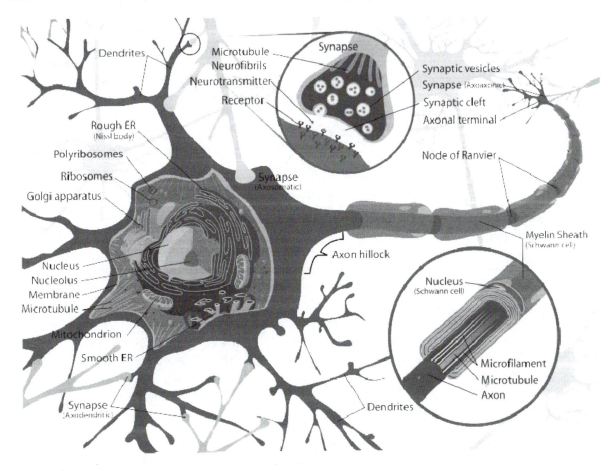

Synapse

The synapse is the site of contact between an axon and dendrite of two neurons. Once activated, neurons exocytose neurotransmitters into the synaptic junction. These neurotransmitters in turn modulate the activity of their postsynaptic targets. Sufficient depolarization of the dendrites of postsynaptic neurons can trigger action potentials in the postsynaptic neurons.

Action potential

An impulse traveling along a neuron is an electrical phenomenon initiated by a temporary change in the permeability of the neuron's cell membrane. Action potentials originate at the axon hillock (i.e., the trigger region), where summation results in threshold depolarization of the neuron. The gradients of sodium and potassium ions across the neuronal membrane are regulated by sodium and potassium channels. Each sodium channel has an activation gate and an inactivation gate, while potassium channels have only one gate. The phases of an action potential are as follows:

- Resting state – The sodium activation gates are closed, sodium inactivation gates are open, and potassium gates are closed. Resting membrane potential is at around -70 mV inside the cell.
- Depolarizing phase – The action potential begins with the activation gates of the sodium channels opening, allowing Na^+ ions to enter the cell and cause a sudden depolarization, which leads to the spike of the action potential. Excess Na^+ ions enter the cell causing a reversal of potential, becoming briefly more positive on the inside of the cell membrane.
- Repolarizing phase – The sodium inactivation gates close and potassium gates open. This causes Na^+ ions to stop entering the cell, and K^+ ions to leave the cell, resulting in repolarization. Until the membrane is repolarized, it cannot be stimulated, which is called the absolute refractory period.
- Return to resting state – Excess potassium leaves the cell, causing a brief hyperpolarization. Sodium activation gates close and potassium gates begin closing. The sodium-potassium pump begins to re-establish the resting membrane potential.

Once an action potential begins, it is self-propagated, and travels down the length of the axon. In addition, it is all-or-none, meaning that there are not differing degrees of action potentials: you either have one or you do not.

Classification of neurons

- Multipolar neurons – Most abundant; somatic and visceral motor and associational.
- Unipolar neurons – Somatic and visceral sensory neurons; cell bodies are located in cranial sensory and dorsal root ganglia; the peripheral process goes out to receptors, and the central process travels into the central nervous system.

Groups of neurons

- Nucleus – Cluster of nerve cell bodies within the central nervous system.
- Ganglion – Cluster of nerve cells bodies outside the central nervous system.
- Cortex – Layered arrangement of nerve cell bodies on the surface of the cerebrum and cerebellum (gray matter).

Supportive elements of the nervous system

The following are the supportive elements of the nervous system:

- Neuroglia (glial cells) – Long described as supporting cells of the CNS, there is also a functional interdependence between neurons and neuroglia.
- Astrocytes – These neuroglia anchor neurons to blood vessels, regulate the micro-environment surrounding neurons, and regulate the transport of nutrients to, and waste from, neurons.

- Microglia – These neuroglia are phagocytic and function to defend the CNS against pathogens. They may also monitor the condition of neurons.
- Ependymal cells – These cells line the fluid-filled cavities of the brain and spinal cord. They play a role in the production, transport, and circulation of the cerebrospinal fluid.
- Oligodendrocytes – These cells each produce myelin sheaths for several neurons in the central nervous system. These myelin sheaths function to protect and insulate axons, as well as enable rapid electrical conduction along axons during the propagation of action potentials, known as saltatory conduction.
- Schwann cells – These cells produce myelin sheaths for individual nerves in the peripheral nervous system. These myelin sheaths function similar to the myelin sheaths produced by oligodendrocytes. In addition, Schwann cells maintain the micro-environment around the axon, and enable them to regenerate and re-establish connections with receptors or effectors.
- Satellite cells – These cells surround the cell bodies of neurons in ganglia. Their role is to maintain the micro-environment, and to provide insulation for the ganglion cells.

Muscle cells

A muscle fiber is a single muscle cell. If we look at a section of a fiber, we can see that it is complete with a cell membrane, called the sarcolemma, and has several nuclei located just under the sarcolemma—it is multinucleated. Each fiber is composed of numerous cylindrical fibrils running the entire length of the fiber.

Myofilaments

The thick and thin myofilaments form the contractile machinery of muscle and are made up of proteins. Approximately 54% of all of the contractile protein (by weight) is myosin. The thick myofilament is composed of many myosin molecules oriented tail-end to tail-end at the center with myosin molecules staggered from the center to the myofilament tip. The second major contractile protein is actin. Actin is a globular protein.

Sarcoplasm

The sarcoplasm (cytoplasm of the muscle cell) contains Golgi complexes near the nuclei. Mitochondria are found between the myofibrils and just below the sarcolemma. The myofibrils are surrounded by smooth endoplasmic reticulum (*sarcoplasmic reticulum*) composed of a longitudinally arranged tubular network (*sarcotubules*). The complex (terminal cistern-T tubule-terminal cistern) formed at this position is known as a *triad*. The T tubules function to bring a wave of depolarization of the sarcolemma into the fiber and thus into intimate relationship with the terminal cisternae.

Excitation

Contraction in a skeletal muscle is triggered by the generation of an action potential in the muscle membrane. Each motor neuron upon entering a skeletal muscle loses its myelin sheath and divides into branches with each branch innervating a single muscle fiber, forming a *neuromuscular junction*. Each fiber normally has one neuromuscular junction, which is located near the center of the fiber. A *motor unit* consists of a single motor neuron and all the muscle fibers innervated by it. The *motor end plate* is the specialized part of the muscle fiber's membrane lying under the neuron.

Contraction

According to the sliding filament theory (Huxley) the sarcomere response to excitation involves the sliding of thin and thick myofilaments past one another making and breaking chemical bonds with each other as they go. Neither the thick nor thin myofilaments change in length. If we could imagine observing this contraction under a light microscope we would see the narrowing of the "H" and "I" bands during contraction while the width of the "A" band would remain constant.

Muscle twitch

A muscle's response to a single maximal stimulus is a muscle twitch. The beginning of muscular activity is signaled by the record of the electrical activity in the sarcolemma. The latent period is the delay between imposition of the stimulus and the development of tension.

Tetanus

When a volley of stimuli is applied to a muscle, each succeeding stimulus may arrive before the muscle can completely relax from the contraction caused by the preceding stimulus. The result is *summation*, an increased strength of contraction. If the frequency of stimulation is very fast, individual contractions fuse and the muscle smoothly and fully contracts. This is *tetanus*.

Energy sources

In any phenomenon including muscular contraction the energy input to the system and the energy output from the system are equal. Let us consider first the energy sources for muscular contraction. The immediate energy source for contraction is ATP, which can be hydrolyzed by actomyosin to give ADP, P_i, and the energy that is associated with cross-bridge motion.

Muscle fibers

Skeletal muscle fibers can be described on the bases of structure and function as follows:
- White (fast) fibers – Contract rapidly; fatigue quickly; energy production is mainly via anaerobic glycolysis; contain relatively few mitochondria; examples are the muscles of the eye.
- Red (slow) fibers – Contract slowly; fatigue slowly; energy production is mainly via oxidative phosphorylation (aerobic); contain relatively many mitochondria; examples are postural muscles.
- Intermediate fibers – Have structural and functional qualities between those of white and of red fibers.

Skeletal muscle cell

The sarcolemma of a skeletal muscle cell is structured to receive and conduct stimuli. The sarcoplasm of the cell is filled with contractile myofibrils, and this results in the nuclei and other organelles being relegated to the edge of the cell. Myofibrils are contractile units within the cell, which consist of a regular array of protein myofilaments. Each myofilament runs longitudinally, with respect to the muscle fiber. There are two types of myofilaments: thick bands and thin bands. The thick bands are made up of multiple molecules of a protein called myosin. The thin bands are made up of multiple molecules of a protein called actin. The thin actin bands are attached to a Z-line or Z-disk of an elastic protein called titin. The titin protein also extends into the myofibril, anchoring the other bands into position. From each Z-line to the next is a unit called the sarcomere.

Epithelial tissue

Epithelial tissue covers the external surfaces of the body and lines the internal tubes and cavities. It also forms the glands of the body. Characteristics of epithelial tissue (epithelium) are as follows:
- Has compactly aggregated cells.
- Has limited intercellular spaces and substance.
- Is avascular (no blood vessels).
- Lies on a connective tissue layer—the basal lamina.
- Has cells that form sheets and are polarized.
- Is derived from all three germ layers.

Epithelial cells may also have specializations at the cell surface, such as the following:
- Microvilli – Fingerlike projections of plasma membranes.
- Cilia – Motile organelles extending into the lumen consisting of specially arranged microtubules.
- Flagella – Similar to cilia. Primary examples are human spermatozoa.
- Stereocilia – Are actually very elongated microvilli.

Types of epithelium

Classification	Location(s)	Function(s)
Simple squamous epithelium	Endothelium of blood and lymphatic vessels; Bowman's capsule and thin loop of Henle in kidney; mesothelium lining pericardial, peritoneal and pleural body cavities; lung alveoli; smallest excretory ducts of glands.	Lubrication of body cavities (permits free movement of organs); pinocytotic transports across cells.
Stratified squamous keratinized epithelium	Epidermis of skin.	Prevents loss of water and protection.
Stratified squamous nonkeratinized epithelium (moist)	Mucosa of oral cavity, esophagus, anal canal; vagina; cornea of eye and part of conjunctiva.	Secretion; protection; prevents loss of water.
Simple cuboidal epithelium	Kidney tubules; choroids plexus; thyroid gland; rete testis; surface of ovary.	Secretion; absorption; lines surface.
Stratified cuboidal epithelium	Ducts of sweat glands; developing follicles of ovary.	Secretion; protection.
Simple columnar epithelium	Cells lining lumen of digestive tract (stomach to rectum); gall bladder; many glands (secretory units and ducts); uterus; uterine tube (ciliated).	Secretion; absorption; protection; lubrication.
Pseudostratified columnar epithelium	Lines lumen of respiratory tract (nasal cavity, trachea and bronchi) (ciliated); ducts of epididymis (stereocilia); ductus deferens; male urethra.	Secretion; protection; facilitates transport of substances on surface of cells.
Stratified columnar epithelium	Male urethra; conjunctiva.	Protection.
Transitional epithelium	Urinary tract (renal calyces and pelvis, ureter and urinary bladder).	Protection.

Connective tissue

Connective tissue is the packing and supporting material of the body tissues and organs. It develops from mesoderm (mesenchyme). All connective tissues consist of three distinct components: ground substance, cells, and fibers. Ground substance is located between the cells and fibers, both of which are embedded in it. It forms an amorphous intercellular material. In the fresh state, it appears as a transparent and homogenous gel. It acts as a route for the passage of nutrients and wastes to and from the cells within or adjacent to the connective tissue. The fiber components of connective tissue add support and strength. Three types of fibers are present: *collagenous*, *elastic*, and *reticular*. Collagen fibers (white fibers) are the most numerous fiber type and are present in all types of connective tissue in varying amounts. Collagen bundles are strong and resist stretching. They are found in structures such as tendons, ligaments, aponeuroses and fascia, which are subjected to pull or stretching activities. Elastic fibers (yellow fibers) are refractile fibers which are thinner (0.2 to 1 µm diameter) than collagen fibers. They are extremely elastic and are located in structures with a degree of elasticity, such as the walls of blood vessels (elastic arteries), true vocal cords and trachea. Reticular fibers are thinner (0.2 to 1 µm diameter) than collagenous fibers. They are arranged in an intermeshing network (reticulum) which supports the organ. Reticular fibers are inelastic. They are found in the walls of blood vessels, lymphoid tissues (spleen and lymph nodes), red bone marrow, basal laminae and glands (liver and kidney).

Cells

The cells of connective tissue are primarily attached and non-motile (*fixed cells*), but some have the ability to move (*wandering or free cells*). The typical cells found in connective tissue are as follows:

- Fibroblasts – Constitute the largest number of cells present in connective tissue. In an actively secreting state, they are flattened stellate-shaped cells with an oval nucleus and basophilic cytoplasm due to the numerous rough endoplasmic reticulum. In the inactive state, they are referred to as *fibrocytes*.
- Mesenchymal cells – Undifferentiated connective tissue cells that have the potential to differentiate into other types of connective tissue cells. They are primarily found in embryonic and fetal tissues; some are thought to be present in adults, abutting the walls of capillaries. They are smaller than fibroblasts, and are stellate in shape.
- Macrophages (histiocytes) – May be fixed or free. Free macrophages may wander through the connective tissue by extending their cell processes. Fixed macrophages are very numerous in loose connective tissue.
- Adipocytes (fat cells) – Found in most connective tissue, either singly or in groups. If the connective tissue layer is primarily composed of fat cells, it is referred to as adipose tissue. An adipocyte is a round, large cell with a distinct, dense nucleus usually located at the periphery of the cytoplasm.
- Mast cells – Ovoid cells with small round nuclei. The cytoplasm contains numerous coarse basophilic granules which also stain metachromatically and are soluble in water. The mast cell granules are composed of *histamine* and an anticoagulant known as *heparin*.
- Plasma cells – Have a characteristic eccentric nucleus which contains chromatin arranged in a definite pattern near the nuclear envelope. This pattern gives a "cartwheel or spoke wheel" appearance. The juxtanuclear cytoplasm appears clear and less basophilic due to the Golgi complex located in this area.
- Reticular cells – Star-shaped cells which join via their processes to form a cellular network. They are found abutting reticular fibers in certain glands and lymphoid tissues.

- Pericytes – Located in the adventitia of blood vessels. They are believed to be totipotential cells which may differentiate into various connective tissue cells as well as into smooth muscle cells.
- White blood cells –Certain white blood cells, or leukocytes, migrate out of the blood into the extracellular ground substance. The main leukocytes found in the connective tissue are lymphocytes, monocytes, eosinophils, basophils, and neutrophils. The leukocytes in connective tissue are similar in structure and function to those in the blood.

ECM

The extracellular matrix (ECM) is a complex structural entity that surrounds and supports cells that are found within mammalian tissues. The ECM is composed of 3 major classes of biomolecules:
- Structural proteins – Collagen and elastin.
- Specialized proteins – Fibrillin, fibronectin, laminin, etc.
- Proteoglycans – These are macromolecules composed of a protein core with long chains of repeating disaccharide units attached, called glycosaminoglycans (GAGs), which together form complexes of extremely high molecular weight.

Collagens are the most abundant proteins found in the animal kingdom, and are the primary component of the ECM. There are at least 12 types of collagen. Of these, types I, II and III are the most abundant, and form fibrils of similar structure. Type IV collagen forms a two-dimensional reticulum, and is a major component of the basal lamina. Collagens are predominantly synthesized by fibroblasts, but they are also synthesized by epithelial cells.

Endocrine system

The endocrine system is a signal transmission system, similar to the nervous system, but differs greatly from the nervous system in its method of signal transduction. The endocrine system is a system of glands spread throughout the body that regulates body growth and function through the secretion of hormones directly into the bloodstream. The secretion of each hormone is regulated by a feedback loop that serves to reduce further hormone secretion.

Hormones secreted by the neurohypophysis

The hormones that are secreted by the neurohypophysis are secreted by neurons from the hypothalamus. These hormones include the following:
- Anti Diuretic Hormone (ADH) – ADH increases the reabsorption of water from the kidneys collecting tubules in response to increasing blood osmolarity. An insufficiency of ADH usually results from the destruction of cells in the hypothalamus, and results in diabetes insipidus, the production of a large volume of dilute urine. This renders the individual unable to concentrate their urine, resulting in frequent dehydration.
- Oxytocin (OT) – OT stimulates uterine smooth muscle contractions during labor, and also triggers milk ejection by the mammary glands. OT is released by hypothalamic neurons in response to physical and chemical stimuli at the end of pregnancy and by infant suckling. OT is also used clinically to induce labor.

Hormones secreted from the adenohypophysis

- Follicle-Stimulating Hormone (FSH) – Gonadotropin that is released in response to gonadotropin-releasing hormone (GnRH). FSH stimulates gametogenesis in both males and females. In females, this involves follicular development and the 1st stage of oogenesis. FSH also stimulates estrogen secretion. In males, FSH stimulates spermatogenesis.
- Luteinizing Hormone (LH) – Gonadotropin also released in response to GnRH. In females, LH stimulates ovulation and progesterone secretion. In males, the same hormone is called interstitial cell-stimulating hormone (ICSH). ICSH stimulates interstitial cells in the testes to secrete testosterone.
- Thyroid-Stimulating Hormone (TSH) – Secreted in response to thyrotropin-releasing hormone (TRH) from the hypothalamus. TSH causes the thyroid to secrete its hormones, T_3 (triiodo-thyronine) and T_4 (thyroxine).
- Adrenal Corticotropic Hormone (ACTH) – Stimulates the release of corticosteroids from the adrenal cortices. ACTH is released in response to corticotropin-releasing hormone (CRH) from the hypothalamus.

Hormones secreted by the enteric endocrine system

Cholecystokinin

This hormone is synthesized and secreted by enteric endocrine cells that are located in the duodenum. Its secretion is strongly stimulated by the presence of partially digested proteins and fats in the small intestine. As chyme floods into the small intestine, cholecystokinin is released into the blood and binds to receptors on pancreatic acinar cells, stimulating them to secrete large quantities of digestive enzymes.

Cholecystokinin (CCK) is a peptide hormone of the gastrointestinal system that is responsible for stimulating the digestion of fat and protein. CCK is secreted by the duodenum, the first segment of the small intestine, and stimulates the release of digestive enzymes and bile from the pancreas and gall bladder, respectively. It also acts as a hunger suppressant. CCK is composed of 33 amino acids, and is very similar in structure and sequence to gastrin, another gut hormone. It is activated post-translationally from the processing of the precursor, preprocholecystokinin. CCK mediates a number of physiological processes, including digestion and satiety. CCK is secreted by the duodenum when fat- or protein-rich chyme leaves the stomach and enters the duodenum. CCK then stimulates the secretion of bile into the small intestine, which serves to emulsify fats, thereby increasing the effectiveness of their enzymatic digestion. As a neuropeptide, CCK mediates satiety by acting on the CCK receptors, which are distributed widely throughout the central nervous system. In humans, CCK administration causes nausea and anxiety, and weakly decreases the desire to eat.

Secretin

This hormone is also a product of endocrinocytes that are located in the epithelium of the proximal small intestine. It is secreted in response to acid in the duodenum, which occurs when acid-laden chyme from the stomach flows through the pylorus. The predominant effect of secretin on the pancreas is to stimulate duct cells to secrete water and bicarbonate. As soon as this occurs, the enzymes secreted by the acinar cells are flushed out of the pancreas, through the pancreatic duct, and into the duodenum.

Secretin is a hormone that is produced by the S cells of the duodenum in response to low pH and fatty acids, and functions to stimulate the secretion of bicarbonate from the bicarbonate producing organs (i.e., the liver, the pancreas, and Brunner's glands) when the pH drops below a set value. This helps to neutralize the gastric acid entering the duodenum from the stomach. Secretin also inhibits acid secretion from the stomach by reducing gastrin release from the G cells of the stomach. For these reasons, secretin is referred to as "Nature's Antacid".

Secretin was also the first substance that was identified to cause a physiological effect in the body after being transported via the blood. It contains 27 amino acids, and is homologous to glucagon.

Gastrin

This hormone, which is very similar to cholecystokinin, is secreted in large amounts by the stomach in response to gastric distention and irritation. Gastrin stimulates parietal cells to secrete acids, and also stimulates pancreatic acinar cells to secrete digestive enzymes.

Insulin

The major function of insulin is to counteract the concerted action of a number of hyperglycemia-generating hormones, and to maintain low blood glucose levels. Insulin also stimulates lipogenesis, diminishes lipolysis, increases amino acid transport into cells, and modulates transcription, altering the cell content of numerous mRNAs. In addition, insulin stimulates growth, DNA synthesis, and cell replication, effects that it has in common with the insulin-like growth factors and relaxin. Insulin is synthesized as a preprohormone in the B cells of the islets of Langerhans. Its signal peptide is removed in the cisternae of the endoplasmic reticulum, and it is packaged into secretory vesicles in the Golgi, folded into its native structure, and then locked into this conformation by the formation of 2 disulfide bonds. Specific protease activity cleaves the center third of the molecule, which dissociates as C peptide, leaving the amino terminal B peptide disulfide-bonded to the carboxy-terminal A peptide. Insulin secretion from B cells is principally regulated by plasma glucose levels.

Glucose metabolism and insulin

An example of the relationship between glucose metabolism and insulin can be seen by examining insulin-dependent diabetes mellitus (IDDM). Uncontrolled IDDM leads to increased hepatic glucose output. First, liver glycogen stores are mobilized, and then hepatic gluconeogenesis is used to produce glucose. Insulin-deficiency also impairs non-hepatic tissue utilization of glucose. In particular, in adipose tissue and skeletal muscle, insulin stimulates glucose uptake by inducing the insertion of glucose transporter proteins into the plasma membranes of these tissues. Reduced glucose uptake by peripheral tissues, in turn, leads to a reduced rate of glucose metabolism. In addition, the level of hepatic glucokinase is regulated by insulin. Therefore, a reduced rate of glucose phosphorylation in hepatocytes leads to increased delivery to the blood. Other enzymes that are involved in anabolic metabolism of glucose are also affected by insulin. The combination of increased hepatic glucose production and reduced peripheral tissues metabolism leads to elevated plasma glucose levels. When the capacity of the kidneys to absorb glucose is surpassed, glucosuria ensues. Glucose is an osmotic diuretic and an increase in renal loss of glucose is accompanied by loss of water and electrolytes, termed polyuria. The result of the loss of water leads to the activation of the thirst mechanism (polydipsia), while the negative caloric balance that results from the glucosuria and tissue catabolism leads to an increase in appetite and food intake (polyphagia).

Juxtaglomerular apparatus

In the juxtaglomerular apparatus, the kidneys control blood pressure through the secretion of renin by granular cells. Renin secretion is increased by a fall in Na^+ load (i.e., a fall in $[Na^+]$), prostaglandins, sympathetic nerve activity, circulating catecholamines, and a fall in blood pressure. Renin secretion is decreased by a rise in [Cl-], angiotensin II, antidiuretic hormone (ADH), and increased blood pressure. Blood pressure can also be sensed by stretch receptors on the afferent arterioles. The mesangial cells are phagocytic and remove macromolecules that escape from the capillaries. They can contract and may modify the surface area of the capillaries available for filtration.

Renin-angiotensin system

The renin-angiotensin system plays an important role in regulating blood volume, arterial pressure, cardiac function, and vascular function. While the pathways for the renin-angiotensin system have been found in a number of tissues, the most important site for renin release is the kidney. Sympathetic stimulation (acting via β-1-adrenoceptors), renal artery hypotension, and decreased sodium delivery to the distal tubules all stimulate the release of renin by the kidney. Renin is an enzyme that acts upon a circulating substrate, angiotensinogen, which undergoes proteolytic cleavage to form the decapeptide, angiotensin I (AI). Vascular endothelium, particularly in the lungs, has an enzyme, angiotensin converting enzyme (ACE), which cleaves off two amino acids to form the octapeptide, angiotensin II (AII).

Renin

Renin is a proteolytic enzyme that is secreted into the blood by the granular cells. It converts angiotensinogen into angiotensin I. An enzyme, called angiotensin converting enzyme (ACE), converts angiotensin I to angiotensin II (AII). AII is a powerful vasoconstrictor. It constricts the blood vessels, and raises the peripheral resistance, thereby acting to restore blood pressure. AII also increases the secretion of aldosterone, leading to Na^+ reabsorption. Thus, when blood pressure falls, Na^+ delivery to the distal tubule will fall. This is sensed by the macula densa cells, which signal the granular cells to secrete renin. This results in an increase in circulating AII, which increases peripheral resistance, and in turn increases blood pressure. β-1 receptors on granular cells increase renin release when stimulated by catecholamines. Sympathetic nerve activity can also increase renin release.

Angiotensin II

AII has several very important functions:
- Constricts resistance vessels (via AII receptors), thereby increasing systemic vascular resistance and arterial pressure.
- Acts upon the adrenal cortex to release aldosterone, which in turn acts upon the kidneys to increase sodium and fluid retention.
- Stimulates the release of vasopressin (antidiuretic hormone, ADH) from the posterior pituitary, which acts upon the kidneys to increase fluid retention.
- Stimulates the thirst centers within the brain.
- Facilitates norepinephrine release from sympathetic nerve endings, and inhibits norepinephrine reuptake by nerve endings, thereby enhancing sympathetic adrenergic function.
- Stimulates cardiac and vascular hypertrophy.

Aldosterone

The mineralocorticoids get their name from their effect on mineral metabolism. The most important of them is the steroid aldosterone. Aldosterone acts on the kidneys, promoting the reabsorption of sodium ions (Na^+) into the blood. Water follows the salt, and this helps to maintain normal blood pressure. Aldosterone also acts on the sweat glands to reduce the loss of sodium in perspiration, and acts on the taste buds to increase their sensitivity to sources of sodium. Aldosterone secretion is stimulated by the following:

- A drop in the level of sodium ions in the blood.
- A rise in the level of potassium ions in the blood.

ANP

Atrial natriuretic peptide (ANP) increases atrial pressure, and decreases Na^+ reabsorption in the kidneys. The predominant signal for ANP release is atrial wall stretch, or atrial distension, due to volume expansion. Hypoxia is also a potent stimulus for ANP release. In addition, increased heart rate, sympathetic stimulus, and metabolic factors may mediate this effect. Enhanced ANP release resulting from hyperosmolality with volume expansion has also been demonstrated. ANP exerts its effects by binding to specific membrane-bound receptors. Three natriuretic peptide receptors have been identified. The ANP_A and ANP_B receptors have guanylate cyclase activity, and mediate the biological effects of the natriuretic peptides. The ANP_C receptor functions mainly as a clearance receptor, removing ANP from the circulation. All natriuretic peptides are bound by the ANP_C receptor. ANP and BNP act through the ANP_A receptor, while CNP acts through the ANP_B receptor. The half-life of ANP is 2 to 5 minutes in humans, and its metabolic clearance rate is about 14 to 25 (mL/min)/kg. The hormone is eliminated either enzymatically, or through the clearance receptor. The ANP_C receptor internalizes ANP, and delivers it to lysosomes for degradation, while the receptor itself is recycled.

ADH

Antidiuretic hormone (ADH, vasopressin), is a nine-amino acid peptide that is secreted from the posterior pituitary. Within hypothalamic neurons, the hormone is packaged in secretory vesicles with a carrier protein called neurophysin, and both are released upon hormone secretion. Decreased blood volume can also stimulate the secretion of ADH. The single most important effect of ADH is to conserve body water by reducing the output of urine. A diuretic is an agent that increases the rate of urine formation. Injection of small amounts of ADH into a person or animal results in antidiuresis, or decreased formation of urine, and the hormone was named for this effect. ADH binds to receptors in the distal or collecting tubules of the kidney, and promotes reabsorption of water back into the circulation. In the absence of ADH, the kidney tubules are virtually impermeable to water, and it flows out as urine. ADH stimulates water reabsorption by inducing the insertion of aquaporins (water channels) into the membranes of kidney tubules. These channels transport solute-free water through tubular cells, and back into the blood, leading to a decrease in plasma osmolarity, and an increase in urine osmolarity.

Bone growth hormones

Hormones that Regulate Bone Growth are as follows:
- Growth Hormone (GH) – Synthesized, stored, and secreted from the anterior pituitary, this hormone is necessary for normal growth and development of the skeleton. A deficiency (hyposecretion) of GH during childhood will result in dwarfism, while an excess (hypersecretion) of GH during childhood will result in giantism. Hypersecretion during adulthood will produce acromegaly, a disorder in which the shape of many bones, especially those in the face, becomes exaggerated.
- Thyroid Hormones (e.g., thyroxine) – Regulate the metabolism of most cells, including those within bone tissue.
- Testosterone – This and other androgens are important for growth in the mass and density of bone.
- Estrogens – These hormones are important for growth in the length of bone, as well as for bone maintenance.
- Parathyroid Hormone (PTH) – This hormone functions to regulate calcium homeostasis. Calcium is necessary in the blood for many functions. When the level of calcium in the blood decreases, PTH is secreted to increase the level of calcium back to normal. PTH utilizes several methods in order to increase calcium levels in the blood:
    - Increased Vitamin D production – Vitamin D is a hormone whose precursor is produced in the skin in response to sunlight, and is then processed in the liver and kidneys to become active vitamin D3. Vitamin D3 increases calcium absorption in the gut. Without this vitamin, calcium is not absorbed to any great degree.
    - Increased reabsorption of calcium in the kidneys – Much calcium is lost in urine. Thus, when more calcium is needed in the blood, this is an important source.
    - Reabsorption of bone – PTH increases osteoclastic activity to release calcium into the blood.
- Calcitonin - Normally important only in children, this hormone is secreted by special cells in the thyroid. It functions to stimulate both the uptake of calcium into growing bone tissue and the deposition of bone matrix. It has been used in osteoporosis patients in order to aid in their uptake of calcium.

GH

Growth hormone (GH, somatotropin) secretion is controlled by both GH-releasing hormone (GHRH) and GH-inhibiting hormone (GHIH, somatostatin), which are secreted by the hypothalamus. GH regulates the growth and development of the musculoskeletal system and other tissues. It stimulates amino acids to be used for protein synthesis, and causes lipolysis to provide fatty acids for catabolism. For these reasons, it is sometimes abused to stimulate muscle growth and catabolize fat. Negative feedback results from GH itself, and also from mediators called somatomedins (somatomedin is also known as insulin-like growth factor 1) produced by the liver, muscles, and other tissues. Positive feedback is produced by strenuous exercise, and energy demanding activities. Childhood hypersecretion of GH causes the excessive growth seen in giantism, while adulthood hypersecretion causes acromegaly, a condition in which the bones are exaggerated in shape. Childhood hyposecretion causes dwarfism.

Somatostatin

There are two forms of somatostatin, referred to as SS-14 and SS-28, reflecting their peptide length. Both forms of somatostatin are generated by the proteolytic cleavage of prosomatostatin, which itself is derived from preprosomatostatin. Five stomatostatin receptors have been identified and characterized, all of which are members of the G protein-coupled receptor superfamily. Somatostatin was named for its effect of inhibiting the secretion of growth hormone (GH) from the pituitary gland. Experimentally, all known stimuli for GH secretion are suppressed by somatostatin administration. Ultimately, GH secretion is controlled by the interaction of somatostatin and GH-releasing hormone (GHRH), both of which are secreted by hypothalamic neurons. Cells within the pancreatic islets secrete insulin, glucagon, and somatostatin. Somatostatin appears to act primarily in a paracrine manner in order to inhibit the secretion of both insulin and glucagon. It also has the effect of suppressing pancreatic exocrine secretions, by inhibiting cholecystokinin-stimulated enzyme secretion, and secretin-stimulated bicarbonate secretion. Somatostatin is secreted by scattered cells within the gastrointestinal epithelium, and by neurons in the enteric nervous system.

Parathyroid hormone

Parathyroid hormone is secreted by the parathyroid glands, which are small bodies near the thyroid gland. The secretion of this hormone is regulated by the serum calcium level:
- If the serum calcium level decreases, the parathyroid secretes PTH.
- If the serum calcium level increases, PTH production is inhibited.

PTH serves two functions:
- PTH promotes the normal bone resorption process, which is adversely affected by calcitonin.
- PTH also stimulates the excretion of phosphates by the kidneys (inhibits resorption), and enhances calcium resorption, which in turn stimulates osteoblasts and osteoclasts.

Estrogen

Estrogen is the primary female sex hormone. It is a steroid hormone and is named after its ability to regulate the estrous cycle in animals. The effects of estrogen are as follows:
- Feedback inhibition of follicle-stimulating hormone (FSH).
- Reduce hot flashes.
- Less gain of abdominal fat.
- Increase high-density lipoprotein (HDL) cholesterol.
- Decrease low-density lipoprotein (LDL) cholesterol.
- Helps vaginal atrophy.
- Increases myometrial excitability.
- Fewer osteoporotic fractures.
- Decrease risk of colon cancer.
- Improves pelvic musculature.
- Helps regulate luteinizing hormone (LH) secretion.
- Prevents collagen loss in skin (fewer wrinkles).
- Questionable effects on Alzheimer's disease.

Progesterone

Progesterone is an example of a progestogen. This hormone plays a vital role in pregnancy. After ovulation, the corpus luteum secretes progesterone, which prepares the lining of the uterus for implantation of the fertilized ovum. Progesterone is then released by the placenta throughout pregnancy in order to suppress ovulation. For this reason, progesterone was the model on which the first oral contraceptives were built. Progesterone itself is not a good oral contraceptive because it is degraded within the digestive system. Therefore, massive doses of progesterone are required to prevent pregnancy if it is taken orally.

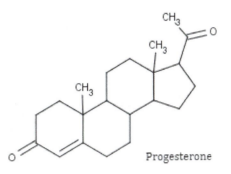

Progesterone

Prolactin

Prolactin is a polypeptide hormone that is synthesized in, and secreted by, specialized cells of the anterior pituitary gland. The anterior pituitary gland is stimulated by thyrotropin-releasing hormone (TRH), and inhibited by dopamine. Prolactin inhibits gonadotropin-releasing hormone (GnRH) synthesis, therefore indirectly inhibiting ovulation.

Peptide hormones

The particular steroid hormone class synthesized by a given cell type depends upon its complement of peptide hormone receptors, its response to peptide hormone stimulation, and its genetically expressed complement of enzymes. The following peptide hormones are responsible for stimulating the synthesis of the corresponding steroid hormones:
- Luteinizing Hormone (LH) – Progesterone and testosterone.
- Adrenocorticotropic Hormone (ACTH) – Cortisol.
- Follicle Stimulating Hormone (FSH) – Estradiol.
- Angiotensin II/III (AII and AIII) – Aldosterone.

The thyroid hormones are thyroxine (also called T_4 because it contains four iodine atoms) and triiodothyronine (also called T_3 because it contains three iodine atoms). These are released into the blood stream.

Mnemonic: "PET CAT"
Progesterone, Estrogen, Testosterone, Cortisol, Aldosterone, Thyroxine.

Nervous system

The structural divisions of the nervous system are as follows:
- Central Nervous System (CNS) – The brain and the spinal cord.
- Peripheral Nervous System (PNS) – The nerves, ganglia, receptors, etc.

The functional divisions of the nervous system are as follows:
- Voluntary Nervous System (a.k.a. Somatic Division) – Responsible for willful control of somatic effectors (skeletal muscles), and conscious perception. Mediates voluntary reflexes.
- Autonomic Nervous System – Responsible for control of autonomic effectors (smooth muscle, cardiac muscle, and glands). Mediates visceral reflexes.

The following are the functions of the nervous system:
- Integration of body processes.
- Control of voluntary effectors (skeletal muscles), and mediation of voluntary reflexes.
- Control of involuntary effectors (smooth muscle, cardiac muscle, and glands), and mediation of autonomic reflexes (heart rate, blood pressure, glandular secretion, etc.).
- Response to stimuli.
- Responsible for conscious thought and perception, emotions, personality, and the mind.

> ➢ **Review Video: Nervous System**
> Visit *mometrix.com/academy* and enter *Code:* **708428**

Thalamic nuclei

The functions of the different thalamic nuclei are described below:
- Lateral Geniculate Nucleus (LG) – Part of the visual information pathway. It receives information from the superior colliculus, and then relays it to the visual areas of the cortex in the occipital lobe.
- Medial Geniculate Nucleus (MG) – Processes auditory information. It receives messages from the inferior colliculus, and then transfers them to the auditory areas of the cortex in the temporal lobe.
- Ventral Posterolateral Nucleus (VPL) – Involved in the processing of somatosensory information. Messages come in from the spinothalamic tract and the medial lemniscus, and are passed on to the somatosensory areas of the cortex in the parietal lobe. This nucleus mediates the sensations of pain and temperature, as well as proprioception.
- Ventral Posteromedial Nucleus (VPM) – Also handles sensory information. It receives input from the trigeminothalamic tract, which it then passes on to the somatosensory areas of the cortex in the parietal lobe. Sensory information mediated by the trigeminal nerve is processed in this area.
- Ventral Lateral and Ventral Anterior Nuclei (VL/VA) – The motor relay nuclei of the thalamus. They process motor information.

- 122 -

Reticular formation

The reticular formation is a set of interconnected nuclei that are located throughout the brain stem. Its dorsal tegmental nuclei are located in the midbrain, its central tegmental nuclei are located in the pons, and its central and inferior nuclei are located in the medulla. The reticular formation has two components:

- Ascending reticular formation (a.k.a. Reticular Activating System) – Responsible for the sleep-wake cycle, thus mediating various levels of alertness. This part of the reticular system projects to the mid-line group of the thalamus, which also plays a role in wakefulness. From the thalamus, information is sent to the cortex.
- Descending reticular formation – Involved in autonomic nervous system activity, as it receives information from the hypothalamus. The descending reticular formation also plays a role in motor movement.

Interneurons of the reticular formation receive some of the corticobulbar fibers from the motor cortex. It is those fibers that innervate the three cranial nerves involved in eye movement. Other corticobulbar fibers innervate cranial nerves directly. The descending reticular nuclei in the brain are involved in reflexive behavior, such as coughing and vomiting.

Control of respiration

The respiratory center is located in the medulla of the brainstem, with contributions from the pons. Within the medulla are the dorsal respiratory group (DRG) and the ventral respiratory group (VRG). The DRG sends stimuli to the muscles of inspiration: the diaphragm, the external intercostals, etc. The VRG sends stimuli to the muscles of expiration: the internal intercostals and the abdominal muscles. Since the muscles of expiration are only active during forced expiration, the VRG is also only active during forced expiration. Conversely, the DRG is active during both quiet and forced respiration. The pons sends stimuli to the medulla in order to regulate the rate and depth of respiration. The pneumotaxic center increases the rate of respiration by shortening inspirations. The apneustic center increases the depth, and reduces the rate, of respiration by prolonging inspirations. While the function of the apneustic center is established, its location is not.

The following are the inputs to the respiratory control center:

- Peripheral chemoreceptors – Respond to increased carbon dioxide, and decreased pH. Although the peripheral chemoreceptors include receptors to oxygen, oxygen levels are secondary stimuli at best, and are normally not important in triggering increased respiration.
- Central chemoreceptors – Located in the medulla, their primary stimuli are decreased pH and increased carbon dioxide. pH is especially important since carbon dioxide does not readily diffuse into the brain tissue, but affects it through its impact on hydronium ions.
- Muscle contraction – When you exercise, there is a direct stimulus to the respiratory center from active muscles and joint receptors. This causes increased respiration before blood chemistry actually changes enough to demand it.
- Higher brain centers – From the voluntary motor center, for voluntary control over respiration; and from the hypothalamus, for control in response to emotional stimuli and body temperature.
- Vagal afferents – The only autonomic part of the respiration center, these afferents send stimuli from stretch and irritant receptors in the lungs. The irritant receptors act to produce coughing, hiccups, etc.

Cardiac control center

The inputs of the cardiac control center are:
- Baroreceptors in the aortic and carotid sinuses – The baroreceptor reflex is responsible for the moment-to-moment maintenance of normal blood pressure.
- The hypothalamus – Efferent signals from the hypothalamus stimulate the cardiac control center in response to exercise, emotions, "fight or flight" activity, or temperature.

The following are the outputs of the cardiac control center:
- Cardioaccelatory center – Stimulates the sympathetic cardiac accelerator nerves. These fibers innervate the sinoatrial (SA) node, the atrioventricular (AV) node, and the ventricular myocardium (VM). The effect of such stimulation on the SA and AV nodes is an increase in their depolarization rate by reducing their resting membrane polarization. The effect of such stimulation on the VM is an increase in its contractility, thus increasing its force and volume of contraction. Sympathetic stimulation increases both the rate and the volume of the heart.
- Cardioinhibitory center – Stimulates the parasympathetic vagus nerve. The vagus nerve innervates the SA and AV nodes, and only sparingly innervates the atrial myocardium. It does not innervate the VM.
- Parasympathetic division – Controls the heart at rest, keeping its rhythm slow and regular. This is referred to as normal vagal tone. During stress (i.e., exercise, emotions, the "fight or flight" response, or temperature), parasympathetic effects are inhibited, and the sympathetic division is activated.

Cushing's triad and intracranial pressure

Cushing's triad, which includes bradycardia, hypertension (with widened pulse pressure), and a change in respiratory pattern, is seen in head injuries with increased intracranial pressure (ICP). Head injuries rarely cause hypotension, except in spinal cord injuries (hypotension with bradycardia). Therefore, other causes of hypotension must be sought. Normal ICP ranges from 0 to 15 mmHg, depending on the total volume of brain tissue and the total volume of cerebrospinal fluid (CSF). Normal fluctuations in ICP are due to the translocation of CSF into the subarachnoid space, and to increased CSF absorption.

Cerebrum

The cerebrum, or cortex, is the largest part of the human brain, and is associated with higher brain function, such as thought and action. The cerebral cortex is divided into four sections, called lobes:
- Frontal lobe – Associate with reasoning, planning, parts of speech, movement, emotions, and problem solving.
- Parietal lobe – Associated with movement, orientation, recognition, and perception of stimuli.
- Occipital lobe – Associated with visual processing.
- Temporal lobe – Associated with perception and recognition of auditory stimuli, memory, and speech.

Internal capsule

The internal capsule lies between the lenticular and the caudate nuclei. It is a group of myelinated, ascending and descending fiber tracts, including the pyramidal tract that connects the cortex to other parts of the central nervous system. The capsule itself ends within the cerebrum, but the axons that pass through it continue down to the brain stem and the spinal cord. They descend through the midbrain within two large bundles, called the cerebral peduncles, or crus cerebri. Because so many axons join together to pass through this area, the internal capsule is sometimes referred to as a bottleneck of fibers. This makes it a very bad place to get a lesion. The striata, a branch of the middle cerebral artery, brings blood to the internal capsule. The striata is called the "Artery of Stroke" because it is prone to hemorrhage, and supports so many important nerve fibers. If there is a problem with the blood supply in this area, many efferent and afferent tracts can be damaged. Despite its close proximity to the caudate nucleus and the lenticular nucleus, the internal capsule is not part of the basal ganglia.

Brainstem

The components of the brainstem are as follows:
- The midbrain, pons, and medulla are collectively called the brainstem.
- The mesencephalon contains the midbrain.
- The metencephalon includes the pons and cerebellum.
- The myelencephalon contains the medulla oblongata.

Note: The diencephalon contains the thalamus, the hypothalamus, and the epithalamus.

Blood-brain barrier

The choroid plexus and the arachnoid membrane act together at the barriers between the blood and cerebrospinal fluid (CSF). On the external surface of the brain, the ependymal cells fold over onto themselves in order to form a double-layered structure, which lies between the dura and pia, called the arachnoid membrane. Within the layers of the arachnoid membrane is the subarachnoid space, which participates in CSF drainage. Passage of substances from the blood through the arachnoid membrane is prevented by tight junctions. The arachnoid membrane is generally impermeable to hydrophilic substances, and its role is forming the blood-CSF barrier is largely passive. The choroid plexus forms the CSF, and actively regulates the concentration of molecules in the CSF. The choroid plexus consists of highly vascularized, "cauliflower-like" masses of pia mater tissue that dip into pockets formed by ependymal cells. The ependymal cells, which line the ventricles, form a continuous sheet around the choroid plexus. While the capillaries of the choroid plexus are fenestrated, non-continuous, and have gaps between the capillary endothelial cells that allow for the free movement of small molecules, the adjacent choroidal epithelial cells form tight junctions that prevent most macromolecules from effectively passing from the blood into the CSF.

Cranial nerves

- Olfactory – Smell.
- Optic – Vision.
- Oculomotor – Eyelid and eyeball movement.
- Trochlear – Innervates the superior oblique muscles, which turn the eyes downward and laterally.

- Trigeminal – Chewing, face, mouth, touch, and pain.
- Abducens – Turns the eyes laterally.
- Facial – Controls most facial expressions, secretion of tears and saliva, and taste.
- Vestibulocochlear – Hearing and equilibrium sensation.
- Glossopharyngeal – Senses carotid blood pressure and controls taste.
- Vagus – Senses aortic blood pressure, slows heart rate, stimulates digestion, and controls taste.
- Spinal Accessory – Controls the trapezius and sternocleidomastoid, and swallowing movements.
- Hypoglossal – Controls tongue movements.

Vagus nerves

The vagus nerves are cranial nerves that begin in the brain, descend through the neck, and enter the thorax by passing anteriorly to the large arteries, and posteriorly to the large veins: the left vagus passes in front of the aortic arch, and behind the left brachiocephalic vein; the right vagus passes in front of the right subclavian artery, and behind the superior vena cava. In the superior mediastinum, the vagus nerves give off recurrent laryngeal nerves. However, because the arteries of the thorax develop asymmetrically, they have different paths: the right laryngeal nerve recurs or passes under the right subclavian artery on its way back up to the larynx, which it supplies, while the left recurrent nerve passes under the aortic arch. Both of the recurrent laryngeal nerves innervate the trachea and the esophagus, as well as the larynx. Both of the vagus nerves give off cardiac branches in the neck, and in the thorax. These branches enter the superficial and deep cardiac plexuses to mingle with sympathetic fibers before innervating the heart. Both vagus nerves pass posteriorly to the root of the lung, and contribute to the pulmonary plexuses of nerves before continuing on to the esophageal plexus. Fibers from both nerves intermingle with each other, and with sympathetic fibers in the plexus, before being reformed as anterior and posterior vagal trunks, which pass through the diaphragm on their way to the celiac plexus in the abdomen.

LARP = Left – Anterior; Right – Posterior

Lumbar plexus

The lumbar plexus (LP) is formed by the ventral rami of the first 3, and the greater part of the 4th, lumbar nerves, with a communication from the 12th thoracic nerve. It is on the internal surface of the posterior abdominal wall, ventral to the transverse processes of the lumbar vertebrae, and its branches pierce the psoas. The branches of the LP are as follows:
- Iliohypogastric (L1, T12)
- Ilioinguinal (L1)
- Genitofemoral (L1,2)
- Lateral femoral cutaneous (L2,3)
- Obturator (L2,3,4)
- Accessory obturator (L3,4) (present 29% of the time)
- Femoral (L2,3,4)

The ventral rami of the spinal nerves that form the LP divide within the plexus to form anterior and posterior divisions. The motor branches of the nerves generally do the following:
- Anterior division – Innervate muscles that flex, adduct, or medially rotate.
- Posterior division – Innervate muscles that extend, abduct, or laterally rotate.

In the lower extremity, the anterior divisions that supply the flexor musculature course along the posterior aspect of the extremity because of a developmental medial rotation of 180 degrees.

Enteric plexuses

There are two major functional components of the enteric plexuses:
- Myenteric plexus (of Auerbach) – The larger plexus. As the name suggests, it is located within the muscle layers of the bowel's muscularis externa, and is found throughout the gastrointestinal tract.
- Submucosal plexus (of Meissner) – The smaller plexus. Motor fibers from the submucosal plexus pass to the epithelial crypt cells, where they stimulate secretion. There are additional connections that enter the submucosal plexus from the myenteric plexus. The stomach and esophagus lack a submucosal plexus.

There are surprising similarities between the enteric nervous system (ENS) and the central nervous system. In fact, the similarities are extensive enough that the ENS has been called the "Second Brain". Particularly important are the glial cells that are associated with the ENS. Enteric glia wrap around and support entire bundles of axons that originate from enteric nerves.

Arm nerves

The four key nerves of the arm are:
- Musculocutaneous nerve – Supplies all of the muscles in the anterior (flexor) compartment of the arm. In the interval between the biceps and brachialis, it becomes the lateral cutaneous nerve of the forearm, which supplies a large area of forearm skin.
- Radial nerve – Supplies all of the muscles in the posterior compartment of the arm. It descends inferolaterally behind the deep brachial artery, travels posteriorly along the medial side of the arm, and then enters a groove around the humerus, known as the radial sulcus. It divides into deep and superficial branches: deep branch – entirely muscular in distribution; superficial branch – entirely cutaneous, supplying the dorsum of the hands and digits.
- Median nerve – No branches in the arms. It initially runs along the lateral side of the brachial artery, crossing it at the middle of the arm. It descends into the cubital fossa, deep to the bicipital aponeurosis.
- Ulnar nerve – No branches in the arms. Passes anterior to the triceps on the medial side of the brachial artery. Passes posterior to the medial epicondyle, and medial to the olecranon, to enter forearm.

Upper thigh and pelvis nerves

The nerves of the upper thigh and pelvis are:
- Iliohypogastric nerve (L1) – Supplies the skin in the lower anterior abdominal wall.
- Ilioinguinal nerve (L1) – Supplies the skin of the groin.
- Lateral cutaneous nerve of the thigh (L2,3) – Supplies the skin of the lateral thigh.

- Femoral nerve (L2,3,4) – Supplies both the skin and the muscles, including the iliacus muscle.
- Genitofemoral nerve (L1,2) – Supplies the cremasteric muscle and skin on the medial thigh.
- Obturator nerve (L2,3,4) – Travels through obturator foramen in order to supply the lower limb.

Receptors

All receptors are transducers, which means that they respond to a stimulus by changing (transducing) it into a generator or receptor potential. A receptor potential is like the graded potentials that occur at a synapse. Graded potentials can result in an action potential produced in a neuron leading to the brain. Various stimuli can often produce a generator potential, including electrical, physical, chemical, and others.

- Exteroceptors – Respond to stimuli from outside of the body, such as light, sound, pressure, stretch, odor, temperature, pain, etc.
- Interoceptors or visceroceptors – Respond to stimuli that arise from within the body, such as chemical stimuli, deep pressure, and many others.
- Proprioceptors – Respond to muscle or tendon stretch, and help the body monitor position (body sense).

Mechanoreceptors, thermoreceptors, photoreceptors, chemoreceptors, and nociceptors

- Mechanoreceptors – Respond to a mechanical stimulus, such as touch, pressure, stretch, sound, vibration, or vestibular orientation.
- Thermoreceptors – Respond to temperature change, such as hot and cold.
- Photoreceptors – Respond to light, such as photopic (visual color spectrum) or scotopic (dim) light.
- Chemoreceptors – Respond to various chemicals, such as glucose, oxygen, carbon dioxide, hormones, and many, many more.
- Nociceptors – Pain receptors for any noxious stimulus.

Central chemoreceptors

The central chemoreceptors are cells in the floor of the fourth ventricle (part of the brain stem) that respond to the pH of the cerebrospinal fluid (CSF), and the output from these cells influences breathing. The normal pH of the body is 7.4, while values higher than this represent alkaline conditions in the body, and pH values of less than 7.4 represent acidic conditions. An acidic CSF causes hyperventilation, and this is the reason for dyspnoea with conditions such as diabetic ketoacidosis. An alkaline CSF inhibits the respiratory center. Carbon dioxide in the blood can rapidly diffuse into the CSF, and there is a balance between the level of carbon dioxide, bicarbonate, and hydronium ions in the CSF. If the carbon dioxide in the blood increases (e.g., following exercise), then the carbon dioxide, bicarbonate, and hydronium ion concentrations increase correspondingly in the CSF. This increase in the acidity of CSF causes hyperventilation, which lowers the carbon dioxide concentration in the blood.

Peripheral chemoreceptors

The carotid and aortic bodies are small pieces of tissue that contain peripheral chemoreceptors, which respond to the oxygen and carbon dioxide concentrations in arterial blood. The carotid body is the more important of the two, and is situated at the division of the common carotid artery into the external and internal carotid arteries in the neck. The aortic body is found on the aortic arch. The information from the carotid body is carried along the glossopharyngeal nerve (9th cranial nerve), and the information from the aortic body is carried along the vagus nerve (10th cranial nerve), to the respiratory center. The output from the carotid body is thought to provide information in order to allow for the immediate regulation of breathing, breath-by-breath, by the respiratory center. In normal people, if the arterial blood that reaches the carotid body has a partial pressure of oxygen of 80 mmHg (10 kPa) or a carbon dioxide partial pressure of more than approximately 40 mmHg (5 kPa), then there is an immediate, marked increase in breathing. These limits can be modified by disease or age. For example, people with chronic bronchitis may tolerate an increased concentration of carbon dioxide, or a decreased concentration of oxygen, in the blood.

Arterial baroreceptors

Arterial baroreceptors are located in the carotid sinus, and in the aortic arch. The sinus nerve, a branch of the glossopharyngeal nerve (9th cranial nerve), innervates the carotid sinus. The sinus nerve synapses in the brainstem. The aortic arch baroreceptors are innervated by the aortic nerve, which then combines with the vagus nerve (10th cranial nerve) while traveling to the brainstem. Therefore, bilateral vagotomy denervates the aortic arch baroreceptors. Arterial baroreceptors are sensitive to the stretching of the walls of the vessels in which the nerve endings lie. Increased stretching augments the firing rate of the receptors and nerves, and recruits additional afferent nerves. The receptors of the carotid sinus respond to pressures ranging from 60-180 mmHg. Receptors within the aortic arch have a higher threshold pressure, and are less sensitive than the carotid sinus receptors. Therefore, the carotid sinus receptors are normally the dominant arterial baroreceptor. Maximal carotid-sinus sensitivity occurs near the normal mean arterial pressure. This "set point" changes during hypertension, heart failure, and other disease states. Receptors are sensitive to the rate of pressure change, and to the mean pressure. Therefore, at a given mean arterial pressure, decreasing the pulse pressure (systolic minus diastolic pressure) decreases the baroreceptor firing rate. This is important during conditions in which pulse pressure and mean pressure decrease, such as hemorrhagic shock.

Peripheral nervous system

The peripheral nervous system is made up of a somatic portion and an autonomic portion. The somatic portion is made up of cranial nerves and spinal nerves. The autonomic portion innervates all smooth muscle, cardiac, muscle and glands. The autonomic system is further divided into the sympathetic (i.e., fight or flight) and the parasympathetic nervous systems (i.e., maintains homeostasis).

Reflex arc

The typical pathway of a reflex may be outlined as follows:
- Sensory receptor on dendrite of dorsal root ganglion cell →
- Ganglion cell →
- Axon cell →
- Dorsal root →
- Dorsal horn of the spinal cord →
- Either directly to a motor cell in the ventral horn or via internuncial (association) neurons to a ventral horn motor cell →

- Axon via ventral root →
- Spinal nerve →
- Effector organ (e.g., muscle).

Olfactory system

The olfactory system is a highly specialized mucus membrane located in the roof of each nasal cavity. The olfactory neurons detect odorants by way of G protein-coupled receptors and transmit the signals through the piriform plate, directly to the olfactory bulbs. The four primary odors that are perceived are fragrant, acidic, burnt, and rancid.

Gustatory system

In higher vertebrates the sense of taste is generally restricted to the oral cavity (tongue and epiglottic region). The taste buds are located in vallate, foliate, and fungiform papillae. Each taste bud is specialized for a specific taste molecule, which is determined by its expression of a specific G protein-coupled receptor. While only five primary molecules of taste perception have been identified, there are several hundred specific G protein-coupled taste receptors. The five primary tastes that are perceived are sweet, sour, bitter, salty, and umami.

Ear

The ear is an auditory organ for the sense of hearing, monitors the effects of gravity and position of the head. The auditory functions of the ear are the following:
- Reception and conduction of sound waves.
- Amplification of sound waves.
- Transduction of the waves into nerve impulses.
- Transmission of the impulse to conscious centers.

Incus

The incus is the anvil-shaped bone in the middle ear (incus is Latin for anvil). It consists of a body and two crura. The body (corpus incudis) is somewhat cubical, but compressed transversely. On its anterior surface is a deeply concavo-convex facet, which articulates with the head of the malleus. The two crura diverge from one another at nearly right angles. The short crus (crus breve, or short process) is somewhat conical in shape, projects almost horizontally backward, and is attached to the fossa incudis in the lower and back parts of the epitympanic recess. The long crus (crus longum, or long process) descends nearly vertically behind, and parallel to, the manubrium of the malleus. After bending medially, it ends in a rounded projection, called the lenticular process, which is tipped with cartilage, and articulates with the head of the stapes.

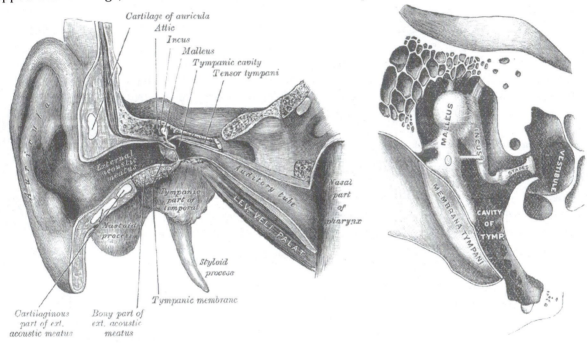

Stapes

The stapes is the stirrup-shaped bone in the middle ear (stapes is Latin for stirrup). It consists of a head, a neck, two crura, and a base. The head (capitulum stapedis) presents a depression, which is covered by cartilage, and articulates with the lenticular process of the incus. The neck, the constricted part of the bone that succeeds the head, gives insertion to the tendon of the stapedius muscle. The two crura (crus anterius and posterius) diverge from the neck, and are connected at their ends by a flattened oval plate, called the base (basis stapedis). The base forms the foot-plate of the stirrup, and is fixed to the margin of the fenestra vestibuli by a ring of ligamentous fibers. Of the two crura, the anterior is shorter and less curved than the posterior.

Cochlea

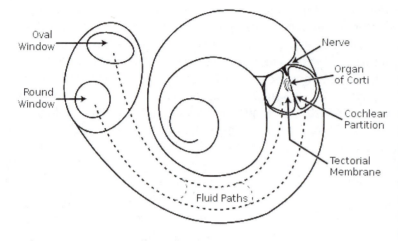

The cochlea is the auditory portion of the inner ear. The cochlea is shaped like a snail, with a spiral-shaped cavity, and gets its name from the Latin word for snail shell. Within the spiral cavity, the organ of Corti is the core component responsible for the detection of auditory stimuli. Once sound waves are transmitted through the inner-ear ossicles, they are transmitted through the oval window and into the perilymph of the scala vestibuli. On the opposite side of the cochlea is the scala tympani, which abuts the round window and allows for reverberations within the cochlea in order to assure stimulation of the inner-ear hair cells. Between the scala vestibuli and the scala tympani is the endolymph-filled scala media. At the base of the scala media is the basilar membrane, on which the inner and outer hair cell nerves are attached. Above the hair cells is a movable membrane, known as the tectorial membrane, which vibrates in response to sound waves transmitted through the endolymph, and transduces them into mechanical stimuli by dislocating specific hair cells. Since lower frequency sound waves travel further through the lymph of the cochlea, and vice versa, the perceived frequencies of sound waves decrease as the hair follicles become increasingly distal to the oval window.

Eye

The visual system is made up of the eye and the complex nerve pathways for interpretation of visual stimuli by the cerebral cortex and subcortical centers. The eyes function as follows:
- Refract light rays and focus them on the retina for the production of an image.
- Convert light rays into a nervous impulse.
- Transmit impulses to the visual centers of the brain for interpretation.

Rods and cones

The photoreceptors of the eye consist of the rods and cones. The rods are rectangular-shaped photoreceptors that are responsible for the detection of scotopic, or dim, light. The impulses transmitted by these receptors are perceived as low-resolution, predominantly black and white images. The cones are pyramidal-shaped photoreceptors that are responsible for the detection of photopic, or normal, light. The impulses that are transmitted by the cones are perceived as normal high-resolution, colored images. The outer segments of both the rods and cones have many layered membrane shelves, which are actually modified cilia containing many opsin molecules. The opsin molecules are modified G protein-coupled receptors that change shape upon absorption of light molecules and serve to transduce light waves into chemical impulses. The opsin molecules of the rods are called rhodopsins, while the opsin molecules of the cones are called photopsins.

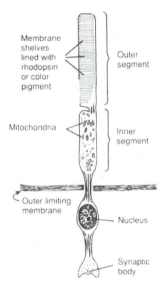

Circulatory system

The functions of the circulatory system are as follows:
- To conduct nutrients and oxygen to the tissues.
- To remove waste materials by transporting nitrogenous compounds to the kidneys and carbon dioxide to the lungs.
- To transport chemical messengers (hormones) to target organs and modulate and integrate the internal milieu of the body.
- To transport agents which serve the body in allergic, immune, and infectious responses.
- To initiate clotting and thereby prevent blood loss.
- To maintain body temperature.
- To produce, carry and contain blood.
- To transfer body reserves, specifically mineral salts, to areas of need.

- 133 -

General components and structure

The circulatory system consists of the heart, blood vessels, blood, and lymphatics. It is a network of tubular structures through which blood travels to and from all the parts of the body. In vertebrates this is a completely closed circuit system, as William Harvey (1628) once demonstrated. The heart is a modified, specialized, powerful pumping blood vessel. Arteries, eventually becoming arterioles, conduct blood to capillaries (essentially endothelial tubes), and venules, eventually becoming veins, return blood from the capillary bed to the heart.

Course of circulation

The course of circulation is as follows:
- Systemic route:
  - Arterial system – Blood is delivered by the pulmonary veins (two from each lung) to the left atrium, passes through the bicuspid (mitral) valve into the left ventricle and then is pumped into the ascending aorta; backflow here is prevented by the aortic semilunar valves. The aortic arch toward the right side gives rise to the brachiocephalic (innominate) artery, which divides into the right subclavian and right common carotid arteries. Next, arising from the arch is the common carotid artery, and then the left subclavian artery. The subclavians supply the upper limbs. As the subclavian arteries leave the axilla (armpit) and enter the arm (brachium), they are called brachial arteries. Below the elbow these main trunk lines divide into ulnar and radial arteries, which supply the forearm and eventually form a set of arterial arches in the hand which give rise to common and proper digital arteries. The descending (dorsal) aorta continues along the posterior aspect of the thorax giving rise to the segmental intercostals arteries. After passage "through" (behind) the diaphragm, it is called the abdominal aorta. At the pelvic rim, the abdominal aorta divides into the right and left common iliac arteries. These divide into the internal iliacs, which supply the pelvic organs, and the external iliacs, which supply the lower limb.
  - Venous system – Veins are frequently multiple, and variations are common. They return blood, originating in the capillaries of peripheral and distal body parts, to the heart.
- Hepatic portal system - Blood draining the alimentary tract (intestines), pancreas, spleen, and gall bladder does not return directly to the systemic circulation, but is relayed by the hepatic portal system of veins to and through the liver. In the liver, absorbed foodstuffs and wastes are processed. After processing, the liver returns the blood via hepatic veins to the inferior vena cava and from there to the heart.
- Pulmonary Circuit - Blood is oxygenated and depleted of metabolic products, such as carbon dioxide, in the lungs.
- Lymphatic Drainage - A network of lymphatic capillaries permeates the body tissues. Lymph is a fluid similar in composition to blood plasma, and tissue fluids not reabsorbed into blood capillaries are transported via the lymphatic system eventually to join the venous system at the junction of the left internal jugular and subclavian veins.

Heart

The heart is a highly specialized blood vessel that pumps approximately 70-80 times per minute, and propels about 4,000 gallons (about 15,000 liters) of blood to the tissues daily. It is composed of the following:

- Endocardium – Lining coat; epithelium.
- Myocardium – Middle coat; cardiac muscle.
- Epicardium – External coat or visceral layer of pericardium; epithelium and mostly connective tissue.
- Impulse conducting system – Conducts electrical signals to the cardiac nodes.

Each heartbeat is myogenic (i.e., originating within the heart), and autorhythmic (i.e., depolarizing spontaneously).

The heart has 4 valves that ensure unidirectional blood flow:

- Right AV Valve (Tricuspid).
- Left AV Valve (Mitral/Bicuspid).
- Pulmonary Semilunar Valve.
- Aortic Semilunar Valve.

Cardiovascular system

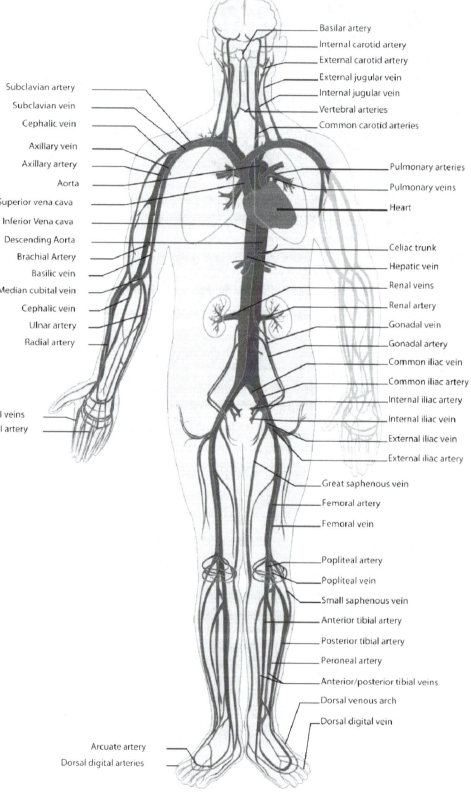

Basilar artery
Internal carotid artery
External carotid artery
External jugular vein
Internal jugular vein
Vertebral arteries
Common carotid arteries

Subclavian artery
Subclavian vein
Cephalic vein
Axillary vein
Axillary artery
Aorta
Superior vena cava
Inferior Vena cava
Descending Aorta
Brachial Artery
Basilic vein
Median cubital vein
Cephalic vein
Ulnar artery
Radial artery

Pulmonary arteries
Pulmonary veins
Heart

Celiac trunk
Hepatic vein
Renal veins
Renal artery
Gonadal vein
Gonadal artery
Common iliac vein
Common iliac artery
Internal iliac artery
Internal iliac vein
External iliac vein
External iliac artery

Palmar digital veins
Digital artery

Great saphenous vein
Femoral artery
Femoral vein

Popliteal artery
Popliteal vein
Small saphenous vein
Anterior tibial artery
Posterior tibial artery
Peroneal artery
Anterior/posterior tibial veins
Dorsal venous arch
Dorsal digital vein

Arcuate artery
Dorsal digital arteries

- 136 -

Cardiac nodes

The cardiac nodes are as follows:
- Sinoatrial node – Pacemaker potential; initiates depolarization; sets heart rate.
- Fibrous skeleton – Insulates the atria from the ventricles.
- Atrioventricular (AV) node – The electrical gateway to the ventricles.
- AV bundle and bundle branches – The pathway for signal conduction from the AV node.
- Purkinje fibers – Spread upward from apex throughout the ventricular myocardium.

Cardiac nerves

Modification of the intrinsic rhythmicity of the heart muscle is produced by cardiac nerves of the sympathetic and parasympathetic nervous system. Stimulation of the sympathetic system increases the rate and force of the heartbeat and dilates the coronary arteries. Stimulation of the parasympathetic (vagus nerve) reduces the rate and force of the heartbeat and constricts the coronary circulation. Visceral afferent (sensory) fibers from the heart end almost wholly in the first four segments of the thoracic spinal cord.

Sinus bradycardia

Sinus bradycardia may occur due to any of the following:
- Sick Sinus Syndrome or Sinoatrial (SA) Node Disease.
- Heart Block – Occurs when the signal from the SA node is slowed or stopped at the AV node, or in the ventricular conducting system. Heart block is classified as first, second, or third degree, and the decrease in heart rate correlates to the degree of heart block.
- Increase in Parasympathetic (Vagal) Tone – For instance, due to training in athletes. This is a normal response. The heart rate increases with exercise or atropine.
- Parasympathetic (Vagal) Stimulation – For instance, with carotid sinus stimulation. Stimulation of carotid sinus baroreceptors results in increased parasympathetic stimulation that decreases the heart rate.
- Acute Myocardial Infarctions.
- Digitalis and Beta-Blockers.

Blood flow through the heart

The flow of blood through the heart is explained below:
- Deoxygenated blood from the body (systemic division) enters the heart through the superior and inferior vena cavae.
- Blood enters the right atrium from the vena cavae.
- Blood flows through the tricuspid valve and into the right ventricle.
- The right ventricle pumps blood through the pulmonary semilunar valve and into the pulmonary trunk to the pulmonary arteries.
- Blood flows to the lungs where it is oxygenated.
- Blood returns to the heart through the pulmonary veins and into the left atrium.
- From the left atrium, blood flows through the mitral (bicuspid) valve and into the left ventricle.
- The left ventricle pumps blood through the aortic semilunar valve to the aorta, and then to the systemic division.

EDV

End diastolic volume (EDV) is simply the "full" volume of blood in the heart, and is often referred to as "preload". Since the heart fills with blood from venous return flow, anything that affects the venous return flow of blood will change the EDV. For example, hemorrhagic blood loss drops volume, and reduces venous return. As a result, the heart does not fill completely, and the EDV goes down. The drop in EDV reduces stroke volume, producing a weak or "thready" pulse. The lower stroke volume reduces the cardiac output and blood pressure, reducing baroreceptor stimulation, and allowing the heart rate to increase.

ESV

End systolic volume (ESV) refers to the amount of blood remaining in the heart (ventricle) at the end of a beat. Notice that ESV indicates that the heart does not empty completely with each beat. There will always be a small amount of blood left in the ventricles at the end of each beat. Subtracting this "leftover" volume from the full volume (EDV) gives the amount ejected (SV). Anything that affects the ventricles capacity to empty upon contraction affects ESV. For example, weakened cardiac muscle would reduce the strength of contraction, and thus increase the ESV. A myocardial infarction (MI) would have that effect. If the heart fails to empty completely, stroke volume falls as less blood enters blood vessels, and cardiac output drops, causing a drop in blood pressure. Chronic hypertension is another example. Systemic hypertension results in increased pressure in systemic arteries, into which the left ventricle must empty. As systemic pressures go up, the heart must contract more strongly in order to eject a normal stroke volume. A point can be reached beyond which the ventricle fails to generate enough force to empty completely against the high arterial pressure ("afterload"). The blood that is not ejected remains in the ventricle, and increases the ESV. Notice that an increase in ESV results in a corresponding decrease in stroke volume.

Stroke volume and ejection fraction

Stroke volume (SV) is the volume of blood that is ejected by the heart, or a ventricle, with each beat or stroke. SV is related to the clinical term "ejection fraction", since both describe the same volume, but express it differently. Ejection fraction (EF) is the percentage of "full volume" (V_{Full}) that is ejected with each heartbeat:

$$EF = \frac{SV}{V_{Full}} \times 100$$

Since the ventricles never empty completely with each beat, SV is described by the following equation:
$$SV = EDV - ESV$$
Where:
EDV = End diastolic volume.
ESV = End systolic volume.

Cardiac output

Cardiac output is simply the amount of blood that is pumped by the heart (or a ventricle), expressed in milliliters per minute. The effect of heart rate on cardiac output is easily understood. Since the heart ejects blood with each beat, the more beats per minute, the more blood is ejected in that time interval. If output increases or decreases, the pressure will change accordingly, as dictated by the equation for cardiac output. Recall that heart rate is controlled by the vasomotor center of the medulla in response to changes in systemic blood pressure. Baroreceptors in the aortic arch and carotid sinus detect increased blood pressure, and act reflexively, via the vasomotor center, to slow heart rate via parasympathetic nerves to the sinoatrial (SA) node, or "pacemaker". Absence of baroreceptor activity has the opposite effect, increasing the heart rate and the resultant blood pressure.

Formula for Cardiac Output:
CO = SV x R
Where:
CO = Cardiac output.
SV = Stroke volume.
R = Rate in beats per minute.

Fick's principle

Fick's principle has frequently been used to measure cardiac output (CO) using oxygen levels and the pulmonary circulation.

Fick's equation for CO is as follows:

$$CO = \frac{O_{2\,Uptake}}{[O_{2\,Arterial}] - [O_{2\,Venous}]}$$

Where:
$O_{2\,Uptake}$ = The uptake of oxygen by the lungs, which is the auxiliary entry route of oxygen.
$[O_{2\,Venous}]$ = The rate of entry of oxygen into the pulmonary circulation by the blood-borne route, which is equal to the CO multiplied by the (systemic) mixed-venous oxygen content.
$[O_{2\,Arteriole}]$ = The rate that oxygen leaves the pulmonary compartment, which is equal to the CO multiplied by the (systemic) arterial oxygen content.

Cardiac cycle

The cardiac cycle is the sequence of events in one heartbeat. The alternating contraction and relaxation of the heart is repeated about 70-80 times per minute, and the duration of one cycle is about 0.8 seconds. There are three phases of the cardiac cycle, which succeed one another during the cycle. The contraction phases are called systole, and the relaxation phase is called diastole. Unless otherwise specified, systole and diastole both refer to left ventricle; however, each chamber has its own systole and diastole. The durations of the individual phases are as follows:

- Atrial systole – 0.1 seconds.
- Ventricular systole – 0.3 seconds.
- Diastole – 0.4 seconds.

The period of rest for each chamber is 0.7 seconds for the atria and 0.5 seconds for the ventricles; so, in spite of its activity, the heart is at rest longer than at work.

The phases of the cardiac cycle are as follows:

- Quiescent period – Period when all chambers are at rest and filling. The atrioventricular (AV) valves are open, and the semilunar valves are closed. 70% of ventricular filling occurs during this period.
- Atrial systole – Pushes the last 30% of blood into the ventricle.
- Atrial diastole – The atria begin filling.
- Ventricular systole – First, the AV valves close, causing the initial heart sound; then, after the iso-volumetric contraction phase, the semilunar valves open, permitting the ventricular ejection of blood into the arteries.
- Ventricular diastole – As the ventricles relax, the semilunar valves close first, producing the second heart sound; then, after the isovolumetric relaxation phase, the AV valves open, allowing for ventricular filling.

Signal conduction and systole

One heartbeat is equivalent to each depolarization. The resting SA node fires every 0.8 sec, or about 75 bpm, resulting in atrial systole. The AV node delays the signal 100 msec, allowing ventricles to fill with blood. The AV bundle and Purkinje fibers deliver signals to the ventricles, resulting in ventricular systole.

ECG

The following are the basics of an electrocardiogram (ECG):

- P wave – Small, upward wave; indicates atrial depolarization.
- QRS complex – Initial downward deflection, followed by a large, upright wave, followed by a small, downward wave; represents ventricular depolarization; masks atrial repolarization; an enlarged R portion indicates enlarged ventricles; an enlarged Q portion indicates a probable heart attack.
- T wave – Dome-shaped wave; indicates ventricular repolarization; flat when insufficient oxygen; elevated with increased potassium levels.
- P-R interval – The interval from the beginning of the P wave to the beginning of the QRS complex; represents the conduction time from initial atrial excitation to initial ventricular excitation; a good diagnostic tool for AV node function; normally < 0.2 sec.
- S-T segment – The time from the end of the S wave to the beginning of the T wave; represents the time between the end of the impulse spreading through the ventricles and ventricular repolarization; depressed when insufficient oxygen; elevation may indicate myocardial infarction.
- Q-T interval – The time for singular depolarization and repolarization of the ventricles; conduction problems, myocardial damage, or congenital heart defects can prolong this.

Note: An ECG can show the following dysfunctions: heart enlargement, conduction pathways, myocardial infarction, and electrolyte/hormone imbalances.

QRS complex

The QRS complex represents the time it takes for depolarization of the ventricles. In normal sinus rhythm, each P wave is followed by a QRS complex. Activation of the anterioseptal region of the ventricular myocardium corresponds to the negative Q wave. The Q wave is not always present. Activation of the rest of the ventricular muscle from the endocardial surface corresponds to the rest of the QRS wave. The R wave is the point when half of the ventricular myocardium has been depolarized. Activation of the posteriobasal portion of the ventricles gives the RS line. The normal QRS duration range is from 0.04 sec to 0.12 sec, measured from the initial deflection of the QRS from the isoelectric line, to the end of the QRS complex. Normal ventricular depolarization requires normal function of the right and left bundle branches. A block in either the right or left bundle branch delays depolarization of the ventricles, resulting in a prolonged QRS duration. Pumping of blood begins when ventricular pressure exceeds aortic pressure, causing the semilunar valves to open. This is normally at the end of the QRS complex, and the start of the ST segment.

Schematic representation of a normal ECG

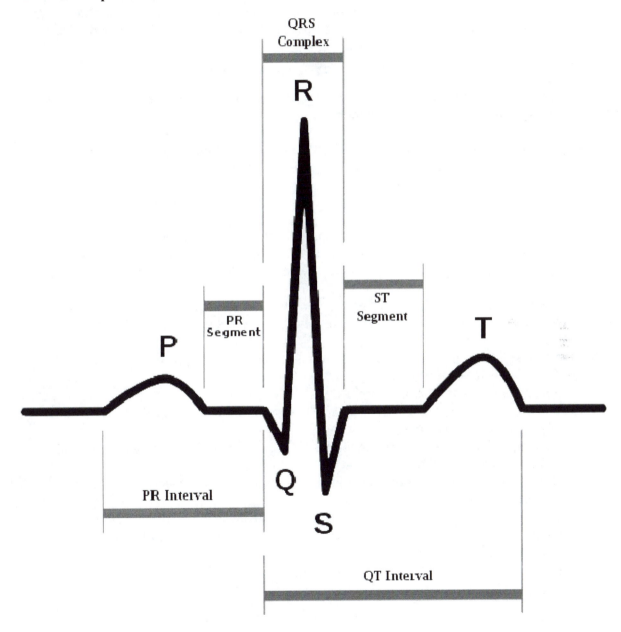

Blood

Blood is the medium in which dissolved gases, nutrients, hormones and waste products are transported. Blood is composed of a straw-colored liquid, called plasma, which contains suspended cells. The different specialized cells that are found in blood are:
- Red blood cells
- White blood cells
- Platelets

Approximately 90% of plasma is water (blood's solvent), with the rest is composed of dissolved substances, primarily proteins (e.g., albumin, globulin, and fibrinogen). Plasma typically accounts for 55% of blood by volume, and the remaining 45% is primarily composed of red blood cells. Approximately 8% of total body weight is blood.

Composition

Blood has numerous functions, such as gas transport, hemostasis, and defense against disease, all of which are brought about by its various components.
- Plasma – The liquid portion of blood.
  - Fluid – Mostly water with dissolved substances, including electrolytes, gases (O_2, CO_2, etc.), nutrients, wastes, and regulatory molecules.
  - Plasma Proteins:
    - Albumin – Most abundant protein (~65%). Responsible for blood osmolarity and viscosity.
    - Fibrinogens or Clotting Proteins – Prothrombin, fibrinogen, etc.
    - Globulins – Found as antibodies, as well as storage and transport proteins.
- Red Blood Cells – Carriers of O_2 in the blood via hemoglobin. Responsible for the pigmentation of blood.
- White Blood Cells – The lymphocytes of the immune system (e.g., T cells, B cells, macrophages, natural killer cells, etc.). Responsible the adaptive immune response, allowing for the killing of specific microbes.
- Monocytes – Respond to necrotic cell material by migrating to necrotic tissues and differentiating into macrophages.
- Neutrophils – Phagocytosis of microbes.
- Eosinophils – Phagocytosis; defense against helminthic parasites; and allergic reactions.
- Basophils – Allergic reactions.
- Complement – Defense against pyogenic bacteria; activation of phagocytes; clearing of immune complexes; and lytic attack on cell membranes.
- Platelets – Anucleated cell fragments that are key components of hemostasis and the formation of blood clots.
- Coagulation Factors – Responsible for coagulation in coordination with platelets.
- Vitamin K – Essential cofactor in normal hepatic synthesis of some clotting factors.
- Plasmin – Lyses fibrin and fibrinogen.
- Antithrombin III – Inhibits IXa, Xa, XIa, XIIa, IIa, and VIIa.

Plasma

Plasma contains clotting agents, and will form a blood clot upon exposure to air. The clear fluid that is exuded from clotted whole blood, and clotted plasma, is called serum. Interstitial fluid contains much less protein than plasma, at around 2% by volume, compared to 7% in plasma. This is because most of the plasma protein molecules are too large to pass through the capillary walls and into the interstitial area. The small amount of protein that does leak through is eventually taken up by the lymphatic system, and is ultimately returned to the blood. Plasma proteins form three major groups, and these groups have various functions:

- Albumin (55% of total plasma protein).
- Fibrinogen (7% of total plasma protein).
- Globulins (38% of total plasma protein).

The relative proportions of plasma proteins can vary in certain diseases, and electrophoretic tracings that show such changes can be a useful diagnostic aid. Most of the plasma proteins are produced by the liver. The gamma globulins are produced by cells of the body's immune system.

Plasma response to blood vessel injury

Blood vessel injury generates numerous responses. Endothelial retraction of the injured vessel results in subendothelial collagen exposure. This generates the platelet release reaction, which produces serotonin, thromboxane A2, and platelet phospholipid. Thromboxane A2 causes platelet aggregation, and the formation of the primary hemostatic plug. However, this is easily washed away by bloodflow or further damage. Vessel injury also releases tissue factor, which along with platelet phospholipid activates the coagulation cascade. During coagulation, factor XIIIa converts loose fibrin polymers into stable fibrin polymers. The primary hemostatic plug causes platelet fusion, which along with stable fibrin polymers forms a stable secondary hemostatic plug.

Blood clotting

If damage occurs to a blood vessel, circulating platelets immediately get trapped at the injury site. On accumulation, the platelets plug the leak in the vessel, providing a first step in damage control. This mechanism is supplemented by blood coagulation, or clotting, which is the most important means of defense against bleeding. Plasma contains several dissolved proteins. One of those, fibrinogen, is a rod-shaped, soluble protein that, in the presence of the catalyst, thrombin, gets converted to an insoluble protein, fibrin. Fibrin molecules produce a tangled net of fibers (by adhering end-to-end and side-to-side), which immobilizes the fluid portion of blood, causing it to solidify. This net also traps the red blood cells. The combined action of the platelets and the "fibrin web" is sufficient to prevent a dangerous loss of blood. In cases where the formation of fibrin, and therefore the formation of a clot, is impaired (e.g., hemophilia), a person is at great risk of bleeding to death.

Thrombosis

Thrombosis is a clot formation within a blood vessel. Predisposing factors to thrombosis include damage to the vascular wall, stasis of blood flow, or altered blood coagulability or composition. Damage to the vascular wall causes a hemostatic response to form a stable hemostatic plug (clot), while the stasis of blood increases the likelihood of clotting, as does changed blood coagulability or composition (e.g., increased viscosity). A thrombosis may occur on the arterial or venous side of the circulation.

Embolism

Embolism is the process whereby a thrombus (clot) that is formed in one part of the circulation breaks off and passes into another part of the circulation. An embolism may also occur in the arterial or venous side of the circulation. The term, embolism, is also used to describe emboli of non-blood origin, such as air, fat, or other fluid.

Plasma pH

A pH of between 6.8 and 7.8 is required for survival. A plasma pH outside of this range is usually lethal. For maintenance of health, however, the pH range is much narrower, requiring between 7.35 and 7.45. The plasma pH is normally kept within this range despite continuous production of metabolic acid. Maintenance of pH levels is very important since pH affects the electrical charges on chemical substances, especially proteins. A small change in pH reflects a huge change in $[H^+]$. Changes in pH can result in decreased enzymatic activity, which affects almost all body systems, particularly metabolic systems. In addition, the activity of transmembrane channels and pumps may also be altered, and thus the cells of the nervous system are particularly affected by the pH of their milieu. Therefore, if pH is not kept within the range of 7.35-7.45, bodily functions begin to deteriorate. If pH extends beyond 6.8 or 7.8, these deteriorations are usually enough to be lethal.

Plasma potassium and arterial pH

Cells exchange potassium (K^+) and hydronium (H^+) ions with plasma. In metabolic acidosis, the plasma K^+ concentration increases, even though the body K^+ concentration may become depleted. In metabolic alkalosis, the plasma K^+ concentration may decrease. However, while cells initially gain K^+, chronic alkalosis may result in a loss of body K^+ because of increased K^+ excretion by renal principal cells. This occurs due to increased sodium (Na^+) ion delivery to this segment, encouraging the exchange of Na^+ for cellular K^+, with K^+ staying in the lumen in order to maintain electroneutrality. Chronic K^+ depletion can result in alkalosis where decreased K^+ secretion by depleted principal cells results in a greater portion of the Na^+ that is delivered to the distal tubule being reabsorbed in exchange for secreted H^+ ions. The corresponding transfer of cellular bicarbonate (HCO_3^-) to the plasma explains the paradoxical association of an acidic urine with an alkaline plasma.

Red blood cells

Red blood cells (RBCs), also called erythrocytes, are the familiar discoid-shaped cells that make up 99% of the cells in blood. They are the principal carriers of the red-colored hemoglobin molecules. Hemoglobin is an iron-containing protein, and binds about 97% of all oxygen in the body. Since oxygen is not very soluble in water, if oxygen were simply dissolved in blood plasma, not much could be carried by the bloodstream. Each hemoglobin molecule binds to four oxygen molecules, and consequently hemoglobin permits human blood to carry more than 70x the amount of oxygen that it could carry otherwise. The unique surface shape of red blood cells is nature's design to maximize surface area in order to facilitate absorption and the release of oxygen. The cell membranes of RBCs contain different proteins that are responsible for the different blood types. There are primarily two types of proteins that are found on the cell surface of RBCs: protein A and B. Different combinations of these proteins, and their antibodies, results in four types of blood:
- Type A – Have protein A, and antibodies to protein B.
- Type B – Have protein B, and antibodies to protein A.
- Type AB – Have both protein A and B, but neither of the antibodies.
- Type O – Have neither proteins, but have both of the antibodies.

Reduced red blood cell formation

Reduced red blood cell (RBC) formation can be caused by decreased erythropoietin secretion, or in response to erythropoietin secretion, resulting in decreased numbers of committed stem cells, and increased maturation time. This can be caused by chronic disease, such as malignant disease, inflammatory conditions such as rheumatoid arthritis, or chronic renal failure. A lack of precursor cells can also result in reduced RBC formation. This can arise due to increased demands for precursors, such as occurs during growth and pregnancy, or due to bleeding and loss of precursors, such as occurs during menstruation and hemorrhage. Marrow defects can also lead to reduced RBC formation, as an adequate marrow microenvironment is necessary for erythropoiesis (e.g., the environment must include burst promoting factors). Marrow suppression can be caused by tumors, radiotherapy, chemotherapy, infection, or particular drugs.

Vitamin B_{12} and folic acid in red blood cell production

Vitamin B_{12} and folic acid are important in the final stages of red blood cell (RBC) development. They are essential for the production of DNA in RBCs. Decreased production of DNA in RBCs results in a failure of nuclear maturation and division, which slows proliferation. Folic acid is present as part of polyglutamates in the blood, which are broken down to mono-glutamates in the upper GI tract. During absorption, they are converted to methyltetrahydrofolate monoglutamate, which is the main form found in the blood. Vitamin B_{12} converts methyltetrahydrofolate monoglutamate to tetrahydrofolate, the substrate that is used for the synthesis of folate polyglutamates in cells. These intracellular folate polyglutamates are the active form of folate, and act as coenzymes for DNA synthesis, which is necessary for RBC production.

Erythropoietin

Erythropoietin is essential for fetal erythropoiesis, and is produced in response to hypoxia and anemia. Cord blood erythropoietin is purely fetal, and reflects tissue oxygenation. It has been found to be increased in many complicated pregnancies with underlying fetal hypoxia. Erythropoietin could be used as a marker of fetal hypoxia because its concentration rises rapidly by increased production in response to hypoxia. Its measurement might enable more accurate timing of hypoxic injury. In addition, erythropoietin levels have been well correlated with perinatal brain damage, and may facilitate the treatment of high-risk neonates. Erythropoietin has also been used successfully in anemia of prematurity, decreasing the transfusion requirement. However, studies are still needed to determine the optimal doses of erythropoietin and iron supplementations that are required for maximizing the red blood cell response. Erythropoietin has been examined as a potential maternal therapy in various disorders during pregnancy, such as end-stage renal disease, severe antepartum iron-deficiency anemia, and postpartum anemia. Erythropoietin has been found to be effective and well tolerated in these conditions.

Bilirubin

Bilirubin is the main bile pigment that is formed from the breakdown of heme in red blood cells. The broken down heme travels to the liver, where it is secreted into bile. Normally, a small amount of bilirubin circulates in the blood. Serum bilirubin is considered a true test of liver function, as it reflects the liver's ability to take up, process, and secrete bilirubin into the bile. When the reticuloendothelial system breaks down old red blood cells, bilirubin is one of the waste products. This "free bilirubin" is in a lipid-soluble form that must be made water soluble in order to be excreted. The free, or unconjugated, bilirubin is carried by albumin to the liver, where it is converted, or conjugated, and made water soluble. Once it is conjugated into a water-soluble form, bilirubin can be excreted in the urine. An enzyme, glucuronyl transferase, is necessary for the conjugation of bilirubin. Either a lack of glucuronyl transferase, or the presence of drugs that interfere with its function, impairs the ability of the liver to conjugate bilirubin. The terms "direct" and "indirect" reflect the way the two types of bilirubin react to certain dyes. Conjugated bilirubin is water soluble, and reacts directly when dyes are added to the blood specimen. The non-water-soluble, free bilirubin does not react to the reagents until alcohol is added to the solution.

Hemoglobin formation

Each hemoglobin (Hb) molecule consists of 4 polypeptide chains, called globins, and 4 heme groups. Hb synthesis begins in the proerythroblasts of the bone marrow, and continues into their reticulocyte stage. Heme synthesis begins in the mitochondria with succinyl-CoA, condensing with glycine to form porphobilinogen. Porphobilinogen exits the mitochondria to form uroporphyrinogen, which is converted to coproporphyrinogen, which then enters the mitochondria to form protoporphyrin. Iron is brought into the cell by transferrin, and ferrous iron is inserted into the protoporphyrin molecule in order to form the heme group (x4).

Hemoglobin oxygenation and oxidation

Oxygenation is the loose, reversible binding of Hb with O_2 molecules, forming oxy-Hb. Hb oxygenation is the principle method of O_2 uptake from the lungs to the red blood cells for transport to the tissues. Each Hb molecule has the capacity to bind to four O_2 molecules since there are four heme molecules in each Hb. O_2 binds loosely with the coordination bonds of the iron atom in the heme; not the two positive bonds of the iron atom. As a result, the iron atom is not oxidized, and oxygen can be carried to the tissues in molecular form, rather than ionic form. Oxidation of Hb involves the conversion of the functional ferrous (Fe^{2+}) heme iron atom to the non-functional ferric (Fe^{3+}) form. This is called methemoglobin. This oxidized form of Hb cannot bind or transport oxygen. Such oxidation of Hb may occur as a result of exposure to toxic chemicals, such as nitrites, aniline dyes, or oxidative drugs.

Partial pressure of O_2 and O_2 content

Partial pressure of O_2 (pO_2, also called oxygen tension)
The pO_2 is proportional to the amount of O_2 that is dissolved in the blood. Differences in the pO_2 are of significance in determining the rate of diffusion between the blood and the tissue. The units for the pO_2 are mmHg.

O_2 content
The O_2 content is the total amount of O_2 per dL of blood, and includes both dissolved and hemoglobin (Hb)-bound O_2, though the dissolved [Hb] is typically negligible. The units for the O_2 content are mL O_2/dL blood, often written as mL/dL or Vol%. By convention, volume units are substituted for molar units (moles/liter), although the latter can be calculated using the gas law.

Oxygen-hemoglobin dissociation curve

The affinity of hemoglobin (Hb) for oxygen (O_2) increases as successive molecules of O_2 bind. More molecules bind as the partial pressure of O_2 (pO_2) increases, until the maximum amount that can be bound is reached. As this limit is approached, very little additional binding occurs, and the curve levels out as the Hb becomes saturated with O_2. Hence, the curve has a sigmoidal, or S shape. At pressures above about 60 mmHg, the standard dissociation curve is relatively flat, which means that the oxygen content of the blood does not change significantly, even with large increases in the pO_2. To get more O_2 to the tissue, one would require blood transfusions to increase the Hb count (and therefore the O_2-carrying capacity), or supplemental O_2 that would increase the O_2 that is dissolved in the plasma. The pO_2 in the blood at which the Hb is 50% saturated (known as the p50), is typically around 26.6 mmHg for a healthy person. In the presence of disease or other conditions that change the affinity of Hb for O_2, and shift the curve to the right or left, the p50 changes accordingly. An increased p50 indicates a rightward shift of the standard curve, which means that a larger pO_2 is necessary to maintain a 50% O_2 saturation. This indicates a decreased affinity.

Anemia and compensatory mechanisms to restore oxygen levels

Anaemia refers to any condition where there is reduced oxygen carrying capacity due to a fall in hemoglobin (Hb) concentration, with resultant tissue hypoxia. It is defined as a Hb concentration of < 13.5 g/dL in males, < 11.5 g/dL in females, < 15 g/dL in newborns to three-month olds, and < 11 g/dL in infants and adolescents from three-months to puberty. Anaemia results when compensatory mechanisms fail to restore oxygen levels to meet tissue demands. The following compensatory mechanisms are seen: arteriolar dilatation, increased cardiac output, increased anaerobic metabolism, increased Hb dissociation, increased erythropoietin output, and internal redistribution of blood flow. If these compensatory mechanisms are adequate, oxygen levels are restored. If not, anaemia ensues, with cardiac effects, poor exercise tolerance, lethargy, pallor, headaches, angina on effort, and claudication.

Carbonic anhydrase and chloride shift

Carbonic anhydrase
Carbonic anhydrase is an enzyme that is found in red blood cells (RBCs) that catalyzes the reversible production of carbonic acid (H_2CO_3) from water (H_2O) and carbon dioxide (CO_2):
- This reaction is favored by the high pCO_2 in the tissue capillaries; and, as a result, the CO_2 that is produced by the tissues is converted into H_2CO_3 in the RBCs.
- H_2CO_3 then ionizes to form hydronium ions (H^+) and bicarbonate (HCO_3^-).
- Since much of the H^+ is buffered by hemoglobin, while much of the HCO_3^- is free to diffuse outwardly, an electrical gradient is established that draws Cl^- into the RBCs. This is called the chloride shift.
- A reverse chloride shift occurs in the lungs. In this process, the low pCO_2 favors the conversion of H_2CO_3 into CO_2, which can be exhaled.

Chloride shift
As HCO_3^- is formed, it diffuses out of the RBCs. Cl^- then diffuses into the RBCs in order to maintain electroneutrality. This is the chloride shift, or Hamburger shift. The chloride shift is rapid, and is complete before the cells exit the capillaries. The osmotic effect of the extra HCO_3^-, and Cl^- in venous RBCs, causes the venous RBC volume to increase slightly. For this reason, venous hematocrit slightly exceeds arterial hematocrit.

Lymphatic system

The functions of the lymphatic system are:
- To filter and absorb the excess tissue fluid, and to return it back into circulation.
- To transport dietary lipids via lacteals.
- To carry out immune responses.

Lymph
Clear, watery fluid resembling interstitial fluid.

Lymph capillaries
Begin as blind-ended capillaries consisting of simple squamous epithelium, allowing for one-way movement of fluid.

Paracortex of a lymph node
The paracortex contains lymphocytes, accessory cells, and supporting cells, and is the predominant site of T lymphocytes within the lymph node:
- T cells – The various types of T cells enter the lymph nodes from the blood via the high endothelial venules (HEVs). When activated, they form lymphoblasts, which divide to produce T-cell clones that respond to specific antigens. Activated T cells then pass into the circulation to reach peripheral sites. Note: Poor development of the paracortex can be found in DiGeorge syndrome.
- Accessory cells – Interdigitating cells are numerous in the paracortex, and they act as antigen-presenting cells.

Medulla of a lymph node
The medulla comprises the large blood vessels, the medullary cords, and the medullary sinuses. The medullary cords are rich in plasma cells, which produce antibodies that pass out of the node via the efferent lymph vessel. Macrophages are also numerous within the medulla.

White blood cells

White blood cells (WBCs), also called leukocytes, serve as "sanitary engineers", cleaning up dead cells and tissue debris that would otherwise accumulate and lead to problems. There are five classes of WBCs:
- Neutrophils – 40-70%.
- Lymphocytes – 20-40%.
- Monocytes – 2-10%.
- Eosinophils – 1-6%.
- Basophils – < 1%.

Many infections stimulate the body to release large numbers of protective leukocytes into the bloodstream, causing the WBC count to rise.

T lymphocytes

- All T Cells:
  - CD3 molecule.
  - T-cell receptor (Ag recognition).
  - Involved in both humoral and cell-mediated responses.
- Helper T Cells (TH):
  - CD4 molecules.
  - Recognizes antigen presented within class II MHC molecules.
  - Promotes differentiation of B cells and cytotoxic T cells.
  - Activates macrophages.
- Suppressor T Cells (TS):
  - CD8 molecules.
  - Downregulates the activities of other cells.
- Cytotoxic T Cells (CTL):
  - CD8 molecules.
  - Recognizes antigen presented within class I MHC molecules.
  - Kills cells expressing the appropriate antigen.

B lymphocytes

The surface components of B lymphocytes are:
- Surface Immunoglobulins – Responsible for antigen recognition.
- Immunoglobulin Fc Receptors – Binds to immunoglobulins.
- Class II MHC Molecules – Responsible for antigen presentation.

The functions of B lymphocytes are as follows:
- Direct antigen recognition.
- Differentiation into antibody-producing plasma cells.
- Antigen presentation within class II MHC molecules.

Killer cells

Natural Killer Cells (NK Cells) – A type of cytotoxic lymphocytes that are a major component of the innate immune system. These cells are responsible for triggering the apoptosis of tumor cells, and cells that are infected by viruses. They trigger apoptosis by binding to the affected cells via antigens presented by CD1 molecules, and releasing cytoplasmic granules of proteins called perforin, which creates holes in the cell membrane and triggers subsequent cell death.

Cytotoxic T Cells (Killer T Cells, or KT Cells) – A subgroup of T cells that trigger the apoptosis of tumor cells, and cells that are infected by viruses. These cells recognize target cells by the antigens that are presented in class I MHC molecules that are presented on the cell surface.

Natural Killer T Cells (NKT Cells) – A subset of T cells that resembles both NK cells and KT cells by having traditional T-cell receptor complexes (similar to KT cells, though limited in diversity), as well as recognizing lipids and glycolipids presented by CD1 molecules, rather than MHC complexes (similar to NK cells). NKT cells respond to activation by rapidly releasing cytokines that suppress immune responses, and have been found to target tumor cells and the prevention of autoimmune diseases.

Accessory cells

The accessory cells are responsible for phagocytosis, cell killing, and antigen presentation:
- Macrophages:
    - Immunoglobulin Fc receptor.
    - Complement component C3b receptor.
    - Class II MHC molecule.
    - Bind Fc portion of immunoglobulin (enhances phagocytosis).
    - Bind complement component C3b (enhances phagocytosis).
    - Antigen presentation within class II MHC.
    - Secrete IL-1 promoting T-cell differentiation and proliferation.
    - Can be "activated" by T-cell lymphokines.
- Dendritic cells:
    - Class II MHC molecule.
    - Antigen presentation within class II MHC.
- Polymorphonuclear cells (PMNs):
    - Immunoglobulin Fc receptor.
    - Complement component C3b receptor.
    - Bind Fc portion of immunoglobulin (enhances phagocytosis).
    - Bind complement component C3b (enhances phagocytosis).

Risk factors for infection

Risk factors for infection can be divided into two groups:
- Inadequate Primary Defenses:
    - Broken skin or mucosa.
    - Traumatized tissue.
    - Decreased ciliary action.
    - Obstructed urine flow.
    - Altered peristalsis.
    - Change in the pH of secretions.
    - Decreased mobility.
- Inadequate Secondary Defenses:
    - Reduced hemoglobin.
    - Suppression of white blood cells (WBCs) by drugs or disease.
    - Suppressed inflammatory response.
    - Low WBC count, called leukopenia.

Host defenses against viral infection

A number of host defenses contribute to the prevention and/or elimination of viral infections. Prior to infection, non-specific defenses include the following:
- Anatomical barriers.
- Viral inhibitors in fluids and tissues.

After infection, non-specific defenses include the following:
- Fever – Viral replication is strongly influenced by temperature.
- Inflammatory processes – Edema, leukocyte accumulation, local hyperthermia, reduced oxygen tension, altered cell metabolism, etc.
- Production of interferon – This substance is produced by infected cells. It then reacts with other cells, activating an RNA endonuclease that causes mRNA degradation, and inducing the phosphorylation of eIF2, which essentially turns off cellular protein synthesis.

Specific host defenses include the following:
- Antiviral antibodies – These may prevent adsorption to target cells.
- Cytotoxic T lymphocytes – These recognize virally infected cells and trigger their destruction, reducing viral production.

First line of defense against bacterial infection

The first line of defense is part of the innate (primary) immune response, which is a non-specific form of defense against infection:
- Skin – Provides a barrier to the entry of bacteria. Fatty acids, lactic acids of sweat, and sebaceous secretions also contribute to the first line of defense.
- Mucous lining of the respiratory and GI tracts – Traps bacteria, and the trapped particles are removed by coughing and sneezing, which is aided by ciliated epithelial cells.
- Tears, saliva, and urine – Contain antibiotic enzymes and acids that kill bacteria.
- Normal Bacterial Flora – In humans, the intestinal bacterial flora defends against infectious bacteria by competitive inhibition: they compete for nutrients, space to grow, etc.

Exotoxins

Exotoxins are plasma-soluble substances (usually proteins) that are usually secreted by Gram-positive bacteria. Many, if not most, of these are actually coded for by temperate phage genes, rather than bacterial genes. There are four general types of exotoxins:
- Cytotoxins – Cause direct damage to cells.
- Neurotoxins – Impair nerve function.
- Enterotoxins – Cause intestinal symptoms.
- Leukocidins – Kill leukocytes (e.g., streptolysin, a toxin produced by *Streptococci*).

Endotoxins are Gram-negative bacterial cell-wall components (usually lipopolysaccharides). There are also mycotoxins (produced by fungi), such as ergot, phalloidin, psilocybin, and aflatoxin.

Endotoxins

The physiological responses to endotoxin are as follows:
- Macrophages release cytokines (e.g., IL-1β and TNFα) that stimulate the production of prostaglandins, fever, weakness, and aches.
- A decrease in circulating neutrophils as they aggregate and stick to blood vessel walls, which causes them to release toxic granules and damage the endothelial cells.
- Blood clots in the peripheral vasculature (disseminated intravascular coagulation); and, rarely, internal hemorrhaging or multiple organ system failure (MOSF) occurs.
- Bradykinin release triggers vasodilation, which increases vascular permeability.

- Hypotension (severe drop in blood volume) causes a vascular collapse, called endotoxic shock or septic shock.
- MOSF – Lungs (acute respiratory distress syndrome (ARDS)), kidneys (kidney failure), brain (mental delirium), and liver (liver failure).

Phagocytosis

Phagocytosis is carried out by polymorphonuclear leukocytes (mainly acting on pyogenic bacteria), and by macrophages (mainly on bacteria, viruses, and protozoa that are capable of intracellular life). There are many different forms of macrophages that carry out phagocytosis: Kupffer cells in the liver, alveolar macrophages in the lungs, microglia in the brain, osteoclasts in the bones, mesangial glomerular cells in the kidneys, etc. Complement facilitates phagocytosis, as adherence reactions activate phagocytic cells to engulf and destroy microbes. Microbes bind to the phagocyte receptors, a process that can be aided by opsonins (factors that bind to both the microbes and the phagocytic cells in order to facilitate their uptake). Membrane protrusions, called pseudopodia, form around the microbes, which are ingested to form a phagosome. The phagosome fuses with lysosomes, which contain enzymes and granules that will kill and digest the microbe. The degradation products are then released from the phagocyte.

Secondary immune response

The secondary immune response is also known as adaptive immunity. It develops after exposure to an antigen, and comes into play when microbes penetrate the barriers of the innate immune response. Resistance is improved upon repeated infection with the same pathogen. Adaptive immunity is highly specific. The cells involved are the lymphocytes (B and T cells), which differentiate and proliferate in response to an antigenic stimulus, and macrophages, which function to trap, process, and present antigens to T lymphocytes for activation. There are four important features of the secondary immune response:
- Specificity
- Adaptiveness
- Self-recognition
- Memory

There are two categories of secondary immune response:
- Humoral immunity – Mediated by B cells against extracellular pathogens.
- Cell-mediated immunity – Mediated by T cells against intracellular pathogens.

Antigen and antibody relationship

An antigen (Ag) is a molecule that elicits a specific immune response when introduced into an animal. More specifically, antigenic (immunogenic) substances have the following characteristics:
- Generally Large Molecules (> 10 kDa in molecular weight).
- Structurally Complex (proteins are usually very antigenic).
- Accessible (the immune system must be able to contact the molecule).
- Foreign (not recognizable as self).

An antibody (Ab) is a glycoprotein that is produced in response to an Ag, which is specific for the Ag, and binds to it via non-covalent interactions. The term "immunoglobulin" is often used interchangeably with "antibody", though the distinction between the two is that immunoglobulin

(Ig) is used more generally for classes of antibodies, while Ab is used for an Ig that has a specific Ag. Igs come in different forms, and are classified based upon their structure: IgA, IgD, IgE, IgG, or IgM.

Antibody isotypes

The following are antibody isotypes:
- IgM – Activates complement and is the 1st antibody in development and response.
- IgD – A B-cell receptor.
- IgG – Involved in placental transfer, binds to mast cell surfaces, activates complement, and is involved in opsonization and antibody-dependent cell cytotoxicity. There are four subclasses, called IgG1, IgG2, IgG3, and IgG4.
- IgE – Binds to mast cell surfaces, and is involved in allergic responses.
- IgA – There are two subclasses, called IgA1 and IgA2. Also found as dimers in secretions (sIgA).

Autoimmunity

Autoimmunity refers to the reaction of the immune system to the body's own tissues. It can be organ-specific (e.g., type I diabetes mellitus) or non-organ-specific (e.g., lupus erythematosus). Human major histocompatibility molecules are located on the surface of all cells that function to distinguish self from non-self. In humans, these molecules are referred to as human leukocyte antigens (HLAs). The immune system generally recognizes its own HLAs and does not attack these cells. However, if the body fails to recognize cells or tissues as self, or fails to eliminate the antibodies that react to self-antigens, then an autoimmune response may be generated.

Nosocomial infections

Nosocomial infections are infections where the spread of the infection is favored or promoted by a hospital environment. There are 3 types of nosocomial infections:
- Exogenous infections – Caused by microorganisms that are not found in normal flora. Examples include *Aspergillus* and *Salmonella*.
- Endogenous infections – Where microorganism overgrowth causes a different area of the body to become infected. Examples include *Enterococci* (GI) in a wound site or *E. coli* (GI) within the urinary tract via a Foley catheter.
- Iatrogenic infections – Infections that are caused by medical procedures. Examples include urinary tract infection after Foley catheter insertion or bacteremia after intravenous (IV) insertion.

Nutrition

The environment must supply its organisms with adequate nutrients via the food supply. No organism is independent of the environment, but based upon nutritional self-sufficiency we can classify organisms as either autotrophs or heterotrophs. Heterotrophs include all animals; autotrophs include all organisms that carry out photosynthesis and can manufacture organic constituents from inorganic material.

Heterotrophs

A heterotroph is an organism that requires organic substrates to get its carbon for growth and development. This is in contrast to autotrophs, which use carbon dioxide as their sole source of carbon. All animals, fungi, and many bacteria are heterotrophic. Some parasitic plants have also become fully or partially heterotrophic, though carnivorous plants are still autotrophic, even though they use a flesh diet to augment their nitrogen supply.

Autotrophs

An autotroph is an organism that utilizes carbon dioxide as a source of carbon in order to produce organic compounds, using either light or reactions of inorganic chemical compounds as a source of energy. This is in contrast to heterotrophs, which require organic compounds as a source of carbon, rather than carbon dioxide. Plants and other organisms that use photosynthesis are photolitho-autotrophs, while bacteria that utilize the oxidation of inorganic compounds, such as hydrogen sulfide or ferrous iron, are chemolithoautotrophs. Autotrophs are a vital part of the food chain. They take in energy from the sun, or from inorganic sources, and convert it into organic molecules that can be used to carry out biological functions within their own cells, or can be used by other organisms (called heterotrophs) as food. Thus, heterotrophs (animals, fungi, as well as most bacteria and protozoa) depend on autotrophs for energy, and for the raw materials they use to make complex organic molecules. Heterotrophs obtain energy by breaking down organic molecules that they obtain from food.

Carbohydrates

Of primary importance in human nutrition are the monosaccharides, disaccharides, and polysaccharides. Monosaccharides are generally simple 5- or 6-carbon sugars that cannot be broken down into smaller units. Common examples include glucose and fructose.

Glycogen

Glycogen is a polysaccharide that is found most abundantly in the liver and muscles. Although it is the same molecule in both tissues, it has 2 quite different primary functions in these tissues. In muscle tissues, glycogen is employed as a fuel source (i.e., a source for the production of adenosine triphosphate (ATP)) during brief periods of high energy consumption. During times of energy abundance (e.g., after a meal), the liver takes up glucose from the blood stream, as well as nutrients that it can convert into glucose (primarily amino acids, galactose, fructose, lactate, pyruvate, and glycerol, but not fatty acids), and then converts these nutrients to glycogen. Conversely, when blood glucose levels fall, the liver catabolizes glycogen into glucose via a series of exquisitely regulated hydrolytic reactions, referred to as glycogenolysis.

Proteins

Few free amino acids are available in the diet. Amino acid intake is primarily in the form of proteins (high molecular weight heteropolymers of amino acids). Amino acids are necessary for the production and maintenance of protoplasm.

Amino acids

The categories of amino acids are as follows:
- Glucogenic – Amino acids that give rise to a net production of pyruvate or TCA-cycle intermediates, such as α-ketoglutarate or oxaloacetate, all of which are precursors for glucose via gluconeogenesis. All amino acids, except for lysine and leucine, are at least partly glucogenic.
- Ketogenic – Lysine and leucine are the only amino acids that are solely ketogenic, giving rise only to acetyl-CoA or acetoacetyl-CoA, neither of which can bring about net glucose production.
- Glucogenic and Ketogenic – A small group of amino acids, comprised of isoleucine, phenylalanine, threonine, tryptophan, and tyrosine. They give rise to both glucose and fatty acid precursors, and are thus characterized as being both glucogenic and ketogenic.

Finally, it should be recognized that amino acids have a third possible fate. During times of starvation, the reduced carbon skeletons of amino acids are used for energy production, with the result being that they are oxidized in order to produce CO_2 and H_2O.

Essential and nonessential amino acids

Essential amino acids cannot be produced by the body, and are thus required to be obtained from dietary sources. These include the following amino acids: isoleucine, leucine, lysine, methionine, phenylalanine, threonine, tryptophan, valine, histidine, tyrosine, and selenocysteine. Nonessential amino acids can be produced by the body, and are thus not essential to be obtained from dietary sources. These include the following amino acids: alanine, arginine, aspartate, cysteine, glutamate, glutamine, glycine, proline, serine, asparagine, and pyrolysine.

Glutamine

Glutamine is the most abundant amino acid in the bloodstream. It is considered a "conditionally" essential amino acid because it can be manufactured in the body, but under extreme physical stress the demand for glutamine exceeds the body's ability to synthesize it. Most of the glutamine in the body is stored in muscles, followed by the lungs, where much of the glutamine is manufactured. Glutamine is important for removing excess ammonia, a common waste product in the body. In the process of picking up ammonia, glutamine donates it when needed to make other amino acids, as well as sugar and the antioxidant glutathione.

Several types of important immune cells rely on glutamine for energy: the immune system would be impaired without it. Glutamine also appears to be necessary for normal brain function and digestion. Adequate amounts of glutamine are generally obtained through the diet alone, because the body is also able to make glutamine. However, certain medical conditions can deplete glutamine levels, including injuries, surgery, infections, and prolonged stress. When the body is stressed, such as from injuries, infections, burns, trauma, or surgical procedures, steroid hormones, such as cortisol, are released into the bloodstream. Elevated cortisol levels can deplete glutamine stores in the body.

> ➢ **Review Video: Amino Acids**
> *Visit mometrix.com/academy and enter Code:* **190385**

- 155 -

Fats

Fats may be grouped into simple lipids, compound lipids, and lipids derived from simple and compound lipids by hydrolysis. Fats are composed of three fatty acid molecules joined to a molecule of glycerol.

Omega-3 fatty acids

Omega-3 fatty acids are considered essential fatty acids, which means that they are essential to human health, but cannot be manufactured by the body. For this reason, omega-3 fatty acids must be obtained from dietary sources, including fish and certain plant oils. Also known as polyunsaturated fatty acids (PUFAs), omega-3 and omega-6 fatty acids play a crucial role in brain function, as well as normal growth and development.

There are three major types of omega-3 fatty acids that are ingested in foods and used by the body:
- α-Linolenic Acid (ALA).
- Eicosapentaenoic Acid (EPA).
- Docosahexaenoic Acid (DHA).

Once eaten, the body converts ALA into EPA and DHA, the two types of omega-3 fatty acids that are more readily used by the body. Extensive research indicates that omega-3 fatty acids reduce inflammation, and help prevent certain chronic diseases, such as heart disease and arthritis. These essential fatty acids are highly concentrated in the brain and appear to be particularly important for cognitive and behavioral function. In fact, infants who do not get enough omega-3 fatty acids from their mothers during pregnancy are at risk for developing vision and nerve problems. Omega-3 fatty acids help reduce inflammation, and most omega-6 fatty acids tend to promote inflammation.

Vitamins

Vitamins are organic substances that are needed in minute quantities, often playing a role as part of an enzymatic system. Vitamins are used up during metabolic activities, and must be constantly replaced.

Water-soluble and fat-soluble vitamins

Water-soluble vitamins: Vitamins, such as vitamin C and the B vitamins, are stored in the body for only a brief period of time, and are then excreted by the kidneys. The one exception to this is vitamin B_{12}, which is stored in the liver. Water-soluble vitamins need to be taken daily. Vitamin C (ascorbic acid) and the B complex group make up the nine water-soluble vitamins. The B-complex group consists of the following vitamins: B_1 (thiamine), B_2 (riboflavin), B_3 (niacin), B_6 (pyridoxine), and B_{12} (niacin, pantothenic acid, biotin, folic acid, and cobalamin).

Fat-soluble vitamins: Vitamins that are absorbed into the circulation together with fat from the intestine. Any disease or disorder that affects the absorption of fat, such as celiac disease, could lead to a deficiency of these vitamins. Once absorbed into the circulation, these vitamins are carried to the liver where they are stored. Vitamins A, D, E, and K make up the fat-soluble vitamins. Vitamins A, D, and K are stored in the liver, and vitamin E is distributed throughout the body's fatty tissues.

Vitamin A (fat soluble)
- Sources – Dairy products, eggs, and liver. Can be converted by the body from the β-carotene found in green vegetables, carrots and liver.
- Uses – Maintains the health of the epithelium, and acts on the retina's dark adaptation mechanism.
- Deficiency – Leads to keratinisation of the nasal and respiratory passage epithelium, and night blindness.

Vitamin B_1 (thiamine, water soluble)
- Sources – Yeast, egg yolk, liver, wheat germ, nuts, red meat, and cereals.
- Uses – Carbohydrate metabolism.
- Deficiency – Leads to fatigue, irritability, and loss of appetite. Severe deficiency can lead to beriberi and Wernicke-Korsakoff syndrome. Alcoholism can also lead to severe deficiency.

Vitamin B_2 (riboflavin, water soluble)
- Sources – Dairy products, liver, vegetables, eggs, cereals, fruit, and yeast.
- Uses – Intracellular metabolism.
- Deficiency – Leads to a painful tongue, fissures to the corners of the mouth, and chapped lips.

Vitamin B_3 (niacin, water soluble)
- Sources – Dairy products, poultry, fish, lean meats, nuts, and eggs. Legumes, enriched breads, and cereals also supply some niacin.
- Uses – Necessary for many aspects of health, growth, and reproduction. Niacin assists in the functioning of the digestive system, skin, and nerves. It is also important for the conversion of food to energy. It can be prescribed as a treatment for elevated total cholesterol, and other types of lipid disorders, but should only used with medical supervision due to the potential side effects of an overdose, including liver damage, peptic ulcers, and skin rashes.
- Deficiency – Leads to pellagra, with symptoms including inflamed skin, digestive problems, and mental impairment.

Vitamin B_5 (pantothenic acid, water soluble)
- Sources – Found in all living things, and widely distributed in food, so deficiency is rare.
- Uses – Helps the body to convert carbohydrates into glucose (sugar), plays a role in the breakdown of fats and carbohydrates for energy, critical to the manufacture of red blood cells as well as sex and stress-related hormones produced in the adrenal glands, important in maintaining a healthy digestive tract, and it helps the body to use other vitamins more effectively (particularly B_2 (riboflavin)). Pantethine, an active, stable form of vitamin B_5, has been gaining attention in recent years as a possible treatment for high cholesterol. Panthenol, another form of vitamin B_5, is often found in hair care products because of the belief that it makes hair more manageable, softer, and shinier.
- Deficiency – Leads to fatigue, insomnia, depression, irritability, vomiting, stomach pains, burning feet, and upper respiratory infections.

Vitamin B_6 (pyridoxine, water soluble)
- Sources – Meats, whole-grain products, vegetables, nuts, and bananas.
- Uses – Essential for normal brain development and function, important for maintaining healthy nerve and muscle cells, aids in the production of DNA and RNA, necessary for proper absorption of vitamin B_{12}, necessary for the production of red blood cells and

immune cells, relieves symptoms associated with premenstrual syndrome (PMS), enhances the activity of the immune system and the body's ability to withstand stress, and works closely together with vitamins B_9 and B_{12} to control blood levels of the amino acid homocysteine.
- Deficiency – Leads to muscle weakness, nervousness, irritability, depression, difficulty concentrating, and short-term memory loss.

Vitamin B_9 (folic acid, water soluble)
- Sources – Beans and legumes, citrus fruits and juices, wheat bran and other whole grains, dark green leafy vegetables, poultry, pork, shellfish, and liver.
- Uses – Works along with vitamin B_{12} and vitamin C to help the body digest and utilize proteins, and to synthesize new proteins when they are needed. It is necessary for the production of red blood cells and for DNA synthesis. Folic acid also helps with tissue growth and cell function. In addition, it helps to increase appetite when needed, and stimulates the formation of digestive acids. Synthetic folic acid supplements may be used in the treatment of disorders associated with folic acid deficiency and may also be part of the recommended treatment for certain menstrual problems and leg ulcers.
- Deficiency – Leads to poor growth, graying hair, inflammation of the tongue (glossitis), mouth ulcers, peptic ulcer, and diarrhea. It may also lead to certain types of anemias.

Vitamin B_{12} (water soluble)
- Sources – Liver, red meat, dairy products, and fish. Only found in animal products.
- Uses – Essential for the manufacturing of genetic material in cells. Involved in the production of erythrocytes.
- Deficiency – Leads to pernicious anemia. Schilling test can identify deficiency.

Vitamin C (ascorbic acid, water soluble)
- Sources – Green vegetables and fruits.
- Uses – Essential for the maintenance of bones, teeth, gums, ligaments, and blood vessels. It is also necessary for ensuring a normal immune response to infection. Helps with iron absorption, and cross-links collagen. Cofactor for dopamine.
- Deficiency – Leads to scurvy.

Vitamin D (fat soluble)
- Sources – Fish liver oils and dairy produce. Vitamin D is also produced in the skin when it is exposed to sunlight.
- Uses – Has a role in the absorption of calcium, which is essential for the maintenance of healthy bones.
- Deficiency – Leads to rickets, hypocalcemic tetany, and osteomalacia. Excess factors that can cause hypercalcemia include sarcoidosis, Paget's disease, malignancy, hyperparathyroidism, and milk-alkali syndrome.

Vitamin K (fat soluble)
- Sources – Green vegetables.
- Uses – Used by the liver for the formation of prothrombin.
- Deficiency – Leads to bleeding due to delayed clotting times caused by a lack of clotting factors. Patients may show signs of bruising easily, and have nosebleeds. Deficiency can be caused by prolonged use of antibiotics. Warfarin is a vitamin-K antagonist, and will induce an acute deficiency.

Minerals

Minerals are also utilized by the tissues of the body. Among the most common minerals are calcium, phosphorus, potassium, sodium, magnesium, chlorine, manganese, iodine, iron, zinc, copper, cobalt, bromine, and fluorine.

Kilocalories

The kilocalorie (kcal) is the unit of heat used in measuring the value of foods for producing heat and energy in the human body. It is equivalent to the amount of heat that is required to raise the temperature of one kilogram of water one degree Celsius. At 20°C, 1 kcal = 4.182×10^3 J.

Digestive System

Chemical and enzymatic properties of digestion and absorption

Carbohydrates
- Salivary amylase enzymatically digests 50% of dietary starch, but is inactivated by the acidic environment of the stomach.
- Pancreatic amylase completes starch digestion in the small intestine. The products of starch digestion are oligosaccharides and maltose.
- Sodium-glucose transporters (SGLT) of absorptive cells regulate the transport of glucose and galactose across the intestinal epithelia.
- Fructose is absorbed by facilitated diffusion, and then converted to glucose within the absorptive cells.

Proteins
- Pepsin digests a portion of dietary protein in the acidic stomach.
- Pancreatic proteases and brush-border enzymes complete protein digestion in the small intestine.
- The products of protein digestion are peptides and amino acids.

Lipids
- Lingual lipase digests 10% of dietary fat in the acidic stomach.
- Pancreatic lipase completes fat digestion in the small intestine.
- Bile emulsifies fat for efficient enzymatic digestion.
- The products of fat digestion are fatty acids and monoglycerides.

Oral cavity

The oral cavity:
- Receives food and perceives taste, odor, texture, and temperature.
- Grinds foodstuffs to facilitate the action of enzymes.
- Adds enzymes, mucus and moisture, and shapes the bolus for the process of swallowing.

Saliva

Saliva is both digestive and protective. It is added to food ingested within the oral cavity, and has the following functions:
- Dissolves food.
- Initiates starch digestion.
- Lubricates food.
- Kills bacteria with antibacterial enzymes.

Saliva is composed of the following:
- Water
- Electrolytes
- Enzymes
- Mucin

- Glycoproteins
- Blood group proteins
- Gamma globulins

Pharynx and esophagus

The oral and laryngeal pharynx and the esophagus are essentially conduits for food to reach the stomach.

Anterior triangle of the neck

The anatomy of the anterior triangle of the neck is as follows:
- Viscera – The lower pharynx, larynx, esophagus, and trachea.
- Glands – The thyroid, parathyroid, submandibular, and lower portion of the parotid.
- Muscles:
  - Suprahyoid Group – Stylohyoid, digastric, mylohyoid, and geniohyoid.
  - Infrahyoid Group – Thyrohyoid, omohyoid, sternohyoid, and sternothyroid.
- Nerves:
  - Vagus (and its laryngeal branches).
  - Accessory (briefly).
  - Ventral Rami of the Cervical Plexus.
  - Ansa Cervicalis.
  - Cutaneous Branches of the Cervical Plexus.
  - Phrenic, Hypoglossal, and Sympathetic Chain.
- Vessels:
  - Common, Internal, and External Carotid Arteries.
  - 1st six branches of the External Carotid Artery.
  - Internal and External Jugular Venous System.

Stomach

Food is received, stored, and churned within the stomach. Once food enters the stomach, gastric acid is added, and the digestive process that began in the mouth is continued. Also, intrinsic factor (anti-pernicious anemia factor) is secreted.

Gastric acid

Gastric acid is the main secretion of the stomach, containing H_2O, hydrochloric acid (HCl), and several enzymes (mainly pepsinogen, the proenzyme of pepsin). Gastric acid is produced by the parietal cells (wall cells) of the gastric mucosa, and about 2-3 liters are secreted within a 24-hour period. The pH of gastric acid is between 2-3, with the acidity being maintained by the H^+/K^+-ATPase proton pump. The parietal cells also release bicarbonate into the blood stream during the process. Gastric acid production is regulated by both the autonomic nervous system, and several hormones. In addition, the parasympathetic nervous system, via the vagus nerve, and the hormone gastrin stimulate the parietal cells to produce gastric acid.

Conversely, vasoactive intestinal peptide, cholecystokinin, and secretin all inhibit production. In atrophic gastritis and achlorhydria, there is decreased gastric acid production, and thus decreased disinfectant properties of the gastric milieu, which leads to an increased risk of infections of the digestive tract (such as with a food borne infection by *Vibrio vulnificus*). In diseases that feature excessive vomiting, patients develop hypochloremic metabolic alkalosis, which is a decreased blood acidity that is caused by H^+ and Cl^- depletion.

The composition of gastric acid is as follows:
- Water
- Hydrochloric acid (HCl)
- Inorganic salts
- Mucus
- Enzymes (e.g., pepsin, renin, and lipase)

Bicarbonate

Bicarbonate (HCO_3^-) is a polyatomic ion that is produced by the mucosal cells of the duodenum and the stomach. It is the intermediate form in the deprotonation of carbonic acid (H_2CO_3): removing the first proton from H_2CO_3 produces HCO_3^-; removing the second proton produces carbonate (CO_3^{2-}). Salts that contain the bicarbonate ion are also referred to as bicarbonates, such as sodium bicarbonate ($NaHCO_3$, or baking soda). Bicarbonates are more correctly named hydrogen carbonates in the chemical nomenclature system. Occasionally, they are referred to as "acid carbonates". Bicarbonates will release carbon dioxide (CO_2) when exposed to an acid, such as acetic acid (vinegar). This is used to cause breads to rise when cooking, as well as to propel toy rockets. The HCO_3^-/CO_3^{2-} ionic system also functions as a buffer system in the blood.

Intrinsic factor

Intrinsic factor is a glycoprotein that is produced by the parietal cells of the stomach, and is necessary for the absorption of vitamin B_{12}. In all mammals, vitamin B_{12} is necessary for the maturation of erythrocytes, and a deficiency of this vitamin can lead to the development of anemia. For this reason, problems with the function of intrinsic factor can cause pernicious anemia.

Pepsin

Pepsin is a digestive protease that is produced by the chief cells of the stomach, and degrades food proteins in the stomach. Pepsin is first expressed in an inactive proform, called pepsinogen, which contains an additional 44 amino acids that are cleaved off outside of the secreting cell in order to avoid the digestion of intracellular proteins. Pepsin is most active at pH 2-4, and is permanently inactivated above pH 6. The other important digestive proteases are trypsin and chymotrypsin.

Anatomy

The anatomy of the stomach is as follows:
- Gastroesophageal region – The junction between the stomach and the esophagus.
- Fundus – The blind portion of the stomach, above its junction with the esophagus. This portion is thin-walled compared to the rest of the stomach, and has few secretory cells. As the bolus of food enters this area first, some action of salivary amylase may continue briefly.
- Body of the stomach – This is where extensive gastric pits are located that possess the secretory cells of the stomach.
- Pylorus – This narrowed region leads through the pyloric sphincter and into the duodenum.

<u>Epithelial cells</u>
Four major types of secretory epithelial cells cover the surface of the stomach, and extend down into the gastric pits and glands:

- Mucous cells – Secrete an alkaline mucus that protects the epithelium against shear stress and acid.
- Parietal cells – Secrete H^+ and intrinsic factor.
- Chief cells – Secrete pepsin, a proteolytic enzyme.
- G cells – Secrete the hormone gastrin.

Liver

The liver has the following functions:

- Manufacturing:
  - Blood proteins – Albumen, fibrinogen, prothrombin, etc.
  - Clotting proteins – Produces 12 clotting factors, including plasmin.
  - Urea – Nitrogenous waste from amino acid metabolism.
  - Bile – Excretory for the bile pigments, responsible for the emulsification of fats.
- Storage:
  - Glycogen – Carbohydrate fuel.
  - Iron – As hemosiderin and ferritin.
  - The fat-soluble vitamins A, D, E, and K.
- Detoxification – Alcohol, drugs, medicines, and environmental toxins.
- Protein metabolism:
  - Transamination – Removal of the amine from one amino acid, and using it to produce a different amino acid.
  - Deamination – Removal of the amine group in order to catabolize the remaining keto acid (the amine group enters the blood as urea, which is excreted through the kidneys).
- Glycemic regulation – The management of blood glucose.
- Glycogenesis – The conversion of glucose into glycogen.
- Glycogenolysis – The breakdown of glycogen into glucose.
- Gluconeogenesis – The manufacture of glucose from non-carbohydrate sources, mostly protein.

Arterial and venous blood flow

<u>Arterial blood flow</u>
The common hepatic artery is a branch of the celiac trunk. After branching off from the gastroduodenal artery, it becomes the proper hepatic artery, which divides into the right and left hepatic arteries (30% of the blood flow into the liver is through these arteries, while the rest is through the portal vein). There is great variation in the origin of these vessels, which can be quite disturbing to the medical doctor. The caudate and quadrate lobes may receive their blood from the middle hepatic artery. This variable artery usually takes its origin equally from either the left or the right hepatic artery (90%), or rarely from another source (10%).

Venous blood flow

The hepatic portal vein supplies about 70% of the blood to the liver. It carries nutrient-rich blood from the GI tract to the liver for metabolism or storage. It is formed by a union of the superior mesenteric vein and the splenic vein. The inferior mesenteric vein may join either of the other two veins, or enter at their junction. Hepatic veins drain blood from the liver directly into the inferior vena cava.

High-density lipoproteins

High-density lipoproteins (HDLs) are synthesized *de novo* in the liver and the small intestine, primarily as protein-rich, disc-shaped particles. These newly formed HDLs are nearly devoid of any cholesterol and cholesteryl esters. The primary apoproteins of HDLs are apoA-I, apoC-I, apoC-II and apoE. Cholesterol-rich HDLs return to the liver, where they are endocytosed. Hepatic uptake of HDLs, or reverse cholesterol transport, may be mediated through an HDL-specific apoA-I receptor, or through lipid-lipid interactions. Macrophages also take up HDLs through apoA-I-receptor interaction. HDLs can then acquire cholesterol and apoE from the macrophages, and cholesterol-enriched HDLs are then secreted from the macrophages. The addition of apoE to these HDLs increases their uptake and catabolism by the liver. HDLs also acquire cholesterol by extracting it from cell surface membranes. This process has the effect of lowering the level of intracellular cholesterol, since the cholesterol that is stored within cells as cholesteryl esters will be mobilized to replace the cholesterol that is removed from the plasma membrane.

Low-density lipoproteins

In the circulation, low-density lipoproteins (LDLs) are produced from very-low-density lipoproteins (VLDLs) by lipoprotein lipase. LDLs are the primary plasma carriers of cholesterol for delivery to all tissues. LDLs are taken up by cells via LDL receptor-mediated endocytosis, which occurs predominantly in the liver (75%), adrenals, and adipose tissue. The specific apoprotein for the LDLs is apoB-100, and the interaction of the LDLs with LDL receptors requires the presence of apoB-100. Upon endocytosis, the endocytosed membrane vesicles (endosomes) fuse with lysosomes, in which the apoproteins are degraded, and the cholesterol esters are hydrolyzed to yield free cholesterol. The cholesterol is then incorporated into the plasma membranes as necessary. Excess intracellular cholesterol is re-esterified by acyl-CoA-cholesterol acyltransferase (ACAT) for intracellular storage. The activity of ACAT is enhanced by the presence of intracellular cholesterol. Insulin and triiodo-thyronine (T_3) increase the binding of LDLs to liver cells, whereas glucocorticoids (e.g., dexamethasone) have the opposite effect. The precise mechanism for these effects is unclear, but they may be mediated through the regulation of apoB-100 degradation.

Bile

Bile is a complex fluid that contains water, electrolytes, and a battery of organic molecules, including bile acids, cholesterol, phospholipids, and bilirubin. Gastrin triggers the secretion of bile, which flows through the biliary tract, and into the small intestine. There are two fundamentally important functions of bile in all species:

- Bile contains bile acids, which are critical for the digestion and absorption of fats and fat-soluble vitamins by the small intestine.
- Many waste products are eliminated from the body by their secretion into bile, and their subsequent elimination in feces.

Adult humans produce approximately 400 to 800 mL of bile per day, and other animals produce proportionately similar amounts. The secretion of bile can be considered to occur in two stages:

- Initially, hepatocytes secrete bile into canaliculi, from which it flows into bile ducts. This hepatic bile contains large quantities of bile acids, cholesterol, and other organic molecules.
- As bile flows through the bile ducts, it is modified by the addition of a watery, bicarbonate-rich secretion from ductal epithelial cells.

Gallbladder

The gallbladder stores bile that is produced by the liver. When demand exists, bile is released and flows into the cystic duct, which connects with the common bile duct (formed by union of the common hepatic and cystic ducts). The common bile duct empties into the second part of the duodenum.

Pancreas

Pancreatic lipase, amylase and proteases are controlled by the presence of foodstuffs and hormones. As acid chyme enters the duodenum from the stomach, secretin is released, and fluid and bicarbonate are secreted. Pancreatic juice has the following functions:

- Neutralizes the acid chyme in the duodenum.
- Provides enzymes for the digestion of proteins, carbohydrates, and fats.

The islets of Langerhans are the endocrine portion of the pancreas. Three cell types can be identified, as follows:

- A, or alpha, cells, which are presumed to produce glucagons.
- B, or beta, cells, which are more numerous than A cells, and produce insulin.
- D, or delta, cells; their significance is uncertain but they might represent multipotent resting cells.

Anatomy

The anatomy of the pancreas is as follows:

- Location: The pancreas is entirely retroperitoneal.
- Parts of the pancreas:
  - Head – Found in the curve formed by the 1st, 2nd, and 3rd parts of the duodenum.
  - Uncinate process – A prolongation of the head toward the left.
  - Neck, body, and tail – Located in the splenorenal ligament (usually touches the spleen).
  - Ducts – The pancreas has a main duct that joins the common bile duct to drain through the ampulla of Vater, and into the second part of the duodenum at the major duodenal papilla. An accessory duct may drain into the duodenum, proximal to the main duct, through the minor duodenal papilla.
- Arterial supply: The splenic artery gives numerous branches to the body of the pancreas. Three of the larger ones are the dorsal pancreatic artery, the great pancreatic artery (pancreatica magna), and the caudal pancreatic artery. The superior and inferior pancreaticoduodenal arteries supply most of the blood to the head of the pancreas via their anterior and posterior branches.

Glucagon

Glucagon is a hormone produced by the alpha cells of the pancreas, which functions to release glycogen that is stored in the liver and muscles, helping to maintain the level of glucose in the blood. Glucagon injections are used to treat serious insulin reactions in people with diabetes. Binding of glucagon to the glucagon receptor turns glycogen phosphorylase on, converting it into its active form, phosphorylase A, which breaks down glycogen polymers into glucose-1-phosphate.

Small intestine

Digestion is completed and most absorption takes place in the small intestine. The small intestine stretches nearly 20 feet, and includes the duodenum, the jejunum, and the ileum. The surface area is increased by circular folds (the plicae circularis), finger-like villi, and the presence of microvilli (brush border) on the cell surfaces. At the base of the villi are the intestinal crypts, also called the intestinal glands because they are the source of the secretory cells of the mucosa. These cells are constantly renewed by mitosis, and push up along the villi until they exfoliate from the surface, cycling with about a 5-day turnover. Intestinal enzymes are released from the surface of the mucosal cells by exocytosis. These enzymes are called brush-border enzymes because they cling to the surface of microvilli. The three portions of the small intestine differ in subtle ways:
- The duodenum is the only portion with Brunner's glands in its submucosa, which produce an alkaline mucus.
- The ileum has Peyer's patches, concentrated lymph tissue in the submucosa.
- Goblet cells are progressively more abundant the further one travels along the small intestine.

Arterial blood supply of the gut

- Visceral branches of abdominal aorta – Median, unpaired.
    - Celiac trunk (left gastric, splenic, and gastroduodenal).
    - Superior mesenteric artery.
    - Inferior mesenteric artery.
- Dorsal body wall – Visceral, paired.
- Dorsal body wall branches – Paired.

The foregut includes the stomach, the 1st and 1/2 of the 2nd part of the duodenum, and is supplied by the celiac trunk.

Portal vein system

The portal vein system begins in small venules all along the intestinal tract, and ends in venous sinusoids in the liver. Here, the nutrient-rich blood is processed and detoxified before leaving the liver through hepatic veins, which drain into the inferior vena cava. The portal system is a valveless system of veins. This means that blood can flow in any direction, depending on pressure differences within the system. The portal vein is formed by the union of superior mesenteric and splenic veins. The inferior mesenteric vein can drain into the splenic vein, or into the place where the splenic vein joins the superior mesenteric vein. Tributaries of the portal vein include the pyloric from the duodenum, the coronary (left gastric) from the lesser curvature of the stomach (it receives lower esophageal veins), the cystic from the gall bladder, and the paraumbilical from the region of the anterior abdominal wall around the umbilicus.

Chylomicrons

Chylomicrons are assembled in the intestinal mucosa as a means to transport dietary cholesterol and triacylglycerols to the rest of the body. The predominant lipids of chylomicrons are triacylglycerols. The apolipoproteins that predominate before the chylomicrons enter the circulation include apoB-48, and apoA-I, II and IV. ApoB-48 combines only with chylomicrons. Chylomicrons leave the intestine via the lymphatic system, and enter the circulation at the left subclavian vein. In the bloodstream, chylomicrons acquire apoC-II and apoE from plasma HDLs. In the capillaries of adipose tissue and muscle, the fatty acids of chylomicrons are removed from the triacylglycerols by the action of lipoprotein lipase (LPL), which is found on the surface of the endothelial cells of the capillaries. The apoC-II in the chylomicrons activates LPL in the presence of phospholipid. The free fatty acids are then absorbed by the tissues, and the glycerol backbone of the triacylglycerols is returned, via the blood, to the liver and kidneys. Glycerol is converted into the glycolytic intermediate dihydroxyacetone phosphate (DHAP). During the removal of fatty acids, a substantial portion of phospholipid, apoA and apoC, is transferred to HDLs. Chylomicrons function to deliver dietary triacylglycerols to adipose tissue and muscle, and dietary cholesterol to the liver.

Large intestine

The function of the large intestine is to reabsorb water and electrolytes in order to preserve their balance within the body, and to propel food along for elimination (egestion). The large intestine (colon) is much shorter in length, while larger in diameter, than the small intestine. The longitudinal muscle of the colon is arranged into three distinct bands, called the taenia coli, which cause the colon to buckle, producing the haustra. These are pouches that increase the surface area of the colon for the absorption of water and electrolytes. The first part of the colon is a blind pouch, called the cecum. The ileum enters the cecum at the ileocecal sphincter (valve). Attached to the cecum is the vermiform (worm-like) appendix, a vestigial remnant of the larger cecum seen in other mammals. The appendix has a concentration of lymph tissue, and is filled with lymphocytes, but its removal has not been demonstrated to have any negative effect on the immune system. The cecum leads in sequence to the ascending colon, the transverse colon, the descending colon, and then the sigmoid colon, before finally entering the rectum. The rectum possesses skeletal muscle which functions during the defecation reflex.

Intestinal motility

Intestinal motility facilitates the following:
- The mixing of food with secretions and enzymes.
- The contact of foodstuffs with the intestinal mucosa
- Propulsion along the tube (peristalsis).

This process is controlled by the nervous system, hormonal secretions, and intestinal distension and similar phenomena. Epinephrine (from the adrenal) inhibits contraction; serotonin (from the small intestines) stimulates contractions.

Innervation of the intestinal tract

The nerves supplying the intestinal tract affect smooth muscle, glands, endocrine tissue, and control motility and secretion. Motility or *peristalsis* is a wave of compression (contraction) that is followed by a regional relaxation. The gut musculature (smooth) is controlled by the autonomic nervous system.

Effects of sympathetic innervation
- Some excitation of salivary secretion.
- A decrease of motility and secretion in the stomach and small intestines due mainly to the vasoconstrictive action.
- An inhibition of muscular contraction and intrinsic ganglion cell activity due to the release of the neurotransmitters epinephrine and norepinephrine.

Effects of parasympathetic innervation
- Stimulation of motility and secretion via its supply of the intrinsic plexi and the release of the neurotransmitter acetylcholine.
- Release of gastrin.

Excretory System

Kidneys

Structure and functions

The kidneys are composed of several layers, and are each covered by a fibrous capsule, called the renal capsule. The outer layer of the kidneys is the cortex, which contains the major (upper) portion of the nephrons. The middle layer of the kidneys is the medulla, which is composed of the triangular-shaped pyramids, and the renal columns. The pyramids contain the collecting tubules and the loops of Henle, the lower portion of the nephrons. These tubules run nearly parallel to one another, and give the pyramids a grain that leads to their points, or papillae. The renal columns are regions between the pyramids through which blood vessels run to and from the cortex. The papilla of each pyramid projects into a funnel-shaped area, known as the calyx. The calyces (plural of calyx) collect the urine that is released from the papillae, and allow it to drain into a large area, known as the renal pelvis, and then into the ureters. The nephrons are the functional units of the kidneys: they individually and collectively perform the functions of the kidneys.

Blood supply

The blood supply to the kidneys is paramount to their function. The two kidneys receive between 15-20% of the body's systemic blood flow at rest. The renal arteries branch into lobar, and then interlobar arteries, which pass through the renal columns in the direction of the renal cortex. Arcuate arteries branch into the cortex, and lead to the interlobular arteries, which evenly distribute the blood supply throughout the cortex to the afferent arterioles that serve the nephrons. Blood flow that leaves the nephrons returns through veins of the corresponding names.

Glomerulus

The processes in the glomerulus are as follows:

- The filtration coefficient is high because of a high permeability and a large surface area.
- The reflection coefficient is high (about 1.0), and the filtrate is a true ultrafiltrate, as the glomerular capillaries are essentially impermeable to protein (oncotic pressure in the filtrate is zero).
- The hydrostatic pressure in the capillaries is high, and does not decrease much along the length of the capillary.
- Because of the large loss of fluid, and the impermeability to protein, the oncotic pressure in the capillary increases along its length. This increased oncotic pressure is important in the reabsorption from the proximal tubule into the peritubular capillaries.
- There is a net outward filtration pressure, often along the whole length of the capillary.

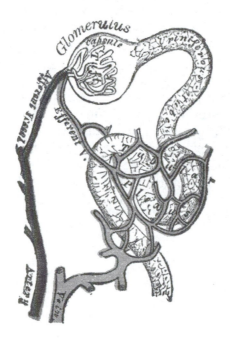

Renal tubule

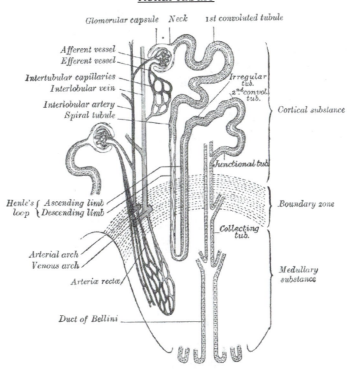

Proximal convoluted tubule

A large amount of nutrients and water are filtered from the blood in the glomerulus. It is necessary to reabsorb most of the nutrients and water, but leave wastes in the tubule, or death would result from dehydration and starvation. Selective reabsorption occurs in the proximal convoluted tubule. Glucose, vitamins, important ions, and most amino acids are reabsorbed from the tubule back into the capillaries near the proximal convoluted tubule. These molecules are moved into the peritubular capillaries by active transport, a process that requires energy. Cells of the proximal convoluted tubule have numerous microvilli and mitochondria, which provide surface area and energy. When the concentration of some substances in the blood reaches a certain level, the substance is not reabsorbed; it remains in the urine. This process prevents the composition of the blood from fluctuating by regulating the levels of glucose and inorganic ions, such as sodium, potassium, bicarbonate phosphate, and chloride. Urea remains in the tubules.

Descending and ascending aspects of the loop of Henle

The descending loop of Henle is highly permeable to water. Water moves out of the tubule by osmosis, and into the medullary interstitial fluid for reabsorption. The descending limb epithelial cells do not have the appropriate protein channels on them for active water transport. In the ascending loop of Henle, the sodium-potassium pumps work non-stop to pump sodium out into the medullary interstitial fluid. This is a major contributing factor to the reason why the medullary interstitial fluid has a solute concentration gradient. As the positive ions leave the ascending limb cells, the negative ions, such as chloride, tend to follow.

Note: The ascending limb is NOT permeable to water. This is unusual, as most cells will allow some water to slip through at any time. However, these cells are specialized to prevent it. Even their tight junctions between cells are excessively tight so that water will not slip between the cells.

Early distal convoluted tubule and collecting tubules
- Early Distal Convoluted Tubule (DCT)
  - Reabsorption of sodium ions.
  - Reabsorption of calcium ions.
  - Reabsorption of chloride ions.
  - Reabsorption of H_2O (regulated by vasopressin).
- Collecting Tubules (CT)
  - Reabsorption of sodium ions.
  - Secretion of hydrogen ions (for blood pH homeostasis).
  - Secretion of potassium ions.
  - Reabsorption of H_2O (regulated by vasopressin).

Both the DCT and the CT are involved in the reabsorption of water.

Renal plasma flow

$$RPF = \frac{(U_x \times V)}{(P_a - P_v)}$$

Where:
U_x = The urine concentration of solute X.
V = The urine flow rate.
P_a = The arterial plasma concentration of the substance X.
P_v = The venous plasma concentration of the substance X.

However, in practice, it is very difficult to measure the P_v of a substance since catheterization of the renal vein is required, which is an uncommon procedure. Therefore, *para*-aminohippurate (PAH) is used because nearly 100% is secreted in the urine. Using PAH, P_v can be eliminated, and the effective RPF (eRPF) can be calculated as follows:

$$eRPF = \frac{(U_{PAH} \times V)}{P_{PAH}}$$

Where:
U_{PAH} = The urine concentration of PAH.
P_{PAH} = The arterial plasma concentration of PAH.

Note: Renal blood flow (RBF) = $\dfrac{RPF}{(1 - [Hematocrit])}$

Renal clearance

As substances in the blood pass through the glomeruli, they are filtered to different degrees. The extent to which they are removed from the blood is called "clearance". The clearance is the number of liters of plasma that are completely cleared of a substance by the kidneys per unit time (mL/min). The idea of complete clearance is hypothetical since almost no substance would be completely cleared. However, clearance measurements are extremely important clinically.

The clearance (C_x) of a substance (X) is given by the following equation:

$$C_x = \frac{U_x \times V}{P_x}$$

Where:
U_x = The concentration of X in the urine in mg per mL (or mmol/L).
P_x = The concentration of X in the plasma in mg per mL (or mmol/L).
V = The urine flow rate in mL per minute.

If a substance is completely cleared (hypothetical), then clearance equals the glomerular filtration rate (GFR). This means that the substance had neither been secreted nor reabsorbed during its passage down the renal tubule. If the clearance is < GFR, then net reabsorption has occurred. Any solute that is fully reabsorbed has a clearance of zero. Solutes that have a clearance > GFR have undergone net secretion, as well as filtration.

Net filtration pressure

NFP = ΔP – Δπ
Where:
ΔP = Hydrostatic pressure gradient.
Δπ = Oncotic pressure gradient.

The NFP can be calculated by subtracting the factors that promote filtration from the factors that oppose filtration. Specifically, the NFP can be calculated as follows:

NFP = GBHP – CHP – BCOP
Where:
GBHP = Glomerular blood hydrostatic pressure.
CHP = Capsular hydrostatic pressure.
BCOP = Blood colloid osmotic pressure.

Under typical conditions, the NFP is positive on the order of 10 mmHg, favoring filtration.

Free water clearance

$$C_{H_2O} = V - C_{osm}$$

Where:
V = The urine flow rate.

C_{osm} = The osmolar clearance = $U_{osm} \times \dfrac{V}{P_{osm}}$

Dilute urine, excreted in the absence of antidiuretic hormone (ADH), can be thought of as being made up of two fluid volumes:
- A volume that contains the urine solutes at the same concentration as in plasma, and called the osmolar clearance (C_{osm}).
- Pure water excreted with no solutes, called positive free water clearance (V).

Concentrated urine, produced in the presence of ADH, can be thought of as the difference between two volumes:

- The volume of plasma from which the urinary solutes derive (C_{osm}).
- The (smaller) volume of urine actually excreted (V).

The difference, $C_{osm} - V$, represents water free of solutes, retained in the body due to the action of ADH. This is called the negative free water clearance, or tubular free water reabsorption.

Total body weight, extracellular fluid, and intracellular fluid

Total Body Weight (TBW)
TBW = ECF + ICF
Where:
ECF = Extracellular fluid volume.
ICF = Intracellular fluid volume.

Extracellular Fluid
ECF = IV + PV
Where:
IV = Interstitial volume.
PV = Plasma volume.

Muscle and Skeletal Systems

Classification of muscles

A muscle cell not only has the ability to propagate an action potential along its cell membrane, as does a nerve cell, but also has the internal machinery to give it the unique ability to contract. Most muscles in the body can be classified as striated muscles in reference to the fact that when observed under a light microscope the muscular tissue has light and dark bands or striations running across it. Although both skeletal and cardiac muscles are striated and therefore have similar structural organizations, they do possess some characteristic functional differences. In contrast to skeletal muscle, cardiac muscle is a functional syncytium. This means that although anatomically it consists of individual cells the entire mass normally responds as a unit and all of the cells contract together. In addition, cardiac muscle has the property of automaticity, which means that the heart initiates its own contraction without the need for motor nerves. Non-striated muscle consists of multi-unit and unitary (visceral) smooth muscle. Visceral smooth muscle has many of the properties of cardiac muscle. To some extent it acts as a functional syncytium (e.g., areas of intestinal smooth muscle will contract as a unit. Smooth muscle is part of the urinary bladder, uterus, spleen, gallbladder, and numerous other internal organs. It is also the muscle of blood vessels, respiratory tracts, and the iris of the eye.

Skeletal muscles

In order for the human being to carry out the many intricate movements that must be performed, approximately 650 skeletal muscles of various lengths, shapes, and strength play a part. Each muscle consists of many muscle cells or fibers held together and surrounded by connective tissue that gives functional integrity to the system. Three definite units are commonly referred to:
- Endomysium – Connective tissue layer enveloping a single fiber.
- Perimysium – Connective tissue layer enveloping a bundle of fibers.
- Epimysium – Connective tissue layer enveloping the entire muscle.

Difference from cardiac muscles

Skeletal muscle is found attached to the bones for movement. Its cells are long, multi-nucleated cylinders. They acquired this characteristic because they develop from the fusion of small, single cells into long units. The cells may be many inches long, but they vary in diameter, averaging between 100 and 150 microns. Skeletal muscle cells are independent cells that are separated from one another by connective tissue, and must each be stimulated by the axons of nerves. Cardiac muscle is the muscle found in the heart. It is composed of much shorter cells than skeletal muscle, and these cells branch to connect to one another. These connections are by means of gap junctions, called intercalated disks, which allow for electrochemical impulses to simultaneously pass to all of the connected cells. This causes the cells to form a functional network, called a syncytium, in which the cells function as a single unit.

Smooth muscle

Visceral muscle is located within the walls of internal organs and blood vessels. Visceral muscle is called smooth muscle because it has no striations, and is thus smooth in appearance. It is organized as layers within the mucous membranes of the respiratory and digestive systems, as distinct bands within the walls of blood vessels, or as sphincter muscles. Single unit smooth muscle is also connected into syncytia, similar to cardiac muscle, and is partly myogenic. Within the walls of the stomach, intestines, and blood vessels, smooth muscle cells form multi-unit muscle tissue that is regulated by the autonomic nervous system, and thus involuntary. Such multi-unit smooth muscle tissue is responsible for the continual rhythmic contractions of the stomach and the intestines.

Muscle attachment and function

For coordinated movement to take place, the muscle must attach to either bone or cartilage or, as in the case of the muscles of facial expression, to skin. The portion of a muscle attaching to bone is the tendon. A muscle has two extremities, its origin and its insertion.

Movement

The following are terms to describe movement:
- Flexion – Bending, most often ventrally to decrease the angle between two parts of the body; it is usually an action at an articulation or joint.
- Extension – Straightening, or increasing the angle between two parts of the body; a stretching out or making the flexed part straight.
- Abduction – Movement away from the midsagittal plane (midline); to adduct is to move medially and bring a part back to the mid-axis.
- Circumduction – Circular movement at a ball and socket (shoulder or hip) joint, utilizing the movements of flexion, extension, abduction, and adduction.
- Rotation – Movement of a part of the body around its long axis.
- Supination - Refers only to the movement of the radius around the ulna. In supination the palm of the hand is oriented anteriorly; turning the palm dorsally puts it into pronation. The body on its back is in the supine position.
- Pronation – Refers to the palm of the hand being oriented posteriorly. The body on its belly is the prone position.
- Inversion – Refers only to the lower extremity, specifically the ankle joint. When the foot (plantar surface) is turned inward, so that the sole is pointing and directed toward the midline of the body and is parallel with the median plane, we speak of inversion. Its opposite is eversion.
- Eversion – Refers to the foot (plantar surface) being turned outward so that the sole is pointing laterally.
- Opposition – One of the most critical movements in humans; it allows us to have pulp-to-pulp opposition, which gives us the great dexterity of our hands. In this movement the thumb pad is brought to a finger pad. A median nerve injury negates this action.

Muscle names

Position and location
- Pectoralis major and minor – Pectoral region of thorax; major is larger.
- Temporalis – Temporal region of head.
- Infra- and supraspinatus – Below and above spine of scapula.
- External and internal intercostals – Intercostal spaces.

Principal action
- Pronators (e.g., pronator quadratus) – Refers to palm down and supinator to palm up; quadratus refers to the shape.
- Flexors and extensors – Flexors and extensors of digits.
- Levator scapulae – Elevator of the scapula (shoulder).

Shape
- Trapezius – Trapezoidal in shape.
- Rhomboid major and minor – Rhomboidal in shape.

Number of divisions (heads) and position
- Biceps brachii – Two-headed muscle in anterior brachium.
- Triceps brachii – Three-headed muscle in posterior brachium.

Size, length, and shape
- Flexor pollicis longus and brevis – Long and short flexors of the thumb.
- Rhomboid major and minor – Major is larger in size; rhomboidal in shape.

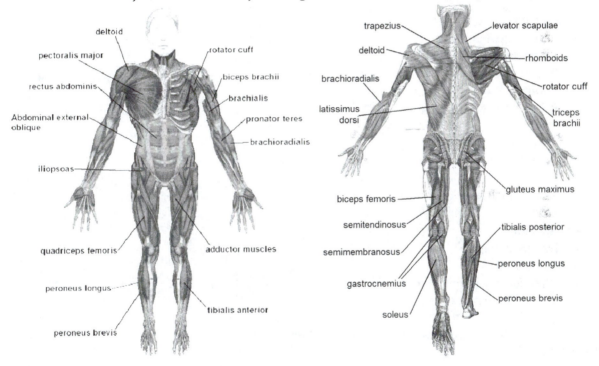

Attachment sites
- Sternocleidomastoid – Extends from sternum and clavicle to the mastoid process.
- Sternohyoid – Extends from sternum to hyoid bone.

Mastication muscles

The muscles of mastication (chewing) are inserted into the mandible, and are innervated by the motor root of V3:
- Temporalis – Closes jaw.
- Masseter – Closes jaw.

- Medial (Internal) pterygoid – Closes jaw and moves jaw from side to side (opposite).
- Lateral (External) pterygoid – Opens, protrudes, and moves jaw from side to side (opposite).

The pterygoid muscles are so named because they arise from the medial and lateral sides of the lateral pterygoid plate of the sphenoid bone. The lateral pterygoid muscle can open the jaw because it inserts into the neck of the mandible, and into the articular disc. Upon contraction, it pulls the head of the mandible anteriorly, causing it to hinge on the articular disc in such a way that the jaw opens. Alternating action of the pterygoids on both sides can move the jaw from side to side. Thus, with proper synchronization, these muscles produce the grinding movements of chewing. The buccinator, although a muscle of facial expression (innervated by VII), aids in maintaining the position of food within the oral cavity during chewing. The temporo-mandibular joint is a double synovial joint with an intervening disc. It has two functions: the upper part functions as a gliding joint, and the lower part functions as a hinge joint. This joint is frequently damaged when the teeth are misaligned.

Borders of the abdomen

The following are the borders of the abdomen:
- Superior – The diaphram.
- Inferior – Continuous with the pelvis.
- Anterior – The lower part of the thoracic cage superiorly, as well as the musculature of anterior abdominal wall.
- Posterior – The lumbar vertebrae and intervertebral discs, the 12th rib, the quadratus lumborum muscles, the psoas, and the iliac crest.

Hesselbach's triangle

The boundaries of Hesselbach's triangle are as follows:
- Lateral edge of the rectus abdominus.
- Inferior epigastric vessels.
- Inguinal ligament.

Hernias that occur within the triangle are said to be direct, while hernias that occur lateral to the triangle borders are said to be indirect.

Umbilical, diaphragmatic hiatal, and femoral hernias

Umbilical hernia
During development, there is a natural herniation of the bowel into the umbilical cord. The bowel returns to the abdominal cavity before birth. However, on occasion, the linea alba fails to fuse properly, resulting in a weak area that is subject to herniation (congenital umbilical hernia). An umbilical hernia in adults occurs when the umbilicus becomes greatly stretched, allowing omentum or intestines to pass through it. This condition is referred to as an acquired umbilical hernia.

Diaphragmatic hiatal hernia
A diaphragmatic hiatal hernia is an abnormal opening in the diaphragm that permits herniation of abdominal viscera into the thoracic cavity. Congenital diaphragmatic hernias are present at birth (hernias of Bochdalek), and are due to a failure of the diaphragm to develop properly. Acquired

diaphragmatic hernias are located at the esophageal hiatus, and usually result in a portion of the stomach protruding into the thoracic cavity.

<u>Femoral hernia</u>
A femoral hernia is a protrusion of abdominal viscera or omenta into the femoral canal lateral to the lacunar ligament. Because of the sharp concave edge of this ligament, these hernias are subject to strangulation (compression that results in a loss of blood supply, which could lead to gangrene).

Groin hernias

The following is the Nyhus classification of groin hernias:
- Type I – Indirect inguinal hernia. The internal inguinal ring is normal (i.e., pediatric hernia).
- Type II – Indirect inguinal hernia. The internal inguinal ring is dilated with the posterior inguinal wall intact.
- Type III:
  - Direct inguinal hernia. Posterior wall defects.
  - Indirect inguinal hernia. The internal ring is dilated with a large medial encroachment on the transversalis fascia of the Hesselbach's triangle (i.e., massive scrotal sliding hernia).
  - Femoral hernia.
- Type IV – Recurrent hernia.
  - Direct.
  - Indirect.
  - Femoral.
  - Other.

Skeletal system

The skeletal system of vertebrates is an *endoskeleton*—that is, it is within the body—as compared to an *exoskeleton*, which is characteristic of arthropods. The human skeletal system provides the following:
- Support.
- Protection of vital organs.
- Sites for muscle attachment.
- Storage site of body calcium and phosphates.
- Sites for blood cell formation.

The *human skeleton* consists of bone and cartilage. The bones form the main rigid structure of the skeleton. The human skeleton consists of about 206 bones, some of which are fused while others are joined together at sites that permit various degrees of movement. The sites of junction, or articulation, whether movable or immovable, are known as *joints*. The human skeleton is divided into an *axial skeleton* and an *appendicular skeleton*.

Adult human skeleton

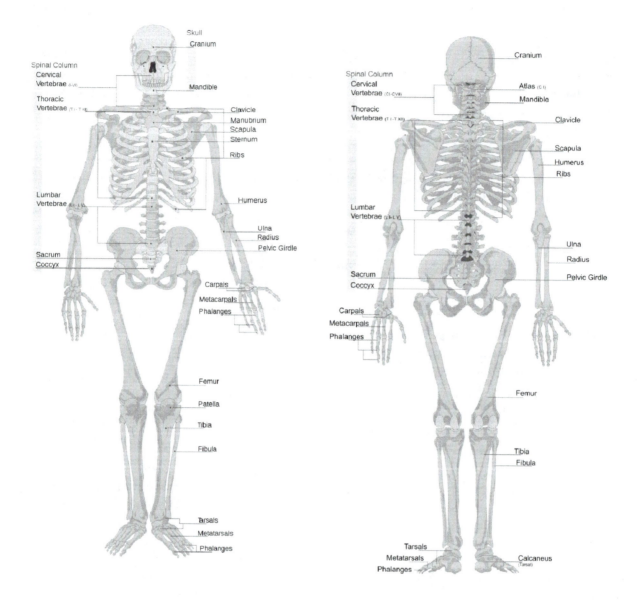

Axial skeleton

The axial skeleton consists of 80 bones forming the trunk (spine and thorax) and skull.

Vertebral column

The main trunk of the body is supported by the spine, or vertebral column, which is composed of 26 bones, some of which are formed by the fusion of a few bones. The vertebral column from superior to inferior consists of 7 cervical (neck), 12 thoracic and 5 lumbar vertebrae, as well as a sacrum, formed by fusion of 5 sacral vertebrae, and a coccyx, formed by fusion of 4 coccygeal vertebrae.

Ribs and sternum

The axial skeleton also contains 12 pairs of *ribs* attached posterior to the thoracic vertebrae and anterior either directly or via cartilage to the *sternum* (breastbone). The ribs and sternum form the *thoracic cage*, which protects the heart and lungs. Seven pairs of ribs articulate with the sternum (*fixed ribs*) directly, and three do so via cartilage; the two most inferior pairs do not attach anteriorly and are referred to as *floating ribs*.

Skull

The skull consists of 22 bones fused together to form a rigid structure which houses and protects organs such as the brain, auditory apparatus and eyes. The bones of the skull form the *face* and *cranium* (brain case), and consist of 6 single bones (*occipital, frontal, ethmoid, sphenoid, vomer* and *mandible*) and 8 paired bones (*parietal, temporal, maxillary, palatine, zygomatic, lacrimal, inferior concha* and *nasal*). The *lower jaw* or *mandible* is the only movable bone of the skull (head); it articulates with the temporal bones.

Other parts

Other bones considered part of the axial skeleton are the *middle ear bones* (*ossicles*) and the small U-shaped *hyoid bone* that is suspended in a portion of the neck by muscles and ligaments.

Appendicular skeleton

The *appendicular skeleton* forms the major internal support of the appendages—the *upper* and *lower extremities* (limbs).

Pectoral girdle and upper extremities

The arms are attached to and suspended from the axial skeleton via the *shoulder* (*pectoral*) *girdle*. The latter is composed of two *clavicles* (*collarbones)* and two *scapulae* (*shoulder blades*). The clavicles articulate with the sternum; the two *sternoclavicular joints* are the only sites of articulation between the trunk and upper extremity. Each upper limb from distal to proximal (closest to the body) consists of hand, wrist, forearm and arm (upper arm). The *hand* consists of 5 *digits* (fingers) and 5 *metacarpal* bones. Each digit is composed of three bones called *phalanges*, except for the thumb, which has only two bones.

Pelvic girdle and lower extremities

The lower *extremities*, or legs, are attached to the axial skeleton via the *pelvic* or *hip girdle*. Each of the two coxal, or *hip bones* comprising the pelvic girdle is formed by the fusion of three bones— *illium, pubis,* and *ischium*. The coxal bones attach the lower limbs to the trunk by articulating with the sacrum.

The Human Skeletal System	
Part of the Skeleton	**Number of Bones**
Axial Skeleton	80
Skull	22
Ossicles (malleus, incus and stapes)	6
Vertebral column	26
Ribs	24
Sternum	1
Hyoid	1
Appendicular Skeleton	
Upper extremities	126
Lower extremities	64
	62

Bone

Bone is a specialized type of connective tissue consisting of cells (*osteocytes*) embedded in a calcified matrix, which gives bone its characteristic hard and rigid nature. Bones are encased by a *periosteum*, which is a connective tissue sheath. All bone has a central marrow cavity. *Bone marrow* fills the marrow cavity or smaller marrow spaces, depending on the type of bone. There are two types of bone in the skeleton: *compact bone* and *spongy* (cancellous) bone. Compact bone lies within the periosteum, forms the outer region of bones, and appears dense due to its compact organization. The living osteocytes and calcified matrix are arranged in layers, or *lamellae*. Lamellae may be circularly arranged surrounding a central canal, the *Haversian canal*, which contains small blood vessels. Spongy bone consists of *bars, spicules* or *trabeculae*, which forms a lattice meshwork. Spongy bone is found at the ends of long bones and the inner layer of flat, irregular and short bones. The trabeculae consist of osteocytes embedded in calcified matrix, which in definitive bone has a lamellar nature. The spaces between the trabeculae contain bone marrow.

Bone cells
The cells of bone are osteocytes, osteoblasts, and osteoclasts:
- Osteocytes are found singly in *lacunae* (spaces) within the calcified matrix and communicate with each other via small canals in the bone known as *canaliculi*. The latter contain osteocyte cell processes. The osteocytes in compact and spongy bone are similar in structure and function.
- Osteoblasts are cells that form bone matrix, surround themselves with it, and thus are transformed into osteocytes. They arise from undifferentiated cells, such as mesenchymal cells. They are cuboidal cells that line the trabeculae of immature or developing spongy bone.
- Osteoclasts are cells found during bone development and remodeling. They are multinucleated cells lying in cavities, *Howship's lacunae*, on the surface of the bone tissue being resorbed. Osteoclasts remove the existing calcified matrix releasing the inorganic or organic components.

Bone matrix
Matrix of compact and spongy bone consists of collagenous fibers and ground substance, which constitute the organic component of bone. Matrix also consists of inorganic material, which is about 65% of the dry weight of bone. Approximately 85% of the inorganic component consists of calcium

phosphate in a crystalline form (hydroxyapatite crystals). Glycoproteins are the main components of the ground substance.

Major types of human bones

Type of Bone	Characteristics	Examples
Long bones	Width less than length.	Humerus, radius, ulna, femur, and tibia.
Short bones	Length and width close to equal in size.	Carpal and tarsal bones.
Flat bones	Thin, flat shape.	Scapulae, ribs, sternum, and bones of cranium (occipital, frontal, parietal).
Irregular bones	Multifaceted shape.	Vertebrae, sphenoid, and ethmoid.
Sesamoid	Small bones located in tendons of muscles.	---------

Joints

The bones of the skeleton articulate with each other at *joints*, which are variable in structure and function. Some joints are immovable, such as the *sutures* between the bones of the cranium. Others are *slightly movable joints*; examples are the *intervertebral joints* and the *pubic symphysis* (joint between the two pubic bones of the coxal bones).

Types of joints

Joint Type	Characteristic	Example
Ball and socket	Permits all types of movement (abduction, adduction, flexion, extension, and circumduction); it is considered a universal joint.	Hips and shoulder joints.
Hinge (ginglymus)	Permits motion in one plane only.	Elbow and knee, inter-phalangeal joints.
Rotating or pivot	Rotation is only motion permitted.	Radius and ulna, atlas and axis (first and second cervical vertebrae).
Plane or gliding	Permits sliding motion.	Between tarsal bones and carpal bones.
Condylar (condyloid)	Permits motion in two planes that are at right angles to each other (rotation is not possible).	Metacarpophalangeal joints, temporomandib-ular.

Adjacent bones at a joint are connected by fibrous connective tissue bands known as *ligaments*. They are strong bands that support the joint and may also act to limit the degree of motion occurring at a joint.

Respiratory System

Respiratory system

The respiratory system is composed of a conduit for air and an air-blood interface for gaseous exchange in the alveoli of the lungs. Respiration refers to the gaseous exchanges that occur between the body and the environment.

Lungs

The two lungs, which contain all the components of the bronchial tree beyond the primary bronchi, occupy most of the space in the thoracic cavity. The lungs are soft and spongy because they are mostly air spaces surrounded by the alveolar cells and elastic connective tissue. The only point of attachment for each lung is at the hilum, or root, on the medial side. This is where the bronchi, blood vessels, lymphatics, and nerves enter the lungs. The right lung is shorter, broader, and has a greater volume than the left lung. It is divided into three lobes, and each lobe is supplied by one of the secondary bronchi. The left lung is longer and narrower than the right lung. It has an indentation, called the cardiac notch, on its medial surface for the apex of the heart. The left lung has two lobes. Each lung is enclosed by a double-layered serous membrane, called the pleura. The visceral pleura is firmly attached to the surface of the lung. At the hilum, the visceral pleura is continuous with the parietal pleura that lines the wall of the thorax. The small space between the visceral and parietal pleurae is the pleural cavity.

Respiratory bronchioles

Respiratory bronchioles are similar in construction to terminal bronchioles, except that the walls are periodically interrupted by alveoli, which are capable of gas exchange. When the proportion of interspersed alveoli increases to the degree where they occupy the majority of the surface of the airway, the passages are called alveolar ducts. Alveolar ducts end in clusters of alveoli, called alveolar sacs. The alveolus can be considered as the unit of gas exchange. Its walls are composed of two epithelial cell types: type-I and type-II pneumonocytes.

Type-I and Type-II pneumonocytes

Type-I Pneumonocytes are squamous pulmonary epithelial cells that form about 95% of the alveolar surface. They are extremely thin, and form part of the blood-air interface, where the gasses diffuse through the cell. Type-II Pneumocytes are cuboidal, and are generally located at the junctions between alveoli. They secrete phospholipid-rich pulmonary surfactant. Small numbers of sensory brush cells, fibroblasts, and macrophages are also present in the interstitial spaces. Alveoli are in intimate contact with capillaries of the pulmonary vasculature.

Gas exchange in the alveoli

Gas exchange takes place only in the alveoli and not in the tracheobronchial tree. The diffusion pathway for alveolar gas may be listed as follows:
- Surfactant (lowers surface tension)
- Alveolar epithelium
- Interstitium (fused basement membranes)

- Capillary endothelium (epithelium)
- Plasma
- Red blood cells

Oxygen transport

Oxygen is transported mainly in the form of oxyhemoglobin. The O_2 Content of Blood (OCB) can be calculated using the following equation:

$$OCB = (15\text{ g Hb}/100\text{ ml Blood}) \times (1.36\text{ ml }O_2/\text{g Hb}) \times (O_2\text{ Saturation Factor }(\%)) \times (0.0032\text{ p}O_2\text{ (torr)})$$

Four factors affect the affinity of hemoglobin for oxygen:
- pH
- Temperature
- Concentration of 2,3-diphosphoglycerate (DPG)
- Carbon dioxide

Carbon dioxide transport

While some carbon dioxide remains in plasma, most diffuses into red blood cells. Bicarbonate ions that are produced in the red blood cells diffuse into the plasma because of the concentration gradient.

Chemical regulation of respiration

The chemical stimulants of physiological importance that affect respiration are as follows:
- Increased arterial pCO_2 (hypercapnia).
- Decreased arterial pO_2 (hypoxia).
- An increased arterial hydrogen-ion concentration (acidosis).

V/Q ratio

The V/Q ratio expresses the balance between alveolar ventilation and capillary blood flow. When ventilation matches blood flow, carbon dioxide is eliminated, and the blood becomes fully saturated with oxygen. In the normal lungs, gravitational forces affect the V/Q ratio; when a person stands, the V/Q ratio is 3 in the apex of the lung, and 0.6 in the base. In the overall lung, the V/Q ratio is assumed to be ideal, and equals 1. When capillary blood flow is in excess of ventilation, the V/Q ratio is less than 1, and arterial hypoxemia results. When V/Q mismatch worsens, the minute ventilation increases, which produces either low or normal arterial pCO_2. The hypoxemia that is caused by low V/Q areas is responsive to supplemental oxygen administration. The more severe the V/Q imbalance, the higher the concentration of inspired oxygen that is needed to raise the arterial pO_2. In the extreme case, when V/Q equals 0, pulmonary blood flow does not participate in gas exchange because the perfused lung unit receives no ventilation. This is referred to as intrapulmonary shunting, and is calculated by comparing the oxygen content in arterial blood, mixed venous blood, and pulmonary capillary blood.

Mnemonic: "FEV ONE"
F – Fibrosing mediastinitis, E – Effusion, V – Vasculitis, O – One pulmonary artery (or hypoplasia), N – Neoplasm, E – Embolism.

Contribution of respiration to pH regulation

The respiratory system functions as a physiological buffer, which acts rapidly and keeps pH levels from changing too much, until the slowly responding kidneys can eliminate the imbalance. The respiratory system can do this because it can excrete the volatile acid CO_2. Increased CO_2 production by metabolizing tissues is detected by chemoreceptors, which drive the respiratory system to match CO_2 exhalation to the rate of production. The pH change brought about by the change in pCO_2 also affects rate of alveolar ventilation. If pH falls below 7.4, ventilation increases. Alternatively, if pH rises above 7.4, ventilation decreases. Increased [H^+] stimulates the respiratory center to increase ventilation. This results in a decrease in [CO_2], and therefore decreases [H^+]. Alveolar ventilation rates then decrease again. The opposite occurs with decreased [H^+], which will stimulate the respiratory center to decrease ventilation. In this way the respiratory system returns pH in the right direction towards normal. Respiratory pH regulation is 50-75% effective. It cannot return pH all the way back to normal when a disturbance outside of the respiratory system alters the pH.

Anatomic dead space and physiologic dead space

Anatomic dead space is the total volume of the conducting airways, from the nose or mouth down to the level of the terminal bronchioles, and averages about 150 mL in humans. The anatomic dead space fills with inspired air at the end of each inspiration, but this air is exhaled unchanged. Thus, assuming a normal tidal volume of 500 mL, about 30% of this air is "wasted" in the sense that it does not participate in gas exchange. Physiologic dead space includes all of the non-respiratory parts of the bronchial tree that are included in anatomic dead space, but also factors in alveoli, which are well ventilated, but poorly perfused, and are therefore less efficient at exchanging gas with the blood. Because atmospheric pCO_2 is practically zero, all of the CO_2 that is expired in a breath can be assumed to come from the communicating alveoli, and none from the dead space. By measuring the pCO_2 in the communicating alveoli (which is the same as that in the arterial blood), and the pCO_2 in the expired air, one can use the Bohr equation to compute the "diluting", non-CO_2-containing volume, which is, in other words, the physiologic dead space.

Bohr equation for physiologic dead space

$$\frac{V_D}{V_T} = \frac{(P_{ACO_2} - P_{ECO_2})}{P_{ACO_2}}$$

Where:

V_D = Dead space.

V_T = Tidal volume.

P_{ACO_2} = Arterial partial pressure of CO_2.

P_{ECO_2} = Expiratory partial pressure of CO_2.

Removal of inhaled products

Large particles are filtered by hairs and mucous material in the nose and respiratory tract. Air is also warmed and humidified.

Diaphragm

The diaphragm is a dome-shaped, musculo-fibrous septum that separates the thorax from the abdomen. Its peripheral part consists of muscular fibers that originate from the circumference of the inferior aperture of the thorax, and converge to be inserted into a central tendon. The muscle fibers may be grouped into three parts, according to their origins: the sternal, the costal, and the lumbar. The sternal part arises by two muscular slips from the dorsum of the xiphoid process. The costal part arises from the inner surfaces of the last 6 ribs. And, the lumbar part arises from the medial and lateral arcuate ligaments (lumbo-costal arches), and from crura. The medial and lateral arcuate ligaments are thickenings of transversalis fascia on the psoas and quadratus lumborum muscles. The lateral arcuate ligament forms the lateral lumbocostal arch. The crura are tendinous at their origins, and blend in with the anterior longitudinal ligament of the vertebral column.
The central tendon of the diaphragm is a strong aponeurosis situated near the center of the muscle, partially blended with the fibrous pericardium. The diaphragm receives both sensory and motor innervation from the C3, C4, and C5 through the phrenic nerve (the C3, C4, and C5 keep the diaphragm alive).

Respiration muscles

Diaphragm
Contraction causes descent of the central tendon. This decreases intrathoracic pressure and increases the volume of the thoracic cavity, resulting in air being drawn into the lungs.

Accessory muscles used in forced respiration
- Scalenus Muscles
- Sternocleidomastoid
- Levator Costarum
- Serratus Inferior, Posterior and Superior
- Quadratus Lumborum
- Intercostals: External, Internal, and Innermost

Inspiration and expiration

During inspiration the thoracic cavity expands, its volume increases, and air rushes into the respiratory tract due to the creation of negative pressure; the musculature involved is the diaphragm. Normal expiration is passive and involves no great muscular contraction.

Positive- and negative-pressure breathing

Gases flow from regions of higher pressure to those of lower pressure. For inspiration to occur, the alveolar gas pressure must be less than the atmospheric pressure. Normal breathing is a form of negative-pressure breathing.

Neuronal control and integration of breathing

Normal spontaneous breathing is under control of motor neurons (primarily the phrenic nerves), which innervate the respiratory muscles. Brain impulses regulate and modulate the process. Voluntary activity originates in the cerebral cortex, while automatic (autonomic) control originates in the pons and medulla of the brain.

Skin System

Skin

The skin and the specialized organs that are derived from the skin (i.e., hair, nails and glands) form the integumentary system.

Functions

The skin functions by surfacing the body and thus protecting it from dehydration, as well as from damage by the elements in the external environment. The skin also helps to maintain normal bodily activities.

Structure

Skin consists of the *epidermis* and the *dermis* (*corium*). Deep to the dermis, and therefore the skin, is the *hypodermis*, which is also known as the *subcutaneous* or superficial connective tissue of the body.

The epidermis is derived from the ectoderm and is composed of a keratinized stratified squamous epithelium. *Thick skin* denotes skin with a thicker epidermis, which contains more cell layers when compared to *thin skin*. The epidermis ranges in thickness from 0.07 millimeter to 1.4 millimeters. In addition, the epidermis consists of specific cell layers, as follows: Stratum basale or germinativum, Stratum spinosum, Stratum granulosum, Stratum lucidum, and Stratum corneum.

Hair

Hairs are long, filamentous keratinized structures that are derived from the epidermis of the skin. The structure of hair consists of a *shaft* and a *root*. The hair follicle consists of two sheathes: the *epithelial root sheath* and the *connective tissue root sheath*. Growth of a hair depends on the viability of the epidermal cells of the hair matrix, which lie adjacent to the dermal papilla in the hair bulb. The matrix cells abutting the dermal papilla proliferate and give rise to cells that move upward to become part of the specific layers of the hair root and the inner epithelial root sheath. Hairs are oriented at a slight angle to the skin surface, and are associated with *arrector pili muscles*. These smooth muscle bundles extend from the dermal root sheath to a dermal papilla. Contraction results in the hairs standing up and the skin surrounding the hair rising up.

Nails

Nails are translucent plates of keratinized epithelial cells on the dorsal surface of distal phalanges of fingers and toes.

Glands

Glands are specialized organs that are derived from the skin. There are two basic types of glands: sebaceous and sweat. Sebaceous glands are *simple, branched alveolar (acinar) glands* with a *holocrine* mode of secretion. Sweat is a watery fluid containing ammonia, urea, uric acid and sodium chloride. There are two types of sweat glands: eccrine and apocrine. The eccrine sweat glands are *simple, coiled tubular glands* with a *merocrine* mode of secretion. The apocrine sweat glands are *very large glands* that are thought to have a *merocrine* mode of secretion.

Reproductive System and Development

Reproductive organs

Male
- Seminiferous tubules of the testes
- Epididymis
- Vas deferens
- Seminal vesicles
- Prostate
- Prostatic urethra
- Membranous urethra
- Penile urethra
- Glans penis

Female
- Ovaries
- Oviduct
- Uterus
- Vagina
- The breasts (accessory organs)

Epididymis, vas deferens, and urethra

Epididymis
The epididymis lies in the scrotum, and is about 3.8-cm long, while the duct is actually about 6-meters long. The epididymis is subdivided into a head, a body, and a tail, which become surrounded by an increasingly thick layer of smooth muscle. The tail of the epididymis is continuous with the vas deferens. The duct is lined by a pseudostratified epithelium, in which the cells have non-motile stereocilia. The epididymis stores spermatozoa, which finish their maturation by acquiring motility here.

Vas deferens and ejaculatory duct
The vas deferens is a highly muscular tube that begins at the epididymis and runs into the pelvic cavity, through the inguinal canal. A total of 45-cm long, it is easily palpable in the spermatic cord, increasing the ease of vasectomy, an operation in which the vas deferens is cut, rendering the patient infertile. At its termination at the prostate, it widens a bit, forming a portion called the ampulla. At this point, it merges with the duct of the seminal vesicle to form the ejaculatory duct, which traverses the prostate to end in the urethra.

Urethra
The urethra is subdivided into prostatic, membranous, and penile urethral portions. The prostatic portion is the first part that traverses the prostate, and receives the ejaculatory ducts. As the urethra passes through the pelvic diaphragm, it is called the membranous part, which then enters the penis, forming the penile portion.

Leydig and Sertoli cells

Leydig Cells are the target cells for luteinizing hormone (LH), and increase their secretion of testosterone in response. Some of this testosterone remains locally to affect Sertoli cells, while most of it is released into the blood stream, where it circulates to affect other organs of the male reproductive system, as well as other tissues and organs. Sertoli Cells are the target cells for follicles-stimulating hormone (FSH), and increase their functions in support of spermatogenesis in response. The combination of testosterone from Leydig cells and FSH results in a number of changes, such as an increase in the amount of androgen binding protein (ABP) and an increase in metabolic support for spermatocytes. ABP chaperones testosterone to developing spermatocytes and throughout the male reproductive tract.

Production and maturation of sperm

The following are the stages in sperm production from germ cells:
- Meiosis to produce haploid cells.
- Loss of most of the cytoplasm.
- Development of the flagellum.
- Formation of the acrosomal tip, which aids in penetration of the egg.

These events require about 60 days, and occur in the seminiferous tubules, the epididymis, and the vas deferens. Sperm are stored in the vas deferens.

Sperm maturation requires a temperature below core body temperature. This is possible because the testes are suspended in a scrotum that hangs outside of the main body cavity, keeping their temperature about 3 degrees Celsius cooler than the core body temperature. In addition, the scrotum has a muscular wall that contracts in cold weather to keep temperature from getting too low. Since a lower temperature is required for sperm development, raising the temperature will reduce sperm production.

Erection

Normally the penis is flaccid because the venous spaces in erectile tissues are empty as a result of constriction of the arteries supplying these spaces. As a result, blood is shunted via arteriovenous channels, thereby bypassing these regions. Upon sexual excitement, mediated by the parasympathetic nervous system, these arteries dilate, allowing the venous spaces to fill with blood, giving rise to an increase in pressure, and an enlargement of the penis, called an erection. This vasodilation is mediated by the release of nitric oxide (NO), a potent vasodilator. The parasympathetic nerves also stimulate the secretions of the bulbourethral glands, which produce mucus that not only neutralizes any acidic urine that may be present, but also results in the release of this mucus from the penis, aiding in lubrication. A variety of inputs, including both sensory and mental, can lead to the stimulation of vasodilatory parasympathetic nerves, leading to erection. Failure to achieve an erection is called impotence, which can result from a variety of factors, ranging from vascular to nerve, psychological, or even temporary factors, such as alcohol or certain drugs.

Uterus

The following are the layers of the uterus:
- Endometrium – The lining of the mucosa.
- Myometrium – Consists of several thick smooth muscle layers that are capable of great enlargement during pregnancy.
- Epimetrium – The outer peritoneal covering (visceral peritoneum).

The following are the parts of the uterus:
- Fundus – The part of the uterus superior to the entrance of the uterine tubes.
- Body – The bulk of the uterus between the fundus and the cervix. It contains most of the uterine cavity.
- Isthmus – A slight constriction between the body and the cervix.
- Cervix – The inferior neck of the uterus that protrudes into the vagina. It contains the cervical canal that connects the uterine cavity with the vaginal canal. The lower opening of the cervical canal is the cervical os. The cervix may be divided into supravaginal and vaginal portions.

Uterine tube

- Infundibulum – The lateral, expanded portion of the uterine tube that has many small finger-like projections, called fimbriae, which are closely apposed to the ovary. It also contains an ostium that opens into the peritoneal cavity. Through the ostium, the ovum enters the uterine tube. This opening is also clinically important since it provides a possible route of infection from the vagina into the peritoneal cavity, and it affords the potential for abnormal fertilization of an ovum and a subsequent ectopic (outside of the uterus) pregnancy in the abdominal cavity.
- Ampulla – The intermediate portion of the tube.
- Isthmus – The medial, constricted portion of the tube.
- Intramural (intrauterine) – The portion located in the wall of the uterus. It is continuous with the uterine cavity.

Blood supply of the ovaries

The ovarian artery originates from the abdominal aorta near the L2 vertebral level, and anastomoses with the uterine artery in the broad ligament. The ovarian veins drain from the pampiniform plexus of the ovary. The right ovarian vein drains directly into the inferior vena cava, while the left drains into the left renal vein. The ovaries produce eggs and secrete sex hormones (estrogen and progesterone). They are attached to the posterior aspect of the broad ligament of the uterus. In nulliparous females (females who have never borne children), they are usually located in the ovarian fossae, which are shallow depressions that are bounded by the external iliac vessels, the obliterated umbilical arteries, and the ureters. Alternatively, in parous females (females who have borne children), their position varies.

Placental barrier and the role of relaxin

The placental barrier between maternal and fetal blood is similar in structure to the respiratory membrane in the lungs, and does not exclude alcohol, nicotine, or toxins from crossing into the fetal blood circulation. With the exception of a rare rupturing of the capillary walls, which may occur at delivery, fetal and maternal blood do not mix. The placenta also functions as an endocrine organ, producing steroid and peptide hormones, as well as prostaglandins, which play an important role in the onset of labor. By the end of the eighth week, the placenta takes over the production of progesterone and estrogen from the corpus luteum. Other hormones that are produced by the placenta include human chorionic gonadotropin, insulin-like growth factors I and II, placental lactogen, prolactin, oxytocin, and relaxin. The hormone relaxin prepares the cervix and pelvic ligaments for birth by inducing them to "relax" and become more pliable for delivery, dilating the cervix to about 10 cm. Oftentimes, labor can also be induced by physically stretching the cervix.

Breast

The anatomy of the breast is as follows:
- Cooper's ligaments – Suspensory ligaments, or connective tissue, that connects the skin to the underlying fat.
- Lactiferous sinuses – Place where the milk is stored; deep to the areola; the dilated portion of the lactiferous ducts.
- Lactiferous ducts – The ducts into which milk is secreted; directly deep to the nipple.
- Areola – Darkened region around the nipple; appears lighter in women who have not borne a child; contains sebaceous glands that secrete protective substances (not milk) during pregnancy.
- Mammary glands – Lobules of glandular tissue that arise from the lactiferous ducts; any deep tissue that is not fatty is glandular tissue.

Menstrual cycle

The phases of the menstrual cycle are as follows:
- Day 1 – The menstrual cycle begins (bleeding starts).
- Day 5 – Sperm can live for 7 days in the female.
- Day 12-16 – A mature egg is released from an ovary into the fallopian tubes.
- Day 16-21 – The egg moves towards the uterus. The egg must be fertilized during this time period or menstruation will result.
- Day 24 – The endometrial lining deteriorates.
- Day 28 – The cycle ends, and bleeding begins again with Day 1.

Embryogenesis

The following are weeks 2 - 40 of fetal development:
- Week 2 – Conception is the moment when the sperm penetrates the ovum. Once fertilized, the ovum is called a zygote, until it reaches the uterus 3 to 4 days later. A bilaminar disk forms during week 2.
- Week 4 – The embryo may float freely in the uterus for about 48 hours before implantation. Upon implantation, complex connections between the mother and the embryo develop in order to form the placenta. The neural plate and the primitive streak form from 3 to 8 weeks. In addition, the heart starts to beat during week 4.
- Week 6 – The embryo is about 1/5 of an inch in length. The tiny heart is beating. The head, mouth, liver, and intestines begin to take shape. And, brain waves are produced by week 6.

- Week 10 – The embryo is now about one inch in length. The limbs, hands, feet, fingers, toes, and facial features become apparent. The nervous system is responsive, and many of the internal organs begin to function. In addition, male or female characteristics begin to appear.
- Week 14 – The fetus is now three-inches long, and weighs almost an ounce. The muscles begin to develop, and eyelids, fingernails, toenails, and sex organs form. Spontaneous movements can be observed.
- Week 18 – The fetus is now about five-inches long. The fetus blinks, grasps, and moves its mouth. Hair grows on the head and body.
- Week 22 – The fetus now weighs approximately half a pound, and spans about 10-inches from head-to-toe. Sweat glands develop, and the external skin has turned from transparent to opaque.
- Week 26 – The fetus can now inhale, exhale, and even cry. Eyes have completely formed, and the tongue has developed taste buds. Under intensive medical care, the fetus has over a 50% chance of survival outside of the womb.
- Week 30 – The fetus is usually capable of living outside of the womb, and would be considered premature at birth.
- Week 40 – This marks the end of the normal gestational period. The child is now ready to live outside of its mother's womb.

Gastrulation

Gastrulation is a dramatic restructuring of the animal embryo during the gastrula phase. Gastrulation varies in different phyla. The following description concerns the gastrulation of triploblasts, or animals with three embryonic germ layers. At the beginning of gastrulation, the embryo is hollow, with an animal pole and a vegetal pole. The cells of the vegetal pole begin to divide and bud inwards, forming a hollow called the archenteron (literally, primitive gut) on the outside surface of the gastrula. Some of the cells of the vegetal pole detach and become mesenchymal cells. The mesenchymal cells divide rapidly, migrate to different parts of the blastocoel, and form filopodia (extensions of the cellular membrane) that help to pull the tip of the archenteron towards the animal pole. Once the archenteron reaches the animal pole, a perforation forms, and the archenteron becomes a digestive tract, passing all the way through the embryo. The three embryonic germ layers have now formed. The endoderm, consisting of the archenteron, will develop into the digestive tract. The ectoderm, consisting of the cells on the outside of the gastrula that played little part in gastrulation, will develop into the skin and the central nervous system.

Pectinate line

The pectinate line is the division of the hindgut anal canal (endoderm) and the ectoderm by an invagination of the skin. The upper anal canal, superior to the pectinate line, is endodermal hindgut. The lower anal canal, inferior to the pectinate line, is ectoderm. They are both supplied by different vessels, nerves, etc. The pectinate line can be identified by looking for the anal columns, longitudinal folds of mucosa that demarcate the upper anal canal.

Derivatives of the ectoderm, mesoderm, endoderm, and notochord

The ectoderm will ultimately form:
- Surface Ectoderm – the adenohypophysis and epithelial components of the skin.
- Neuroectoderm – The brain and spinal cord, CNS neurons, and the pineal gland.

- Neural crest – The autonomic nervous system, Schwann cells, and the pia mater.
- The sensory organs in the body and special sensory organs in the head.

The mesoderm will form:
- Most of the skeleton.
- The heart and blood vessels.
- The kidneys.
- The linings of internal body cavities.
- The spleen and adrenal cortices.

The endoderm will form the gut tube epithelium and its derivatives.

The notochord will form the vertebral column.

Key fetal structures that turn into adult structures

Fetal Structure	Adult Structure
Umbilical Arteries	Median Umbilical Ligament
Notochord	Nucleus Pulposes
Ductus Arteriosus	Ligamentum Arteriosum
Foramen Ovale	Fossa Ovalis
Allantois, Urachus	Median Umbilical Ligament
Ductus Venosus	Ligamentum Venosum
Umbilical Vein	Ligamentum Teres Hepatis

Umbilical cord

The umbilical cord is the flexible, cord-like structure that connects a fetus, at the abdomen, to the placenta. It contains two umbilical arteries and one vein that transport nourishment to the fetus, and remove its wastes. The length of the umbilical cord varies from no cord (achordia) to 300 cm, with diameters of up to 3 cm. Umbilical cords are helical in nature, with as many as 380 helices. An average umbilical cord is 55-centimeters long, with a diameter of 1-2 cm and 11 helices to the fetal left. 6% of cords are shorter than 35 cm, and 94% of cords are shorter than 80 cm. Causes of differences in cord length are unknown. Cords with a single umbilical artery occur in fewer than 1% of singletons, and 5% of cases with at least one twin. The incidence of single umbilical artery can be underestimated with gross examination of the cord, especially if the portion close to the placenta is examined, because the arteries often fuse close to the placenta. Single umbilical arteries are found twice as often in Caucasian women than in African and Japanese women. Diabetes increases the risk significantly. Two-vessel cords are also found more frequently in fetuses aborted spontaneously. And, the male-to-female ratio is 0.85:1. Single umbilical artery is believed to be caused by atrophy of a previously normal artery, presence of the original artery of the body stalk, or agenesis of one of the umbilical arteries.

Blood flow through the fetal heart

Blood from the mother enters the fetus through the vein in the umbilical cord. It goes first to the liver, and splits into three branches. The blood then reaches the inferior vena cava, a major vein that is connected to the heart. Blood enters the heart through the right atrium, the chamber on the upper right side of the heart. Most of the blood flows to the left side through a special fetal opening between the left and right atria, which is called the foramen ovale. Blood then passes into the left ventricle (lower chamber of the heart), and then to the aorta (the large artery that exits from the heart). After exiting the heart through the aorta, the blood is circulated to the head and upper extremities. The blood then returns to the right atrium of the heart via the superior vena cava. About one-third of the blood that enters the right atrium does not flow through the foramen ovale, but instead stays in the right side of the heart, and eventually flows into the pulmonary artery. Since the placenta does the work of exchanging oxygen (O_2) and carbon dioxide (CO_2) through the mother's circulation, the fetal lungs are not used for breathing. Thus, instead of circulating the blood to the lungs, the fetal circulation shunts (bypasses) most of the blood away from the lungs.

Heart development

The heart begins development by the fusion of two separate heart tubes into a single heart tube. As this tube elongates, it develops dilations and constrictions, which will become parts of the atria and ventricles of the adult heart. The primitive heart initially has only a single atrium and ventricle. The atria become distinct from the ventricles by development of endocardial cushions and atrioventricular valves. Endocardial cushions are swellings that grow out from the dorsal and ventral walls of the single heart tube in the area that marks the separation of the tube into atrium and ventricle. The valves develop by a very complicated process in the region of these endocardial cushions. Separation of the single atrium into right and left atria involves the development of partitions called septa. The 1st septum, called the septum primum, grows down from the wall of the common atrium, and ultimately fuses with the endocardial cushion, separating the primitive atrium into a right and left side. For a very brief time before it fuses, there is a small opening between the two chambers, called the foramen (ostium) primum. Before this foramen closes, perforations occur higher up on septum primum that join to form another opening, called the foramen (ostium) secundum. A 2nd septum, called the septum secundum, grows down on the right side of the 1st septum, and covers the foramen secundum.

Blood pressure before and after birth

Before birth, blood pressure is greater in the right atrium than in the left, and the blood passes freely from the right atrium to the left atrium through the foramen ovale. However, after birth, because of an increase in pressure in the left atrium, the septum primum is forced against the foramen ovale, fuses to the septum secundum, and effectively prevents blood from passing between the two chambers. Division of the single ventricle, into right and left ventricles, occurs when the muscular interventricular septum grows up from the floor of the ventricle, and fuses with the endocardial cushions that mark the boundary between atria and ventricles. The membranous part of the interventricular septum marks the site of this fusion, and is the last region of the ventricular wall to close.

Neural tube

The neural tube is the embryonal structure that gives rise to the brain and spinal cord. During gestation, the human neural tube gives rise to three vesicles: the rhombencephalon, the mesencephalon, and the prosencephalon. Formation of the neural tube is the result of an invagination of the ectoderm following gastrulation. This process is induced by signaling molecules that are produced in the notochord and the basal plate. Normally, the closure of the neural tube occurs around the 30th day after fertilization. However, if something interferes, and the tube fails to close properly, a neural tube defect will occur. Among the most common tube defects are anencephaly, encephalocele, and spina bifida. The incidence of a neural tube defect is 2.6 in 1,000 individuals worldwide.

Meckel's diverticulum

A Meckel's diverticulum is a common congenital (present before birth) formation that consists of a small pouch, called a diverticulum, which is located off of the wall of the small intestine. The diverticulum may contain stomach or pancreatic tissue. A Meckel's diverticulum is a remnant of structures within the fetal digestive tract that were not fully reabsorbed before birth. Approximately 2% of the population has a Meckel's diverticulum, but only a few develop symptoms. Symptoms include diverticulitis, or bleeding in the intestine. Symptoms often occur during the first few years of life, but can occur in adults as well. The tests for Meckel's diverticulum include a stool smear for occult blood (stool guaiac), hematocrit, or hemoglobin, and a technetium scan. Surgery to remove the diverticulum is recommended if bleeding develops. In rare cases, the segment of small intestine that contains the diverticulum is surgically removed, and the ends of intestine are sewn back together. Iron replacement may be needed to correct anemia. And, if bleeding is significant, a blood transfusion may be necessary.

Genetics

Mendelian concepts

Gregor Mendel discovered the concept of genetics and the inheritance of traits by carefully analyzing the numerical proportions of hybrid plant species in his garden. He found it essential to work with as great a number of plants as possible in order to overcome chance. His research enabled him to detect three principles of heredity:

Mendel's first law
Mendel's first law is the principle of uniformity. It states that if two plants that differ in just one trait are crossed, the resulting hybrids will be uniform in the chosen trait. This depends upon whether the traits are the uniform feature of either one of the parents' traits (a dominant-recessive pair of characteristics) or whether it is intermediate.

Mendel's second law
Mendel's second law is the principle of segregation. It states that the individuals of the second filial (F2) generation will not be uniform, but that the traits will segregate. Depending upon whether it is a dominant-recessive crossing or an intermediate crossing, the resulting ratios will be 3:1 or 1:2:1. According to this principle, hereditary traits are determined by discrete factors (now called genes) that occur in pairs, one of each pair is inherited from each parent. The concept of independent traits explains how a trait can persist from generation to generation without blending with other traits. It also explains how the trait can seemingly disappear and then reappear in later generations. The principle of segregation was consequently of the utmost importance for understanding both genetics and evolution.

Mendel's law of segregation essentially has three parts:
- Alternative versions of genes account for variations in inherited characteristics. This is the concept of alleles.
- Alleles are different versions of genes that impart the same characteristic. For example, each human has a gene that controls height, but there are variations among these genes in accordance with the specific height the gene "codes" for.
- For each characteristic, an organism inherits two genes, with one derived from each parent. This means that, when somatic cells are produced from two gametes, one allele comes from the mother, and one from the father.

If the two alleles differ, then the dominant allele is fully expressed in the organism's appearance. The other, although inactive, still segregates during gamete production.

Mendel's third law
Mendel's third law is also called the principle of independent assortment. It states that every trait is inherited independently of the others: the two alleles of an organism separate during gamete formation, and randomly reunite during fertilization. This allows for new combinations of genes to arise that did not previously exist, thus ensuring variation. We know today that this principle is only valid in the case of genes that are not coupled; i.e., genes that are not located on the same chromosome.

Ploidy and euploidy

Ploidy indicates the number of copies of the basic number of chromosomes. The basic number of chromosomes in an organism is called the monoploid number (1x). The ploidy of cells can vary within an organism. In humans, most cells are diploid (2x, containing one set of chromosomes from each parent), though sex cells (sperm and oocytes) are haploid (0.5x). In contrast, tetraploidy (4x, four sets of chromosomes), a type of polyploidy, is not uncommon in healthy plant species. Euploidy is a species' normal number of chromosomes per cell. For example, the euploid number of chromosomes in a human cell is 46.

Allele, penetrance, and expressivity

An allele is a particular version of a given DNA sequence, implying more than one possible version or copy. All existing alleles result from a process of evolution, with either gradual or drastic change. There can be more than two possible alleles for a given gene locus, but only two at a time, in a given diploid individual. Multiple alleles can mean many different possible combinations and phenotypes for individuals. Penetrance is the percentage of individuals with a genotype who actually show the trait. If only 80% of people with the genotype actually develop the trait, then you could pass on a trait without showing it, even if the trait is dominant. Expressivity is the degree to which the trait is expressed. For example, a genetic defect causing intellectual disability, such as Fragile X, can result in individuals with a very wide range of intellect, and you cannot predict the degree of expression.

Polygenic traits

The distribution of individuals within a population with different trait values for polygenic (quantitative) traits typically forms a bell-shaped curve. There are three main ways that selection can act on a population, given a distribution of traits such as this:

- Directional selection – The situation in which one extreme form of the trait has highest fitness.
- Stabilizing selection – The situation in which the average form of the trait has higher fitness than does either extreme.
- Disruptive selection – The situation in which both extreme forms of the trait have higher fitness than does the average.

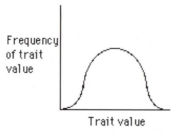

The results of selection on quantitative traits generally make sense: the forms that have highest fitness become most common. As shown, directional selection results in a change in the mean value of the trait toward the form that has the highest fitness. Stabilizing selection results in the loss of the extreme forms of the trait. This means that there is a decrease in genetic variation. Eventually, genetic variation may be lost, as all individuals will have the alleles for the average trait value of the highest fitness. At that point, any phenotypic variation would depend on direct environmental effects rather than on genetic differences among individuals, and the heritability of the trait would be zero, or at least very low. Disruptive selection results in an increase in both extremes, and a loss of intermediate forms.

Over a long period of time, directional selection will result in a shift in the frequency of individuals with different traits until the average form has highest fitness. At this point, the situation becomes one of stabilizing selection, and the extreme forms of the trait will be lost. So, directional selection will eventually lead to a situation where genetic variation will be lost (heritability will become zero) and all individuals will have the alleles for the highest fitness form of the trait.

Autosomal dominant diseases

Autosomal dominant (AD) diseases are those in which both heterozygous and homozygous dominant individuals express the abnormal phenotype. One copy of the mutant gene is sufficient for expression of the abnormal phenotype. In fact, in many AD diseases, the homozygous genotype is incompatible with life. Some examples of AD diseases include familial hypercholesterolemia, Huntington's disease, achondroplasia, and Marfan syndrome.

Several distinct characteristics of AD inheritance include the following:
- Every individual has an affected parent (except in cases of new mutations or incomplete penetrance).
- Males and females are equally likely to inherit the allele and be affected. This is because these alleles are on autosomes, for which each male and female has two copies (in contrast to X-linked diseases).
- The recurrence risk (the probability that a genetic disorder that is present in one patient will recur in another family member) for each child of an affected parent is 50%. For a dominant disorder, only one copy is necessary for development of the disease. Therefore, if one parent is heterozygous for a particular gene, their offspring will either inherit the gene, or they will not, with each outcome equally likely.
- Normal siblings of affected individuals do not pass the trait on to their offspring. If an affected individual's siblings are not affected, they do not carry the mutation and cannot pass it on to their own offspring.

Autosomal recessive diseases

Autosomal recessive (AR) diseases are those in which only individuals whom are homozygous for the mutant allele develop the disease. Those who are heterozygous are phenotypically normal. Some examples of AR diseases include cystic fibrosis, sickle cell anemia, Tay-Sachs, and albinism. Several characteristics of AR diseases include the following:
- Males and females are equally likely to be affected. This is because these are genes on autosomes, of which each male and female has two copies. Sex-linked disorders show different patterns in this respect, since males are XY and females are XX.
- The trait is often found in clusters of siblings, but not in their parents or offspring.
- The more rare a trait is in the general population, the greater the chance that it was from a co-sanguineous mating (inbreeding). If the trait is rare, the probability of two unrelated individuals both carrying the gene, mating, and then having an affected child is very low. If two individuals have a common ancestor, the likelihood that they both carry the same mutated allele is higher than the probability in the general population (assuming that their common ancestor carried the mutation).

- All offspring of an affected person are obligate carriers. Since the affected person is homozygous for the mutated allele, all of their children will inherit one copy of it, and will be carriers of the mutation.

Phenylketonuria

Phenylketonuria (PKU) is an inherited error of metabolism that is caused by a deficiency in the enzyme phenylalanine hydroxylase. Loss of this enzyme results in intellectual disability, organ damage, unusual posture, and can severely compromise pregnancy (in cases of maternal PKU). Classical PKU is an autosomal recessive disorder that is caused by mutations in both alleles of the gene for phenylalanine hydroxylase (PAH), which are found on chromosome 12. In the body, PAH converts the amino acid phenylalanine into tyrosine. Mutations in both copies of the gene for PAH mean that the enzyme is inactive, or is less efficient, and the concentration of phenylalanine in the body can build up to toxic levels.

In some cases, mutations in PAH will result in a phenotypically mild form of PKU, called hyperphenylalanemia. Both diseases are the result of a variety of mutations in the PAH locus. In the cases where a patient is heterozygous for two mutations of PAH (i.e., each copy of the gene has a different mutation), the milder mutation will predominate.

X-linked recessive diseases

X-linked recessive diseases are diseases in which a female must have two copies of the mutant allele in order for the mutant phenotype to develop. Many X-linked recessive disorders are well known, including color blindness, hemophilia, and Duchenne muscular dystrophy. Typical features of X-linked recessive inheritance are as follows:
- They are never passed from father to son.
- Males are much more likely to be affected because they only need one copy of the mutant allele to express the phenotype.
- Affected males get the disease from their mothers, and all of their daughters are obligate carriers because they must inherit the father's X-chromosome, which contains the mutant allele.
- Sons of heterozygous females have a 50% chance of receiving the mutant allele.
- These disorders are typically passed from an affected grandfather to 50% of his grandsons.

Mitochondrial inheritance

Mitochondria are cellular organelles that are involved in energy production and conversion. They have a small amount of their own mitochondrial DNA (mtDNA). Although it is a relatively small proportion of our total DNA, it is still subject to mutation, and several diseases that are associated with mutations in mtDNA have been found, such as exercise intolerance, Leber's optic atrophy, and Kearns-Sayre syndrome. The inheritance patterns of mtDNA are unique because mtDNA is inherited almost entirely maternally. This is because the relatively large ovum has many copies of mitochondrial DNA, but the sperm has very few copies, and most of these are lost during fertilization. Due to this unique feature of mtDNA inheritance, there are a couple constraints on the inheritance patterns of mtDNA disorders:
- All children of affected males will not inherit the disease.
- All children of affected females will inherit it.

DNA mutations

Types of DNA mutations are as follows:
- Point mutation – A simple change in one base of a genetic sequence.
- Frame-shift mutation – A mutation where one or more bases are inserted or deleted, shifting the reading frame of the genetic sequence, and potentially altering or inactivating one or more genes.
- Deletion – A mutation that results in a missing segment of DNA. These may affect only a single gene, or may affect numerous genes.
- Insertion – A mutation that results in the addition of an extra segment of DNA. These can also cause frameshift mutations, and generally result in the production of nonfunctional proteins.
- Inversion – A mutation where an entire section of DNA is reversed. A small inversion may involve only a few bases within a gene, while longer inversions involve large regions of a chromosome containing several genes.
- DNA expression mutation – There are many types of mutations that do not change a protein itself, rather they change where and how much of a protein is made. These types of DNA mutations can result in proteins being made at the wrong time, or in the wrong cell type.
- Silent mutation – The mutation does not alter the peptide sequence.
- Neutral mutation – The mutation codes for a functionally similar amino acid.
- Missense mutation – The mutation codes for a functionally different amino acid.

Analytic methods

Hardy-Weinberg equilibrium
The Hardy-Weinberg equilibrium is the principle that genotype frequencies in a population remain constant unless outside disturbing influences are introduced. In general, if two individuals mate who are heterozygous (i.e., Aa) for a trait, we find the following:
- 25% of their offspring are homozygous for the dominant allele (AA).
- 50% are heterozygous like their parents (Aa).
- 25% are homozygous for the recessive allele (aa), and thus express the recessive phenotype.

Using these principles, the Hardy-Weinberg equilibrium provides us with the following equations to determine the frequencies of particular genotypes:

$A^2 + 2Aa + a^2 = 1$
$A + a = 1$
Where:
A^2 = The fraction of the population that is homozygous for p.
a^2 = The fraction of the population that is homozygous for q.
$2Aa$ = The fraction of the population that is heterozygotes.

Probability
Probability events are possible outcomes of some random processes.
Examples of events:
- You pass 320.
- The genotype of a random individual is Bb.
- The weight of a random individual is less than 150 pounds.

We can define the probability of a particular event, say A, as the fraction of the outcomes in which event A will occur. In written form, we can denote the probability of A by Pr(A) or Prob(A).

For example, when flipping a coin once, the only possible outcomes are heads or tails. If Pr(Heads) is 0.75, then that means that there is a 75% chance that the coin will land on heads. Therefore, Pr(Tails) has to be 0.25, since Pr(Tails) = 1 - Pr(Heads) = 0.25.

Useful rules of probability are as follows:
- Probabilities are between zero (never occur) and one (always occur) – Pr(A) lies between zero and one for all A.
- 2. Probabilities sum to one – The sum of probabilities of all mutually exclusive events is one. For example, if there are n possible outcomes, then Pr(1) + Pr(2) + ... + Pr(n) = 1. Therefore, Pr(1) = 1 - (Pr(2) + ... + Pr(n)).

The AND and OR rules are as follows:
- AND rule – If A and B are independent events (knowledge of one event tells us nothing about the other event), then the probability that BOTH A and B occur is Pr(A and B) = Pr(A) Pr(B). Therefore, probabilities are multiplied with the AND rule.
- OR rule – If A and B are exclusive events (non overlapping), then the probability that EITHER A or B occurs is Pr(A or B) = Pr(A) + Pr(B). Therefore, probabilities are added with the OR rule.

For example, suppose that we are rolling a set of fair dice, and flipping a fair coin. What is the probability of rolling an even number on the dice?

A single roll of a set of fair dice has the possible outcomes of 1, 2, 3, 4, 5, or 6 for each of the die, each with the same probability: 1/6. Rolling an even number means that a 2 OR 4 OR 6 is rolled. These three events (2, 4, 6) are non overlapping, and hence exclusive, so we can use the OR rule, giving Pr(Roll Even) = Pr(2) + Pr(4) + Pr(6) = 3/6 = 1/2.

What is the probability of rolling a 5, and then getting a heads in the coin flip?

The dice roll and coin flip are independent events, as the outcome of one does not influence the outcome of the other. Hence, Pr(Heads AND Roll 5) = Pr(Heads) x Pr(5) = 1/2 x 1/6 = 1/12.

Conditional probability
Conditional probability can be used to compute joint probabilities when A and B are NOT independent (i.e., knowing that A has occurred provides information on whether or not B has occurred). The joint probability of A and B, Pr(A,B), is the product of the probability of B, Pr(B), and the probability of A given B, Pr(A|B). Therefore:

Pr(A,B) = Pr(A|B) Pr(B)
Where:
Pr (A|B) = The conditional probability of A given B = Pr(A,B)/Pr(B).

A and B are said to be independent of one another if Pr(A|B) = Pr(A), so that knowing event B occurred provides us with no information about event A.

An important use for conditional probabilities is to compute the probability of some complex event by conditioning on other events. For example, suppose that event A occurs under one of three other mutually exclusive events, say B, C, and D. Then, $Pr(A) = Pr(A|B) \times Pr(B) + Pr(A|C) \times Pr(C) + Pr(A|D) \times Pr(D)$. For another example, suppose that there are three genotypes with different disease risks, where event A is having the disease, and B, C, and D are three different genotypes. Then, $Pr(A|D)$ is the risk of the disease for genotype D, and so forth. The overall risk of the disease is just the weighted risk over all genotypes.

Disease relative risks
What is the risk that you will have a disease given that your sibling (brother/sister) has the same disease?

This is quantified by the disease relative risk, RR, where:
1. RR = Prob(Sib 1 Affected |Sib 2 is Affected)/Prob(Random Individual Affected).
2. RR = The increase in your risk over that for a random individual.

Note: RR = 1 if Prob(Sib 1 Affected|Sib 2 is Affected) = Prob(Random Individual Affected); i.e., you have no increased risk given a relative has the disease.

Therefore, the disease relative risk is the increase in the conditional probability for a sibling (or other relative) vs. a random individual.

For example, consider diabetes: The probability that a random individual (from the US population) has type-1 diabetes is 0.4 percent. This is also referred to as the population prevalence, K. However, the frequency of diabetes in families with an affected sibling is 6 percent. The resulting relative risk that an individual has diabetes, given that its sibling does, is 6/0.4 = 15.

What is the probability that a pair of sibs both have diabetes?

Pr(Both Siblings Affected) = Pr(2nd Affected|1st is Affected) Pr(1st Affected)
Where:
(2nd Affected|1st is Affected) = RR x K, as RR = Pr(2nd Affected|1st is Affected)/K

Pr(Both Siblings Affected) = (RR x K) x K = (K^2) x RR = 0.06 x 0.004 = 0.00024. Hence, the population frequency of families with both siblings affected is 15 times more common than would be expected by chance (i.e., if the disease is independent of family membership, which is K^2).

Example: Rheumatoid Arthritis

Consider the following data for individuals with rheumatoid arthritis (from del Junco et al, 1984):

	Disease	No Disease	Total
Siblings of Affected Individuals	21	475	496
Spouses of Affected Individuals	12	661	673

1. Prob(2nd Sibling Affected|1st is Affected) = 21/496 = 0.042
2. Prob(Random Affected) = 12/673 = 0.018
3. Relative Risk, RR = 0.042/0018 = 2.374

Evolution

Evolution

Evolution is the change in gene (allele) frequencies over time. Evolution takes place at the population level, not at the individual level. In other words, populations evolve over time, but individuals do not. In terms of evolution, a population is a group of interbreeding individuals of the same species that share a common geographical area. A species is a group of populations that have the potential to interbreed in nature and produce viable offspring. And, a gene pool is the sum total of all of the alleles within a population.

The four processes of evolution are:
- Mutation – Changes in the nucleotide sequences of genomic DNA. Mutations provide new alleles, and are therefore the ultimate source of variation.
- Recombination – The reshuffling of the genetic material during meiosis (i.e., prophase I & metaphase I).
- Natural selection – Differential reproduction, with the fittest species surviving for future reproduction.
- Reproductive isolation – Geographical isolation of a population, allowing for interbreeding only within that population, and the eventual adaptation of that population to their particular environmental surroundings.

Note: Mutation and recombination provide natural variation, which is the raw material for evolution.

Hardy-Weinberg law

Prior to the beginning of the 20th century, biologists believed that natural selection would eventually result in the dominant alleles eliminating the recessive alleles. Therefore, over a period of time, genetic variation would eventually be eliminated in a population. As a challenge to this belief, a geneticist, Punnett, was asked to explain the prevalence of blue eyes in humans despite the fact that it is recessive to brown. However, he was unable to do so, and therefore recruited a mathematician colleague, named Hardy, to explain it. Coincidentally, a physician, named Weinberg, also came up with an explanation similar to Hardy's, thus forming the Hardy-Weinberg law.

The Hardy-Weinberg law states that the frequencies of alleles within a population will remain constant unless acted upon by outside agents or forces. In the absence of outside forces, populations are non-evolving and are said to be in Hardy-Weinberg equilibrium. The following forces will disrupt Hardy-Weinberg equilibrium causing evolution to occur:
- Mutation – By definition, mutations change allele frequencies, causing evolution.
- Migration – If new alleles are brought in by immigration, or old alleles are taken out by emigration, then the frequencies of alleles will change, causing evolution.
- Genetic drift – Random events that occur due to a small population size. Random events have little effect on larger populations.

- Nonrandom mating – For each allele in the population to have an equal chance of uniting with any other allele, and thus for the proportions in the population to remain the same, each individual in the population must have an equal chance of mating with any other individual in the population at random. However, most mating in nature is not random because most individuals choose their partner. Sexual selection is an example of nonrandom mating in which mates are selected on the basis of physical or behavioral characteristics.
- Natural selection – For a population to be in Hardy-Weinberg equilibrium there can be no natural selection, which means that all genotypes must be equal in reproductive success. However, according to Darwin's reasoning:
    - All species reproduce in excess of the numbers that can survive; however, adult populations remain relatively constant. Therefore, there must be a severe struggle for survival.
    - All species vary in many characteristics; and, some of the variants confer an advantage or disadvantage in the struggle for life. Therefore, natural selection favors the survival and reproduction of the more advantageous variants, and the elimination of the less advantageous variants.

Since one or more of these events are always acting upon natural populations, the Hardy-Weinberg equilibrium sets up conditions that are very unlikely to occur in nature. Therefore, evolution is occurring in most natural populations.

Genetic drift

Intense natural selection or a disaster can cause a *population bottleneck*, which is a severe reduction in population size that reduces the diversity of a population. The survivors have very little genetic variability and little chance to adapt if the environment changes. Consider a population of 1 million almond trees with a frequency of *r* at 10%. If a severe ice storm wiped out half of the population, leaving 500,000, then it is very likely that the *r* allele would still be present in the population. However, suppose that the initial population size of almond trees were 10 (with the same frequency of r at 10%). In this case, it is likely that the same ice storm could wipe the *r* allele entirely out of the small population. For another example, by the 1890's, the population of northern elephant seals was reduced to only 20 individuals by hunters. Even though the population has increased to over 30,000 since then, there is no genetic variation in the 24 alleles sampled. A single allele has been fixed by genetic drift and the bottleneck effect. In contrast, southern elephant seals have wide genetic variation because their numbers have never reduced by such hunting. The bottleneck effect, combined with inbreeding, is an especially serious problem for many endangered species because great reductions in their numbers have reduced their genetic variability. This makes them especially vulnerable to changes in their environments and/or diseases.

Sometimes a population bottleneck or migration event can cause a *founder effect*. A founder effect occurs when a few individuals that are unrepresentative of the gene pool start a new population. For example, a recessive allele causes the homozygous recessive condition, dwarfism. In Switzerland, the condition occurs in 1 out of 1,000 individuals, while amongst the 12,000 Amish now living in Pennsylvania the condition occurs in 1 out of 14 individuals. This higher frequency is because all of the Amish are descendants of 30 people whom migrated from Switzerland in 1720, and those 30 individuals carried a higher than normal percentage of genes for dwarfism.

Natural selection

Natural selection is differential reproduction where the fittest species survive environmental challenges. Organisms with more advantageous gene combinations secure more resources, which allow them to leave more progeny. It is a negative force: nature selects against, not for. There are three types of selection:

- Stabilizing selection – Selection maintains an already well adapted condition by eliminating any marked deviations from it. As long as the environment remains unchanged, the fittest organisms will also remain unchanged. For example, fur color in mammals varies considerably but certain camouflage colors predominate in specific environments. Stabilizing selection accounts for "living fossils", which are organisms that have remained seemingly unchanged for millions of years.
- Directional selection – Favors one extreme form over others, which eventually produces a change in the population. Directional selection occurs when an organism must adapt to changing conditions. Industrial melanism in the peppered moth (Biston betularia) during the industrial revolution in England is one of the best document examples of directional selection: when increased soot from the industrial revolution darkened the lichens on tree trunks that the light-colored moths used as a camouflage, the population of the lighter-colored moths decreased rapidly, and the frequency of the dark allele increased from less than 1% to over 98% in just 50 generations. Since the 1950's, attempts to reduce industrial pollution in Britain have resulted in an increase in numbers of light moths.
- Disruptive selection – Occurs when two or more character states are favored. For example, African butterflies (Pseudacraea eurytus) range in color from orange to blue. Both the orange and blue forms mimic other foul tasting species (models), so they are rarely eaten. Natural selection eliminates the intermediate forms because they do not look like the models.

Ultimately, natural selection leads to *adaptation*, which is the accumulation of structural, physiological, or behavioral traits that increase an organism's fitness.

Fitness

Darwin marveled at the "perfection of structure" that made it possible for organisms to do whatever they needed to do to stay alive and produce offspring. He called this perfection of structure *fitness*, by which he meant the combination of all traits that help organisms survive and reproduce in their environment. Fitness is now measured as reproductive success, or the number of progeny left behind who carry on the parental genes. Those who fail to contribute to the next or succeeding generations are unfit.

Diploidy and heterozygosity

Diploidy and heterozygosity help to maintain genetic variation. Even though only exposed alleles (those that cause a phenotypic difference) are subject to natural selection in sexually reproducing organisms, heterozygous diploid organisms may be a repository of rare recessive alleles. Recessive alleles provide "genetic insurance" should the environment change.

Sickle cell anemia

Sickle cell anemia is a potentially fatal disease that results from homozygous recessive alleles that code for one of the four polypeptide chains of hemoglobin, the oxygen-transporting molecule in human blood. The mutant form of hemoglobin causes the red blood cells to collapse, forming a variety of odd shapes, including some that are sickle shaped. As a result, their oxygen carrying capacity is much reduced, and they tend to clog up tiny capillaries. Affected individuals exhibit a variety of symptoms, and they usually have considerably shortened lives. Despite the lethality of the allele, it occurs at frequencies as high as 40% in some parts of tropical Africa. By contrast, it occurs at less than 5% in African Americans, and at 0.1% in Caucasian Americans. The high frequency in tropical Africa is maintained because the heterozygous condition confers resistance to malaria, and natural selection has acted to preserve it in areas traditionally high in malaria.

Note: The same trait may be an advantage in one environment, yet a disadvantage in another.

Adaptive radiation

Adaptive radiation is the evolution of a single evolutionary stock into a number of different species. Starting with a single common ancestor, adaptive radiation allows for the evolution of a variety of species that are adapted to particular elements of their environments. An example of this is the differences in beak sizes and shapes of the 14 different finch species that Darwin discovered in the Galapagos Islands: each species were adapted to different food sources.

Convergent and divergent evolution

Convergent evolution is the independent acquisition over time of similar characteristics in unrelated species that are subject to similar selection pressures (convergence of analogous traits). Divergent evolution is the evolution of differences among closely related species because of differing selection pressures in their particular environments (divergence of homologous traits).

Example of convergent evolution
Spiny anteaters, pangolins and giant anteaters all eat a diet of mainly ants and termites. Each of these animals lives on a different continent and is basically unrelated to each other. Each of them has a long, sticky, wormlike tongue and big claws to dig with. So, despite the fact that each of them has come from a different ancestor, they resemble each other and make a living in a similar way (i.e., they eat ants). Therefore, while the ancestors of these animals were different, these animals have evolved similar ways to exploit a resource that is hard to eat.

Example of divergent evolution
Male wolf spiders can use vibrations or visual signals to attract and mate with females. In two species that came from a common ancestor that used visual and vibratory signals, one uses a visual signal while the other uses vibrations (beating its legs on the ground). One lives in a flat habitat, in which vision is not obscured at all, and uses visual signals; the other lives in a complex forest habitat, in which you cannot see very far, and it uses vibrations to signal. These two species have diverged in their signaling behavior because of different selective pressures acting upon them.

Comparative anatomy

Comparative anatomy is the study of similarities and differences in the anatomy of different organisms, and is very similar to evolutionary biology. Comparative anatomy classifies organisms based upon their anatomical structures, and indicates whether various organisms share a common ancestor. An example of comparative anatomy is the presence of similar bone structures in the forearms of humans, cats, whales, and bats. While it is likely that they all once shared a common function, they all serve different functions today, even with common structural parts: humans–

hands, cats–paws, whales–fins, and bats–wings. This occurs due to descent from a common ancestor, with modifications due to random mutations and natural selection, allowing each organism to better adapt to their particular environment.

Homology and analogy

Two major concepts in comparative anatomy are homology and analogy. Homology (homologous traits) refers to similar characteristics in two animals that are a result of common ancestry (descent). Analogy (analogous traits) refers to similarity (or equivalence) in function, morphology, etc. that has arisen independently (i.e., similar selective pressures have resulted in similar traits in unrelated taxa). Animal species that come from the same ancestor are usually similar (i.e., they share characteristics). This is homology, or similarity, as a result of descent. On the other hand, if different species evolve similar traits to adapt to similar environments, then this is analogy as the result of convergent evolution (i.e., they are similar because it is a good trait, not because of descent).

Anatomical terminology

Anatomical Plane	Orientation
Sagittal	Plane parallel to the sagittal suture; divides the body into left and right portions.
Coronal	Plane that divides the body into dorsal (front) and ventral (back) portions.
Transverse	Axial plane that divides the body into cranial (head) and caudal (tail) portions.

Anatomical Term	Direction
Ipsilateral	On the same side.
Contralateral	On the opposite side.
Superficial	On the outside surface.
Deep	Away from the surface.
Intermediate	Between two structures.
Visceral	Associated with organs within body cavities.
Parietal	Associated with the wall of the body cavity.
Axial	Toward the central axis.
Abaxial	Away from the central axis.
Rostral	Toward the nose/mouth.
Caudal	Toward the tail/posterior (or feet in humans).

Directional Term	Defined Axis	Synonym	Direction
Anterior	Anteroposterior	Rostrocaudal Craniocaudal Cephalocaudal	From head to tail (opposite end).
Posterior			
Dorsal	Dorsoventral		From the spinal column (back) to the belly (front).
Ventral			
Left (lateral)	Left-Right	Dextrosinistral Sinistrodextral	From left to right.
Right (lateral)			
Medial	Mediolateral		From the center of the body to one side or the other.
Lateral			
Proximal	Proximodistal		From the tip of an appendage to where it joins the body.
Distal			

Lines of orientation in the thorax

The lines of orientation in the thorax are as follows:
- Midsternal line – The midline of the body.
- Lateral sternal line – A vertical line along the lateral sternal margin.
- Midclavicular line – A vertical line, parallel to the midsternal line, which runs through a point midway between the center of the jugular notch and the tip of the acromion.
- Midaxillary line – A line that passes vertically from the apex of the axilla down the lateral wall of the thorax.
- Midscapular line – Runs vertically through the apex of the inferior angle of the scapula.

Vertebral levels

- Jugular (Suprasternal) Notch – At the same horizontal level as the lower border of the body of the 2nd thoracic vertebra.
- Sternal Angle – At the level of the disc between the 4th and 5th thoracic vertebrae.
- Xiphisternal Junction – At the level of the intervertebral disc between the 9th and 10th thoracic vertebrae.

General Chemistry

Atomic number and mass number

The number of protons in an atom is known as the atomic number, Z, of the atom. Each element in the periodic table of elements has a different Z. For example, hydrogen (H) has 1 proton, and it's Z = 1. Calcium (Ca) has 20 protons, and it's Z = 20. Gold (Au) has 79 protons, and it's Z = 79. The number of neutrons in an atom is denoted by N. The mass number, A, is defined as the total number of protons and neutrons that are present in an atom. Thus, A = Z + N.

Electron capacity of an atomic shell

To determine the electron capacity of an atomic shell, the formula $2n^2$ is used when n = the shell number, or the principle quantum number. Electrons fill the orbitals and shells from the inside out, beginning with shell one. The valence shell is the outermost shell that is currently occupied, even if it only has one electron. Each shell, numbered from the one closest to the center of the nucleus outward (lowest to highest in energy), can hold up to a specific number of electrons due to its differing sublevel and orbital capacity:

- Shell 1: 2 electron capacity – s sublevel – 1 orbital
- Shell 2: 8 electron capacity – s and p sublevels – 4 orbitals
- Shell 3: 18 electron capacity – s, p, and d sublevels – 9 orbitals
- Shell 4: 32 electron capacity – s, p, d, and f sublevels – 16 orbitals

Octet rule

Because we know that s^2p^6 is the configuration of a noble gas, we assume that an atom is stable when surrounded by 8 electrons (4 electron pairs). This is known as the octet rule, and holds true for atoms of low atomic number (< 20).

Excited state and ground state

In quantum mechanics, an excited state of a system, such as an atom, molecule, or nucleus, is any configuration of the system that has a higher energy than the ground state. In other words, an excited state of a system involves any configuration where there is more energy than the absolute minimum. The lifetime of a system in an excited state is usually short: the spontaneous or induced emission of a quantum of energy, such as a photon or a phonon, usually occurs shortly after the system is promoted to the excited state, returning the system to a state with lower energy (either a less excited state or the ground state).

A simple example of this concept involves the hydrogen atom: the ground state of the hydrogen atom corresponds to having the atom's single electron in the lowest possible orbit (that is, the spherically symmetric "1s" state, which has the lowest possible quantum numbers). By giving the atom additional energy (e.g., by the absorption of a photon of an appropriate energy), the electron is able to move into an excited state. If the photon has too much energy, then the electron will cease to be bound to the atom, and the atom will become ionized. Once the electron is in its excited state, we deem the hydrogen atom to be in its excited state.

Spectroscopy

Spectroscopy is the study of spectra, or the dependence of physical quantities on frequency. Spectroscopy is often used in physical and analytical chemistry for the identification of substances through the spectrum emitted or absorbed. A device for recording a spectrum is called a spectrometer. Spectroscopy can be classified according to the physical quantity that is measured or calculated, or the measurement process. The type of spectroscopy depends upon the physical quantity measured. Normally, the quantity that is measured is an amount or intensity of something.

Absorption and emission spectroscopy

Absorption spectroscopy uses the range of electromagnetic spectra in which a substance absorbs. In atomic absorption spectroscopy, the sample is atomized, and then light of a particular frequency is passed through the vapor. After calibration, the amount of absorption can be related to the concentrations of various metal ions using the Beer-Lambert law. Emission spectroscopy uses the range of electromagnetic spectra in which a substance radiates. The substance first absorbs energy, and then radiates this energy as light. This energy can be from a variety of sources, including collision (due either to high temperatures or otherwise), chemical reactions, and light. Absorption spectroscopy is utilized more commonly than emission spectroscopy.

Periodic table

The following is a diagram of a typical cell on the periodic table:

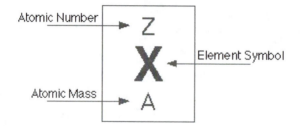

Periods of the periodic table

The periodic table consists of 7 horizontal periods. The lengths of the periods increase with the order of the period. And, elements within a period have consecutive atomic numbers. The 1st period is the shortest period. It consists of just two elements: H and He. The 2nd and 3rd periods have 8 elements each, and are called short periods. The 4th and 5th periods are longer periods, and have 18 elements each. The 6th period has 32 elements, including a 15 element series called the lanthanide series, which is separate from the table. The lanthanide series contains rare-earth elements that show similar properties. The 7th period contains all of the remaining elements, and is incomplete. This period also has a 15 element series called the actinide series, which is separate from the table. The actinide series has a separate identity, and contains uranium and most of the known transuranic elements.

Groups of the periodic table

The vertical columns of the periodic table are called groups. There are 18 groups in the periodic table, and the elements within each group do not have consecutive atomic numbers. The groups are further divided into two groups: A and B. Group 1A to VIII A has all the normal elements, while group 1B to VIII B holds all the transition metal elements. The two final groups are the lanthanide and the actinide series, also known as inner transition elements.

Note: The modern periodic table is approximately divided into metals and non-metals.

Alkali metals

The alkali metals are found in group 1 of the periodic table, formerly known as group IA. These metals are very reactive and do not occur freely in nature. Cesium and francium are the most reactive elements in this group. All of the alkali metals will explode if they are exposed to water. Alkali metals have only one electron in their outer shell, and are therefore ready to lose that one electron in ionic bonding with other elements. As with all other metals, the alkali metals are malleable, ductile, and are good conductors of heat and electricity. In addition, the alkali metals are softer than most other metals. The alkali metals are as follows:

- Lithium
- Sodium
- Potassium
- Rubidium
- Cesium
- Francium

Halogens

The halogens are five non-metallic elements that are found in group 7 of the periodic table. The term "halogen" means "salt-former", and compounds that contain halogens are called "salts". The halogens exist in all three states of matter at room temperature: solids (such as iodine and astatine), liquids (such as bromine), and gases (such as fluorine and chlorine). All halogens have 7 electrons in their outer shells, which gives them an oxidation number of -1. The halogens are as follows:

- Fluorine
- Chlorine
- Bromine
- Iodine
- Astatine

Noble gases

The six noble gases are found in group 18 of the periodic table. These elements were considered to be inert gases until the 1960's, because their oxidation number of 0 prevents them from readily forming compounds. All noble gases have the maximum number of electrons possible in their outer shell (2 for helium, 8 for all of the others), making them very stable. The noble gases are as follows:

- Helium
- Neon
- Argon
- Krypton
- Xenon
- Radon

> **Review Video: <u>Noble Gases</u>**
> *Visit **mometrix.com/academy** and enter **Code: 122067***

Transition metals

The 38 elements in groups 3 through 12 of the periodic table are called "transition metals." As with all metals, the transition elements are both ductile and malleable, and conduct electricity and heat. The interesting thing about transition metals is that their valence electrons, or the electrons that they use to combine with other elements, are present in more than one shell. This is the reason why they often exhibit several common oxidation states. There are three noteworthy elements in the transition metals that are known to produce magnetic fields: iron, cobalt, and nickel.

Metalloids

Metalloids are the elements that are found along the stair-step line that distinguishes metals from non-metals. This line is drawn from between boron and aluminum to the border between polonium and astatine. The only exception to this is aluminum, which is classified under "other metals". Metalloids have properties of both metals and non-metals. Some of the metalloids, such as silicon and germanium, are semi-conductors. This means that they can carry an electrical charge under special conditions. This property makes metalloids useful in computers and calculators. The metalloids are as follows:
- Boron
- Silicon
- Germanium
- Arsenic
- Antimony
- Tellurium
- Polonium

Non-metals

The non-metals are the elements in groups 14-16 of the periodic table. Non-metals are not able to conduct electricity or heat very well. As opposed to metals, the non-metallic elements are very brittle, and cannot be rolled into wires, or pounded into sheets. The non-metals exist in two of the three states of matter at room temperature: solids (such as carbon) and gases (such as oxygen). The non-metals have no metallic luster, and do not reflect light. The non-metals have oxidation numbers of ±4, -3, or -2. The non-metal elements are as follows:
- Hydrogen
- Carbon
- Nitrogen
- Oxygen
- Phosphorus
- Sulfur
- Selenium

Other metals

The 7 elements that are classified as "other metals" are located in groups 13, 14, and 15. While these elements are ductile and malleable, they are not the same as the transition elements. Unlike the transition elements, these elements do not exhibit variable oxidation states, and their valence electrons are only present in their outer shell. All of these elements are solids, have a relatively high density, and are opaque. They have oxidation numbers of +3, ±4, or -3. The "other metals" are as follows:
- Aluminum

- Gallium
- Indium
- Tin
- Thallium
- Lead
- Bismuth

Physical properties of metals

The following are physical properties of metals:
- Physical state – Metals are mostly solids at room temperature. Mercury (Hg) is the only exception: it is liquid at room temperature. The density of metals is high. Only sodium (Na) and potassium (K) have densities that are less than water. Therefore, all metals are hard materials except for sodium and potassium, which are soft metals. Lead is also considered to be a soft metal.
- Brittleness – Metals are not brittle, with the exception of zinc (Zn). Metals do not break easily because of their metallic bonds.
- Melting and boiling points – All metals, other than sodium (Na) and potassium (K), have high melting and boiling points. The melting points of sodium (Na) and potassium (K) are below 100°C, while the melting point of iron (Fe) is about 1540°C.
- Solubility – Pure metals are insoluble in solvents, such as water or any organic solvent. Metals can only be dissolved in acids.
- Sonorousness – Metals make a characteristic sound when hit with an object, and are thus sonorous. The sonorousness of metals depends upon the temperature and density.
- Malleability – Metals can be hammered or beaten into thin sheets without breaking. Malleable means that metallic bonds in the metals do not break easily. Gold (Au) and silver (Ag) are highly malleable elements. Metals can be made into thin foil sheets because of malleability.
- Ductility – Metals can be melted and drawn into thin wires. Because of this property, metals are known as ductile. The ductility property follows from the malleability property. While being drawn into wires, metals are stretched. Because of the strong metallic bonds, the metal atoms do not separate easily. Copper (Cu), aluminum (Al), and Ag are very ductile, because very thin wires can be made out of these elements.
- Tensility – Due to their ductility and malleability properties, metals are very strong. Their bonds do not break easily, as their electrons are shared over an array of metal atoms. This gives metals a very high tensile strength, and therefore metals do not break easily.
- Conduction of heat and electricity – In metals, the bonds are formed by excess or free electrons moving around large arrays of atoms. These electrons are able to conduct electricity and heat. Ag, Cu, and Al are good conductors of heat and electricity, while lead (Pb) is a poor conductor of electricity.

Characteristics of elements in a period

The characteristics of elements in a period are as follows:
- The atomic numbers are consecutive.
- The number of valence electrons in the elements increases incrementally from left to right.
- The elements of the same period have different valencies.
- The atomic radii decrease while going from left to right in a period.
- Metallic character reduces while going from left to right in a period.

- 215 -

- Chemical reactivity is highest at the two extremes, and is the lowest in the center. The reactivity on the left extreme is the most electro-positive, while the reactivity on the right extreme is the most electronegative.
- Oxides that are formed of elements on the left are basic in nature, while elements on the right are acidic in nature. Oxides of elements in the center are amphoteric.

Characteristics of elements in a group

The characteristics of elements in a group are as follows:
- The atomic numbers are not consecutive.
- The number of valence electrons in the elements are the same within a group.
- The elements of the same group have the same valencies.
- The atomic radii increase while going from top to bottom in a group.
- Metallic character increases while going from top to bottom in metallic groups. In non-metallic groups, the non-metallic nature decreases while going from top to bottom.
- Chemical reactivity increases while going from top to bottom in metallic groups. In non-metallic groups, the chemical reactivity decreases while going from top to bottom.

Valency

The tendency of atoms to donate or accept electrons in order to stabilize their outermost orbits is known as the valency of the element. Valency is the measure of reactivity of the element. Quite a lot of transition metals and non-metals show variable valency. A stable orbit may mean that there are no unpaired electrons left in the outermost orbit. Generally, it is observed that an atom tries to acquire the electronic configuration of its nearest noble gas atom. Amongst the transition metals, iron and nickel show variable valency. Amongst the non-metals, oxygen and nitrogen are good examples. These metals and non-metals combine to give various compounds that have different properties. For example, Fe_2O_3 is different from FeO. In Fe_2O_3, Fe shows a valency of +3, while O shows a valency of –2, and Fe_2O_3 is a magnetic compound. In FeO, Fe shows a valency of +2, and FeO is non-magnetic. Water (H_2O) and hydrogen peroxide (H_2O_2) are both compounds of hydrogen and oxygen. In H_2O, H shows a valence of +1, while O shows a valence of –2. However, in H_2O_2, H has a valency of +1, while O has a valency of –1. Water is a neutral compound, while H_2O_2 is a highly acidic compound.

Ionization energy

Ionization energy is the energy that is required to remove one mole of electrons from one mole of atoms in the gas phase. Ionization energy is a measure of how strongly an atom holds on to its electrons. The first ionization energy, I_1, is the amount of energy that is required to remove the first electron (i.e., to form the neutral atom). More energy is required to remove the second electron (I_2). The remaining electrons experience less $e^- - e^-$ repulsion, and thus experience a greater effective nuclear charge. Therefore, ionization energy continues to increase as successive electrons are removed.

> ➤ **Review Video: Ionization Energy**
> Visit *mometrix.com/academy* and enter *Code: 862908*

Electron affinity

The electron affinity of an element is the energy given off when a neutral atom in the gas phase gains an extra electron to form a negatively charged ion. A fluorine atom in the gas phase, for example, gives off energy when it gains an electron to form a fluoride ion:

$$F(g) + e^- \rightarrow F^-(g) \quad \Delta H^\circ = -328.0 \text{ kJ/mol}$$

Electron affinities are more difficult to measure than ionization energies, and are usually known to fewer significant figures. Electron affinities generally become smaller as we go down a column of the periodic table for two reasons: First, the electron being added to the atom is placed in larger orbitals, where it spends less time near the nucleus of the atom. And, second, the number of electrons on an atom increases as we go down a column, so the force of repulsion between the electron being added and the electrons already present on a neutral atom becomes larger. Electron affinity data are complicated by the fact that the repulsion between the electron being added to the atom and the electrons already present on the atom depends on the volume of the atom. Among the nonmetals in groups VIA and VIIA, this force of repulsion is largest for the very smallest atoms in these columns: oxygen and fluorine.

Electronegativity

Electronegativity is the affinity of an atom for electrons. The atoms of the various elements differ in their affinity for electrons. The Pauling scale is the most commonly used scale for electronegativity. Based upon the Pauling scale, fluorine, the most electronegative element, is assigned a value of 4.0, and values range down to cesium and francium, which are the least electronegative at 0.7.

Atom sizes

The atomic size is not easily defined since the electron orbitals only gradually go to zero as the distance from the nucleus increases. For atoms that can form solid crystals, the distance between adjacent nuclei can give an estimate of the atomic size. For atoms that do not form solid crystals, other techniques are used, including theoretical calculations. As an example, the size of a hydrogen atom is estimated to be approximately 1.2×10^{-10} m. Compare this to the size of the proton, the only particle in the nucleus of the hydrogen atom, which is approximately 0.87×10^{-15} m. Thus, the ratio between the sizes of the hydrogen atom to its nucleus is about 100,000 fold. Atoms of different elements do vary in size, but the sizes are roughly the same to within a factor of 2 or so. The reason for this is that elements with a large positive charge on the nucleus attract electrons to the center of the atom more strongly.

Solid bonds

- Bond Strength – Energy required to break the bond.
- Covalent Bond – The strongest bond.
    o Atoms share valence electrons.
    o Position is fixed – Makes the compound brittle.
- Ionic Bond – Strong bond.
    o Attraction between + and – ions.
    o Lattice energy $(E = kQ_1Q_2/d)$.
    o Position is fixed – Makes the compound brittle.
- Metallic Bond – Variable bond strength.
    o Attraction between ions and valence electrons (electron–sea model).
    o Mobile electrons – Conductor.

- o   Pliable metal ions – Malleable and ductile.
- Molecular Bond – Weak bond.
  - o   Attraction between (+) and (–) regions.
  - o   Three levels – Strongest to weakest:
    - ▪ Hydrogen bond – N, O, and F (small with high electronegativity) bond to H (low electronegative); almost ionic.
    - ▪ Dipole force – Polar molecules.
    - ▪ London dispersion force – Temporary polarization of valence electrons (increases with increased atomic or molecular size).

Ionic bonds

Atomic bonds where electrons are transferred between the constituent atoms of a compound are known as ionic bonds (or electrovalent bonds). The compound formed is called an ionic or electrovalent compound. Generally, ionic bonds are formed between metallic atoms that have extra electrons to spare and non-metallic atoms which are electron deficient. Magnesium oxide (MgO), potassium chloride (KCl), and iron (II) oxide (FeO) are some examples of ionic compounds. Ionic compounds are crystalline in nature, and thus have high melting points. Also, because of the availability of ions, such compounds are good conductors of heat. They form electrolytes when molten or in solution. However, they are non-conductors of electricity when solid, as there are no free ions since they are all locked together in a crystal. When an ion loses an electron, it is called a positive ion, or a cation. When an ion gains an electron, it is called a negative ion, or an anion. In the examples above, Na^+, Mg^{2+}, K^+, and Fe^{2+} are cations, while Cl^-, and O^{2-} are anions.

> ➤ **Review Video: Ionic Bonds**
> *Visit **mometrix.com/academy** and enter **Code: 116546***

Covalent bonds

In an oxygen (O) atom, the electronic configuration is 2 electrons in the K-shell, and 6 electrons in the L-shell. It would rather borrow two electrons from another atom in order to complete its last shell, rather than give up its six electrons. The hydrogen (H) atom has only one electron, and only needs to borrow one extra electron to complete its first shell. Two atoms of H and one atom of O can fulfill each other's needs by sharing electrons in their outermost orbits, forming a water molecule, H_2O. In an H_2O molecule, the electrons are not totally given up, as in the case of Na^+Cl^-, but are instead shared by each of the neighboring atoms.

An atomic bond formed by the sharing of electrons is called a covalent bond. Compounds that are formed due to covalent bonding of atoms are called covalent compounds, and are generally formed between non-metals. Hydrogen gas (H_2), nitrogen gas (N_2), oxygen gas (O_2), and hydrochloric acid (HCl) are examples of covalently bonded compounds. If the neighboring atoms share a pair of electrons, then the covalent bond is a single covalent bond. On the other hand, if they share two or three pairs of electrons, then the covalent bond is double or triple covalent bond, respectively. Compared to ionic bonds, covalent bonds are shorter and more difficult to break. There are two types of covalent bonds: sigma bonds and pi bonds. When the covalent bond is linear, or aligned along the plane containing the atoms, the bond is known as sigma (s) bond. Sigma bonds are strong and the electron sharing is at its maximum. Methane, CH_4, is a good example of sigma bonding, and it has four of them. When the covalent bond is parallel, formed by the overlap of two p-orbital lobes, the bond is known as a pi bond. Relative to sigma bonds, pi bonds are usually weaker because they have less orbital overlap due to their parallel orientation. Single bonds are composed solely of

- 218 -

sigma bonds, while double and triple bonds are composed of one sigma bond and either one or two pi bonds, respectively.

> ➤ **Review Video:** <u>Pi Bonds and Sigma Bonds</u>
> *Visit **mometrix.com/academy** and enter **Code: 316056***

VSEPR theory

The valence shell electron pair repulsion (VSEPR) theory is a model that is used to predict the shape of a molecule based on the assumption that all negatively charged valence electrons repel each other. This model is based on the simple idea, formulated by Lewis and others, that electrons tend to move as far away from one another as possible (like charges repel one another). Because electrons tend to pair with one another if they have opposite spins, we can modify the idea to say that pairs of electrons tend to adopt a geometry that minimizes repulsions. We have noted earlier that only the electrons in the valence shell are involved in bonding, so we only need to worry about those electrons.

Gases

- Phase:
  - o Molecules are free to fill an entire volume.
  - o Molecules are far apart – Compressible.
- Pressure:
  - o Force (weight)/Area.
  - o Air pressure decreases with altitude.
  - o Measuring tools:
    - ▪ Barometer – Measures absolute pressure.
    - ▪ Manometer – Measures pressure differences (gauge pressures).
      $P_{gas} = P_{atmosphere} \pm \Delta H$ in mmHg
- Kinetic Theory for Gases (ideal gas):
  - o Molecules in constant random motion, which is proportional to the temperature:
    - ▪ $E = mu^2/2 = cT$
    - ▪ b. $u = (3RT/MM)^{1/2}$
      Where: $R = 8.31$ kg·m²/s²·mol·K, and MM is in kg.
    - ▪ Temperature/velocity distribution curve.
  - o Molecular volume is zero compared to the volume of the container.
  - o Collisions produce pressure without loss of total kinetic energy.
  - o Molecules do not interact.

Units of pressure

The height of a column of mercury, Hg, in millimeters is a standard way of measuring pressure (mmHg). At sea level, and at standard gravitational acceleration, the air pressure is defined as one atmosphere (atm):
1 atm = 760 mmHg.

There are also additional units of measuring pressure, including newtons (N)/m², pascals (Pa), bars, torr, and pounds per square inch (psi). In terms of atmospheres, the conversions for these units are as follows:
- 1 atm = 101,325 N/m²
- 1 atm = 101,325 Pa (1 Pa = 1 N/m²)
- 1 atm = 1.01325 bars
- 1 atm = 760 torr (1 torr = 1 mmHg)
- 1 atm = 14.7 psi

Gay-Lussac's law of combining gas volumes

The volumes of gases taking part in a chemical reaction show simple whole-number ratios to one another when those volumes are measured at the same temperature and pressure. For example, 1 liter of nitrogen gas (N_2) reacts with 3 liters of hydrogen gas (H_2) to produce 2 liters of ammonia gas (NH_3):
N_2 (g) + 3H_2 (g) → 2NH_3 (g)

Since all of the reactants and products are gases, the molar ratio of N_2 (g):H_2 (g):NH_3 (g) of 1:3:2 is also the ratio of the volumes of gases. Therefore, 10 mL of N_2 would react with 10 x 3 = 30 mL of H_2 to produce 10 x 2 = 20 mL NH_3.

Ideal gas law formula

The ideal gas law formula is pretty accurate for all gases, since we assume that the gas molecules are point masses, and the collisions of the molecules are totally elastic (a completely elastic collision means that the energy of the molecules before a collision equals the energy of the molecules after a collision). The formula becomes less accurate as the gas becomes very compressed and the temperature decreases. There are some correction factors for both of these factors for each gas in order to convert the ideal gas law formula into a real gas law formula, but the ideal gas law is a good estimation of the way that gases act.

The ideal gas law formula is as follows:

$PV = nRT$

Where:

P = The absolute pressure of the gas in atm.
V = The volume of the gas in liters.
n = The moles of gas.
R = The universal gas constant, 0.0821 L·atm/mol·K.
T = The temperature in Kelvin.

Charles' law and Boyle's law

Charles' law gives the manner in which the volume of a gas changes with temperature. The law states that, for a constant pressure on a given mass of gas, the volume is directly proportional to the temperature:

$V \propto T$

Thus, the proportion, V/T, is constant (this constant of proportionality is not the same as that given by Boyle's law).

> **Review Video: Charles' Law**
> Visit *mometrix.com/academy* and enter *Code:* **537776**

Robert Boyle made the following observations in the case of gases:
1. At a constant temperature, the volume of a gas is inversely proportional to the pressure.
2. At a constant temperature, the density of a gas is directly proportional to the pressure.

Boyle's law can be written mathematically as follows:

$PV = k$

Where:

P = The pressure of the system.
V = The volume of the system.
k = A constant representative of the pressure and volume of the system.

Note: Boyle's and Charles' laws only hold for ideal gases.

> **Review Video: Boyle's Law**
> Visit *mometrix.com/academy* and enter *Code:* **115757**

Kinetic theory

The kinetic theory is as follows:
- All matter is composed of atoms, which are the smallest units of each element. A particle of a gas could be an atom or a group of atoms.
- Atoms have an energy of motion that we perceive as temperature. The motion of atoms or molecules can be in the form of linear motion of translation, the vibration of atoms or molecules against one another or pulling against a bond, or the rotation of individual atoms or groups of atoms.
- There is a temperature to which we can extrapolate absolute zero, at which, theoretically, the motion of the atoms and molecules would stop.
- The pressure of a gas is due to the motion of the atoms or molecules of gas striking the object bearing that pressure. These collisions are elastic (without friction), when they are against the side of the container or other particles of gas.
- There is a very large distance between the particles of a gas, relative to the size of the particles, such that the size of the particle can be considered negligible.

Dalton's law of partial pressure

Dalton's law of partial pressure states that the pressure of a mixture of gases is equal to the sum of the "partial" pressures of all of the constituent gases alone. Mathematically, this can be represented as follows:

$Pressure_{Total} = Pressure_1 + Pressure_2 ... + Pressure_n$

> ➢ **Review Video: Dalton's Law of Partial Pressure**
> *Visit **mometrix.com/academy** and enter **Code: 355830***

Hydrogen bonds

Hydrogen bonds occur between molecules that have a permanent net dipole, resulting from hydrogen being covalently bonded to either fluorine, oxygen, or nitrogen. For example, hydrogen bonds operate between molecules of water (H_2O), ammonia (NH_3), hydrogen fluoride (HF), hydrogen peroxide (H_2O_2), alkanols (alcohols) such as methanol (CH_3OH), alkanoic (carboxylic) acids such as ethanoic (acetic) acid (CH_3COOH), and organic amines such as methanamine (methyl amine, CH_3NH_2). Hydrogen bonding is a stronger intermolecular force than either dispersion forces or dipole-dipole interactions because the hydrogen nucleus is extremely small and positively charged, while fluorine, oxygen and nitrogen are very electronegative, so that the electron of the hydrogen atom is strongly attracted to them. This results in a highly positive charge localized on the hydrogen atom, and a highly negative charge localized on the fluorine, oxygen, or nitrogen atom. Therefore, the electrostatic attraction between these molecules will be greater than for the polar molecules that do not have hydrogen bonding.

Dipole-dipole interactions

Dipole-dipole interactions are stronger intermolecular forces than dispersion forces. They occur between molecules that have permanent net dipoles (polar molecules), such as SCl_2, PCl_3, and CH_3Cl. If the permanent net dipole within the polar molecules results from a covalent bond between a hydrogen atom and either fluorine, oxygen or nitrogen, then the resulting intermolecular force is referred to as a hydrogen bond. The partial positive charge on one molecule is electrostatically attracted to the partial negative charge on a neighboring molecule.

Metallic bonds

Metallic bonds are where the valence electrons of metal atoms are shared by more than one neighboring atom. This type of bond occurs in metals only. The metal atoms are held together by a "sea" of electrons floating around. Metals consist of a lattice of positive ions through which a cloud of electrons moves. The positive ions will tend to repel one another, but are held together by the negatively charged electron cloud. The mobile electrons can transfer thermal vibrations from one part of the structure to another (i.e., metals can conduct heat). They are also good conductors of electricity. Metals are malleable and ductile because the positive ions in a metal are not held together by rigid bonds. Instead, they are capable of sliding past one another if the metal is deformed.

> ➢ **Review Video:** <u>Metallic Bonds</u>
> *Visit **mometrix.com/academy** and enter **Code:** 230855*

Van der Waal's bonds

Van der Waals forces are relatively weak electric forces that attract neutral molecules to one another in gases, in liquefied and solidified gases, and in almost all organic liquids and solids. These forces are named for the Dutch physicist, Johannes van der Waals, who first postulated these intermolecular forces in 1873 while developing a theory to account for the properties of real gases. Solids that are held together by van der Waals forces have characteristically lower melting points, and are softer than those that are held together by the stronger ionic, covalent, and metallic bonds.

Van der Waals forces may arise from three sources: First, the molecules of some materials, although electrically neutral, may be permanent electric dipoles. Because of fixed distortion in the distribution of electric charge in the structure of some molecules, one side is always positive, while the other side is negative. The tendency of such permanent dipoles to align with each other results in a net attractive force. Second, the presence of molecules that are permanent dipoles temporarily distorts the electric charge in other nearby polar or nonpolar molecules, thereby inducing further polarization. An additional attractive force results from the interaction of a permanent dipole with a neighboring induced dipole. Third, even though no molecules of a material are permanent dipoles, a force of attraction exists between the molecules, accounting for condensing to the liquid state at sufficiently low temperatures.

Phase changes

A phase change occurs when a structural unit has sufficient energy (temperature) to break its solid bond.

- Pressure vs. temperature graph:
  - Triple point – Three-phase equilibrium.
  - Critical point – Permanent gas.
- Break occurs in two stages – Triple point below atmospheric pressure:
  - Melting (solid → liquid):
    - Bond is weakened, but not altogether broken – Units can slide by each other.
    - Opposite is freezing.
  - Boiling (liquid → gas):
    - Bond is broken – Units are free of all cohesion.
    - Opposite is liquefaction.
- Break occurs in one stage – Triple point above atmospheric pressure: Sublimation (opposite is deposition).
- Melting temperature is pressure dependent – High pressure favors a denser phase.

The process of converting a solid into a liquid is known as melting. The temperature at which melting occurs is called the melting point. The inverse of melting is called freezing, or solidification. If solidification converts the solid into properly structured crystals, then the process is also known as a crystallization process. The process of converting a liquid into a gas is called vaporizing. The inverse of vaporizing is called condensation. The temperature at which the liquid turns into gas is called the boiling point of the substance. Some solids, like solid iodine, carbon dioxide, and naphthalene balls, convert directly into a gaseous state from their solid state. They skip the liquid phase. The process of going directly from a solid state to a gaseous state is known as sublimation. The inverse of sublimation is known as solid condensation, or deposition.

Colligative properties

The term "colligative properties" refers to macroscopic observable properties, such as thermodynamic variables (e.g., vapor pressure, boiling and melting temperatures, etc.).

Raoult's law

Raoult's law relates the vapor pressure of components to the composition of the solution. The law assumes ideal behavior. It gives a simple picture of the situation just as the ideal gas law does. The ideal gas law is very useful as a limiting law. As the interactive forces between molecules and the volume of the molecules approaches zero, the behavior of gases approach the behavior of the ideal gas. Raoult's law is similar in that it assumes that the physical properties of the components are identical. The more similar the components, the more their behavior approaches that described by Raoult's law. Using the example of a solution of two liquids, A and B, if no other gases are present, the total vapor pressure, P_{tot}, above the solution is equal to the sum of the vapor pressures of the two components, P_A and P_B.

$$P_{tot} = P_A + P_B$$

If the two components are very similar, or, in the limiting case, differ only in isotopic content, then the vapor pressure of each component will be equal to the vapor pressure of the pure substance, P_0, times the mole fraction in the solution. This is Raoult's law.

Boiling point elevation

A solution typically has a measurably higher boiling point than that of the pure solvent. For example, the boiling point of pure water is 100°C, while the boiling point of water can be elevated by the addition of a solute, such as a salt. This elevation of the boiling point is referred to as boiling point elevation. A treatment of boiling point elevation is given by Ebbing. The boiling point elevation, ΔT_b, is a colligative property of the solution and for dilute solutions is found to be proportional to the molal concentration, c_m, of the solution:

$\Delta T_b = K_b c_m$

Where:

K_b = The boiling point elevation constant.

Freezing point depression

A solution typically has a measurably lower melting point than the pure solvent. For example, the freezing point of pure water is 0°C, but that freezing point can be depressed by the addition of a solute, such as a salt. This depression of the freezing point is known as freezing point depression. A practical example of freezing point depression is the use of ordinary salt (sodium chloride, NaCl) on icy roads in the winter to help melt the ice from the roads by lowering the freezing point of the ice. A 10% salt solution is said to lower the freezing point from 0°C to –6°C (20°F), and a 20% salt solution is said to lower it to –16°C (2°F). A more formal treatment of freezing point depression is given by Ebbing. The freezing point depression, ΔT_f, is a colligative property of the solution, and for dilute solutions is found to be proportional to the molal concentration, c_m, of the solution:

$\Delta T_b = K_f c_m$

Where:

K_f = The freezing point depression constant.

Osmotic pressure of a dilute solution

The osmotic pressure of a dilute solution is found to obey a relationship of the same form as the ideal gas law:

$$P_{osmotic} = \frac{nRT}{V}$$

In chemistry texts, it is usually expressed in terms of the molarity of the solution, and given the symbol Π.

$\Pi = MR'T$

In these relationships, $R = 8.3145$ J/k·mol is the normal gas constant, and $R' = 0.0821$ L·atm/K·mol is the gas constant expressed in terms of liters and atmospheres.

Osmolarity

Osmolarity is a measure of the osmotic pressure that is exerted by a solution across a perfect semi-permeable membrane (one that allows for the free passage of water, but completely prevents the movement of solutes), as compared to pure water. Osmolarity is dependent on the number of particles in solution, but independent of the nature of the particles. For example, 1 mole of glucose dissolved in 1 liter (L) of water has an osmolarity of 1 osmole (osm)/L. If 1 mole of another sugar, such as sucrose, were added to the same liter of water, then the osmolarity would become 2 osm/L. It does not matter that the solution contains 1 mole each of two different solutes: glucose and sucrose. If 1 mole of NaCl were dissolved in 1 L of water, it would produce a 1 mol/L NaCl solution with an osmolarity 2 osm/L, because NaCl dissociates into Na^+ and Cl^- (two particles) in solution. This is true of all compounds that dissociate in solution.

Properties of colloids

The following are properties of colloids:
- The particles of dispersant are between approximately 5-200 nm in diameter.
- The mixture does not separate upon standing in a standard gravity condition (i.e., one "g").
- The mixture does not separate by common fiber filter, but might be filterable by materials with a smaller mesh.
- The mixture is not necessarily completely homogeneous, but is usually close to being so.
- The mixture may appear cloudy or almost totally transparent; but, if you shine a light beam through it, the pathway of the light is visible from any angle. This scattering of light is called the Tyndall effect
- There usually is not a definite, sharp saturation point at which no more dispersant can be taken by the dispersing agent.
- The dispersant can be coagulated, or separated, by clumping the dispersant particles with heat, or by an increase in the concentration of ionic particles in solution into the mixture.
- There is usually only a small effect of any of the colligative properties due to the dispersant.

Henry's law

In chemistry, Henry's law states that the mass of a gas that dissolves in a definite volume of liquid is directly proportional to the pressure of the gas, provided that the gas does not react with the solvent. William Henry first formulated the law in 1801.

The formula for Henry's law is as follows:
$$e^P = e^{kC}$$
Where:
P = The partial pressure of the gaseous solute above the solution.
C = The concentration of the gas in mol/L.
k = Henry's law constant, which has the units L·atm/mol.

Molecular weight

The unit of the molecular weight (MW), formula weight (FW), or atomic weight is "grams per mole", which provides a relationship between the mass in grams and moles of material. The formula to calculate this relationship is as follows:
$$MW = \frac{m}{n}$$
Where:
m = The mass of the material.
n = The number of moles of material.

Empirical formula and molecular formula

The empirical formula is the formula whose subscripts represent the simplest whole number ratio of atoms in a molecule, or the simplest whole number ratio of moles of each element in a mole of the compound. The simplest formula is usually determined by considering experimental data, hence the name "empirical", which means that it is based upon experimentation. The empirical formula speaks of relative numbers. For example, CH_2 says that there will be twice as many hydrogens as there are carbons in the compound that has this simplest formula.

The molecular formula is a formula whose subscripts represent the exact numbers of atoms of each element per molecule of the compound, or the absolute number of moles of each element per mole of the compound. A molecular formula may be reducible to a simple formula if all of its subscripts are divisible by a common denominator. Some compounds have the same empirical and molecular formula. For example, carbon dioxide has, as its empirical and molecular formula, CO_2. The empirical and molecular formulas for sulfur dioxide are also the same: SO_2. There are many situations where two or more compounds have the same simplest formula, but differ by their molecular formulas.

Chemical formulas

Substances (either compounds or mixtures) can be written as a combination of the symbols for its constituent elements, but have to be written in correct proportion. The written representation of a molecule of a substance, using symbols of the constituent elements, is called the molecular or chemical formula. For example, a molecule of potassium permanganate is written as $KMnO_4$, which means that one molecule of potassium permanganate contains one atom of potassium (K), one atom of manganese (Mn), and four atoms of oxygen (O). A molecule of water is written as H_2O, which means that there are 2 atoms of hydrogen (H) and one atom of oxygen (O). In an ordinary molecule of table salt, or NaCl, there is one atom of sodium (Na) and one atom of chlorine (Cl).

Note: To be able to write a chemical formula, we must first know the chemical reaction that precedes the formation of the compound.

Molecular compounds

Molecular compounds are named differently than ionic compounds. For molecular compounds, a set of prefixes are used that identify the subscript in the formula. For example, in the case of PCl_3, there is one phosphorus atom (P^{3+}) and three chlorides ($3Cl^-$). In order to identify the subscript for chloride, we would use the prefix "tri-" to indicate that there are three chloride ions. Therefore, the molecular name for PCl_3 is Phosphorus Trichloride. Another example would be N_2O_4. In this case, we would use the prefix "di-" in front of the elemental name for nitrogen in order to indicate that there are 2 nitrogen atoms ($2N^{4+}$), and then we would use the prefix "tetra-" in front of the oxide ion to indicate that there are four oxides ($4O^{2-}$). Therefore, the molecular name for N_2O_4 is Dinitrogen Tetroxide.

Metric units

Length
1 centimeter (cm) = 10 millimeters (mm)
1 decimeter (dm) = 10 cm
1 meter (m) = 10 dm
1 decameter (dam) = 10 m

Volume
1 microliter (μL) = 10^{-6} liters (L)
1 milliliter (mL) = 10^{-3} L = 1000 μL
1 liter = 1000 mL
1 centiliter (cL) = 10 mL
1 deciliter (dL) = 10 cL
1 liter = 10 dL
1 cubic cm (cm^3) = 1000 mm^3
1 cubic dm (dm^3) = 1000 cm^3
1 cubic meter (m^3) = 1000 dm^3 = 1000 L

Weight
1 picogram (pg) = 10^{-12} grams (g)
1 nanogram (ng) = 10^{-9} g = 1000 pg
1 microgram (μg) = 10^{-6} g = 1000 ng
1 milligram (mg) = 10^{-3} g = 1000 μg
1 gram = 1000 mg
1 kilogram (kg) = 10^3 g = 1000 g
1 tonne = 1000 kg

Relationships
1 part per million (ppm) = 1 mg/kg = 1 μg/g
1 part per hundred (%) = 1 g/100 g = 1% w/w (weight to weight basis)

SI Prefixes and their Multiplying Factors

yotta (Y) – 1,000,000,000,000,000,000,000,000 = 10^{24}
zetta (Z) – 1,000,000,000,000,000,000,000 = 10^{21}
exa (E) – 1,000,000,000,000,000,000 = 10^{18}
peta (P) – 1,000,000,000,000,000 = 10^{15}
tera (T) – 1,000,000,000,000 = 10^{12}
giga (G) – 1,000,000,000 = 10^9 = a billion
mega (M) – 1,000,000 = 10^6 = a million
kilo (k) – 1,000 = 10^3 = a thousand
hecto (h) – 100 = 10^2 = a hundred
deca (da) – 10 = ten
1
deci (d) – 0.1 = 10^{-1} = a tenth
centi (c) – 0.01 = 10^{-2} = a hundredth
milli (m) – 0.001 = 10^{-3} = a thousandth
micro (μ) – 0.000 001 = 10^{-6} = a millionth
nano (n) – 0.000 000 001 = 10^{-9} = a billionth
pico (p) – 0.000 000 000 001 = 10^{-12}
femto (f) – 0.000 000 000 000 001 = 10^{-15}
atto (a) – 0.000 000 000 000 000 001 = 10^{-18}
zepto (z) – 0.000 000 000 000 000 000 001 = 10^{-21}
yocto (y) – 0.000 000 000 000 000 000 000 001 = 10^{-24}

Gram atomic mass and moles

The amount of substance in grams equal to its atomic mass in grams is called the gram atomic mass. For example, since the atomic mass of Na is 23, the gram atomic mass of Na is 23 gm. Similarly, since the atomic mass of O is 16, the gram atomic mass of O is 16 gm. The gram atomic mass is also known as the gram atomic weight of a substance. It was discovered by Avogadro, that the gram atomic mass of substance contains 6.23×10^{23} atoms. This means that, if you take 23 gm of Na, there will be 6.23×10^{23} atoms of Na. Similarly, if you take 16 gm of O, you will have 6.23×10^{23} atoms of O. Since the sizes of atoms increases with the masses of the atoms, Avogadro's number remains constant for the different atomic masses. The mass of a substance that contains 6.23×10^{23} atoms is also known as the molar mass. Thus, 1 mole of Na will be 23 gm of Na, and 1 mole of O will be 16 gm of O. The amount of substance in grams equal to the molecular mass in grams is called the gram molecular mass. For example, the molecular mass of NaCl is 60. Thus, the gram molecular mass of NaCl is 60 gm. The molecular mass of O_2 is 32, and therefore the gram molecular mass of O_2 is 32 gm. Finally, since the molecular mass of water is 18, the gram molecular mass of water is 18 gm.

Density

The density of a substance determines whether it is in the solid, liquid, or gaseous state. Density is defined as follows:

$$\text{Density} = \frac{\text{Mass of Substance (in gm)}}{\text{Volume of Substance (in cubic cm)}}$$

Generally, if the density is high, then the substance is in solid form. If the density is low, then the substance is in liquid form. If the density is even lower, then the substance is in a gaseous state. It is imperative here that density is also a function of temperature. The density of iron is 7.86 gm/cc.

The density of iron in liquid form (at a temperature of 1537°C) is approximately 7.23 gm/cc. Thus, it can be seen that the solid iron volume expands upon heating and becomes liquid. Other than ice, all substances become more dense when they solidify. Water is the only substance in nature whose volume expands upon solidification. The density of ice is 0.93 gm/cc, while the density of water is 1.0 gm/cc. This is the reason why ice floats on water.

Assigning oxidation numbers

The following explains how oxidation numbers are assigned:
- The oxidation number for elements is always zero. For example, Na (s), O_2 (g), and C (s) all have zero oxidation numbers.
- The oxidation number of monoatomic ions is the same as their charge. This means that for Na^+ the oxidation number is +1, and for Cl^- the oxidation number is -1. Oxygen is assigned a -2 oxidation number in covalent compounds. This refers to compounds such as CO, CO_2, SO_2, and SO_3.
- There is an exception to the previous rule, and it involves peroxides, such as H_2O_2. Here, each O in the O_2^{2-} group has a -1 oxidation number.
- Hydrogen is assigned a +1 oxidation number in covalent compounds. This refers to compounds such as HCl, NH_3, and H_2O.
- In binary compounds, the element with the greatest attraction to electrons gets the negative oxidation number. In other words, the most electronegative of the pair gets the negative number.
- The sum of the oxidation numbers is zero for a neutral compound, and equal to the ionic charge for an ionic species. For example, in H_2O, a neutral species, H is +1, O is -2, and the sum of the two is 0. For CO_3^{2-}, each O is -2, C is +4, and the sum is -2.

Redox titrations

A redox titration (also called oxidation-reduction titration, or potentiometric titration) is a type of titration that is based upon a redox reaction between the analyte and titrant. A redox titration involves the use of a potentiometer. An analyte is the substance or chemical constituent that is being measured in an analytical procedure. For instance, in an immunoassay, the analyte may be the ligand, while in a blood glucose test, the analyte is glucose. A reagent of known concentration and volume, called the titrant, is used to react with a measured volume of reactant. Using a calibrated burette to add the titrant, it is possible to determine the exact amount that has been consumed when the endpoint is reached. The endpoint of a titration is when the pH of the reactant is just about equal to 7, and when the reactant stops reverting back to its original color.

Chemical reactions

The transformation of a substance into a new substance or substances is called a chemical reaction. For example, the chemical reaction for the production of water can be written as: $2H_2 + O_2 \rightarrow 2H_2O$.

Hydrogen atoms exists as a diatomic gas, with 2 hydrogen atoms sticking together, written as H_2. The same is true for oxygen gas (O_2). This means that, for the reaction above, the two elements, hydrogen and oxygen in a diatomic gaseous form, combine in a reaction to produce water molecules. The numbers of atoms of each element have to be balanced before and after the reaction takes place. This is important due to the fact that atoms are neither created nor destroyed in a chemical reaction. The factors on the left-hand side of the equation are called the reactants, while the factors on the right-hand side are called the products. Chemical reactions are generally accompanied by heat changes. A reaction in which heat is evolved is called an exothermic chemical reaction. A reaction in which heat is absorbed is called an endothermic chemical reaction. Chemical reactions, whether exothermic or endothermic, are also categorized as reversible or irreversible reactions. A reaction that can proceed in either direction is called reversible, while a reaction that can proceed in only one direction is called irreversible. For example, if you burn sugar in air, you will get carbon and water. This reaction is irreversible because, if you take carbon and water and mix them together, you will never get the original sugar back!

> ➤ **Review Video: Chemical Reactions**
> *Visit mometrix.com/academy and enter Code: 579876*

Writing chemical equations

The following are considerations for writing chemical equations:
- The number of atoms on the reactant side should be the same as the number of atoms on the product side: the reaction should be balanced.
- A horizontal arrow should indicate the direction in which the reaction is proceeding. Normally, the arrow is from left to right ($\rightarrow$). However, for a reversible reaction, the arrow can be shown from the right to left.
- In the case of precipitation of a compound after the reaction, a vertically downward arrow is indicated ($\downarrow$).
- In the case that a product is gaseous, a vertically upward arrow is indicated ($\uparrow$).
- The physical state of the reactants and products can be shown as follows: (s) = solid, (l) = liquid, and (aq) = aqueous (the compound is dissolved in water).
- The conditions under which the reaction takes place can also be indicated. For example, if heat is required to initiate the reaction (an endothermic reaction), it is written over the horizontal arrow, or on the left side of the equation. Alternatively, if heat is given out by the reaction (an exothermic reaction), it is written on the right side of the equation.
- If any catalyst is used for increasing the reaction rate, then it is written above the horizontal arrow.

Combination reactions

Combination reactions are the simplest type of chemical reaction. Here, two or more types of atoms, molecules, or compounds react or combine to produce products. The following are examples of combination reactions:

$2H_2 + O_2 \rightarrow 2H_2O$
$2Na + Cl_2 \rightarrow 2NaCl$

Decomposition reactions

A chemical reaction where a compound splits or decomposes into simpler substances is called a decomposition reaction. The following examples illustrate decomposition reactions:

$2KClO_3 \xrightarrow{\text{Heat}} 2KCl + 3O_2.$
$2H_2O \xrightarrow{\text{Electricity}} 2H_2 + O_2$

Displacement reactions

A chemical reaction, where one element displaces another by virtue of it being more reactive, is called a displacement reaction. In order to determine which element is more reactive than the other, one has to consider the reactivity of the elements. Displacement reactions are primarily seen when one metallic salt solution reacts with another metal. If the second metal is more reactive than the first, then it replaces the first metal in the salt. The following example illustrates a typical displacement reaction:

$CuSO_4$ (aq) + Zn(s) → $ZnSO_4$ + Cu(s)

A blue copper sulphate solution reacting with solid zinc will give rise to a colorless zinc sulphate solution and solid copper. Thus, Zn displaces Cu in the salt form because Zn is more reactive than Cu.

Isomerization reactions

A chemical reaction where rearrangements of atoms occur within a substance without any change in the molecular formula is called an isomerization reaction. Compounds that have the same molecular formula, but different arrangements of atoms, are known as isomers (isomers are different from allotropes). Isomers occur mostly in organic chemistry. The following example illustrates an isomerization reaction:

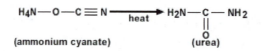

Even though ammonium cyanate and urea have the same chemical formula, their arrangements of atoms inside the molecules differ. They have different structures, and therefore widely differing physical and chemical properties.

Oxidation-reduction reactions

An oxidation reaction involves the addition of oxygen to a reactant, while a reduction reaction involves the addition of hydrogen to a reactant. In a broader perspective, an oxidation reaction is a reaction where an atom or ion loses electrons. Consider the following reaction:

$CuSO_4$ (aq) + Zn (s) → $ZnSO_4$ + Cu (s)

Here, the Zn atom donates two electrons. Since Zn is donating electrons, it is a reducing agent. Zn itself is getting oxidized:

$Zn → Zn^{2+} + 2e^-$

Since Cu is accepting electrons, it is an oxidizing agent, and Cu is getting reduced.

$CuSO_4 → Cu^{2+} + SO_4^{2-}$

$Cu^{2+} + 2e^- → Cu$

Oxidation-reduction reactions are also known as redox reactions. A typical redox reaction is as follows:

$CuO + H_2 → Cu + H_2O$

In the above reaction, the copper oxide loses an oxygen atom, so it is being reduced. The H_2 is gaining an extra oxygen; therefore, it is being oxidized. In this reaction, the CuO is functioning as an oxidizing agent, and the H_2 is functioning as a reducing agent.

The term that is used to describe the degree of oxidation of an element is its oxidation number, or oxidation state.

Haber reaction

The Haber reaction involves the combination of nitrogen gas (N_2) and hydrogen gas (H_2) in order to make ammonia (NH_3):
$$N_2 + 3H_2 \rightarrow 2NH_3$$

The balanced equation requires one nitrogen molecule and three hydrogen molecules in order to make two ammonia molecules. This means that one nitrogen molecule reacts with three hydrogen molecules to make two ammonia molecules.

Enthalpy change

1. The heat content of a chemical system is called the enthalpy (symbol: H).
2. The enthalpy change (ΔH) is the amount of heat that is released or absorbed when a chemical reaction occurs at constant pressure.
3. $\Delta H = H_{products} - H_{reactants}$
4. ΔH is specified per mole of substance, as in the balanced chemical equation for the reaction.
5. The units are usually given as $kJ \cdot mol^{-1}$ (kJ/mol), or sometimes as $kcal \cdot mol^{-1}$ (kcal/mol).
6. 1 calorie (cal) = 4.184 joules (J)
7. Energy changes are measured under standard laboratory conditions: 25°C (298 K) & 101.3 kPa (1 atmosphere).

Exothermic reactions

1. Energy is released.
2. Energy is a product of the reaction.
3. The reaction vessel becomes warmer.
4. The temperature inside of the reaction vessel increases.
5. The energy of the reactants is greater than the energy of the products.
6. $\Delta H = H_{(products)} - H_{(reactants)}$ = negative

For example:
$$N_2\,(g) + 3H_2\,(g) \rightarrow 2NH_3\,(g) + 92.4\ kJ$$
$$N_2\,(g) + 3H_2\,(g) \rightarrow 2NH_3\,(g) \quad \Delta H = -92.4\ kJ \cdot mol^{-1}$$

Endothermic reactions

1. Energy is absorbed.
2. Energy is a reactant of the reaction.
3. The reaction vessel becomes cooler.
4. The temperature inside of the reaction vessel decreases.
5. The energy of the reactants is less than the energy of the products.
6. $\Delta H = H_{(products)} - H_{(reactants)} =$ positive

For example:
$2NH_3\,(g) + 92.4\text{ kJ} \rightarrow N_2\,(g) + 3H_2\,(g)$
$2NH_3\,(g) \rightarrow N_2\,(g) + 3H_2\,(g)$ $\Delta H = +92.4\text{ kJ·mol}^{-1}$

Hess's law

Hess's law states that the heat transferred in a reaction, or the change in enthalpy (ΔH), is the same regardless of whether the reaction occurs in a single step, or in several steps. The method for calculating the enthalpy of the reaction, developed by Hess, is called Hess's law of heat summation. According to this law, if a series of reactions are added together, the net change in the heat of the reaction is the sum of the enthalpy changes for each step. The rules for using Hess's law are as follows:

1. If the reaction is multiplied (or divided) by some factor, then ΔH must also be multiplied (or divided) by that same factor.
2. If the reaction is reversed (flipped), then the sign of ΔH must also be reversed.

> ➢ **Review Video: <u>Hess's Law</u>**
> *Visit **mometrix.com/academy** and enter **Code:** **329059***

Missing mass and heat of combustion

Chemical reactions on a microscopic level are simply the breaking and forming of bonds between the reactant compounds involved in the reaction. It has been observed that a stable compound has less mass (or energy) than the sum of masses of each of the atoms that form the compound. The missing mass is called the binding energy of the compound, and goes to forming the bonds between the atoms. All chemical reactions proceed in the direction of attaining greater binding energy. The greater the binding energy, the more difficult it is to break the compound, and therefore it is more stable. If you plot the energy (or mass) scale vertically, you will see that a compound will be lower on the same scale. The lower down the compound is, the tighter the binding is. In Einstein's famous equation, $E = mc^2$, the missing mass becomes the binding energy of the compound or the molecule.

The heat that is released upon completely burning 1 mole of a compound or substance in air (or oxygen) is known as the heat of combustion of the compound or substance. If the heat of combustion is high, then the compound or substance is a good material for burning.

Bond enthalpy and bond length

We know that multiple bonds are shorter than single bonds. We can also show that multiple bonds are stronger than single bonds, because atoms are held closer and more tightly together as the number of bonds between the atoms increases. Therefore, bond enthalpy increases as bond length decreases.

Calorimetric analysis

One method for determining the energy exchange between the reaction system and its environment is to conduct a calorimetric analysis. A calorimeter is a thermally insulated container where a reaction system can be performed, and the energy exchange between the system and its environment can be measured. The calorimeter and its contents are considered the environment, while the reaction system is a chemical or physical process that occurs within the confines of the calorimeter. The following equation applies:

$$Q_{surr} = Q_{cal} + Q_{contents}$$

The Q_{cal} can be determined if one knows the heat capacity of the calorimeter. This heat capacity can be experimentally determined, and is expressed in kJ/°C. In order to determine the Q_{cal}, you multiply the heat capacity of the calorimeter by the difference between the final and initial temperatures.

Thermal capacity

The thermal capacity of a substance is defined as the amount of heat that is required to raise (or lower) its temperature by 1°C.

Thermal Capacity = Mass × Specific Heat

The thermal capacity of water is very large. This is the reason why it is used as a coolant in many applications, such as in car radiators. It can store within its mass more heat energy before it starts to change its state to steam. Heat energy flows from a hotter body to a colder body when the two bodies are brought into contact. The heat will continue to flow until the temperatures are equalized. No heat flows from one body to the other when they are at equal temperatures. This is called thermal equilibrium.

Specific heat

Heat energy is measured in joules (J). But, more commonly, heat is measured in calories (cal) or in kilocalories (kcal). One kilocalorie is defined as the amount of heat that is needed to raise the temperature of 1 kg of water by 1°C. One calorie = 4.18 joules.

The specific heat of a substance is defined as the amount of heat that is required to raise the temperature of 1 kg of the substance by 1°C. The specific heat is denoted by "s", and its unit of measurement is J/kg°C (joules per kilogram degree centigrade). The specific heat of water is 4180 J/kg°C.

The quantity of heat, Q, that is taken in or given out by a body depends on the mass of the body, the specific heat of the body, and the change in temperature that occurs because of the heat taken in or given out. Thus,

$Q = m \times s \times \Delta T$

Where:

m = the mass of the substance.

s = The specific heat of the substance.

ΔT = The change in temperature

Gibbs free energy

The Gibbs free energy of a system, at any moment in time, is defined as the enthalpy of the system, minus the product of the temperature times the entropy of the system:

$G = H - TS$

The Gibbs free energy of a system is a state function, because it is defined in terms of thermodynamic properties that are state functions. The change in the Gibbs free energy of a system, which occurs during a reaction, is therefore equal to the change in the enthalpy of the system, minus the change in the product of the temperature times the entropy of the system:

$\Delta G = \Delta H - \Delta(TS)$

If the reaction is run at constant temperature, then this equation can be written as follows:

$G = \Delta H - \Delta TS$

There are 4 possible types of reactions with regard to the enthalpic and entropic contribution to the free energy change:

- ΔH = (-), $-T\Delta S$ = (-): Favorable enthalpic change (exothermic), and favorable entropic change (disorder increases).
- ΔH = (+), $-T\Delta S$ = (+): Unfavorable enthalpic change (endothermic), and unfavorable entropic change (disorder decreases).
- ΔH = (-), $-T\Delta S$ = (+): Favorable enthalpic change (exothermic), and unfavorable entropic change (disorder decreases).
- ΔH = (+), $-T\Delta S$ = (-): Unfavorable enthalpic change (endothermic), and favorable entropic change (disorder increases).

Spontaneous reactions often have the following characteristics:

- A negative enthalpy (release of heat energy, $\Delta H < 0$).
- An increase in entropy (increase in disorder, $\Delta S > 0$).

Zeroth law

According to the zeroth law, if two systems are in thermal equilibrium with a third system, then the two systems are also in thermal equilibrium. Two systems are said to be in thermal equilibrium if heat energy is not exchanged between two systems. The concept of temperature is made objective by this law, and is defined as the state of a thermodynamic system that determines the direction of the flow of heat.

Laws of thermodynamics

First law of thermodynamics
The conservation law, states that energy can neither be created nor destroyed. This law provides the basis for all quantitative accounts of energy, regardless of its form, and makes energy the most important concept in physics.

Second law of thermodynamics
Elements in a closed system tend to seek their most probable distribution. In a closed system, entropy always increases.

Third law of thermodynamics
The third law of thermodynamics, or the asymptotic law, states that all processes slow down as they operate closer to the thermodynamic equilibrium, making it difficult in practice to reach that equilibrium. This law suggests that the powerful and fast changes, which are typical of technology and characteristic of living forms of organization, are bound to occur only at levels that are far removed from thermodynamic equilibrium.

Every thermodynamic system possesses an interval energy, U, and has the capacity to do external work, W, which may be called the external energy. If heat energy is supplied (dQ) to a system, then according to the first law of thermodynamics, also known as the law of conservation of energy, it follows that the sum total of changes in the internal and external energy of the system must equal the heat energy supplied to the system:

$dQ = dU + dW$

Where:
    1. dU is an exact differential that depends only on the initial and final states of the system, but not on the path that connects these states.
    2. dQ and dW are inexact differentials, as they depend upon the path between the initial and final states.

> ➤ **Review Video: Laws of Thermodynamics**
> *Visit **mometrix.com/academy** and enter **Code: 253607***

Conversion between Fahrenheit and Celsius

To convert Fahrenheit temperatures into Celsius:
    1. Subtract 32 from the Fahrenheit number.
    2. Divide the answer by 9.
    3. Multiply that answer by 5.

For example, to change 95° Fahrenheit to Celsius:
    1. 95 – 32 = 63
    2. 63 ÷ 9 = 7
    3. 7 × 5 = 35°C

To convert Celsius temperatures into Fahrenheit:
1. Multiply the Celsius temperature by 9.
2. Divide the answer by 5.
3. Add 32 to the answer.

For example, to change 20° Celsius to Fahrenheit:
1. $20 \times 9 = 180$
2. $180 \div 5 = 36$
3. $36 + 32 = 68°F$

Heat conduction

The law of heat conduction, also known as Fourier's law, states that the time rate of heat flow, Q, through an object is proportional to the gradient of the temperature difference:

$$Q = KA \frac{\Delta T}{\Delta x}$$

Where:
K = The conductivity constant, which is dependent upon the nature of the material and its temperature.
A = The transversal surface area.
ΔT = The temperature difference through which the heat is being transferred.
Δx = The thickness of the body of matter through which the heat is passing.

Note: This law forms the basis for the derivation of the heat equation.

Latent heat

The absorption (or release) of heat while changing states is known as the latent heat (L). The latent heat of a substance is the amount of heat that is absorbed (or released) by a unit of mass of a substance in order to change its state without any change in temperature. The MKS unit for latent heat is joules per kilogram, or J/kg.

The latent heat for a solid to liquid transition is known as the latent heat of fusion, while the latent heat for a liquid to gas transition is known as the latent heat of vaporization. If L is the latent heat of a substance, and m is the mass of the substance, then the heat, Q (absorbed or released), that is required to change its state $= Q \times L$. It may be clear, now, that the latent heat of ice (to water) is different from the latent heat of water (to steam).

P-V diagrams

A P-V diagram is a graph that is used to evaluate the efficiency of a thermodynamic process by plotting the pressure, P, versus the volume, V, of the system. The product of pressure and volume represents a quantity of work, and this quantity is represented by the area beneath the P-V curve. Therefore, the area that is enclosed by the four boundaries of the P-V diagram represents the net work that is done by the process during one cycle.

Nature of reactants

We have seen that some elements, because of the way that their electronic configuration occurs, are very reactive. For example, Na, K, and Rb readily give off their electrons, while F, Cl, and Br are elements which quickly accept electrons. On the other hand, noble gases like He, Ne, and Ar are completely chemically inert. Non-metals like C, N, and O also react, but not as vigorously as F, Cl, Br, etc. In most cases, the valence of the reactants will give you a rough estimate of the reaction rates. Reactions produce products by having the reacting molecules come into contact with one another. The more often that they collide, the more likely the chance that product will form. If the reacting molecules move more rapidly, such as in the gaseous state, then the product will be more likely to form. This concept is part of an overriding theory that forms the foundation of all kinetics work, called the collisional theory of reaction rates. Reactions usually occur more rapidly when the reactants are in the gaseous state. The next most favorable reaction condition involves the reacting molecules dispersed in a solution. Reactions do occur in pure liquids or in solid form, but the rates tend to be a lot slower because the reacting molecules are very restricted in their movements among one another, and therefore do not come into contact as often.

The relative reaction rates generally conform to the following order:
Gases > Solutions > Pure Liquids > Solids

Rate of change and the rate constant

The rate of change in the concentrations of the reactants and products can be used to characterize the rate of a chemical reaction. The rate of change in the concentration corresponds to the slope of the concentration-time plot. The rate constant, k, is a proportionality constant in the relationship between the rate and concentrations. This constant has a fixed value at any given temperature, but varies with temperature. For a general reaction, $aA + bB \rightarrow cC + dD$, we would have the following rate law:

$$Rate = k[A]^m[B]^n$$

Catalysts

There are certain substances that, by their mere presence, enhance the rate of reaction. These substances are called catalysts. Catalysts themselves do not participate in the reaction, and remain unchanged. For a reversible and balanced reaction, a catalyst helps the reaction to be more favorable in one direction than the other. There are many examples of catalysts in chemical reactions. For example, if you heat $KClO_3$, it will start to decompose at a very high temperature. However, if a small quantity of MnO_2 is added, the decomposition of $KClO_3$ will occur faster, and at a lower temperature. The chlorophyll in plant leaves acts as a catalyst for the plants to convert energy from the sun into glucose. And, platinum is used as a catalyst for reactions where acids are manufactured.

Homogeneous catalysts
Homogeneous catalysts are catalysts that form a uniform distribution between themselves and the reactant molecules. These catalysts are in a solution together with the reactant molecules. Because they are dispersed within a solution, the surface area of the catalyst is maximized, and, usually, these types of catalysts tend to be more efficient in increasing product formation at a lower temperature. Examples of homogeneous catalysts include any protic acid. A protic acid is an acid that donates hydrogen ions (protons). Sulfuric acid, H_2SO_4, in water catalyzes the dehydration of

alcohols (i.e., the loss of water), in order to produce double-bonded compounds, called alkenes. Phosphoric acid, H_3PO_4, can catalyze the formation of organic esters by combining alcohol and carboxylic acid molecules together, splitting out a water molecule. Aprotic acids, or Lewis acids, also serve as homogeneous catalysts. An aprotic acid is an acid that accepts electrons. Aprotic acids, such as $AlCl_3$, can catalyze substitution reactions in which a hydrogen atom on a benzene ring is replaced by a hydrocarbon group, such as a methyl group, $-CH_3$. This same aprotic acid is also useful in catalyzing the chlorination of an alkene in order to form a dichloroalkane.

Heterogeneous catalysts

Heterogeneous catalysts are sometimes called surface catalysts because they position the reactant molecules on their very surface. Many metals serve as heterogeneous catalysts, in which the reactant molecules have an interface between themselves and the catalyst surface. In the reaction, known as hydrogenation, double bonds between carbons accept two hydrogen atoms, and use the pi electrons between the two carbons in order to attach these hydrogen atoms to the carbon atom. The diatomic hydrogen molecule attaches itself to the surface of a metal catalyst, such as platinum, nickel, or palladium. The double-bonded organic molecule does the same. The single bond between the hydrogen atoms is broken, and so is the pi bond between the two carbons within the organic molecule. The hydrogen atoms then form a single bond between its single electron and one of the two pi electrons that previously constituted the pi bond between the two carbon atoms. Once the hydrogens have been attached, the product molecule disengages from the surface, only to have fresh reactant molecules take its place upon the surface of the metal. Heterogeneous catalysts are, as a rule, not as efficient as homogeneous catalysts.

> **Review Video: Catalysts**
Visit mometrix.com/academy and enter Code: 729053

Reversible and irreversible processes

If a system is taken from one state to another, and can be brought back to the initial state, then the process is called a reversible process. The change from the initial to final state should obviously proceed through the infinitesimal changes, each being a quasi-static state of equilibrium. Some examples are changes in a gas through isochoric, isothermal, or adiabatic changes. If a system is taken from one state to another, but cannot be brought back to the initial state, then the process is called an irreversible process. Some examples are the free expansion of a gas, the dissipation of energy due to friction, or the mixing of two gases or liquids, etc.

Reversible chemical reactions

A chemical reaction in which substances react together to produce resultants, and the resultants in turn react with one another to produce the original substances, is known as a reversible chemical reaction. For example, if calcium oxide is kept in close contact with carbon dioxide, the two substances will slowly unite to make calcium carbonate.
$CaO + CO_2 \rightarrow CaCO_3$

If you heat $CaCO_3$, then you will get back CaO and CO_2.
The two equations can be combined as follows:
$$CaCO_3 \Leftrightarrow CaO + CO_2 \uparrow$$

The horizontal arrow shows that the reaction proceeds in both directions. The vertical arrow indicates that the carbon dioxide gas escapes. Each chemical reaction is characterized by a rate of reaction, which is the rate at which the reactants combine to produce the final product. The rate of a reaction depends on various factors, such as the temperature, the nature of the reacting substances, etc. In a reversible chemical reaction, if the rate of the forward reaction and the rate of backward reaction are the same, we say that the reaction has reached equilibrium.

Law of mass action

The law of mass action is universal, applicable under any circumstance. However, for reactions that are complete, the result may not be very useful. We introduce the mass action law by using a general chemical reaction equation in which reactants, A and B, react to give product, C and D:
$$aA + bB \rightarrow cC + dD$$
Where:
a, b, c, and d = The coefficients for a balanced chemical equation.

The law of mass action states that, if the system is at equilibrium at a given temperature, then the following ratio is a constant:
$$K_{eq} = \frac{[C]^c[D]^d}{[A]^a[B]^b}$$

The square brackets [ ] around the chemical species represent their concentrations. This is the ideal law of chemical equilibrium, otherwise known as the law of mass action.

Reaction quotients and equilibrium constants

If the system is NOT at equilibrium, then the ratio is different from the equilibrium constant. In such cases, the ratio is called a reaction quotient which is designated as Q.
$$Q = \frac{[C]^c[D]^d}{[A]^a[B]^b}$$

A system that is not at equilibrium will tend toward equilibrium, and the requisite changes will alter the Q so that its value approaches the equilibrium constant, K_{eq}.
$$Q \rightarrow K_{eq}$$

K_{eq} is the ratio of products to reactants. Therefore, the larger K is, the more products will be present at equilibrium. Conversely, the smaller K is, the more reactants will be present at equilibrium. If K >> 1, then products dominate at equilibrium, and the equilibrium lies to the right. If K << 1, then the reactants dominate at equilibrium, and the equilibrium lies to the left.

Le Chatelier's principle

When a system at equilibrium is subjected to a disturbance, the composition of the system adjusts so as to minimize the effect of the disturbance. An increase in temperature favors an endothermic reaction. The heat absorbed tends to oppose the increase in temperature. A decrease in temperature favors an exothermic reaction. The heat released opposes the lowering of temperature. Changes in concentration will change the Q so that it no longer equals K, and leads to a shift to restore Q so that it is equal to K.

Reactions generally have the following characteristics:
- For an endothermic reaction heat can be considered as a reactant.
- For an exothermic reaction heat can be considered as a product.
- If $\Delta H > 0$, adding heat favors the forward reaction, while cooling favors the reverse reaction.
- If $\Delta H < 0$, adding heat favors the reverse reaction, while cooling favors the forward reaction.

Radicals

Sometimes, in a chemical reaction of compounds, the constituent elements are not released, but there may be a group of atoms sticking together. These groups are called radicals. Thus, a radical is a component of a compound that consists of groups of atoms. Radicals can be positively or negatively charged. To simplify, ions are called simple radicals, and groups of atomic radicals are called compound radicals. For example, hydroxide (OH) is called a compound radical and is negatively charged. Thus, it is written as OH^-. Other common compound radicals are sulfate (SO_4^{2-}), nitrate (NO_3^-), etc.

Binary ionic compounds

Naming binary ionic compounds involves first naming the element that appears first in the formula, using the name of the element itself, and then naming the second part of the formula, which is usually the anion in an ionic compound, and typically ends in "-ide". If there is a multivalent element involved, such as iron, copper, lead, tin, or mercury, one will have to determine which valence is involved before the name can be established. For example, for $FeCl_3$, we know that Fe has two possible valences. We also know that the total positive charge plus the total negative charge will equal zero. Since we have one Fe, and we know that the halogens in binary compounds are -1, we can determine the valence, x, of Fe as follows:
$$1x_{Fe} + 3x_{Cl} = 0$$
Where:
x_{Fe} = Valence of Fe
x_{Cl} = Valence of Cl = -1

$$1(x_{Fe}) + 3(-1) = 0$$
$$x_{Fe} = +3$$

Therefore, the Fe atom is in the +3 state, and the name of the compound is: Iron (III) Chloride.

Ternary ionic compounds

Naming ternary ionic compounds uses the same procedure as binary ionic compounds. The one big difference is the ending of the name: it is seldom "ide", although in some cases it is. Other more common endings are "ate" and "ite". What is the name of $Be(HSO_3)_2$?

First, identify the element name of Be^{2+}, which is Beryllium. Next, identify the HSO_3^- ion, which is Hydrogen Sulfite. Finally, add the two together to get the name: Beryllium Hydrogen Sulfite.

Standard solutions

There are two types of standard solutions: molar solutions and normal solutions. A molar solution (M) is a solution that contains 1 mole of solute for each liter of solution. One mole of a substance in grams is equivalent to the molecular weight (MW) of that substance (sometimes referred to as the 'gram molecular weight' (gMW)). Thus, a 1 M solution contains 1 gMW of solute per liter of solution. A normal solution (N) is a solution that contains 1 'gram equivalent weight' (gEW) of solute per liter of solution. The gEW is equivalent to the MW, expressed in grams, divided by the 'valency' of the solute.

Concentration units

Concentration units are as follows:
- Mass Percent (%) – (g solute/total g) x 100.
- Mole Fraction (X) – Mole solute/total moles.
- Molality (m) – Mole solute/kg solvent.
- Molarity (M) – Mole solute/L solution.
- Conversion Between Concentration Units:
  - Assume an amount (denominator).
  - Calculate the mass/moles of solute and solvent.
  - Calculate the desired concentration.
- Dilution:
  - $M_1V_1 = M_2V_2$
  - Add sufficient solution to bring the final volume to the total.

Properties of solutions

The properties of solutions are as follows:
- The particles of solute are the size of individual small molecules, or individual small ions. One nanometer is about the maximum diameter for a solute particle.
- The mixture does not separate on standing. In a gravity environment, the solution will not come apart due to any difference in density of the materials in the solution.
- The mixture does not separate by common fiber filter. The entire solution will pass through the filter.
- Once it is completely mixed, the mixture is homogeneous. If you take a sample of the solution from any point in the solution, the proportions of the materials will be the same.
- The mixture appears clear rather than cloudy. It may have some color to it, but it seems to be transparent otherwise.

- The mixture shows no Tyndall effect: light is not scattered by the solution. If you shine a light into the solution, the pathway of the light through the solution is not revealed to an observer outside of the pathway.
- The solute is completely dissolved into the solvent up to a point that is characteristic of the solvent, solute, and temperature. At a saturation point, the solvent can no longer dissolve any more of the solute. If there is a saturation point, the point is distinct and characteristic of the type of materials, as well as the temperature of the solution.
- The solution of an ionic material into water will result in an electrolyte solution. The ions of solute will separate in water to permit the solution to carry an electric current.
- The solution shows an increase in osmotic pressure between it and a reference solution as the amount of solute is increased.
- The solution shows an increase in boiling point as the amount of solute is increased.
- The solution shows a decrease in melting point as the amount of solute is increased.
- A solution of a solid, non-volatile solute in a liquid solvent shows a decrease in vapor pressure above the solution as the amount of solute is increased.

Solubility of ionic compounds in water

The following explains the solubility of ionic compounds in water:
- All compounds of the ammonium ion (NH_4^+), and of alkali metal (group IA) cations, are soluble.
- All nitrates and acetates (ethanoates) are soluble.
- All chlorides, bromides, and iodides are soluble EXCEPT for those of silver, lead, and mercury(I).
- All sulphates are soluble EXCEPT for those of silver, lead, mercury(I), barium, strontium, and calcium.
- All carbonates, sulfites, and phosphates are insoluble EXCEPT for those of ammonium and alkali metal cations.
- All hydroxides are insoluble EXCEPT for those of ammonium, barium, and alkali metal cations.
- All sulfides are insoluble EXCEPT for those of ammonium, alkali metal cations, and alkali earth metal (group II) cations.
- All oxides are insoluble EXCEPT for those of calcium, barium, and alkali metal cations. The soluble ones actually react with the water to form hydroxides (hydrolyse).

Homogenous and heterogeneous mixtures

Substances can also be made up of combinations of compounds, called mixtures. In a mixture, the individual constituents retain their original properties. For example, if you take brine (salt solution), it is a mixture of salt (sodium chloride) and water. If you boil brine, you will be able to separate the two compounds, and will get back pure water and pure salt. If you take lemon sherbet, you will be able to separate lemon juice, water, sugar, and salt from it. In a mixture, the constituents do not chemically combine to give a totally new substance, as happens during the formation of a compound. The example for brine is that of a homogenous mixture, where one compound is completely soluble in the other compound and the mixture displays the same property throughout its bulk. There are also cases where the mixtures consist of compounds that are not soluble with each other, called heterogeneous mixtures. An example of a heterogeneous mixture would be liquid mixtures of oil and water, mud and water, etc. Mixtures can be separated into their constituent parts by various processes such as evaporation, distillation, filtration, etc.

Separation of Mixtures:
- Filtration – Particle size.
- Centrifugation – Density.
- Distillation – State.
- Fractional Distillation – Boiling point.
- Fractional Crystallization – Solubility vs. temperature.
- Chromatography – Solubility, size, and affinity.

Lewis and Bronsted-Lowry acids and bases

A Lewis acid is defined as an electron acceptor, while a Lewis base is defined as an electron donor. The Lewis theory of acids and bases is more general than the "one-sided" nature of the Bronsted-Lowry theory, which defines an acid as a proton donor and a base as a proton acceptor. Keep in mind that the Bronsted-Lowry theory REQUIRES the presence of a solvent, specifically a protic solvent, of which water is the usual example. Since almost all chemistry is performed in water, the fact that this limits the Bronsted-Lowry definition is of little practical consequence. The Lewis definition of an acid and base do not have the constraints that the Bronsted-Lowry theory does, and many more reactions are seen to be acidic or basic in nature when using the Lewis definition than when using the Bronsted-Lowry definition.

Dissociation of water

In pure water, the following equilibrium is established:
$$H_2O\,(l) \rightarrow H^+\,(aq) + OH^-\,(aq)$$

At 25°C, the following is true:
$$K_w = [H_2O] = [H^+][OH^-] = 1.0 \times 10^{-14}$$

The above is called the autoionization of water. The H^+ (aq) ion is simply a proton with no electrons (elemental H has one proton, one electron, and no neutrons). In water, the H^+ (aq) ions form clusters. The simplest cluster is the hydronium ion, H_3O^+ (aq), while some examples of larger clusters are $H_5O_2^+$ and $H_9O_4^+$. $H_9O_4^+$, an H_3O^+ surrounded by three H-bonded water molecules, is currently accepted to be most important hydronium ion structure. Often, H_3O^+ is used to represent the hydronium ion, even though $H_9O_4^+$ is the more accurate formula for this species. Generally, we use H^+ (aq) and H_3O^+ (aq) interchangeably.

pH of solutions

To understand if a given solution is acidic or not, H^+ ion concentration is generally measured. The H^+ concentration is then converted to a logarithmic scale from 1-14, referred to as the pH of the solution. It has been found experimentally that the concentration of H^+ and OH^- in neutral water is 10^{-7} moles per liter. For an acidic solution, the concentration of H^+ ions is $> 10^{-7}$ moles per liter. And, for an alkaline solution, the OH^- concentration is $< 10^{-7}$ moles per liter. In the symbol, pH, p stands for potenz, which means strength (or power), while the H stands for H^+. Together, pH stands for the strength of the H^+ concentration in solution, expressed in moles per liter. The pH of a solution is defined as the negative logarithm of the exponent, or power, of 10 for the H^+ ion concentration. Thus, $[H^+] = 10^{-pH}$ (concentration is shown as a boxed bracket), and $-\log_{10}[H^+] = pH$. In a neutral solution, the pH is 7. In an acidic solution, the pH is between 1 and 7. And, in an alkaline solution, the pH is between 7 and 14. Since the p "factor" is defined as the negative log of the molar concentration of whatever follows the letter p, it can also be combined with other components to be used as a measure of their concentration. Other possible derivatives include the following:

$pCl = -\log[Cl^-]$

$pK_a = -\log(K_a)$

$pK_w = -\log(K_w)$

$pAg = -\log[Ag^+]$

$pOH = -\log[OH^-] = 14 - pH$

Conjugate acid-base pairs

Whatever is left of an acid after the proton is donated is called its conjugate base. Similarly, whatever remains of the base after it accepts a proton is called a conjugate acid. Consider the following reaction:

$$HA\,(aq) + H_2O\,(l) \rightarrow H_3O^+\,(aq) + A^-\,(aq)$$

After HA (acid) loses its proton, it is converted into A^- (base). Therefore, HA and A^- are conjugate acid-base pairs.

After H_2O (base) gains a proton, it is converted into H_3O^+ (acid). Therefore, H_2O and H_3O^+ are also conjugate acid-base pairs.

Conjugate acid-base pairs differ by only one proton: the acid has the extra proton, while the base has one less proton.

Examples:
- HSO_4^- is the conjugate base of H_2SO_4.
- HSO_4^- is the conjugate acid of SO_4^{2-}.
- SO_4^{2-} is not the conjugate base of H_2SO_4.

Strong Bronsted-Lowry acids and bases

Strong acids:
- Are composed of H^+, combined with strongly ionic anions (e.g., Cl^-).
- The strong binary acids are HCl, HBr, and HI.
- Oxyanions are stronger anions than monatomic anions (i.e., $SO_4^{2-} > S^{2-}$).
- The more oxygens, the stronger the acid (i.e., $H_2SO_4 > H_2SO_3$).
- Half of the oxyanions of a particular element form strong acids, with the exception of B, C, and P (all of their oxyacids are weak).

Strong bases:
- Hydroxides of group IA metals.
- Hydroxides of group IIA metals below Mg.

Dissociation of weak acids and the K_a value

The equation for the dissociation of a weak acid, HA, in solution is as follows:

$$HA + H_2O \Leftrightarrow H_3O^+ + A^-$$

And, the equation for determining its K_a value is as follows:

$$K_a = \frac{[H_3O^+][A^-]}{[HA]}$$

K_b value

For a weak base, B, the ionization is as follows:

$$B^- + H_2O \Leftrightarrow HB + OH^-$$

And, the equation for determining its K_b value is as follows:

$$K_b = \frac{[HB][OH^-]}{[B^-]}$$

Buffers

Balanced mixtures of conjugate weak acid-weak base pairs are called buffers. A buffer solution that contains an equal molar quantity of weak acid (HA) and its conjugate base (A⁻) has a pH of the pKa of the weak acid, HA. When OH⁻ is added to the buffer, the OH⁻ reacts with HA to produce A⁻ and water. But, the [HA]/[A⁻] ratio remains more or less constant, so the pH is not significantly changed. When H⁺ is added to the buffer, A⁻ is consumed to produce HA. Once again, the [HA]/[A⁻] ratio is more or less constant, so the pH does not change significantly. As long as the [weak base]/[weak acid] ratio stays within the range of 0.10 to 10.0 (a 100-fold change!), the pH does not change by more than 1.0 unit from the pH of the pKa of the weak acid. Strong acids and bases cannot exist in buffers. Reaction of weak base with an equal number of moles of strong acid results in the creation of an equal number of moles of weak acid, and complete destruction of original weak base. Reaction of weak acid with strong base has exactly the opposite effect.

Titration

Titration is a technique that is used to determine the amount or concentration of a given substance. A solution with a known volume and concentration is used to titrate, or react with, another solution with a known volume, but an unknown concentration. Some type of indicator is used to signal when all of the unknown substance has been reacted. This is commonly called the end point of the titration. The most common type of titration is one that involves an acid and a base reacting with one another. There are also other types of titrations.

> ➤ **Review Video: Titration**
> Visit **mometrix.com/academy** *and enter* **Code: 550131**

Indicators

Litmus paper turns red in acidic media, and blue in alkaline media. For this reason, litmus paper is known as an indicator. An indicator is a chemical that shows the acidity or alkalinity of a solution by means of sharp change in color. Many other indicators also change color when the acidity or alkalinity of the medium fluctuates. One such indicator is phenolphthalein. Phenolphthalein is deep pink in alkaline media, and the pinkness reduces as the alkalinity reduces. It is colorless in an acidic medium.

Neutralization and salts

If the concentration of H^+ and OH^- ions are equal in a solution, then that solution is called a neutral solution. Water, H_2O, is a neutral solution, since the number of H^+ and OH^- ions within H_2O are equal. When acids and bases react with each other, they nullify the effects of acidity and alkalinity within a solution, a process that is called neutralization. The byproducts of neutralization are salt and water. Salt, in chemistry, is a term that denotes all compounds whose positive radical is derived from a base, while its negative radical is derived from an acid. In addition to the salt, the H^+ ion from the acid and the OH^- radical (or ion) from the base form neutral, non-ionized water.

For example:
$NaOH \rightarrow Na^+ + OH^-$ (ionization)
$HCl \rightarrow H^+ + Cl^-$ (ionization)
$NaOH + HCl \rightarrow Na^+ + OH^- + H^+ + Cl^- \rightarrow NaCl + H_2O$ (neutralization)

Titration curves

The progress of a titration is usually monitored with an indicator. Frequently, during a titration, it is also useful to monitor the progress of the titration with a graph. This graph is known as a titration curve. Such a curve reflects the changes in pH that occur as material is added from a buret to the solution in the beaker below the buret. All curves start out with a very slow, or moderate, change in pH, while the base is being added to the acid. As the titration continues, and the endpoint is approached, the pH of the solution will start to change more dramatically. At the endpoint, the line changes most dramatically. Once the endpoint has been passed, the rate of pH change diminishes again, resembling the first part of the graph, except at a higher pH value. If the acid being titrated is weak, then the graph will not be nearly as vertical at the endpoint. The weaker the acid is, the more the graph deviates from being vertical.

Electrolysis and electrolytes

Electrolysis is a chemical process where a substance, in its molten state or in an aqueous solution, is decomposed by the passage of electric current. The complete setup for electrolysis is called an electrolytic cell. This cell consists of a vessel that contains the electrolyte, anode, cathode, battery, and wires. An electrolytic cell is also called a voltameter, since it generates voltage (or current) at its two terminals. Electrodes are the metallic strips that are inserted into the electrolytes for the conduction of electricity. A metal electrode that is connected to the positive terminal of a battery is called an anode (+), while a metal electrode that is connected to the negative terminal of a battery is called a cathode (-). An electrolyte is a compound that allows electric current to pass through itself when either in a molten state or in an aqueous solution. In an electrolysis experiment, solutions of sodium chloride, copper sulphate, dilute sulphuric acids, or acetic acid are common electrolytes. Strong electrolytes allow large electric currents to be passed through them, such as solutions of sodium chloride, copper sulphate, and dilute sulphuric acid. Weak electrolytes are compounds that are poor conductors of electricity when either in a molten state or in an aqueous solution. Non-electrolytes do not allow electric current to pass through themselves in any state, molten or aqueous.

Faraday's law of electrolysis

Faraday's law of electrolysis states that the mass of substance released at any electrode is directly proportional ($\propto$) to the electric charge that is passed through the electrolyte. Thus, if m is the mass of the substance released at the electrode, and Q is the amount of electric charge that is passed through the electrode, then according to Faraday's law of electrolysis:
$Q = I \times t$
Where:
I = Current in amperes.
t = Time in seconds.

m is therefore $\propto$ to I x t:
$m = Z \times I \times t$
Where:
Z = The constant of proportionality, known as the electromechanical equivalent.

The electromechanical equivalent, Z, of a substance is defined as the amount of substance in grams that are liberated at any electrode when one coulomb of charge is passed through an electrolyte.

Electrolysis

The process of electrolysis is as follows:
- Electrolytes dissociate to form negatively charged anions and positively charged cations.
- The ions conduct electricity through the electrolyte.
- Cations are attracted toward the negative electrode. They take the excess electrons from the electrode and neutralize themselves.
- Anions are attracted towards the positive electrode. They give up the excess electrons from the electrode and neutralize themselves.
- The electrolyte dissociates, and the constituent elements of the salt are liberated at the electrodes.

The ions that will be released at the cathode or the anode will depend upon the following factors:
- The Relative Position of the Ion in the Electromechanical Series – The electromechanical series is a representation of how reactive the ion is. For example, in a solution that contains Na^+ and Hg^{2+} ions, the Na^+ ions will be preferentially released, as Na^+ accepts electrons more easily. However, this only happens if the concentration of Hg^{2+} ions is comparatively small. If the electrolyte is made up of NaCl in H_2O, then H^+ ions will be preferentially released, as H^+ is more reactive than Na^+.
- The Concentration of Ions in the Electrolyte – In the above example, if the concentration of Hg^{2+} ions is very large, then it will be preferentially released.
- The Nature of the Electrodes – Some electrode materials are non-corrosive, such as graphite or platinum, and are not affected by the ions surrounding it. However, some electrodes, such as copper, may enhance the release of ions, especially ions like Cu, Ag, Ni, etc.

Galvanic or voltaic cells

The redox reaction in a galvanic cell, or voltaic cell, is a spontaneous reaction. For this reason, galvanic cells are commonly used as batteries. Galvanic cell reactions supply energy that can be used to perform work. The energy is harnessed by situating the oxidation and reduction reactions in separate containers, which are joined by an apparatus that allows electrons to flow. A common galvanic cell is the Daniell cell. The overall chemical reaction of the galvanic cell is as follows:

$$Zn + Cu^{2+} \rightarrow Zn^{2+} + Cu$$

Electrical current in an electrolyte

In a conductor, electrical current flows through the material in its solid form. This is in contrast to an electrolyte, which can carry current in its molten state or in a solution form. Conductors are generally metals, while electrolytes are generally made from ionic compounds and noncovalent compounds (HCl and NH_3 are a few of the exceptions). When a current passes through a conductor, it may get heated up because of its inherent resistance. Other than this physical change, there are no other changes to the conductor. Once the current stops flowing, the conductor returns to its original state. In contrast to this, the cations and anions of an electrolyte go in opposite directions and get neutralized at the positive and negative electrodes, respectively. The chemical change thus produced is irreversible. After the current stops flowing, the electrolyte may change in strength relative to what it had started with. The current through a conductor is due to free electrons that flow and complete the circuit, while the current through an electrolytic cell is due to the flow of ions. For a given conductor or electrolytic cell, the current flowing through the circuit is constant. However, in an electrolytic cell, the current depends upon the strength of the electrolyte, which may change over time.

Periodic Table of the Elements

IA																		0
1 H	IIA											IIIA	IVA	VA	VIA	VIIA		2 He
3 Li	4 Be											5 B	6 C	7 N	8 O	9 F		10 Ne
11 Na	12 Mg	IIIB	IVB	VB	VIB	VIIB	— VIII —			IB	IIB	13 Al	14 Si	15 P	16 S	17 Cl		18 Ar
19 K	20 Ca	21 Sc	22 Ti	23 V	24 Cr	25 Mn	26 Fe	27 Co	28 Ni	29 Cu	30 Zn	31 Ga	32 Ge	33 As	34 Se	35 Br		36 Kr
37 Rb	38 Sr	39 Y	40 Zr	41 Nb	42 Mo	43 Tc	44 Ru	45 Rh	46 Pd	47 Ag	48 Cd	49 In	50 Sn	51 Sb	52 Te	53 I		54 Xe
55 Cs	56 Ba	57 *La	72 Hf	73 Ta	74 W	75 Re	76 Os	77 Ir	78 Pt	79 Au	80 Hg	81 Tl	82 Pb	83 Bi	84 Po	85 At		86 Rn
87 Fr	88 Ra	89 +Ac	104 Rf	105 Ha	106 106	107 107	108 108	109 109	110 110									

* Lanthanide Series:

58 Ce	59 Pr	60 Nd	61 Pm	62 Sm	63 Eu	64 Gd	65 Tb	66 Dy	67 Ho	68 Er	69 Tm	70 Yb	71 Lu

+ Actinide Series:

90 Th	91 Pa	92 U	93 Np	94 Pu	95 Am	96 Cm	97 Bk	98 Cf	99 Es	100 Fm	101 Md	102 No	103 Lr

Organic chemistry

Organic chemistry is a subdiscipline of chemistry that involves the study of the structures, properties, and reactions of carbon-based compounds, hydrocarbons, and their derivatives. In addition to carbon, these compounds may be composed of hydrogen, nitrogen, oxygen, phosphorus, silicon, sulfur, and the halogens. Organic compounds are numerous and diverse, have an enormous range of applications, and form the basis for almost all life processes.

Organic versus inorganic compounds

Organic	Inorganic
Volatile	Non-Volatile
Low Melting Point	High Melting Point
Low Boiling Point	High Boiling Point
Covalent or Van der Waals Bonding	Ionic Bonding
Insoluble in Water	Soluble in Water
Slow Reactions	Fast Reactions

Carbon

The special role of carbon in chemistry is the result of a combination of factors, including the number of valence electrons on a neutral carbon atom, the electronegativity of carbon, and the atomic radius of carbon atoms.

Physical properties of carbon:
- Electronic configuration – $1s^2\ 2s^2\ 2p^2$
- Electronegativity – 2.55
- Covalent radius – 0.077 nm

Carbon has four valence electrons, $2s^2\ 2p^2$, and it must either gain four electrons or lose four electrons in order to reach the noble-gas configuration. The electronegativity of carbon is too small for carbon to gain electrons from most elements in order to form C^{4-} ions, and too large for carbon to lose electrons in order to form C^{4+} ions. Therefore, carbon forms covalent bonds with a large number of other elements, including the hydrogen, nitrogen, oxygen, phosphorus, and sulfur atoms that are found in living systems. Because they are relatively small, carbon atoms can come close enough together to form strong double bonds (C=C), or even triple bonds (C≡C). Carbon also forms strong double and triple bonds to nitrogen and oxygen. It can even form double bonds to elements, such as phosphorus or sulfur, which do not form double bonds to themselves.

Catenation

Carbon atoms are unique amongst all of the elements that are found in nature. In particular, they can form long-chain molecules. The ability of carbon to form long chains is called catenation. Carbon chains are formed because carbon atoms form tetravalent bonds with other carbon atoms. This structure can be repeated endlessly without disturbing the stability of the bonds or the compounds formed. The chains can also form branches, sub-branches, and rings. In addition, the rings can have more rings attached to them. The list is endless. Most amino acids are long-chain carbon molecules. Carbon compounds are classified into two groups:
- Open-chain compounds, or aliphatic compounds.
- Closed-chain compounds, or cyclic compounds.

Organic compounds that form carbon-carbon chains are called aliphatic compounds, such as alkanes, alkenes, and alkynes. They are found in animal and vegetable fats, and do not have a strong aroma. Organic compounds that form closed rings are called cyclic compounds, such as benzene, vanillin, and phenol. Aromatic compounds are cyclic compounds that contain a 6-carbon ring with alternating double and single bonds. As their name suggests, they give off a very strong aroma.

> **Review Video: Catenation**
> Visit ***mometrix.com/academy*** *and enter* ***Code: 295775***

Covalent bonds

When a carbon atom forms a compound, it always forms covalent bonds. There are two types of covalent bonds: sigma bonds and pi bonds. When the covalent bond is linear, or aligned along the plane containing the atoms, the bond is known as sigma (s) bond. Sigma bonds are strong and the electron sharing is at its maximum. Methane, CH_4, is a good example of sigma bonding, and it has four of them. When the covalent bond is parallel, formed by the overlap of two p-orbital lobes, the bond is known as a pi bond. Relative to sigma bonds, pi bonds are usually weaker because they have less orbital overlap due to their parallel orientation. Single bonds are composed solely of sigma bonds, while double and triple bonds are composed of one sigma bond and either one or two pi bonds, respectively.

Hydrocarbons

Hydrocarbons are made up of carbon and hydrogen atoms only. Carbon forms sigma and pi bonds. Chains with all sp^3 hybridization have all single bonds (saturated, 1 sigma), and saturated hydrocarbons are called alkanes. Chains with sp^2 hybridization have double bonds (unsaturated, 1 sigma and 1 pi), and unsaturated hydrocarbons with even 1 double bond, but without triple bonds, are called alkenes. Chains with sp hybridization have triple bonds (unsaturated, 1 sigma and 2 pi), and unsaturated hydrocarbons with even 1 triple bond are called alkynes. Thus, there are three types of hydrocarbons:

- Alkanes – Saturated, connected with 1 sigma bond.
- Alkenes – Unsaturated, connected with 1 sigma and 1 pi bond.
- Alkynes – Unsaturated, connected with 1 sigma and 2 pi bonds.

The golden rule for remembering whether a given hydrocarbon is an alkane, an alkene, or an alkyne is to first count the number of carbon and hydrogen atoms that are present in the molecular formula, and then calculate the result as follows:

- If the number of hydrogen atoms is 2 more than 2x the number of carbon atoms, then the com-pound is an alkane.
- If the number of hydrogen atoms is same as 2x the number of carbon atoms, then the compound is an alkene.
- If the number of hydrogen atoms is 2 less than 2x the number of carbon atoms, then the compound is an alkyne.

The prefixes and suffixes of hydrocarbons are standardized by IUPAC.

Hydrocarbon prefixes and their carbon-atom relationship

Number of Carbon Atoms	Prefix Used
1	Meth-
2	Eth-
3	Prop-
4	But-
5	Pent-
6	Hex-
7	Hept-
8	Oct-
9	Non-
10	Dec-

Straight-chain hydrocarbons are named by combining the prefix for the number of carbon atoms in the chain together with the suffix "-ane" for alkanes, "-ene" for alkenes, or "-yne" for alkynes.

Naming of hydrocarbons with three or more carbon atoms
For hydrocarbons with three or more carbon atoms, branching of the chain is a clear possibility. The IUPAC rules for naming these hydrocarbons are as follows:

- Find the largest chain of carbon atoms.
- Name it similar to straight-chain hydrocarbons. This is called the parent hydrocarbon.
- Find the alkyl group of the branches, or the side chains.

- Number the carbon atoms in the straight chain so that the alkyl groups of the side chain come attached to the smallest-numbered carbon atom of the main chain.
- The position of the alkyl group gets the number of the carbon atom it is attached to.
- The IUPCA name is written first with the number of the side chain, then its alkyl group, and then the parent hydrocarbon.

> ➢ **Review Video: <u>The Basics of Hydrocarbons</u>**
> *Visit **mometrix.com/academy** and enter **Code: 824749***

Alkyl groups

In inorganic chemistry, radicals are atoms or groups of atoms that always stay together in a reaction (e.g., –OH, –SO$_4$, etc.). In organic chemistry, radicals exist but in the form of groups of carbon and hydrogen atoms. A group that is formed by the removal of one hydrogen atom from an alkane molecule is called an alkyl group (e.g., the methyl group is represented as CH$_3$–, while the ethyl group is represented as C$_2$H$_5$–). The structures of the methyl and ethyl groups are shown below.

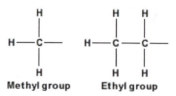

Methyl group   Ethyl group

Aliphatic compounds

Aliphatic compounds are derived from parent hydrocarbons. A hydrocarbon is a compound that is composed of hydrogen and carbon only. By replacing one or more of the hydrogen atoms from a hydrocarbon with a reactive atom from a group of atoms, X, a new compound can be formed. For example, a hydrocarbon R–H can be made to become R–X, where R is the carbon-hydrogen grouping, and X is a functional group. A functional group is an atom, or a group of atoms, which defines the function or the mode of activity of a given carbon compound, R–X. The functional group also determines the properties of the compound. However, aliphatic functional groups cannot be aromatic.

Standard organic functional groups

Functional Group	Name	Example
——OH	Hydroxyl	CH_3CH_2OH (ethanol)
–F, –Cl, –Br, and –I	Alkyl Halide	CH_3Br (methyl bromide)
——NH_2	Amine	CH_3NH_2 (methyl amine)
—C—	Alkyl	$CH_3CH_2CH_3$ (propane)
C≡C	Alkenyl	$CH_3CH = CH_2$ (propene)
——O——	Ether	CH_3OCH_3 (dimethyl ether)
—C—H (with =O)	Aldehyde	CH_3CHO (acetaldehyde)
—C— (with =O)	Ketone	CH_3COCH_3 (acetone)
—C—OH (with =O)	Carboxylic Acid	CH_3CO_2H (acetic acid)
—C—O— (with =O)	Ester	$CH_3CO_2CH_3$ (methyl acetate)
—C—Cl (with =O)	Acyl Chloride	CH_3COCl (acetyl chloride)
—C—NH_2 (with =O)	Amide	CH_3NH_2 (acetamide)

Isomers

Organic compounds that have similar chemical formulas, but different structures, are called isomers. For example, a molecule of butane (C_4H_{10}) can have two structures or configurations: *n*-butane, which is a straight-chain structure, and isobutane, which is a branched-chain structure. Thus, *n*-butane and iso-butane are isomers of each other. A molecule of pentane (C_5H_{12}) can have three different structures: *n*-pentane, iso-pentane, and neo-pentane, all of which are isomers of each other. Because of differences in their structures, and therefore their electronic configurations and bondings, isomers exhibit different physical and chemical properties.

Characteristics of isomers:
- Isomers occur in organic compounds that have more than 3 carbon atoms.
- Organic compounds with 4 carbon atoms have 2 isomers, those with 5 carbon atoms have 3 isomers, those with 6 carbon atoms have 4 isomers, etc.

- As the number of carbon atoms increase, the ways in which the atoms can be arranged can become very complex: straight chains with branches, and branches with sub-branches, can increase the complexity. For example, an organic compound that has 10 carbon atoms will have 75 isomers.

> ➤ **Review Video: <u>Basics of Isomers</u>**
> *Visit **mometrix.com/academy** and enter **Code: 809623***

Organic compound groups

In order to simplify the complexity of organic compounds, they are classified into groups. Just as elements within a group in the periodic table exhibit similar properties, organic compounds that show similar structures, and thus physical and chemical properties, are put together within a group, called a homologous series. They are arranged in increasing order by their molecular weights. In general, a homologous series is a group of organic compounds that have similar structures and chemical properties. The members of the homologous series differ from each other by their number of methylene ($-CH_2-$) groups only. The homologous series for alkanes is methane, ethane, propane, *n*-butane, etc. The series for alkenes is ethene, propene, butene, etc. And, the series for alkynes is ethyne, propyne, butyne, etc.

Key points for organic compounds are as follows:
- Atoms prefer filled valence shells. This rule explains why atoms make bonds, and the type of bonds that are created.
- If a molecule must have an unpaired electron (a.k.a. radical), then it is better to have the unpaired electron distributed over as many atoms as possible through resonance, inductive effects, and hyperconjugation.
- If a molecule must have a charge, then it is better to have the charge distributed over as many atoms as possible through resonance, inductive effects, and hyperconjugation.
- Most reactions involve nucleophiles (molecules with a location of particularly high electron density) attacking electrophiles (molecules with a location of particularly low electron density).
- Steric interactions (atoms bumping into one another) can prevent reactions by keeping the reactive atoms away from one another.
- There must be a reason for a reaction to take place.
- Delocalization ("dispersion of electron density") is always stabilizing, which is why it happens.
- The more reasonable the resonance structures that you can draw, the more stable the species, since this implies that more resonance can take place.
- In valid substitution reactions, you must have a good leaving group. Good leaving groups are the conjugate bases of strong acids (both organic and inorganic).
- You cannot have a positively charged (+) cation in a basic (pH > 10) solution. Only neutral atoms and C^-, N^-, or O^- are allowed.
- You cannot have a negatively charged (-) anion in an acidic (pH < 3) solution. Only neutral atoms and C^+, N^+ or O^+ are allowed.

- If conjugate bases are negatively charged (i.e., with an O⁻, C⁻, or N⁻), then they will be stabilized by electron-withdrawing effects.
- Hydrolysis is the splitting of a bond in a molecule (usually a C–O or C–N bond) by the addition of molecules of water "across" the broken bond.
- Hydration is the addition of molecules of water "across" a double bond (i.e., C=C, C=O, C=N, etc.).

> ➤ **Review Video:** <u>Basics of Organic Compound Groups</u>
> Visit *mometrix.com/academy* and enter *Code:* **889859**

Techniques for analyzing organic compounds

Technique	Nature	Effect
Ultraviolet (UV) Spectrometry	Absorption of radiation in the UV region of the electromagnetic spectrum.	Affects the molecular energy levels of the electrons in atomic and molecular orbitals.
Visible Spectrometry	Absorption of radiation in the visible region of the electromagnetic spectrum.	Affects the energy levels of the electrons in atomic and molecular orbitals.
Infrared (IR) Spectrometry	Absorption of radiation in the IR region of the electromagnetic spectrum.	Changes the vibrational states of the bonds in the molecules.
Mass Spectrometry	This is the exception: it does not involve either absorption or emission of radiation.	The molecule is ionized and broken apart, and then the masses of the fragments (also ions) are measured.
Nuclear Magnetic Resonance (NMR) Spectrometry	Absorption of radiation.	Changes the spin state energy of the nuclei of the hydrogen atoms.

<u>Ultraviolet and visible spectroscopy</u>
Organic molecules absorb light in the ultraviolet region of the electromagnetic spectrum. However, organic molecules with conjugated double bonds tend to absorb light at relatively long wave-lengths. In some cases, the wavelengths fall in the visible region, resulting in highly colored species. Alkenes, for example, are found entirely in the visible region. Commonly, basic biochemical assays, such as Bradford and Lowry assays, utilize the conjugation of organic molecules with transition metals to alter the color of ionic solutions, which in turn affects the absorption of light in the visible region. The differences in absorption, when compared to the absorption of standards of known concentration, can be used to measure the quantities of such organic molecules.

<u>IR spectroscopy</u>
Infrared (IR) radiation of a molecule causes the excitation of the vibrations of covalent bonds within that molecule. These vibrations include the stretching and bending modes. An IR spectrum shows the energy absorptions as one 'scans' the IR region of the electromagnetic spectrum. Most of the information that is used to interpret an IR spectrum is obtained from the functional group region. In practice, it is the polar covalent bonds than are IR "active", and whose excitation can be observed in an IR spectrum. In organic molecules, these polar covalent bonds represent the functional groups. Hence, the most useful information that can be obtained from an IR spectrum regards what functional groups are present within the molecule (NMR spectroscopy typically gives the

hydrocarbon fragments). Remember that some functional groups can be "viewed" as combinations of different bond types. For example, an ester, CO_2R, contains both $C = O$ and $C - O$ bonds, and both are typically seen in an IR spectrum of an ester.

Mass spectrometry

Mass spectrometry involves the measurement of masses of organic compounds and their constituents. In the case of proteins, the peptides are initially digested with specific proteases, and the masses of the individual fragments are then measured and combined into a spectrograph to create a specific fingerprint for that protein. Since no two proteins are identical, the specific mass spectrograph for each protein is unique. This technique can therefore be utilized to determine the identity of unknown proteins within a sample.

NMR

Nuclear magnetic resonance (NMR) spectroscopy is used to determine the numbers and types of atoms that molecules are composed of by exploiting the magnetic properties of atoms and measuring their atomic spins. When interpreting NMR spectroscopy data, the number of signals indicates the number of different types of protons, but be careful about overlapping signals. Downfield shifts mean that the protons are deshielded. Integration only indicates the ratios of the numbers of protons. The signal shape indicates the dynamics of the proton environments. Splitting of a signal into a doublet, triplet, quartet, etc. is due to spin-spin coupling between the nuclei with non-zero nuclear spins. Remember that the multiplicity (doublet, triplet, quartet) does not indicate the number of protons on that carbon: the number of protons is given by the integration. Signal splitting arises only for coupling between nonequivalent nuclei. Hence, ethane is a singlet, and the methyl group of ethanol is only split by the adjacent methylene group.

Liquid-liquid extraction

Liquid-liquid extraction, also known as solvent extraction or partitioning, is a technique for separating compounds based upon their relative solubilities in two different immiscible solvents, typically water and an organic solvent. Generally, when an organic compound is to be isolated from an aqueous solution, the solution is thoroughly mixed with an organic solvent and then centrifuged to separate the two solvents. By then isolating the organic solvent layer, the organic compound can be isolated from the remaining non-organic compounds in the aqueous solution. One example of this technique that is commonly used in life-science and biochemistry laboratories to separate nucleic acid and protein mixtures is called a phenol-chloroform extraction. In phenol-chloroform extractions, a chaotropic agent, such as guanidinium thiocyanate or Trizol, is used to lyse cells while maintaining the integrity of the RNA and DNA in the extracts by denaturing any RNases or DNases. Subsequently, the cell lysates are thoroughly mixed with a phenol:chloroform mixture and then centrifuged to separate the aqueous and organic phases. Following separation, the polar nucleic acids will be found in the aqueous phase (chloroform), while proteins will be found in the organic phase (phenol). To further extract DNA or RNA from the chloroform mixture, nucleic acids can be precipitated using isopropanol and/or ethanol followed by centrifugation. The proteins can be extracted from the phenol mixture by precipitating them using ice-cold acetone and centrifugation.

Distillation

Distillation is a technique for separating liquid mixtures based upon their different volatilities in a boiling solution. Using distillation, a mixture of liquids in a still flask is boiled at a temperature just above the boiling point of the chemical of interest, and the vapor is then allowed to pass through a series of condensation tubes and finally condensed in a collection flask. When the boiling points of the different liquids are relatively close to one another, a fractionating column can be utilized, filled with trays, dishes, wire mesh, or even steel wool, in order to increase the surface area of the column so that the vapor has a greater chance of condensation. Since the higher boiling point liquids will condense more easily at the lower temperatures, the fractionating column allows any impure vapors to condense in the column and return to the flask, while the chemical of interest is allowed to pass through the fractionating column and into the condensation tubes. Distillation is used in a large number of commercial applications. For example, crude oil is distilled to separate it into fractions for specific uses, such as gasoline, kerosene, heating oil, motor oil, and even asphalt. Water is distilled to separate the liquid from impurities, such as salt and other chemicals. And, fermented solutions are also distilled in order to concentrate the alcohol from the initial fermented mash.

Chromatography

Chromatography is a name for a collection of techniques to separate solutions based upon their different rates of travel through a stationary phase. Because different molecules have different sizes and charges, different stationary phases can be utilized to retard the flow of different solutions through the stationary phase based upon these characteristics. In chromatography, the substance of interest is called an analyte, and the graphical output is called a chromatogram, which contains peaks of variable intensities at different time points representative of the different components of the mixture and their rates of travel through the stationary phase. Common chromatographic techniques include the following:

- Paper chromatography – Separates mixtures of solutes based upon size. In this technique, a strip of chromatography paper is placed into a solvent, the solvent is allowed to flow through the paper, and the solutes in the solvent travel through the paper at different rates dependent upon their size, with smaller molecules traveling faster than larger molecules.
- Thin-layer chromatography – Functions similar to paper chromatography, except that a stationary thin layer of absorbent material, such as silica gel, alumina, or cellulose, is used rather than paper.
- Ion-exchange chromatography – Separates mixtures passed through an ionic-resin-filled column based upon charges. The ionic resin may be cationic or anionic.
- Size-exclusion chromatography – Separates mixtures based upon size, with larger molecules moving more quickly than smaller molecules. Using resins filled with small pores, the smaller molecules are retained longer in the resin, while the larger molecules are not retained and pass more quickly through the resin.
- Gas-liquid chromatography – Utilizes gas, such as argon, as the mobile phase. In gas-liquid chromatography, a liquid mixture containing the analyte is injected into a very long, coiled capillary column, and is forced through the column under very high temperature and pressure. As the substance is eluted through the column, smaller molecules travel more quickly than larger molecules.

Alkanes

Alkanes have the general formula C_nH_{2n+2}. In alkanes, the carbon atoms form 4 single bonds (or s (sigma) bonds) to 4 different atoms, and are referred to as saturated hydrocarbons, or paraffins, because they contain no multiple bonds. The simplest hydrocarbon, methane, contains a single carbon atom bonded to 4 hydrogen atoms (CH_4). The alkanes are named by adding the ending "ane" to their root names, such as methane, ethane, propane, etc. The following table gives the names and compositions of the first ten alkanes.

Names and formulas for the alkanes

Formula	Name	Functional Group
CH_4	Methane	CH_3-
C_2H_6	Ethane	C_2H_5-
C_3H_8	Propane	C_3H_7-
C_4H_{10}	Butane	C_4H_9-
C_5H_{12}	Pentane	$C_5H_{11}-$
C_6H_{14}	Hexane	$C_6H_{13}-$
C_7H_{16}	Heptane	$C_7H_{15}-$
C_8H_{18}	Octane	$C_8H_{17}-$
C_9H_{20}	Nonane	$C_9H_{19}-$
$C_{10}H_{22}$	Decane	$C_{10}H_{21}-$

Structural formulas for the alkanes

Methane, ethane, and propane: The structural formulas, which are the actual arrangements of different atoms in space of these substances, are shown below.

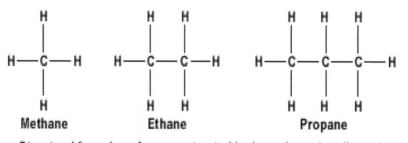

Structural formulae of some saturated hydrocarbons (or alkanes).
They all contain single bonds.

C_2H_6: Since C_2H_6 contains 2 carbon atoms, its prefix is "eth". With 6 hydrogen atoms, the compound conforms to the formula, C_nH_{2n+2}, and is thus an alkane with the suffix "ane". Therefore, C_2H_6 is the molecular formula for ethane. The structural formula for ethane is as follows:

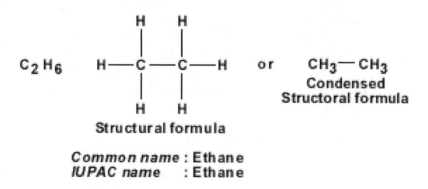

The carbon atoms are saturated, with each having four bonds attached to different atoms.

Butane:

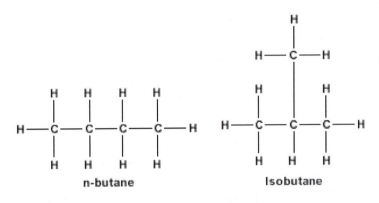

n-butane   Isobutane

The straight-chain butane is called normal butane, or *n*-butane.

Pentane: Pentane (C_5H_{12}) can be represented by three different structural formulas:
- The simple straight-chain pentane is called *n*-pentane.
- Pentane with one branched chain is called isopentane, or 2-methylbutane.
- Pentane with two branched chains is called neopentane, or 2,2-dimethylpropane.

Properties of the alkanes
- Physical state – Lower molecular weight alkanes are gases at room temperature (i.e., methane, ethane, propane, and butane). Higher alkanes, up to those having 17 carbon atoms, are liquids at room temperature, while even higher alkanes are solids at room temperature.
- Melting and boiling points – Homologous alkanes show increases in their melting and boiling points with increased chain length, similar to the behavior of elements within the same group in the periodic table.
- Solubility – Alkanes, like all other organic chemicals, are insoluble in water. Instead, they are soluble in organic liquids. Alkanes are non-polar and are therefore soluble in other non-polar liquids, but they are not soluble in polar liquids, such as water.
- Combustion – Alkanes are flammable, and are easy to catch fire. Complete combustion of an alkane leads to carbon dioxide and water. During combustion, the supply of oxygen has to be sufficient: insufficient oxygen leads to the production of carbon monoxide, and the heat generated is less than when sufficient oxygen is available.
- Reactivity – Alkanes have saturated covalent bonds. Therefore, their reactivity with other chemicals is relatively low.
- Substitution reaction – In alkanes, substitution reactions are easily performed by the replacement of hydrogen atoms with more reactive atoms (e.g., chloride (Cl^-)).

> ➤ **Review Video: Properties of Alkanes**
> *Visit mometrix.com/academy and enter Code:* **903333**

Chemical properties of methane
- Combustion – Methane burns in air with a blue flame. Methane produces a good amount of heat when it undergoes combustion, which is why it is used as a fuel.
- Reactivity – Methane is quite unreactive, except with fluorine, chlorine, etc. With these, it undergoes substitution reactions.

<u>Uses of methane</u>
- Because of its excellent burning capability, methane is used as a cooking gas.
- Methane is used to produce carbon dioxide gas.
- Methane is used to produce carbon black, which is used in rubber production.
- Methane is used as a starting material for other organic compounds, such as methyl chloride, methylene dichloride, chloroform, etc.

Alkenes

Hydrocarbons that contain two hydrogen atoms less than their corresponding alkanes are called alkenes, or olefins. They are called olefins because they react with chlorine to form oil-like derivatives (olefin means oil forming). Alkenes have at least one double bond, and are thus unsaturated carbon compounds. Their general formula is C_nH_{2n}, and their names are derived from the alkanes simply by changing the ending from "ane" into "ene" (e.g., propane → propene). The simplest of alkenes has two carbons connected by a double bond (1 sigma + 1 pi bond), called ethene (H–C=C–H). The table below gives the names and compositions of the first six alkenes.

Alkene	Number of C Atoms	Number of H Atoms	Molecular Formula
Ethene	2	4	C_2H_4
Propene	3	6	C_3H_6
Butene	4	8	C_4H_8
Pentene	5	10	C_5H_{10}
Hexene	6	12	C_6H_{12}
Heptene	7	14	C_7H_{14}

<u>Ethene</u>
A molecule of the simplest alkene, ethene, has five sigma bonds and one pi bond. The structural formula for ethene ($CH_2=CH_2$) is as follows:

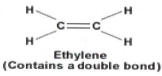

Ethylene
(Contains a double bond)

The next higher alkene is propene (CH_3–$CH=CH_2$). This has one double-bonded carbon atom.

Uses of ethene are as follows:
- Ethene is used for manufacturing organic compounds, such as ethanol and ethylene glycol. Ethylene glycol is used for making artificial fibers, like polyesters.
- Ethene is used for the manufacture of plastics. These plastics are made from the polymerization of ethene into polyethene. Polyethenes are used for making bags, electrical insulation, etc.
- Ethene is used for the artificial ripening of fruits, such as mangos, bananas, etc.

<u>Benzene</u>
Benzene consists of 6 carbon atoms linked together to form a hexagon. Each C atom is attached to two other C atoms and one hydrogen atom, and there are alternating double and single bonds between the C atoms. Experimentally, the C – C bonds in benzene are all the same length, and

benzene is planar. We write resonance structures for benzene in which there are single bonds between each pair of C atoms and the 6 additional electrons are delocalized over the entire ring. This structure is depicted by a hexagon, representing benzene, with a circle contained within the hexagon that represents the delocalized electrons. Benzene belongs to a category of organic molecules that are called aromatic compounds (due to their odor). Aromatic compounds were being extracted from coal tar as early as the 1830s. As a result, many of these compounds were given common names that are still in use today. A few of these compounds are shown below.

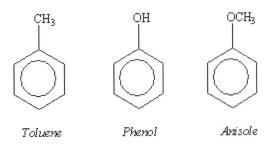

Toluene   Phenol   Anisole

Alkynes

Hydrocarbons that have at least two carbon atoms connected by an unsaturated triple bond are called alkynes. Their general formula is C_nH_{2n-2}, and their names are derived from the alkanes simply by changing the ending from "ane" into "yne" (e.g., propane → propyne). The simplest of alkynes has two carbon atoms connected by a triple bond (1 sigma + 2 pi bonds), called ethyne (H–C≡C–H). The table below gives the names and compositions of the first six alkynes (with 1 triple bond).

Alkyne	Number of C Atoms	Number of H Atoms	Molecular Formula
Ethyne	2	2	C_2H_2
Propyne	3	4	C_3H_4
Butyne	4	6	C_4H_6
Pentyne	5	8	C_5H_8
Hexyne	6	10	C_6H_{10}
Heptyne	7	12	C_7H_{12}

➢ **Review Video: Basics of Alkynes**
Visit mometrix.com/academy and enter Code: 963837

Reactions with hydrocarbons

Combustion of hydrocarbons
Alkanes, alkenes, and alkynes all undergo combustion reactions in the presence of O_2 and heat. Alkanes are less reactive than both alkenes and alkynes, which are generally highly exothermic. Alkanes burn with a blue flame, while both alkenes and alkynes burn with a yellow flame. All three give off carbon monoxide or soot if not burned in the presence of adequate amounts of O_2, and become increasingly difficult to ignite as their number of carbon atoms increase. The equation for complete combustion is as follows:
$C_nH_{2n+2} + (1.5n+0.5)O_2$ → $(n+1)H_2O + nCO_2$

In the absence of sufficient O_2, the following equations may apply:

$$C_nH_{2n+2} + (n+0.5)O_2 \rightarrow (n+1)H_2O + nCO \qquad \text{(Carbon Monoxide)}$$

$$C_nH_{2n+2} + (0.5n+0.5)O_2 \rightarrow (n+1)H_2O + nC \qquad \text{(Soot)}$$

Nucleophilic aliphatic substitution

$$R_2-\underset{R_3}{\overset{R_1}{\underset{|}{\overset{|}{C}}}}-G \ + \ :X \ \xrightleftharpoons{\text{Solvent}} \ R_2-\underset{R_3}{\overset{R_1}{\underset{|}{\overset{|}{C}}}}-X \ + \ :G$$

Where:

$$R_2-\underset{R_3}{\overset{R_1}{\underset{|}{\overset{|}{C}}}}-G \quad = \text{The substrate.}$$

R = The side group, generally an H, alkyl, or aryl.
:X = A nucleophilic reagent.
G = The leaving group.

Halogenation
Halogenation is the reaction of the carbon-carbon double bond in alkenes, such as ethene, with halogens, such as chlorine, bromine, and iodine. Reactions where the chlorine or bromine are in solution (e.g., "bromine water") are slightly more complicated, and are treated separately.

Polymerization
Polymerization is a process whereby long-chain molecules are formed from shorter chains. Alkenes, like ethene, undergo polymerization. Ethene is an unsaturated gas. For making a long-chain polymer, all of its pi bonds can be broken apart, and another ethene can be attached. Then, the pi bond of the second ethene molecule can be broken apart to add another ethene molecule. In this way, a very-long-chain molecule, or polymer, can be produced.

When ethene gas is heated to a temperature $\geq 200°C$, and at a pressure ≥ 2000 atmospheres, it polymerizes to become a solid, called polyethene. A large number of ethene molecules join together to make polythene (the "n" can be as large as 1000), and the molecular weight is very large.

Diels-Alder reaction
The Diels-Alder Reaction is a conjugate-addition reaction of a conjugated diene to an alkene (the dienophile) in order to produce a cyclohexene. Examples of the Diels-Alder reaction can be seen below.

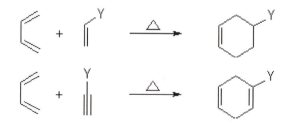

The [4+2]-cycloaddition of a conjugated diene and a dienophile (an alkene or alkyne) is an electrocyclic reaction that involves the 4 π-electrons of the diene and 2 π-electrons of the dienophile. The driving force of the reaction is the formation of new σ-bonds, which are energetically more stable than the π-bonds. In the case of an alkynyl dienophile, the initial adduct can still react as a dienophile if not too sterically hindered. In addition, either the diene or the dienophile can be substituted with cumulated double bonds, such as substituted allenes.

Substituents of aromatic rings

There are three ways in which a pair of substituents can be placed on an aromatic ring. In the ortho (o) isomer, the substituents are in adjacent positions on the ring. In the meta (m) isomer, they are separated by one carbon atom. And, in the para (p) isomer, they are on opposite ends of the ring. The three isomers of dimethylbenzene, or xylene, are shown below.

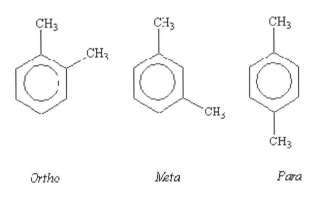

Ortho   Meta   Para

Alcohols

Organic compounds that have the hydroxyl group (–OH) attached to carbon atoms are known as alcohols. Methyl alcohol (CH_3OH) is the simplest of the alcohols. This is also known as methanol. The next higher alcohol is ethyl alcohol (C_2H_5OH), or ethanol.

An alcohol is produced by replacing one hydrogen from an alkane with a hydroxyl group. The two equations below show how methanol and ethanol are made:

$$CH_4 \xrightarrow{\text{Replace one H by OH}} CH_3\text{---}OH$$
Methane   Methyl alcohol
                                 (or Methanol)

$$C_2H_6 \xrightarrow{\text{Replace one H by OH}} C_2H_5\text{---}OH$$
Ethane   Ethyl alcohol
                                 (or Ethanol)

In the IUPAC naming system, the names of alcohols are derived by the replacement of the terminal "e" of the hydrocarbon name with "ol" (e.g., propane → propanol). The IUPAC rules for naming alcohols are as follows:
- Find the alkane from which the alcohol is made, and name it similar to the nomenclature for straight-chain hydrocarbons. This is called the parent hydrocarbon.
- Find where the hydroxyl group is attached: in the branches or in the side chains.

- Number the carbon atoms in the straight chain so that the hydroxyl group of the side chain is attached to the smallest-numbered carbon atom.
- The position of the hydroxyl group gets the number of the carbon atom it is attached to.

> **Review Video: Basics of Alcohols**
*Visit **mometrix.com/academy** and enter **Code: 105795***

Phenols

Phenols are another class of alcohols in which an –OH group is attached to an aromatic ring, as shown in the figure below. Phenols are potent disinfectants. When antiseptic techniques were first introduced in the 1860s by Joseph Lister, it was phenol (or carbolic acid, as it was then known) that was used. Phenol derivatives, such as o-phenylphenol, are still used in commercial disinfectants, such as Lysol.

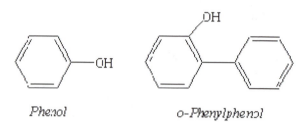

Phenol   o-Phenylphenol

Physical properties of alcohols

The following are physical properties of alcohols:
- Physical state – Alcohols are colorless liquids at ordinary room temperature.
- Odor – Lower members of the alcohol group have a characteristic fruity smell.
- Density – Alcohols are lighter than water.
- Solubility – Alcohols, such as methanol and ethanol, are completely soluble (miscible) in water. Longer-chain members of the alcohol group tend to be less soluble in water.
- Acidic nature – Alcohols are neutral liquids, and have no effect on litmus, or other acidity, tests.
- Conductivity – Alcohols are covalently bonded compounds, and are thus are non-ionic and non-conductors of electricity.

> **Review Video: Physical Properties of Alcohols**
*Visit **mometrix.com/academy** and enter **Code: 926662***

Properties of Methanol

The following are the properties of methanol:
- Methanol is a colorless liquid at room temperature.
- Methanol has a slight fruity odor.
- The boiling point of methanol is 64.5°C.
- Methanol is completely miscible in water.
- The density of methanol is less than water.
- Methanol is a neutral solution, and shows negative results for all acidity tests.
- Methanol is poisonous, and can cause blindness if ingested.

- Methanol is very flammable, and burns with a pale blue flame. It forms carbon dioxide and water upon complete oxidation, or combustion.
- Methanol reacts with Na^+ to give off hydrogen gas.
- Methanol reacts with ethanoic acid to give methyl ethanoate, which is an ester.

Solubilities of alcohols

As a general rule, polar or ionic substances dissolve in polar solvents, while nonpolar substances dissolve in nonpolar solvents. As a result, hydrocarbons do not dissolve in water. They are often said to be immiscible (literally, "not mixable") in water. Alcohols, as might be expected, have properties between the extremes of hydrocarbons and water. When the hydrocarbon chain is short, the alcohol is soluble in water. There is no limit on the amount of methanol (CH_3OH) and ethanol (CH_3CH_2OH), for example, that can dissolve in a given quantity of water. As the hydrocarbon chain becomes longer, the alcohol becomes less soluble in water. One end of the alcohol molecules is so nonpolar in character that it is said to be hydrophobic (literally, "water hating"). The other end contains an –OH group that can form hydrogen bonds to neighboring water molecules, and is thus said to be hydrophilic (literally, "water loving"). As the hydrocarbon chain becomes longer, the hydrophobic character of the molecule increases, and the solubility of the alcohol in water gradually decreases until it becomes essentially insoluble in water.

Nucleophilic substitution reaction

Nucleophilic substitution (S_N1/S_N2) is the reaction of an electron-pair donor (the nucleophile, Nu) with an electron-pair acceptor (the electrophile). An sp^3-hybridized electrophile must have a leaving group (X) in order for the reaction to take place. An example of the nucleophilic substitution reaction can be seen below.

Combustion and oxidation of alcohols

The combustion of alcohols in air occurs very easily (e.g., methanol burns with a blue flame). Alcohols burn in air to give carbon dioxide and water. A large amount of heat is also generated during this chemical reaction. Oxidation differs from combustion in that the oxygen is supplied in a controlled fashion. Oxidation of alcohols gives rise to carbonic acids and water. The reaction of potassium dichloride and dilute sulphuric acid can provide atomic oxygen, or nascent oxygen, giving off methanoic acid and water as reaction products.

Pinacol rearrangement

The pinacol rearrangement reaction is a method of conversion of a 1,2-diol into a carbonyl under acidic conditions. In this reaction, one of the hydroxyl groups is protonated to form a carbocation, followed by the migration of an alkyl group from one of the adjacent carbons. The resultant oxonium ion has an increased relative stability, which serves as the driving force for the reaction.

Protection of alcohols

Since alcohol groups are subject to action by Grignard reagents, alcohol groups can be replaced by substituting groups that are later removed in order to maintain the presence and location of the alcohol group. For example, alcohols are easily sialated under mild conditions to form silyl ethers, which can later be reversed under mildly acidic conditions.

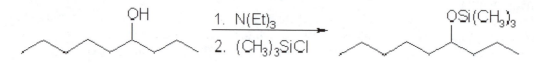

Tosylates

Alcohols can be converted into tosylates using tosyl chloride and a base to "mop-up" the HCl byproduct. Tosylates are good substrates for substitution reactions, used mostly for 1° and 2° ROH (S_N2 reaction). During these reactions, the –OH reacts first as a nucleophile, attacking the electrophilic center of the tosylate, displacing Cl^-, since tosylates have a much better leaving group: the conjugate base of tosic acid, pK_a = -2.8. The advantage of this method is that the substitution reactions are not under strongly acidic conditions. Tosylates react with nucleophiles in much the same way as alkyl halides. Alternatives to tosylates are mesylates (use CH_3SO_2Cl) and triflates (use CF_3SO_2Cl).

Reactions of alcohols with carboxylic acids

Carboxylic acids are organic acids. Alcohols react with carboxylic acids to form sweet-smelling organic compounds, called esters. The reaction of alcohols with carboxylic acids is called esterification. This is one of the major tests to see the presence of an alcoholic group in a sample of liquid mixtures. When methanol is heated with ethanoic acid in the presence of concentrated sulphuric acid, methyl ethanoate (an ester) and water are formed. The concentrated sulphuric acid acts as a catalyst for this reaction.

Alkanol reactions

Types of alkanol reactions are as follows:

- Dehydration (elimination) – The products that are formed depend on the conditions used. For example, alkenes are formed in the presence of H_2SO_4 (H_3PO_4 is better since it does not produce as many by-products), and the correct temperature (hot for primary, warm for secondary, and cool for tertiary). Alcohols lose a water molecule.
- Oxidation – The products depend on the type of alcohol used: primary, secondary, or tertiary. For primary and secondary, a C=O bond replaces the C-OH, but this bond will either be at the end of the carbon chain (an aldehyde), or in the middle (a ketone). Aldehydes can be further oxidized to form carboxylic acids. Tertiary alcohols will not oxidise.
- Substitution – Not very important for the alcohols, except for halogenation using PCl_5, which may be used as an identifying test for the alcohol group.
- Reaction with Active Metals – Alcohols react with active metals, releasing hydrogen. This may also be used as an identifying test for alcohols.
- Esterification – This is the reaction between an alcohol and a carboxylic acid, which forms an ester link (-COO-), holding two carbon chains together. The conditions required for this reaction are concentrated H_2SO_4 and elevated temperatures.

> ➢ **Review Video: Alkanol Reactions**
> Visit **mometrix.com/academy** and enter **Code: 788169**

Mitsunobu reaction

The Mitsunobu reaction allows for the conversion of primary and secondary alcohols to esters, amides, or thioethers. The nucleophile employed should be acidic, since one of the reagents (DEAD, diethylazodicarboxylate) must be protonated during the course of the reaction in order to prevent from side reactions. Examples of the Mitsunobu reaction can be seen below.

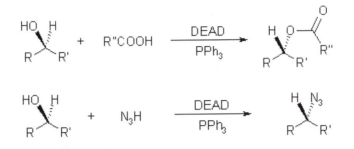

Preparation of aprotic solvents

Substances that cannot act as a source of a proton are said to be aprotic. Because ethers do not contain an –OH group, they are aprotic solvents. Ethers can be synthesized by splitting a molecule of water between two alcohols in the presence of heat and concentrated sulfuric acid.

$$2CH_3CH_2OH \xrightarrow{H^+} CH_3CH_2OCH_2CH_3$$

They can also be formed by reacting a primary alkyl halide with an alkoxide ion.

$$CH_3CH_2CH_2Br + CH_3O^- \longrightarrow CH_3CH_2CH_2OCH_3 + Br^-$$

Aldehydes and ketones

An aldehyde is an organic compound containing the formyl group, which is a carbonyl group bound to a terminal carbon, having the formula R-CHO. A ketone is an organic compound containing a carbonyl group bound to two carbon atoms, having the formula RC(=O)R'. An aldehyde differs from a ketone in that the carbonyl is located at the end of the compound rather than the middle. Both aldehydes and ketones are important in organic chemistry and industry. For example, many fragrances and fixatives are aldehydes, while many sugars and solvents are ketones. Aldehydes are generally named by replacing the suffix of the hydrocarbon with "-al", such as methane → methanal. In some special cases, non-conventional naming standards are used:
- If an aldehyde is added to a ring, then the suffix "–carbaldehyde" is used.
- If replacing the aldehyde group with a carboxyl (–COOH) group would yield a carboxylic acid with a trivial name, then the "–ic acid" ending can be replaced with "–oic acid" in the trivial name.
- If the compound is a natural product or carboxylic acid, then the prefix "n-oxo-" can be used to indicate the position of the aldehyde group, with "n" being the number of the carbon.

Ketones are named by replacing the suffix of the hydrocarbon with "-one", such as hexane → hexone. However, the most important ketones have generally retained trivial names, such as acetone and propriophenone.

Nucleophilic addition at the C=O bond

In aldehydes and ketones, nucleophiles react very readily at the carbonyl bond. During a nucleophile addition reaction, the carbonyl carbon converts from sp^2 to sp^3 hybridization, and the oxygen becomes protonated. If the nucleophile is an alcohol under acidic or basic conditions, then the product is a hemiacetal, which can be further reacted to produce an acetal and water under acidic conditions. If the nucleophile is an amine under acidic conditions, then the product is an imine-enamine tautomer (the imine form has a double-bonded nitrogen, while the enamine form has a single-bonded nitrogen).

Aldol addition/aldol reaction

'Aldol' is an abbreviation of aldehyde and alcohol. An aldol reaction is a reaction where the enolate of an aldehyde or a ketone reacts at the α-carbon with the carbonyl of another molecule, under basic or acidic conditions, in order to obtain β-hydroxy aldehyde or ketone. An example aldol addition/aldol reaction can be seen below.

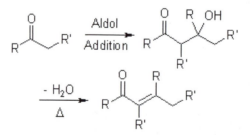

Aldol condensation reaction

In some cases, the adducts obtained from the aldol addition can easily be converted (*in situ*) to α,β-unsaturated carbonyl compounds, either thermally or under acidic or basic catalysis. The formation of the conjugated system is the driving force for this spontaneous dehydration. Under a variety of protocols, the condensation product can be obtained directly, without isolation of the aldol. An example aldol condensation reaction can be seen below.

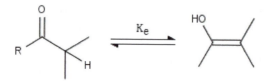

The aldol condensation is the second step of the Robinson annulation.

Keto-Enol tautomerism

Tautomerism refers to an equilibrium between two different structures of the same compound. Usually, the tautomers differ in the point of attachment of a hydrogen atom. One of the most common examples of a tautomeric system is the equilibrium between a ketone and its enol form, called keto-enol tautomerism. An example of this reaction can be seen below.

- 270 -

Wolff-Kishner reduction reaction

The Wolff-Kishner reduction reaction reduces aldehydes and ketones to alkanes. Condensation of the carbonyl compound with hydrazine forms the hydrazone, and treatment with base then induces the reduction of the carbon, coupled with oxidation of the hydrazine to gaseous nitrogen, in order to yield the corresponding alkane. An example of the Wolff-Kishner reaction can be seen below.

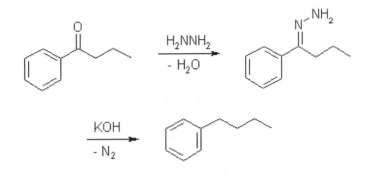

Grignard reagents

Grignard noted that alkyl halides react with magnesium metal in diethyl ether (Et$_2$O) to form compounds that contain a metal-carbon bond. Methyl bromide, for example, forms methyl-magnesium bromide.

$$CH_3Br + Mg \xrightarrow{Et_2O} CH_3MgBr$$

Because carbon is considerably more electronegative than magnesium, the metal-carbon bond in this compound has a significant amount of ionic character. Grignard reagents, such as CH$_3$MgBr, are best thought of as hybrids of ionic and covalent Lewis structures.

$$CH_3-Mg-Br \longleftrightarrow [CH_3^-][Mg^{2+}][Br^-]$$

Grignard reagents are our first source of carbanions (literally, "anions of carbon"). The Lewis structure of the CH$_3^-$ ion suggests that carbanions can be Lewis bases, or electron-pair donors.

Perhaps the most important aspect of the chemistry of Grignard reagents is the ease with which this reaction allows us to couple alkyl chains. Isopropylmagnesium bromide, for example, can be used to graft an isopropyl group onto the hydrocarbon chain of an appropriate ketone, as shown in the figure below.

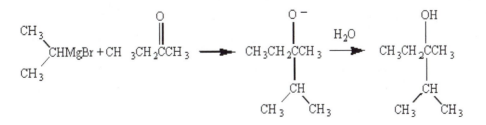

Organic acids

Organic compounds that have the carboxyl group (–COOH) behave like acids, and are thus known as carboxylic acids, or organic acids. The bonds in a carboxyl group are such that the C has a double bond to O, and a single bond to which the hydroxyl group –OH is attached. The simplest carboxylic acid is methanoic acid (HCOOH), commonly called formic acid. The next acid with two carbon atoms is called ethanoic acid (CH_3COOH), or commonly called acetic acid. The carboxylic acids form a homologous series. Two hydrogen atoms of one of the carbon atoms in an alkane are replaced simultaneously by an oxygen atom and a hydroxyl group, to make a carboxylic acid. The oxygen atom is double bonded to the carbon atom. Thus, the general formula for carboxylic acid is R-COOH, where R is an alkyl group, like methyl (CH_3), ethyl (C_2H_5), propyl (C_3H_7), etc. In the case of the simplest of the acids, namely formic acid (H-COOH), the R is a hydrogen atom. The IUPAC names of organic acids are derived from the IUPAC names for their corresponding alkanes. The carboxyl group is given the "oic" suffix, which is then attached to the IUPAC name for the alkane, and the word acid is added to the end. The IUPAC rules for naming carboxylic acids are as follows:

- Find the alkane from which the alcohol is made, and name it similar to the nomenclature for straight-chain hydrocarbons. This is called the parent hydrocarbon.
- Add an "oic" suffix to the name for the alkane by removing the "e" from the alkane name.
- Find where the carboxyl group is attached: in the branches or in the side chains. The –COOH group is generally attached at the end of a branch.

> **Review Video: The Basics of Organic Acids**
> Visit **mometrix.com/academy** and enter **Code: 238132**

The following are the physical properties of organic acids:

- Physical state – The first three organic acids are colorless liquids at ordinary room temperatures. Organic acids having between 4 to 9 carbon atoms are colorless oily liquids at ordinary room temperatures. Carbonic acids with a higher number of carbon atoms are colorless wax-like substances at ordinary room temperatures.
- Odor – The first three members have a very pungent smell. Acids with between 4 to 9 carbon atoms smell pungent like goats butter. Still higher molecular weight organic acids are odorless.
- Solubility – The first four carbonic acids are soluble in water. As the molecular weight increases, their solubility in water decreases. Organic acids with 10 or more carbon atoms are insoluble in water. All organic acids are soluble in organic solvents, such as benzene, ethanol, ether, etc.
- Acidic nature – Organic acids are weak acids, as they can be only partially ionized in water to give H^+ ions. The acidic nature decreases as the homologous series increases. The lower members readily turn blue litmus paper to red.
- Fatty acids – Larger organic acids that have one –COOH group are also called monocarboxylic fatty acids. Most of these acids are produced by the hydrolysis of fats, and are therefore known as fatty acids. They have many industrial uses, especially in the soap and detergent industry.

> **Review Video: Physical Properties of Organic Acids**
> Visit **mometrix.com/academy** and enter **Code: 342179**

The following are chemical properties of organic acids:

- Action on litmus paper – Methanoic and ethanoic acids turn blue litmus paper to red quite easily. This indicates the acidic nature of the compounds. Larger organic acid molecules do not show this test result as readily.
- Reaction with sodium bicarbonate – Organic acid reacts with sodium bicarbonate to release water and carbon dioxide. If ethanol is reacted with sodium bicarbonate, sodium ethanoate,

an ester, is formed along with water and carbon dioxide. The sodium bicarbonate test is a test for the presence of a carboxyl group (–COOH) in a compound because the reaction causes effervescence and the release of carbon dioxide.

- Reaction with alcohols – Esters are formed when alcohols are made to react with organic acids in the presence of concentrated sulphuric acid.

The following are uses of organic acids:

- Organic acids are used in some food items. For example, vinegar is dilute acetic acid. Vinegar is used in many preparations for pickles, salads, sauces, etc.
- Organic acids are used in the manufacture of soaps. Sodium salts of fatty acids are used in the soap and detergent industries.
- Organic acids find use in medicines. For example, acetic acid is used in the production of aspirin.
- Organic acids are used as industrial solvents.
- Organic acids are used in the preparation of perfumes and artificial essences that are used in food manufacturing.
- Acetic acid is used for making cellulose acetate, which is an important starting material for making artificial fibers.
- Acetic acid is also used for the coagulation of latex. This is needed when rubber is made from latex in a rubber manufacturing industry.

Preparation
Organic acids are prepared by oxidation of alcohols. Incomplete oxidation of alcohols leads to organic acids. Incomplete oxidation is achieved by providing nascent oxygen for the reaction. When air is made to pass over heated copper, oxygen from the air can break into atomic or nascent oxygen. This is made to react with an alcohol in order to give organic acid and water. In this manner, copper functions as a catalyst.

$$CH_3OH \ + \ O_2 \ \xrightarrow[\text{Heat}]{\text{Cu}} \ HCOOH \ + \ H_2O$$

Methanol or Methyl alcohol   Oxygen (From air)   Methanoic acid or Formic acid   Water

$$CH_3CH_2OH \ + \ O_2 \ \xrightarrow[\text{Heat}]{\text{Cu}} \ CH_3COOH \ + \ H_2O$$

Ethanol (Ethyl alcohol)   Oxygen (From air)   Ethanoic acid (Acetic acid)   Water

Nucleophilic attack and reduction

Because the ▯-carbon of carboxylic acids is extremely labile due to keto-enol tautomerism, it is very prone to nucleophilic attack and can form a wide variety of compounds, such as amines, halogenated variants, etc. Carboxylic acids can also be reduced to form aldehydes in the presence of the ester and diisobutylaluminum hydride (DIBAL).

Decarboxylation of organic acids

Decarboxylation is the loss of carbon dioxide. Simple carboxylic acids rarely undergo decarboxylation. Carboxylic acids with a carbonyl group at the 3- (or b-) position readily undergo thermal de-carboxylation (e.g., derivatives of malonic acid). An example decarboxylation reaction can be seen below.

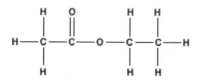

Esterification of organic acids

Esterification is a process where carboxylic acids react with alcohols to yield compounds called esters. Carboxylic acids react readily with alcohols in the presence of a catalytic amount of mineral acids. An example esterification reaction can be seen below.

$$\text{RCOOH} + \text{R'OH} \xleftrightarrow{\text{Mineral Acid}} \text{RCOOR'} + H_2O$$

Esters and acid derivatives

When the functional group is –COOR, where R is an alkyl group, the resultant compound is called an ester. The production of esters is accomplished through esterification, which produces an ester and water. Esterification is performed in the presence of concentrated sulphuric acid, which is a catalyst for the reaction. Ester tests are performed to identify whether an organic mixture has alcohol or an acid. Esters have a very sweet, fruity smell, and naturally occurring esters are found in fruits. The structure of a typical ester, namely ethyl ethanoate, is as follows:

The common names of esters are derived from the organic acid and the alcohol from which they are derived. For example, when acetic acid reacts with ethyl alcohol, the ester that is formed is called ethyl acetate. However, the IPUAC name is different. Acetic acid is called ethanoic acid by the IUPAC rules. Thus, the ester formed is called ethyl ethanoate. The IUPAC names for esters are derived from the prefix of the alcohol and from the name of the acid.

The physical properties of esters are as follows:
- Physical state – Lower molecular weight esters are colorless, volatile liquids. Higher esters are colorless, waxy solids.
- Odor – All esters have a strong fruity smell.
- Solubility – Lower members of the esters are soluble in water. The solubility decreases with increases in the molecular weight of the esters. Esters are also soluble in organic solvents. And, esters themselves are good organic solvents.
- Acidic nature – Esters are neutral to litmus tests.

The uses of esters are as follows:

- Used as artificial perfumes or scents, as they emit a sweet smell.
- Used in making artificial food flavors that are added in many edible items, like ice creams, soft drinks, sweets, etc.
- Used as industrial solvents for making cellulose, fats, paints, and varnishes.
- Used as solvents in the pharmaceutical industries.
- Used as softeners in the plastic and molding industries.

Hofmann's rule

Hofmann's rule implies that steric effects have the greatest influence on the outcome of the Hofmann or similar eliminations. The loss of the β-hydrogen occurs preferably from the most unhindered (least substituted) position [$-CH_3$ > $-CH_2-R$ > $-CH(R_2)$]. The product alkene with the fewest substituents will predominate. Examples of the Hoffman rule can be seen below.

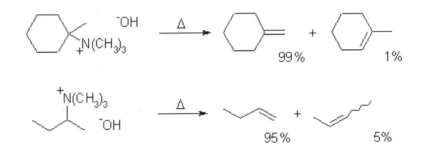

Hydrolysis of esters

Esters break down into the respective organic acids and alcohols from which they were formed. This process is called hydrolysis. When sodium hydroxide is added to an ester, for example to ethyl ethanoate, a salt is formed, sodium ethanoate, along with ethyl alcohol. This reaction is shown below.

$$CH_3COOC_2H_5 \quad + \quad NaOH \quad \xrightarrow{\text{Heat}} \quad CH_3COONa \quad + \quad C_2H_5OH$$

| Ethyl ethanoate or Ethyl acetate | Sodium hydroxide | Sodium ethanoate or Sodium acetate | Ethanol or Ethyl alcohol |

The above reaction is a test for checking if esters are present in any solution. When a few drops of the indicator, phenolphthalein, are added to a solution of ester and NaOH, the solution will show a pink coloration. Heat the solution to speed up the reaction. When the ester has reacted completely, the pink color will disappear.

Hydrolysis of an ester with an alkaline solution, such as sodium hydroxide, is known as saponification (soap making). This reaction is used in the preparation of soaps.

Saponification

Saponification is the hydrolysis of an ester under basic conditions to form an alcohol and the salt of the acid. Saponification is commonly used to refer to the reaction of a metallic alkali (base) with a fat or oil in order to produce soap.

Acetoacetic ester synthesis process

When α-keto acetic acid is treated with one mole of a base, the methylene group, which is more acidic, reacts with the base. And, the reaction with an alkylation reagent gives alkyl products attached to methylene. When this reaction is repeated in the next step, the other hydrogen can also react to a dialkyl product. The two alkylation agents may be the same or different (R', R''). β-keto esters tend to decarboxylate after hydrolysation to β-keto carboxylic acid and heating to give one or two alkyl-substituted ketones, respectively.

Metathesis reactions

Reactions in which none of the atoms undergo a change in oxidation number are called metathesis reactions. Consider the reaction between a carboxylic acid and an amine, for example.

$$CH_3CO_2H + CH_3NH_2 \longrightarrow CH_3CO_2^- + CH_3NH_3^+$$

Or, the reaction between an alcohol and hydrogen bromide.

$$CH_3CH_2OH + HBr \longrightarrow CH_3CH_2Br + H_2O$$

These are metathesis reactions because there is no change in the oxidation number of any atom in either reaction.

Willgerodt-Kindler reaction

The Willgerodt-Kindler reaction allows for the synthesis of amides from aryl ketones, under the influence of a secondary amine and a thiating agent. The mechanism involves the formation of an enamine, which undergoes thiation, and the carbonyl group migrates to the end of the chain via a cascade of thio-substituted iminium-aziridinium rearrangements. An example of the Willgerodt-Kindler reaction can be seen below.

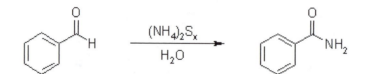

Chelating agents

Certain organic compounds are capable of forming coordinate bonds with metals through two or more atoms of the organic compound. Such organic compounds are called chelating agents. The compound that is formed by the reaction of the chelating agent and a metal is called a chelate. A chelating agent that has two coordinating atoms is called bidentate; one that has three, tridentate; and so on. EDTA, or ethylenediaminetetraacetate, is a common hexadentate chelating agent. Chlorophyll is a chelate that consists of a magnesium ion joined with a complex chelating agent. Heme, part of the hemoglobin in blood, is an iron chelate. Chelating agents are important in textile dyeing, water softening, enzyme deactivation, and as bacteriocides.

Amines

Amines are organic compounds that contain a nitrogen group with a lone pair of electrons. Amines are derivatives of ammonia with one or more hydrogen atoms replaced by alkyl or aryl groups. Amines are named either with either the prefix "amino–" or suffix "–amine" added to the root name of the compound.

Petasis reaction

The petasis reaction is a multicomponent reaction (MCR) that enables the preparation of amines and their derivatives, such as α-amino acids. This reaction is also referred to as the boronic acid Mannich reaction, since it proceeds via an imine, with the organic ligand of the boronic acid acting as the nucleophile, similar to the role of the enolizable ketone component in the original Mannich reaction. Examples of the Petasis reaction can be seen below.

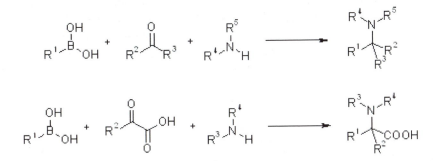

Sandmeyer reaction

The Sandmeyer reaction allows for the substitution of an aromatic amino group via preparation of its diazonium salt and subsequent displacement with a nucleophile (e.g., Cl^-, I^-, CN^-, RS^-, HO^-, etc.). Many Sandmeyer reactions proceed under copper (I) catalysis, while the Sandmeyer-type reactions with thiols, water, and potassium iodide do not require catalysis. An example of a Sandmeyer reaction can be seen below.

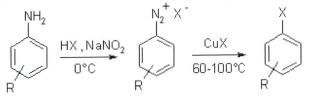

X= CN, Br, Cl, SO₃H

Hofmann elimination

Hofmann elimination is sometimes referred to as Hofmann degradation. This elimination reaction of alkyl trimethyl amines proceeds with anti-stereochemistry, and is generally suitable for producing alkenes with one or two substituents. The reaction follows Hofmann's rule. An example of a Hofmann elimination can be seen below.

Carbohydrates

Carbohydrates are organic compounds that consist only of carbon, hydrogen, and oxygen. In general, the hydrogen to oxygen ratio in carbohydrates is 2:1, although carbohydrates are not technically hydrates of carbon; rather, they are more akin to polyhydroxy aldehydes and ketones. Carbohydrates are also referred to as saccharides, and are classified as either monosaccharides, disaccharides, oligosaccharides or polysaccharides. Mono- and disaccharides, which are composed of one and two carbohydrates, respectively, are referred to as sugars. Oligo- and polysaccharides are composed of longer, more complex chains of sugars (i.e., oligo = 2 to 10; poly = 11+), which are important for energy storage and the production of a wide variety of biological molecules. Common carbohydrates are:

- Glucose (monosaccharide) – Blood sugar.
- Fructose (monosaccharide) – Fruit sugar.
- Sucrose (disaccharide) – Table sugar, composed of glucose and fructose.
- Lactose (disaccharide) – Milk sugar, composed of glucose and galactose.
- Oligofructose (oligosaccharide) – Short chain of fructose molecules naturally found in fruits.
- Oligogalactose (oligosaccharide) – Short chain of galactose molecules naturally found in milk; considered to be a prebiotic.
- Starch (polysaccharide) – Polymer of glucose used to store energy in plants and fruits.
- Glycogen (polysaccharide) – Polymer of glucose used to store energy in animals.
- Cellulose (polysaccharide) – Polymer of hundreds to thousands of glucose subunits used for the structural composition of plants.
- Chitin (polysaccharide) – Polymer of *N*-acetylglucosamine that forms the cell walls of fungi and the exoskeletons of arthropods.

> ➤ **Review Video: Carbohydrates**
> Visit *mometrix.com/academy* and enter *Code:* **601714**

Structure of carbohydrates

Originally, scientists considered any compound that conformed to the formula $C_m(H_2O)_n$ to be carbohydrates, including formaldehyde (CH_2O). However, today, carbohydrates are considered to be any compound that conforms to the formula $(CH_2O)_n$, where n is greater than or equal to three.

Typically, carbohydrates have the structure H-$(CHOH)_x$-(C=O)-$(CHOH)_y$-H, which is essentially an aldehyde or ketone with hydroxyl groups on each carbon atom that is not part of the aldehyde or ketone functional group. However, not all compounds that conform to this formula are considered to be carbohydrates (e.g., inositol (($CH_2O)_6$)), and not all carbohydrates conform to this formula (e.g., fucose and deoxyribonucleic acid). In solutions, carbohydrates naturally exist in equilibrium between open- and closed-chain structures. For example, the open chain structure for glucose is as follows:

Glucose

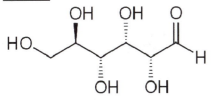

The open-chain structure of glucose forms four closed-chain, cyclic isomers by a nucleophilic addition reaction between the C-1 aldehyde group and either the C-4 or the C-5 carbon, yielding a hemiacetal group (i.e., -C(OH)H-O-). The four cyclic isomers of glucose are as follows:

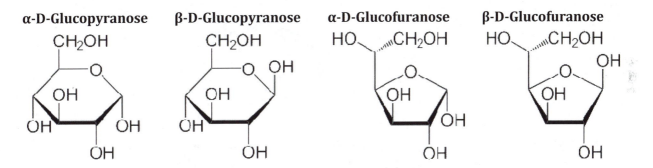

Note: The α- and β-cyclic isoforms of glucose differ by the final orientation of the hydroxyl group on the C-1 carbon. The hydroxyl group of the α-isoform is in the *trans* arrangement, meaning that it is opposite to the plane of the sugar molecule; while the hydroxyl group of the β-isoform is in the *cis* arrangement, meaning that it is on the same side as the plane of the sugar. Because of the different orientations of only the C-1 hydroxyl group of the glucose molecule, each of these isoforms are chiral, meaning that they have a mirror image that is non-superposable.

Glycosidic linkages

Chains of carbohydrates are formed by covalent bonds referred to as glycosidic linkages, which are formed by a dehydration reaction between two hydroxyl groups of the sugar molecules. This reaction yields two sugar molecules linked together by an oxygen atom and results in the release of a water molecule. Glycosidic bonds can still take place if the hydroxyl group is replaced by a thiol or amine group; however, instead of being referred to as O-glycosidic bonds, they are referred to as either S-glycosidic or N-glycosidic bonds, respectively. An example of a disaccharide, linked by an O-glycosidic bond can be seen below.

Lactose

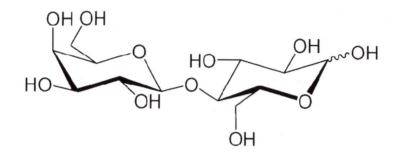

Glucose

Glucose ($C_6H_{12}O_6$) is a simple monosaccharide, and is an important source of energy in all biological systems. The name, glucose, is derived from the Greek word for sweet. All cells utilize glucose as their primary source of energy, and as a metabolic intermediate. Glucose is produced in plants as one of the primary products of photosynthesis, and is believed to be the most widely utilized monosaccharide in nature because of its stability and lower tendency to react with the amino groups of proteins. While there are many isomers of glucose, all of which can be divided into two stereoisomeric groups (i.e., dextrorotary (D, right handed) and levorotary (L, left handed), only the dextrorotary isoforms exist in nature. Because of this, glucose is sometimes referred to as dextrose, although this name is strongly discouraged due to confusion when discussing the levorotary isoforms.

Glycogen

Glycogen is a highly branched polymer of glucose in which most of the glucose residues are linked to each other by alpha-1,4-glycosidic bonds to form a linear backbone. Interspersed along the linear backbone, at intervals of 4-10 glucose residues, are branches created by alpha-1,6-glycosidic bonds. As a result of the extensive branching, the glycogen molecule has a frond-like and highly branched configuration with an open helical tertiary structure. The helix, in turn, is organized into spherical particles with a molecular weight of 10-15 million Daltons (60,000 glucose residues per particle), and the spherical particles, in turn, are organized into large granules. The granules range in size from 10-40 nm and are located in the cellular cytosol.

<u>Structure</u>

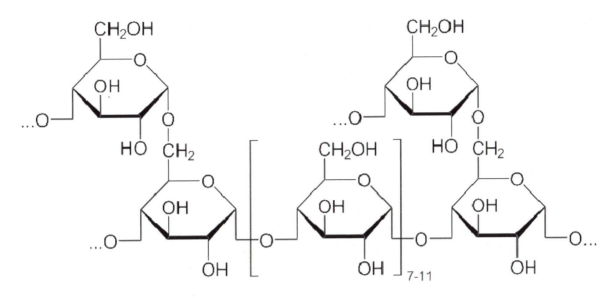

Ribose

Ribose ($C_5H_{10}O_5$) is a simple, five-carbon monosaccharide with all of the hydroxyl groups on the same side of the molecule in the Fisher projection. Ribose, along with its epimer arabinose, are derived from gum Arabic; and, similar to glucose, are only found as dextrorotary isoforms in nature. Ribose is a very important carbohydrate for biological systems, and serves as the backbone for a large number of important biological compounds, including the following:

- Ribonucleic Acid (RNA) – Nucleic acids that are transcribed from DNA and then used for a variety of purposes, such as the template for ribosomes to produce proteins (messenger RNA), short sequences for silencing transcriptional activity (microRNAs), short sequences for triggering the degradation of mRNAs (silencing or short-hairpin RNAs), adapter molecules between mRNAs and amino acids (transfer RNAs), ribosomal structural molecules (ribosomal RNAs), etc. RNA is composed of chains of ribonucleotides, each consisting of a nucleobase, a ribose sugar, and a phosphate group.
- Deoxyribonucleic Acid (DNA) – Nucleic acids that store long-term genetic information. DNA is composed similar to RNA, except with deoxyribose in the place of ribose, which is derived from the removal of an oxygen atom from ribose, and thymine in the place of uracil.
- Adenosine Triphosphate (ATP) – Important for the storage and transmission of energy. Derived from the phosphorylation of the ribonucleoside, adenosine.
- Nicotinamide Adenine Dinucleotide (NADH) – A coenzyme used to carry electrons. Derived from two ribonucleosides linked by a pair of phosphate groups.
- Cyclic Adenosine Monophosphate (cAMP) and Cyclic Guanosine Monophosphate (cGMP) – Used as second messengers for many biological processes. Derived from ATP and GTP by the ester linkage of the first phosphate group to the C-3 hydroxyl group of the ribose molecule, catalyzed by phosphodiesterase.

Reactions of Monosaccharides

Ring formation

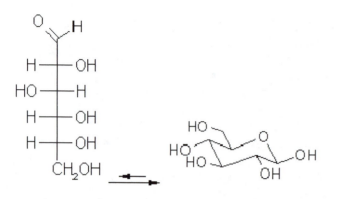

Oxidation reaction

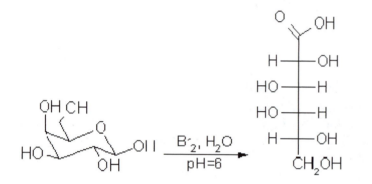

Mutarotation

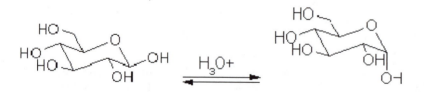

Ester formation

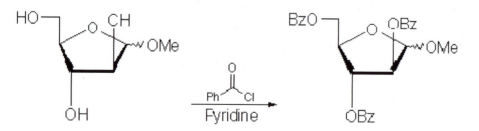

Amino acids and proteins

Amino acids are organic compounds that contain an amine group, a carboxylic acid group, and a side chain that is specific to each molecule. Amino acids are primarily composed of carbon, hydrogen, oxygen, and nitrogen, and generally conform to the formula $H_2NCHRCOOH$, where R represents the specific side chain of the amino acid. In most amino acids, the amine group is attached to the α-carbon, and they are thus referred to as α-amino acids; however, they can be also be found with the amine group bound to a different carbon, such as the γ-carbon in γ-amino acids.

Amino acids are the building blocks of proteins, which are chains of amino acids. Each protein is composed of a specific sequence of amino acids. Since proteins are composed of 20 standard amino acids (as well as nonstandard amino acids on occasion) and vary in length from 20 amino acids to tens of thousands of amino acids, there are literally an infinite number of possible combinations. However, the proteins that are naturally produced within cells are limited to what is encoded by the genome, including alternative splice forms; and, are composed of domains and motifs of conserved amino acid sequences that confer specific functions to the proteins. Collectively, the proteins that are encoded by the genome control or participate in virtually every process within living cells.

Note: Amino acid chains of between 3-20 amino acids are called peptides, while amino acid chains of greater than 20 amino acids are called polypeptides.

> ➤ **Review Video: Amino Acids**
> *Visit* ***mometrix.com/academy*** *and enter* ***Code:*** **190385**

Amino acid side chains

Nonpolar R-groups

Glycine (G)

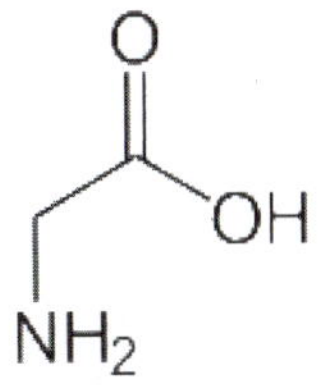

Alanine (A)

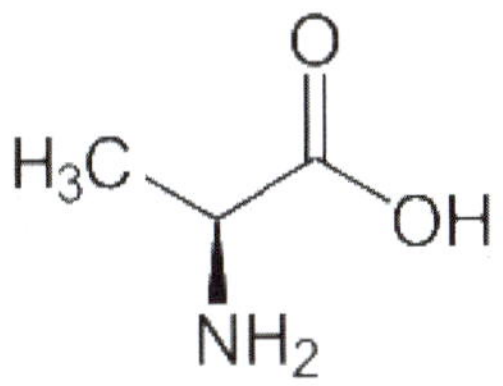

Valine (V)

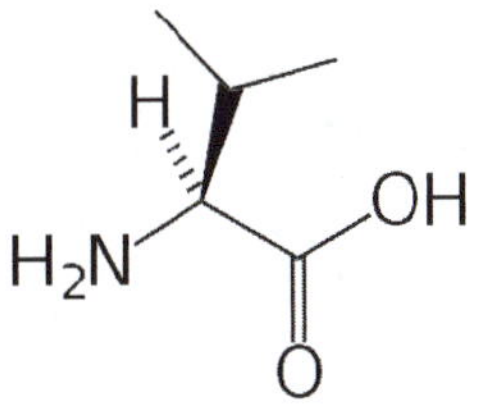

Leucine (L)

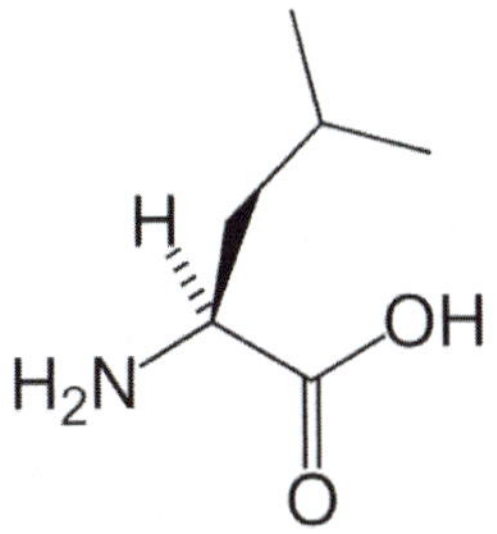

Isoleucine (I)

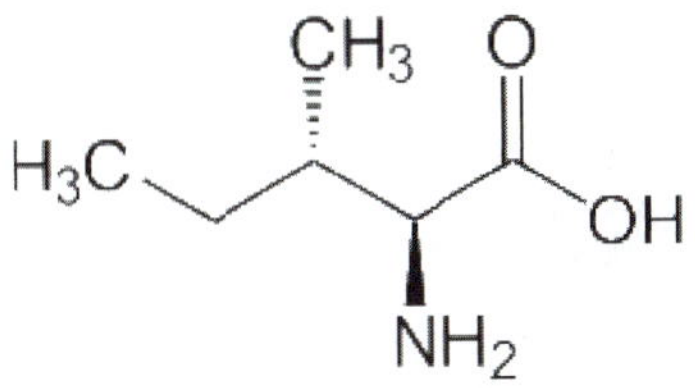

Proline (P)

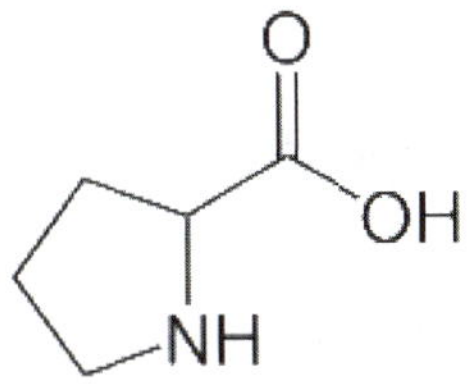

Polar, uncharged R-groups

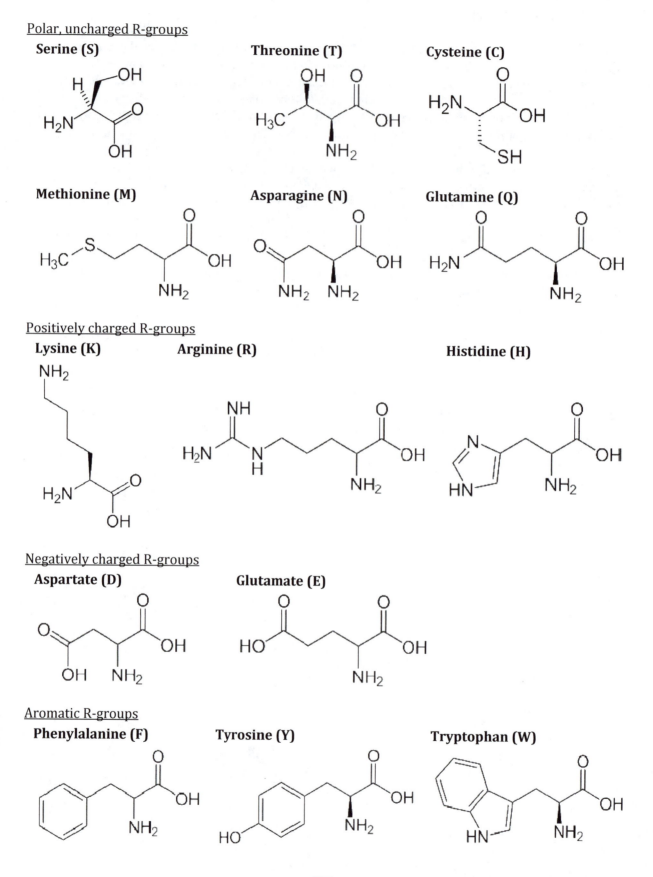

Serine (S)

Threonine (T)

Cysteine (C)

Methionine (M)

Asparagine (N)

Glutamine (Q)

Positively charged R-groups

Lysine (K)

Arginine (R)

Histidine (H)

Negatively charged R-groups

Aspartate (D)

Glutamate (E)

Aromatic R-groups

Phenylalanine (F)

Tyrosine (Y)

Tryptophan (W)

Peptide bond formation

Proteins are formed by the polymerization of amino acids. The polymerization of amino acids occurs through the formation of peptide bonds, where the amine group of one amino acid reacts with the carboxylic acid group of another amino acid to form an amide bond. In cells, this reaction occurs first by the ATP-dependent ester linkage of an amino acid to a specific tRNA by an aminoacyl tRNA synthetase, producing an aminoacyl tRNA. The aminoacyl tRNA then serves as a substrate for ribosomes, which catalyze the bond formation between the carboxylic acid group of the growing peptide chain and the ester bond of the aminoacyl tRNA. The result of this process is the formation of a peptide bond and the release of a water molecule. Because of the directionality of the peptide bond formation, proteins are synthesized from the N-terminus towards the C-terminus.

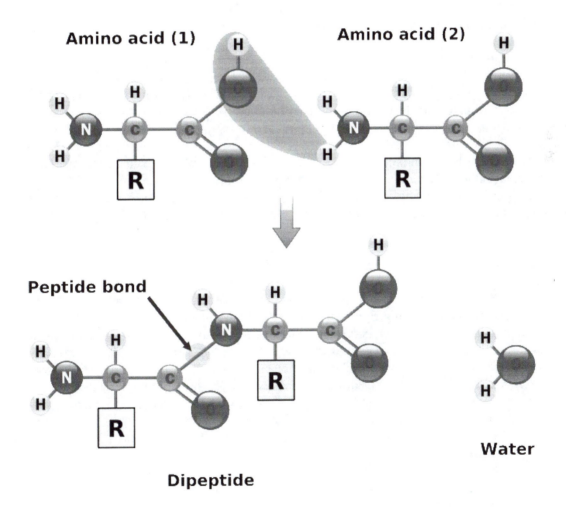

Protein folding

As the growing peptide chain exits the ribosome, the linear sequence of amino acids is folded into secondary and tertiary structures based upon hydrophobicity, hydrogen bonding, van der Waal's forces, and disulfide bridges. The folding of proteins also requires chaperones:

- Chaperones (also called chaperonins) are needed every time a protein remains unfolded, or becomes unfolded to cross a membrane (or refolds on the other side). Two or more types of chaperones are involved in protein folding, and different ones are found in different parts of the cell.
- There are two major types (families) of chaperones: HSP60 or HSP70, depending on their molecular weight (60 kDa vs. 70 kDa), and mode of action.
- The major chaperone inside of the endoplasmic reticulum is a member of the HSP70 family, called binding immunoglobulin protein (BiP).

Primary and secondary structures

Primary structure refers to the linear number and order of the amino acids present in a peptide or protein. The convention for the designation of the order of amino acids is that the N-terminal end (i.e., the end bearing the residue with the free α-amino group) is to the left (and the number 1 amino acid), while the C-terminal end (i.e., the end with the residue containing a free α-carboxyl group) is to the right. The secondary structure is the ordered array of amino acids of a protein into regular conformational substructures, typically α-helices or β-strands, which are bound together by hydrogen bonding. Within a single protein, different regions of the polypeptide chain may assume different secondary conformations, and these conformations are determined by the primary amino acid sequence.

Tertiary and quanternary structures

The tertiary structure of a protein is the overall shape of the protein that is formed by salt bridges, hydrogen bonding, disulfide bonding, and posttranslational modifications between the secondary structures of a protein. The tertiary structure is what determines the overall functions of a protein, and denaturation of this structure will usually inactivate the protein. The quanternary structure of a protein is the structure of a macromolecular complex of proteins composed of more than one tertiary protein subunit. An example of a quanternary structure is the functional hemoglobin molecule, which is composed of multiple globular heme subunits held together by hydrogen bonding. While all proteins have tertiary structures, not all proteins have quanternary structures.

Hydrolysis of peptide bonds

Peptide bonds are metastable and can be broken spontaneously in the presence of water by a reaction, called amide hydrolysis. This reaction releases 8-16 kJ/mol, but occurs very slowly. In living organisms, this reaction is usually catalyzed by enzymes called peptidases.

Lipids

Lipids are hydrophobic or amphipathic molecules, including fats, sterols, monoglycerides, diglycerides, triglycerides, phospholipids, etc. The biological functions of lipids include energy storage, membrane structure formation, and cell signaling. Because of the amphipathic nature of phospholipids, cell membranes can be formed, where the hydrophilic regions are oriented towards the aqueous solutions both inside and outside of the membrane, and the hydrophobic regions are sandwiched together within the membrane, creating a barrier to entry/exit for the cells. The formation of a membrane allows for cellular and subcellular compartmentalization, which allows for the very creation of all living beings. Fatty acids are the basic building blocks of most lipids, and are composed of long hydrocarbon chains that terminate in a carboxylic acid group. Fatty acids that contain only single bonds are referred to as saturated, while fatty acids with one or more double bonds are referred to as unsaturated. Fatty acids can be synthesized by chain elongation using acetyl-CoA and malonyl- or methylmalonyl-CoA groups in a process called fatty acid synthesis.

> **Review Video: Lipids**
*Visit **mometrix.com/academy** and enter **Code: 269746***

The following molecules are composed of fatty acids:
- Glycerolipids – Formed by the mono-, di-, and trisubstitution of fatty acids to a glycerol molecule. An example of an unsaturated triglyceride can be seen below.

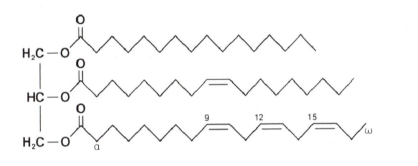

- Phospholipids – Formed by the di-substitution of fatty acids to a glycerol molecule containing one phosphate group. An example of a phospholipid, phosphatidylcholine, can be seen below.

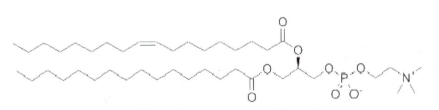

- Sphingolipids – A complicated family of lipids formed from a sphingoid base composed of a serine residue bound to a fatty acid residue. The sphingoid base is then converted into ceramides, phosphosphingolipids, glycosphingolipids, and other compounds. An example of a sphingolipid, sphingosine, can be seen below.

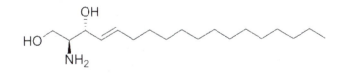

Common saturated fatty acids

Common Name	Chemical Structure	Carbon:Double Bond Ratio
Caprylic Acid	$CH_3(CH_2)_6COOH$	8:0
Capric Acid	$CH_3(CH_2)_8COOH$	10:0
Lauric Acid	$CH_3(CH_2)_{10}COOH$	12:0
Myristic Acid	$CH_3(CH_2)_{12}COOH$	14:0
Palmitic Acid	$CH_3(CH_2)_{14}COOH$	16:0
Stearic Acid	$CH_3(CH_2)_{16}COOH$	18:0
Arachidic Acid	$CH_3(CH_2)_{18}COOH$	20:0
Behenic Acid	$CH_3(CH_2)_{20}COOH$	22:0
Lignoceric Acid	$CH_3(CH_2)_{22}COOH$	24:0
Cerotic Acid	$CH_3(CH_2)_{24}COOH$	26:0

Common unsaturated fatty acids

Common Name	Chemical Structure	D^x	C:D	n-x
Myristoleic Acid	$CH_3(CH_2)_3CH=CH(CH_2)_7COOH$	$cis\text{-}\Delta^9$	14:1	n-5
Palmitoleic Acid	$CH_3(CH_2)_5CH=CH(CH_2)_7COOH$	$cis\text{-}\Delta^9$	16:1	n-7
Sapienic Acid	$CH_3(CH_2)_8CH=CH(CH_2)_4COOH$	$cis\text{-}\Delta^6$	16:1	n-10
Oleic Acid	$CH_3(CH_2)_7CH=CH(CH_2)_7COOH$	$cis\text{-}\Delta^9$	18:1	n-9
Elaidic Acid	$CH_3(CH_2)_7CH=CH(CH_2)_7COOH$	$trans\text{-}\Delta^9$	18:1	n-9
Vaccenic Acid	$CH_3(CH_2)_5CH=CH(CH_2)_9COOH$	$trans\text{-}\Delta^{11}$	18:1	n-7
Linoleic Acid	$CH_3(CH_2)_4CH=CHCH_2CH=CH(CH_2)_7COOH$	$cis,cis\text{-}\Delta^9,\Delta^{12}$	18:2	n-6
Linoelaidic Acid	$CH_3(CH_2)_4CH=CHCH_2CH=CH(CH_2)_7COOH$	$trans,trans\text{-}\Delta^9,\Delta^{12}$	18:2	n-6
α-Linolenic Acid	$CH_3CH_2CH=CHCH_2CH=CHCH_2CH=CH(CH_2)_7COOH$	$cis,cis,cis\text{-}$ $\Delta^9,\Delta^{12},\Delta^{15}$	18:3	n-3
Arachidonic Acid	$CH_3(CH_2)_4CH=CHCH_2CH=CHCH_2CH=CHCH_2CH=CH(CH_2)_3COOH$	$cis,cis,cis,cis\text{-}$ $\Delta^5,\Delta^8,\Delta^{11},\Delta^{14}$	20:4	n-6
Eicosapentaenoic Acid	$CH_3CH_2CH=CHCH_2CH=CHCH_2CH=CHCH_2CH=CHCH_2CH=CH(CH_2)_3COOH$	$cis,cis,cis,cis,cis\text{-}$ $\Delta^5,\Delta^8,\Delta^{11},\Delta^{14},\Delta^{17}$	20:5	n-3
Erucic Acid	$CH_3(CH_2)_7CH=CH(CH_2)_{11}COOH$	$cis\text{-}\Delta^{13}$	22:1	n-9
Docosahexaenoic Acid	$CH_3CH_2CH=CHCH_2CH=CHCH_2CH=CHCH_2CH=CHCH_2CH=CHCH_2CH=CH(CH_2)_2COOH$	$cis,cis,cis,cis,cis,cis\text{-}$ $\Delta^4,\Delta^7,\Delta^{10},\Delta^{13},\Delta^{16},\Delta^{19}$	22:6	n-3

Terpenes

Terpenes are a diverse group of organic compounds that are produced in plants, primarily conifers, as well as some insects. Terpenes are the primary components of resins and essential oils, and are used commercially for both their aromatic and flavorful qualities. Structurally, terpenes and terpenoids consist of one or more units of isoprene, C_5H_8, and conform to the formula $(C_5H_8)_n$. Terpenes are also used as the building blocks for a wide variety of compounds in nearly every living creature, including steroids, which are derivatives of the triterpene, squalene. However, the

- 288 -

products are not terpenes or terpenoids in the literal sense because they do not contain the characteristic number of carbon atoms.

Steroids

Steroids are a group of lipids that contains a characteristic arrangement of four cycloalkane rings joined to one another. The core structure of steroids consists of 20 carbon atoms joined together to create 3 cyclohexane rings and 1 cyclopentane ring. Steroids differ by the functional group that attaches to their core structure, as well as the oxidation states of the rings. Some examples of steroids include cholesterol, estradiol, testosterone, and dexamethasone.

Steroid core structure

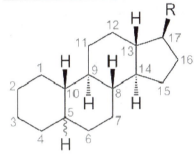

Cholesterol

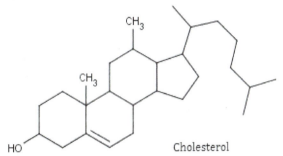

Cholesterol

Analysis of the structure of cholesterol indicates that its formula is $C_{27}H_{46}O$, which does not fit the pattern that is expected for a terpenoid. The most important property of this molecule is the fact that, with the exception of the –OH group on the lower left-hand corner of the molecule, there is nothing about its structure that would suggest that it is soluble in water.

Phosphorus compounds

Phosphorus is essential for life. Organophosphorus compounds contain carbon-phosphorus bonds, while organophosphate compounds contain phosphorus linked to carbon through an ester linkage ($-C-O-P(OH)_3$). In the form of phosphate, phosphorus is a critical component of DNA, RNA, ATP, cAMP, and phospholipids, among a wide variety of organophosphate compounds.

Phosphoric acids

The most basic phosphoric acid is H_3PO_4. When 1 or 2 hydrogens are removed from phosphoric acid, dihydrogen phosphate, $H_2PO_4^{1-}$ (1st conjugate base), and hydrogen phosphate, HPO_4^{2-} (2nd conjugate base), are formed. When all three hydrogen atoms are removed from phosphoric acid, the resulting compound is referred to as phosphate, PO_4^{3-} (3rd conjugate base). Phosphate is a very important functional group in organic chemistry and biochemistry, essential for most energy-dependent chemical reactions.

Phosphoric acid monomers can be linked together to form polyphosphate-anhydride compounds through a condensation reaction that results in two phosphoric acid residues linked together by an ester linkage, along with the release of a water molecule. Common polyphosphate compounds are as follows:

- Pyrophosphate – Two phosphoric acid subunits.
- Tripolyphosphate – Three phosphoric acid subunits.
- Tetrapolyphosphate – Four phosphoric acid subunits.
- Trimetaphosphate – Three phosphoric acid subunits linked together into a cyclical ring.
- Phosphoric anhydride – Four phosphoric acid subunits linked together into a spherical complex.

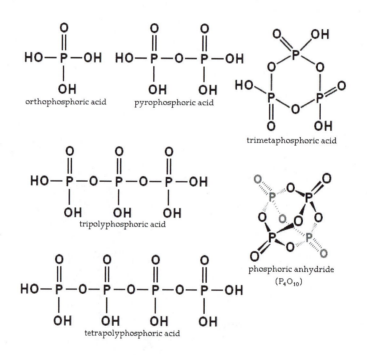

Phosphoester and phosphodiester linkages

Phosphates and polyphosphates can also be linked to other organic compounds, such as nucleotides or nucleic acids. In the case of nucleotides, the binding of one or more phosphates functions to store energy that can later be used for enzymatic reactions, due to the amount of energy that is stored in the phosphor-ester linkages.

Given the repulsion of the phosphate groups to one another, when pyrophosphate or tripolyphosphate are linked to a nucleotide, forming ADP or ATP in the case of adenosine, the energy that is stored in the second and third bonds increases dramatically.

Hydrolysis of these high-energy bonds by living systems allows such energy to be harnessed to power enzymatic processes. The amounts of energy that are released by hydrolysis of the third or second bonds of ATP, releasing inorganic phosphate (P_i) or pyrophosphate (PP_i), respectively, are as follows:

$$ATP + H_2O \rightarrow ADP + P_i \qquad \Delta G° = -30.5 \text{ kJ/mol}$$

$$ATP + H_2O \rightarrow AMP + PP_i \qquad \Delta G° = -45.6 \text{ kJ/mol}$$

As can be seen by the above reactions, the energy that is released by the second and third bonds is only 50% greater than the energy released by the third bond alone.

In the case of nucleic acids, phosphates are used to link nucleotides via phosphodiester linkages. Phosphodiester linkages are very strong covalent bonds that are formed between a phosphate group and two 5-carbon carbohydrate rings. In DNA, the carbohydrates are deoxyribose, while in RNA, the carbohydrates are ribose. Because phosphodiester linkages form the backbone of nucleic acids, they are essential to all known life.

Wittig reaction

The Wittig reaction allows for the preparation of an alkene by the reaction of an aldehyde or ketone with triphenol phosphonium ylide, also called Wittig reagent, which is generated from a phosphonium salt. The geometry of the resulting alkene depends upon the reactivity of the ylide. If R is Ph, then the ylide is stabilized, and is not as reactive as when R is an alkyl. Stabilized ylides give (E)-alkenes, whereas non-stabilized ylides lead to (Z)-alkenes. Examples of the Wittig reaction can be seen below.

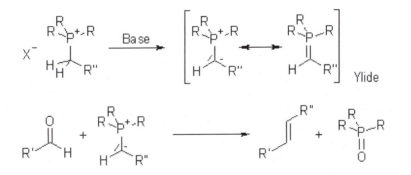

Physics

Scalars and vectors

A scalar is a physical quantity whose definition does not in any way depend on direction in space. Scalars include time, mass, volume, temperature, density, and others. The size of a scalar quantity is represented as a number. In physical equations, scalars obey the algebra of numbers. A vector is a physical quantity that depends on direction in space. A vector has both size and direction, and both must be specified to uniquely characterize the vector. Vector quantities include displacement, velocity, acceleration, momentum, angular momentum, and others. Since surface area has spatial orientation, it must often be treated as a vector. Direction also matters with vectors. Two vectors are only said to be equal if their sizes and directions are the same.

Components of vectors
When dealing with vectors algebraically, it is useful to represent a vector by its components. The components of vectors are the projections of those vectors onto chosen coordinate axes. The components of a vector are usually treated as scalar quantities. While the coordinate axes can be any lines, we customarily use the axes of a Cartesian coordinate system, specifying the x, y, and z components of the vector. When this is done, any vector in the space is uniquely defined by specifying the coordinate axes and the vector's components along those axes (x, y, and z). Sometimes, it is even useful to have a set of coordinate axes that are not orthogonal (perpendicular), as long as the axes "span the space" (are able to uniquely represent any vector in the space by its components). This requirement is met if the three axes do not all lie in the same plane, and if no two are collinear.

Distance and displacement

Distance and displacement are both used to describe the extent of a body's motion. Distance is a scalar quantity that represents the length of the path that a body follows when moving from one point to another, while displacement is a vector that represents the relative position of two points in space. The size of a displacement vector is the distance between the points, while its direction is the direction of the line segment that joins the points. When we speak of displacement of a body during a time interval, the displacement is a vector that is drawn from the earlier (initial) position to the later (final) position of that body.

Speed and velocity

Speed is a scalar quantity, while velocity is a vector that describes the speed and direction of a body in motion. The velocity vector is defined as follows:

$$v = \frac{\Delta x}{\Delta t}$$

Where:
Δx = The displacement vector.
Δt = The infinitesimal time interval.

For example: If a car is moving at 60 mph, and it is going north, then the velocity would be 60 mph north.

Average speed

The average speed, $\overline{v}$, of an object is the average rate at which it travels a particular distance. If a car's average speed is 65 mph, then this means that the car's position will change on average by 65 miles every hour. The average speed is a rate. In kinematics, a rate is always a quantity divided by the time taken to get that quantity, or the elapsed time. Since average speed is the rate that the position changes, the average speed equals the distance traveled divided by the elapsed time, as follows:

$$\overline{v} = \frac{d}{t}$$

Where:
d = The distance traveled.
t = The elapsed time.

For example: If a car travels between two towns that are 60 miles apart in 2 hours, then what is its average speed?

$$\overline{v} = \frac{60 \text{ miles}}{2 \text{ hours}} = 30 \text{ mph}$$

Average velocity

The average velocity is merely one half of the sum of if the initial and final velocities. Therefore, the average velocity, $\overline{v}$, can be calculated as follows:

$$\overline{v} = \frac{v_f + v_i}{2}$$

Where:
v_f = The final velocity.
v_i = The initial velocity.

Acceleration

Acceleration is a vector that represents the rate at which velocity changes over a defined period of time, and is defined as follows:

$$a = \frac{v_f - v_i}{t}$$

Where:
v_f = The final velocity.
v_i = The initial velocity.
t = The elapsed time.

The concepts of velocity and acceleration are linked together, but they are linked incorrectly in many people's minds. Many people think that if an object has a large velocity, then it must have a large acceleration; if it has a small velocity, then it must have a small acceleration; or, if its velocity is zero, then its acceleration must also be zero. This is wrong! Acceleration is the rate at which velocity changes, which means that acceleration tells you how fast the velocity is changing. A large acceleration tells you that the velocity is changing quickly; a small acceleration tells you that the velocity is changing slowly; and, an acceleration of zero tells you that the velocity is not changing at all. However, while acceleration tells you how the velocity changes, it does not tell how much the velocity is: an object may have a large velocity, but a small (or zero) acceleration, and vice versa. Many people also have the misguided notion that positive acceleration means speeding up, while negative acceleration means slowing down. By studying examples of the calculations of accelerations, you can conclude that if the velocity and acceleration are in the same direction, then the object is speeding up. Conversely, if the velocity and acceleration are in opposite directions, then the object is slowing down.

Mass

Mass is an intrinsic property of a body. Gravitational mass is measured by determining the gravitational force on a body relative to a mass standard. Inertial mass is determined and defined by Newton's third law. So far, as we know, gravitational and inertial mass are the same.

The net force on a body is the vector sum of all real forces acting on that body, and no other forces. This statement assumes that the scenario is within an inertial frame of reference.

Relationship to Newton's first and second laws
If F is the net real force on a body, and a is the acceleration of the center of mass of that body, then $F = ma$. This is Newton's first and second laws in the special case where the mass does not change.

According to Newton's first law, when the net force on a body is zero:
- A body at rest will remain at rest.
- A moving body will continue to move with constant speed in a straight line.

This is also known as the law of inertia. Inertia is defined as the tendency of a body to oppose any attempt to put it in motion; or, if it is moving, to change its speed or direction of motion. Inertia is a passive property, and thus only opposes forces.

Newton's first two laws are embodied in this more general statement: The rate of change of momentum of a body is proportional to the net force acting upon it. In equation form, $F = \Delta(mv)/\Delta t$. This is a vector equation, and applies even in cases where the mass may change in size.

Newton's third law

Newton's third law states that if body A exerts a force on body B, then B exerts an equal size and oppositely directed force on A. This can be written as follows: $F_{AB} = -F_{BA}$. Remember that forces are vectors, and the two forces of Newton's third law act on different bodies.

Law of universal gravitation

Every object in the universe attracts every other object with a force that is directed along the line of centers for the two objects, which is proportional to the product of their masses, and inversely proportional to the square of the separation between the two objects. Considering only the magnitude of the force, and momentarily putting aside its direction, the law of universal attraction can be stated as follows:

$$F = G \frac{m_1 m_2}{r^2}$$

Where:
F = The magnitude of the gravitational force between two objects.
G = The gravitational constant, 6.67×10^{-11} N·m²·kg⁻².
m_1 = The mass of the first object.
m_2 = The mass of the second object.
r = The distance between the two objects.

Thus, gravity is proportional to the mass of each object, but has an inverse square relationship to the distance between the centers of each mass. If the objects have spatial extent, then the force has to be calculated by integrating the force over the extents of the two bodies. It can be shown that, for an object with a spherically symmetric distribution of mass, the integral gives the same gravitational attraction on outside masses as if the object were a point mass.

Centripetal force

The centripetal force that acts on a rotating body is simply the radial component of the net force acting on that body. The radial component of a force is the vector component in the direction of a line drawn from the body to the center of rotation. The centripetal force is neither a "new" force, to be added to the real forces when finding the net force, nor is it a fictitious force. It is a real vector component of real forces.

Note: We are assuming that the analysis is being carried out in an inertial coordinate system. In advanced courses, one sometimes does such problems in a rotating coordinate system. Such systems are non-inertial, so Newton's second law for real forces does not apply.

The equation for centripetal force is as follows:

$$F_{centripetal} = ma_{centripetal}$$

Where:

$$a_{centripetal} = \frac{v^2}{r}$$

v = The velocity in meters per second.
r = The radius of the circle in meters.

Therefore, $F_{centripetal} = m \dfrac{v^2}{r}$

Weight

Weight is the force exerted on an object by the acceleration of gravity. It is dependent upon the mass of the object, but mass and weight are not the same. Weight also takes into account the local gravitational acceleration, so an object with a given mass can have a different weight depending on its location. On Earth, the gravitational acceleration, g, is 9.8 m/s². The equation for weight is as follows:

$$F = mg$$

Where:
m = The mass of the object.
g = The gravitational acceleration.

Friction

Friction acts in a direction to oppose the slipping or sliding motion of bodies at their contact surface. Forces due to friction are tangential to the contact surface where the bodies touch. The force of static friction, F_s, can be calculated as follows:
$$F_s = \mu_s R$$
Where:
μ_s = The coefficient of static friction.
R = The normal force.

The force of kinetic friction, F_k, can be calculated as follows:
$$F_k = \mu_k R$$
Where:
μ_k = The coefficient of kinetic friction.
R = The normal force.

The coefficient of friction, μ, varies widely from surface to surface.

Note: The short phrase, "friction opposes motion", should not be used because it can be misleading. The frictional force that is exerted by the floor on your feet acts in the direction of your walking motion. This frictional force on your feet helps to prevent your feet from slipping backward as they might on ice. The frictional force of the pavement acting upon your automobile's wheels is also forward in the direction of the auto's motion. Frictional forces and forces due to rolling resistance are the only forces that sustain your car's forward motion. Friction relates to two surfaces regardless of whether they are at rest or sliding.

> ➢ **Review Video: Friction**
> Visit *mometrix.com/academy* and enter *Code:* **716782**

Rolling resistance

Rolling resistance results from elastic or non-elastic deformations of bodies in contact, even if they are not slipping or sliding. To illustrate the difference between rolling resistance and friction, consider a ball or cylinder rolling on an infinite horizontal plane. Will it roll forever? No. Why? Not simply because of friction. Friction is, by definition, a force acting tangential to the surface. However, friction would act parallel to the plane in this situation. If such a tangential force acted opposite to the motion of the ball, then this would decrease the ball's forward velocity, but it would have a torque that would be in a direction to increase the angular velocity of the ball, which is contradictory. Conversely, if the tangential force were in a direction to decrease the angular velocity, then it would have a torque that would increase the forward linear velocity, which is likewise contradictory. However, elastic forces that are associated with deformations at the contact surface are not parallel to the plane, and they may not be quite perpendicular to the plane. They can provide the necessary torque, in the correct sense, to slow the ball's rotation, provide the vertical force to balance the weight, and a horizontal force to slow the forward motion of the center of mass. Both friction and rolling resistance are usually present where two bodies are in contact. We sometimes carelessly combine their effects and call it "friction". Sometimes, we can get by with that without introducing errors, but we should be more careful.

Pulleys

A pulley is a grooved wheel that turns around an axle (fulcrum), while a rope or a chain is used in the groove to lift heavy objects. A pulley changes the direction of the force: Instead of lifting up, you can pull down using your body weight against the resistance (the load that you are lifting). A pulley may be fixed, moveable, or used in combination. The simple pulley gains nothing in force, distance, or speed, but it changes the direction of the force. A fixed pulley (attached to something that does not move, such as the ceiling or wall) acts as a first-class lever, with the fulcrum located at the axis; instead of a bar, the pulley uses a rope. A moveable pulley acts as second-class lever, while the load (resistance) is between the fulcrum and the effort.

> ➤ **Review Video: Pulleys**
> *Visit **mometrix.com/academy** and enter **Code: 495865***

Torque

Torque expresses the ability of a force to cause the rotation of a body around a particular axis of rotation. While torque is a vector quantity, it may be treated as a signed scalar when all of the forces of concern lie in a common plane, as is the case with rotating wheels. Torque is defined as the perpendicular force times the distance from the fulcrum. Torque can be calculated as follows:

$\tau = F_\perp d$

Where:

$F_\perp$ = The perpendicular force applied to the object.

d = The position vector relative to the fulcrum.

Torque in static systems

The torque concept is useful in both static and dynamic systems, but nothing rotates in static systems, so the net torque on each part of the system is zero. When the forces on a body do not lie in a single plane, we must treat torque as a vector. The vector that represents the torque is oriented along a line perpendicular to that plane, and passes through the center of torques. If, as you look at this plane, the torque would produce a clockwise rotation, then the torque vector is pointing toward you. If the torque would produce a counter-clockwise rotation, then the torque vector points away from you. The right hand rule is a useful mnemonic for getting this right: if you curl your fingers around the line of the torque with your fingers curling in the direction of the rotation, then your thumb points in the direction of the torque. When a body is at rest, the net force on the body is zero, and the net torque on the body is also zero. Furthermore, the net torque on the body is zero no matter what center of torque is chosen. That simply means that the body does not rotate about any axis because it does not rotate at all.

When the net torque on a body is zero:
- A body that is not rotating will continue without rotation.
- A body that is rotating will continue rotating with the same angular speed.

If the net (total) force on a body has zero components in one direction, then the body will not move in that direction. If the vector sum of all forces and the sum of all torques acting on a body are zero, then that body is not accelerating.

Levers

A lever is a simple machine that magnifies force. Levers are comprised of a rigid bar (lever arm), a pivot point (fulcrum), a load force, and an effort force. The effort force creates a torque around the fulcrum, and the magnitude of this torque is dependent upon the magnitude of the force and its distance from the fulcrum. This torque must be balanced by the torque created by the load force. Changing the distance from the fulcrum to the load force changes the amount of force magnification. There are three main types of levers: first class, second class, and third class. A first-class lever has the fulcrum located between the effort force and the load force on the lever arm. An example of this type of lever is a pair of pliers. A second-class lever has the load force located between the effort force and the fulcrum on the lever arm. An example of the second class of lever is a pair of nutcrackers. A third-class lever has the effort force located between the fulcrum and the load force on the lever arm. An example of this type of lever is a pair of tongs.

> ➤ **Review Video: <u>Levers</u>**
> *Visit **mometrix.com/academy** and enter **Code: 994753**

Momentum

The momentum, P, of a body is the product of its mass times velocity, and is therefore a vector quantity. The net momentum of the parts of a closed system remains constant no matter what is going on within the system. This is known as the conservation of momentum, and follows from Newton's third law. Mathematically, we may express momentum, P, with the following formula:
$P = m \times v$
Where:
m = The mass of the object.
v = The velocity of the object.

Small objects, such as bullets and small dogs, have large momentums due to their velocity. Large objects, such as trains and tractor trailers, have large momentums even when moving slowly due to their large mass. A general set of relationships between the mass, velocity, and momentum may be expressed as follows:
- Large Mass = Large Momentum
- Small Mass = Small Momentum
- Large Velocity = Large Momentum
- Small Velocity = Small Momentum

Impulse

When you apply a force on an object, you also exert an impulse on it. When something exerts a force on you, it also exerts an impulse on you. Forces and impulses always go together. In addition, impulse is a vector quantity, and has the same direction as the applied force. Impulses are also directly proportional to the applied force: more force means more impulse. Double the force, double the impulse; triple the force, triple the impulse; etc. However, impulse is not the same as force: impulse also depends on how long the force is applied. Thus, more time = more impulse. Impulse is directly proportional to the time for which the force is applied: twice as long means twice the impulse, while three times as long means three times the impulse. Therefore, the impulse that is exerted on an object depends directly on both how much force is applied, and how long the force is applied. Impulse is the product of the force and time:

$\text{Impulse} = (\text{force}) \times (\text{time}) = F \times t$

Work

Work is a measure of the energy that is expended to move something, and is a scalar quantity. Work equals the force applied to an object in the direction of the displacement multiplied by the net distance that the object has moved. If there is no motion, then no work is done, no matter how much force is applied. Work that is done on a machine or system either increases the energy stored by the system or makes something move. Work can be calculated as follows:

$\text{Work} = F_d d$

Where:
F_d = The component of the force in the direction of the displacement.
d = The displacement of the object.

The definition of work is independent of time. This means that a student who walks up a flight of stairs does the same amount of work as he would if he runs up the stairs. In each case, the force exerted and the distance that the student moves is the same. The only difference is the time that is taken to do the work.

> ➤ **Review Video: Work**
> *Visit **mometrix.com/academy** and enter Code: **681834***

Work-kinetic energy theorem

The work-kinetic energy theorem states that the net work done on an object, W_{net}, is equivalent to the change in kinetic energy of the object, ΔKE:

$W_{net} = \Delta KE$

Where:
$KE = 1/2mv^2$

Power

Power is defined as the work done per unit time, and is the rate at which work is performed. Power is calculated as follows:

$\text{Power} = \dfrac{\text{Work}}{\text{Time}}$

Several common units for power are watts (W), horsepower (hp), ergs per second (erg/s), and foot-pounds per minute (ft-lb/min). One watt is equivalent to one Joule per second (J/s), while one horsepower is equivalent to 33,000 ft-lb/min.

Kinetic energy

Kinetic energy (KE) represents the amount of work that is done to set a body in motion. It also represents the amount of work that a body of mass, m, can do as a result of its motion with speed, v. The KE of an object in motion can be calculated as follows:

$$KE = \frac{1}{2}mv^2$$

Where:
m = The mass of the object.
v = The velocity of the object.

Note: We have defined KE in terms of the amount of work that is required to set a body in motion. The units of KE are therefore the same as the units for work: joules or foot-pounds.

Potential energy

Potential energy (PE) refers to the potential of a system to do work by virtue of its position. The PE that is possessed by an object is the amount of work that the object is capable of doing simply because of the energy that is stored up by its position. For an object on earth, the force that is required to lift an object is equal to the body's weight, mg. If we lift this object to a height, h, then we do work. As a result, we can calculate the PE as follows:

$$PE = mgh$$

Where:
m = The mass of the object.
g = Gravitational acceleration = 9.8 m/s² = 32.2 ft/s²
h = The height of the object.

Note: h is the difference between two heights, and it measures how far the object has been lifted above a certain level. The units of PE are the same as those for work: joules or foot-pounds.

> ➤ **Review Video: <u>Potential and Kinetic Energy</u>**
> Visit ***mometrix.com/academy*** and enter ***Code: 491502***

Gravitational potential energy

Gravitational potential energy is a convenient concept when dealing with bodies or systems in a gravitational field. It allows one to treat the body as "possessing" energy due to its position in the field, thereby avoiding the need for including the gravitational source as part of the system. The gravitational potential energy of a body at a certain position is simply the work that must be done on the body to move it to that position from a fixed reference position. Gravitational potential energy is the potential energy of a body divided by the mass of the body. The work done when moving a body from point A to B in a gravitational field is independent of the path along which it moves between A and B. In addition, the potential energy difference between those points is independent of the path. Therefore, it follows that the change in potential energy around any closed-loop path is zero. This is an example of conservation of energy.

Conservation of energy

Energy can be present in many forms: kinetic, thermal, nuclear, various kinds of potential energy, and others. But, when all forms are accounted for and measured, the total energy of a closed system is conserved, or remains constant.

Wavelength, period, and frequency

Wavelength
The distance from crest (high point) to crest, or from trough (low point) to trough, is called the wavelength (l).

Period
The period is the time required to make one cycle or vibration. Since the frequency is the number of crests or troughs per unit time, and the period is the time between the passage of two successive crests or troughs, the relationship between frequency, f, and period, T, is reciprocal: $f = 1/T$, while $T = 1/f$.

Frequency
A measure of the number of waves or motions per unit time. In the case of a pendulum, the frequency is determined by how rapidly the pendulum swings. If the pendulum makes one complete swing per second, then the frequency is 1 vibration/s, or 1 cycle per second. The units for frequency are hertz (1 Hz = 1 cycle/s).

Hooke's law

Hooke's law states that the amount that an elastic body stretches is in direct proportion to the force that is acting upon it. This force can be calculated as follows:
$F = -kx$
Where:
k = The spring constant.
x = The displacement of the spring from its equilibrium point.

Note: The magnitude of the force cannot be negative. The sign (+/–) is the direction of the vector.

Forces that are measured by spring balances are calculated using this principle.

Energy transformation of a pendulum

The motion of a pendulum is a classic example of the conservation of mechanical energy. A pendulum consists of a mass, known as a bob, attached by a string to a pivot point. As the pendulum moves, it sweeps out a circular arc, moving back and forth in a periodic fashion. Neglecting air resistance, which would be small for an aerodynamically shaped bob, there are only two forces that act upon the pendulum bob:
- Gravity – The force of gravity acts in a downward direction, and does work upon the pendulum bob. However, gravity is an internal force, or conservative force, and thus does not serve to change the total amount of mechanical energy of the bob.

- Tension – Tension is an external force, and if it acts upon the pendulum bob, it serves to change the total mechanical energy of the bob. However, the force of tension does not do work since it always acts in a direction perpendicular to the motion of the bob: at all points in the trajectory of the pendulum bob, the angle between the force of tension and its instantaneous displacement is always 90 degrees.

As the pendulum swings, energy transformation allows for the conservation of energy, and thus continued motion, by continually transforming energy back and forth between mechanical and gravitational energy.

Transverse and longitudinal waves

Transverse waves
For transverse waves, the displacement of the medium is perpendicular to the direction of propagation of the wave. A ripple on a pond and a wave on a string are easily visualized transverse waves. Transverse waves cannot propagate in a gas or a liquid because there is no mechanism for driving motion perpendicular to the propagation of the wave.

Longitudinal waves
In longitudinal waves, the displacement of the medium is parallel to the propagation of the wave. A wave in a "slinky" is a good visualization. Sound waves in air are longitudinal waves.

Resonance

Resonance is the tendency of a system to absorb more oscillatory energy, when the frequency of the oscillations matches the system's natural frequency of vibration (its resonant frequency), than it does at other frequencies. Examples are the acoustic resonances of musical instruments, the tidal resonance of the Bay of Fundy, orbital resonance as exemplified by some of the Jovian moons, the resonance of the basilar membrane in the biological transduction of auditory input, and resonance in electronic circuits. A resonant object, whether mechanical, acoustic, or electromagnetic, will probably have more than one resonant frequency (especially harmonics of the strongest resonance). It will be easy to vibrate at those frequencies, and more difficult to vibrate at other frequencies. And, it will "pick out" its resonant frequency from a complex excitation, such as an impulse or a wideband noise excitation. In effect, it is filtering out all frequencies other than its resonance.

Standing waves

The modes of vibration that are associated with resonance in extended objects, such as strings and air columns, have characteristic patterns called standing waves. These standing wave modes arise from the combination of reflection and interference such that the reflected waves interfere constructively with the incident waves. An important part of the condition for this constructive interference for stretched strings is the fact that the waves change phase upon reflection from a fixed end. Under these conditions, the medium appears to vibrate in segments or regions, and the fact that these vibrations are made up of traveling waves is not apparent – hence the term "standing wave". The behavior of the waves at the points of minimum and maximum vibrations (nodes and antinodes) contributes to the constructive interference that forms the resonant standing waves. Standing waves in air columns also form nodes and antinodes, but the phase changes involved must be separately examined for the case of air columns. The term, node, describes a point where the medium does not move, while the term, anti-node, describes a point of maximal vibration.

Beat frequencies

When two sound waves of different frequencies approach your ear, the alternating constructive and destructive interference causes the sound to be alternatively soft and loud, a phenomenon that is called "beating" or "producing beats". The beat frequency is equal to the absolute value of the difference in frequency of the two waves.

Refraction and diffraction

Refraction is a change in the direction of waves as they pass from one medium to another. Refraction, or the bending of the path of the waves, is accompanied by a change in the speed and wavelength of the waves. Diffraction is a change in the direction of waves as they pass through an opening, or around a barrier, in their path.

Amplitude, decibels, and speed

Amplitude
The amplitude of a sound wave is the same thing as its loudness. Since sound is a compression wave, its loudness, or amplitude, corresponds to how much the wave is compressed. It is sometimes called the pressure amplitude.

Decibel
A common measurement of loudness is the decibel (dB), which is really 1/10 of a bel. The bel is a unit of measurement for sound, named after the inventor of the telephone, Alexander Graham Bell. It is a complex unit that varies with the ratio of the logarithms of loudness.

Speed
The speed or velocity of sound in air is approximately 344 m/s, 1130 ft/s, or 770 mph at room temperature, 20°C (70°F). The speed varies with the temperature of air, such that sound travels slower at higher altitudes, or on cold days.

Attenuation

Attenuation is the decrease in intensity of a signal, beam, or wave as a result of absorption of energy, and of scattering out of the path to the detector, but not including the reduction due to geometric spreading.

Doppler effect

The Doppler effect is the apparent change in frequency or wavelength of a wave that is perceived by an observer moving relative to the source of the waves. For waves that propagate in a wave medium, such as sound waves, the velocity of the observer and the source are reckoned relative to the medium in which the waves are transmitted. It is important to note that the effect does not result because of an actual change in the frequency of the source.

Ultrasound

Ultrasound is sound with a frequency that is greater than the upper limit of human hearing, approximately 20 kilohertz (kHz). Some animals, such as dogs, dolphins, and bats, have an upper limit that is greater than that of the human ear, and thus can hear ultrasound. Ultrasound has industrial and medical applications. Medical ultrasonography can visualize muscle and soft tissue, making it useful for scanning the organs, and obstetric ultrasonography is commonly used during pregnancy. Typical diagnostic ultrasound scanners operate in the frequency range of 2 to 13 megahertz. More powerful ultrasound sources may be used to generate local heating in biological tissue, with applications in physical therapy and cancer treatment. Focused ultrasound sources may also be used to break up kidney stones or for cataract treatment by phacoemulsification.

Solids and liquids

The following are principles of solids and liquids:
- Solids that are undisturbed preserve their shape, while liquids flow to conform to the shape of their container – Solids have rigidity and elasticity, but can be deformed by compression, stretching, and shear. In contrast, most liquids strongly resist being compressed; and, to a first approximation, may be considered to maintain constant volume over a wide range of pressures.
- Liquids seek their own level – More precisely, any two connectable points on the surface of a liquid at rest are at the same height.
- Liquid pressure is a scalar quantity – A liquid that contacts a solid surface is responsible for a force on that surface. The force is perpendicular to the surface, and is of size, $F = PA$, where P is the liquid pressure, and A is the area of the surface. The area must be small enough that the pressure is essentially constant over the surface. This is, in fact, the definition of pressure, which is, in calculus form, $P = \Delta F / \Delta A$.
- Pressure, at a given point in a liquid, exerts force on an infinitesimal area at that point, which is the same size no matter what the orientation of that area – This is often abbreviated in the potentially misleading slogan: "Pressure acts equally in all directions."
- Any two connectable points in a liquid are at the same pressure if they are at the same height.

Density

A substance can be identified by its properties, such as color, odor, or crystalline structure. An important distinguishing attribute of any substance is its density. Density tells us how much of a substance occupies a given volume, and it can be used to identify solids, as well as liquids. For example, we know that 1 kg of lead will occupy less volume than 1 kg of water, which would occupy less volume than 1 kg of air under standard conditions. Furthermore, we know that 1 m³ of lead would contain more mass than 1 m³ of water, which would contain more mass than 1 m³ of air under standard conditions. The density of a material is defined as the mass per unit volume. It can be calculated as follows:

$$d = \frac{m}{V}$$

Where:
m = The mass of the material.
V = The volume of the material.

Specific gravity

The specific gravity (SG), or relative density, of a substance is defined as the ratio of the density of the substance to the density of water. Specific gravity can be calculated as follows:

$$SG = \frac{\rho}{1 \text{ gm·cm}^{-3}}$$

Where:
ρ = The density of the substance.

Since it is defined as a ratio of densities, specific gravity is a unitless quantity. Objects that have a specific gravity of less than one will float when placed in water, which means that it is less dense than water.

Archimedes' principle

Archimedes' principle states that, for a body floating on or immersed in a liquid, the liquid exerts a net upward "buoyant" force due to the pressure differences on its surfaces. Horizontal forces that are due to pressure add to zero, but vertical components do not because of height differences. Using the principles above, one can derive a simple result: the buoyant force on the object is equal to the weight of the liquid that the object has displaced.

Warning: There must be liquid underneath the body for there to be an upward buoyant force on it. The buoyant force is due to pressure differences. It is not the result of the "desire" of the displaced water to return to its original place.

Hydrostatic pressure

Hydrostatic pressure is the pressure exerted by a fluid due to its weight. The buoyancy force on a body that is fully immersed in a static fluid is attributable to the pressure summed (integrated) over the body's surface. The pressure is isotropic in that case: it acts in all directions equally. This is not true in the case of fluid flow.

Pressure is a measure of the force that is exerted per unit area, and can be calculated as follows:

$$Pressure = \frac{Force}{Area}$$

Consider the simple example of pushing your thumb against your nose with a force, F. Such an action may be uncomfortable, but it is doubtful that you will seriously injure yourself. Now, try pushing against your nose with the same force, F, but this time use a sharp nail instead of your thumb. In each case, the applied force is the same, but the experience would be much more painful when using a nail. This is because the force that is exerted by the nail is over a much smaller area than when using your thumb. The units of pressure are a force divided by an area. As with volume, there are many units of pressure that are commonly used today, such as pascals (Pa = N/m^2), pounds per square inch (psi), bars, millimeters of Hg (mmHg), and standard atmospheres (atm).

Pascal's law

Pascal's law states that pressure applied to an enclosed fluid is transmitted undiminished to every portion of the fluid, and to the walls of the containing vessel. Pascal's principle, put more simply, means that an incompressible fluid transmits pressure. This is the basis for the hydraulic lever. In a hydraulic lever, for example, if you apply a force over the given area of the left-hand piston, then this force is transformed into a pressure that is transmitted through the hydraulic fluid or oil. This pressure is then transformed back in to an output force over the given area for the right-hand piston. The following formula calculates the difference in applied forces of a hydrolic system, dependent upon the difference in surface areas:

$$F_2 = F_1 \left(\frac{A_2}{A_1} \right)$$

Where:
F_1 = The input force.
A_1 = The surface area of the input piston.
A_2 = The surface area of the output piston.

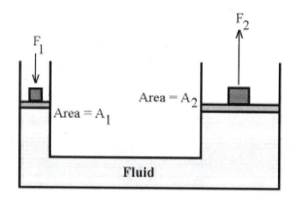

Pressure and depth

Pressure, P, at any depth, h, is the weight of the liquid above that depth divided by the area. The formula for the pressure on an object that is submerged in a fluid is calculated as follows:

$$P = \frac{\text{Weight}}{\text{Area}} = \frac{mg}{A} = \frac{\rho Vg}{A} = \frac{\rho Ahg}{A} = \rho hg$$

Where:
m = The mass of the fluid = ρV
g = Gravitational acceleration = 9.8 m/s^2 = 32.2 ft/s^2
ρ = The density of the fluid.
V = The volume of the fluid above the object = Ah
A = The area of the fluid above the object.
h = The height of the fluid above the object.

Poiseuille's law

According to Poiseuille's law, the laminar flow of a liquid through a circular tube is determined by the following formula:

$$q = \frac{\pi r^4}{8\mu}\left(\frac{p_1 - p_2}{L}\right)$$

Where:
q = The discharge.
L = The length of the pipe.
p_1, p_2 = The pressure at the pipe ends.
m = The dynamic viscosity of the liquid.
r = The radius of the pipe.

Continuity equation

The equation of continuity is a hydrodynamic equation that expresses the principle of the conservation of mass in a fluid. It equates the increase in mass of a hypothetical fluid volume to the net flow of mass into the volume:

$$\frac{\delta\rho}{\delta t} + \nabla\cdot(\rho u) = 0 \text{; or}$$

$$\frac{D\rho}{Dt} + \rho\nabla\cdot u = 0$$

Where:
ρ = The fluid density.
u = The velocity vector.

Under the quasi-static approximation, with pressure as a vertical coordinate, the equation takes the following form:

$$\nabla_\rho \cdot v + \frac{\delta\omega}{\delta p} = 0$$

Where:
p = The pressure.
v = The velocity vector.
∇_ρ = The del operator in the isobaric surface.

Cohesion and adhesion

Cohesion and adhesion phenomena are two effects seen mainly where liquids are in the picture. For example, the formation of water droplets is due to cohesion forces acting between the water molecules. A cohesive force is a force that holds together the like atoms, ions, or molecules of a single body. Attraction between unlike surfaces is due to adhesion. For example, if you put water into a test tube and watch the level of the water, the meniscus is upwardly curved. This is because the water molecules on the top surface are experiencing an attractive force with the glass test tube. An adhesive force is a force that holds two separate bodies together. Instead of water, if you put mercury into a test tube, you will see that the mercury level has an inverted hump. This means that the cohesive forces within the mercury atoms are higher than the adhesive forces between the mercury atoms and glass. A number of phenomena can be explained in terms of adhesion and cohesion. For example, the surface tension in liquids results from cohesion, and capillary action results from a combination of adhesion and cohesion. The hardness of a diamond is due to the strong cohesive forces between the carbon atoms of which it is made. And, the friction between two solid bodies partly depends upon adhesion.

Nonionic and anionic surfactants

A surfactant that dissociates in water and releases cations and anions is called an ionic surfactant. In contrast, a surfactant that does not dissociate is called a nonionic surfactant. Sorbitan monopalmitate is an example of a nonionic surfactant. An anionic surfactant has an anionic hydrophilic group. Anionic surfactants generally include "soaps" (fatty acid soaps), alkylsulfonic acid salts (the main component of synthetic detergent, such as linear alkyl benzene sulfonate (LAS)), and fatty alcohol sulfates (the main component of shampoos or old neutral detergents). Ammonium laurate, triethanolamine sterate, and docusate sodium are all examples of anionic surfactants.

Elastic limit of a solid

Most solid objects that are subjected to an applied stress will return to their original shape and dimensions, provided that the stress is below a characteristic threshold for the material of which they are made. This limit is called the elastic limit, or sometimes the yield point. Beyond this stress level, plastic deformation occurs, wherein the atomic or molecular structure changes shape permanently. The elastic limit of a substance depends very little on the Young's modulus, or Poisson ratio. However, the elastic limit can vary by as much as an order of magnitude between the softest and hardest steels.

Coefficient of thermal expansion

Most solids expand when heated. The reason for this is that it gives atoms more room to bounce around with the large amount of kinetic energy that they have at higher temperatures. The coefficient of thermal expansion is generally defined as the fractional increase in the length per unit rise in temperature. The exact definition varies, dependent upon whether it is specified at a precise temperature (true coefficient of thermal expansion), or over a temperature range (mean coefficient of thermal expansion).

Shear stress

The response of a solid to a shear stress is similar to the response to a pressure: the sample changes shape, but does not continue to change if the shear stays constant. If the shear is removed, then the sample returns to its original shape. It turns out that the word "shape" is advisable, since the volume of the sample does not change in response to a shear stress. The measure of shear stress is defined as the sheer force divided by the area to which it is applied. In order to study the shear stress most simply, the forces are applied in pairs so that the net force on the object is zero, and it is not accelerated. We may imagine a force towards the right applied to the top of a cubic sample, and an equal magnitude force towards the left applied to the bottom of the sample. This stress is called a simple shear.

Tension

Tension is an external stress that tends to pull an object apart. If the force of tension is greater than the inward force of the object, then the object will stretch. Many objects, such as ropes and cables, can only be loaded with tension. If these objects are compressed, then they deform.

Compression

Compression is an external stress applied to an object that presses together. If the force of the compression is greater than the outward force of the object, then the volume of the object will be decreased. Gases are easily compressed, while solids and liquids are less easily compressed if at all.

Conductors

Conductors are materials that contain movable charges of electricity. When an electrical potential difference is impressed across separate points on a conductor, the mobile charges within the conductor are forced to move, and an electric current between those points appears in accordance with Ohm's law. While many conductors are metallic, there are many non-metallic conductors, as well. Under normal conditions, all materials offer some resistance to flowing charges, which generates heat. Thus, the proper design of an electrical conductor includes an estimate of the temperature that the conductor is expected to endure without damage, as well as the quantity of electrical current. The motion of charges also creates an electromagnetic field around the conductor that exerts a mechanical force on the conductor. Non-conducting materials lack mobile charges, and are called insulators. A material can be an electrical conductor without being a thermal conductor, although a metal can be both an electrical conductor and a thermal conductor. Electrically conductive materials are usually classified according to their electrical resistance: ranging from high to null resistance, there are semiconductors, ordinary metallic conductors (also called normal metals), and superconductors.

Charging by conduction and induction

Charging by conduction is the mechanism of charging an uncharged body by bringing it directly into contact with another charged body. In conduction, the charges flow from one body into the other until the two bodies that are in contact reach equilibrium in terms of charges.

> ➤ **Review Video: Charging by Conduction**
> *Visit mometrix.com/academy and enter Code:* **502661**

Charging by induction is the mechanism of charging an uncharged body by bringing it near another charged body, but not into contact with it. In the process of induction, the charges do not flow from one body to the other. The body into which the charges are being induced does not acquire extra charge.

> ➤ **Review Video: Charging by Induction**
> *Visit mometrix.com/academy and enter Code:* **520959**

Law of conservation of charge

The law of conservation of charge (current rule) states that the charge that flows into a junction must be equal to the charge that flows out of that junction. This law also applies to current, as the total current that flows into a junction must be equal to the total current that leaves that junction. This rule is a consequence of the fact that the flow of charge is conserved in steady-state flow. If less charge flowed out of any circuit junction than flowed into the junction, then there would be a buildup of charge at that junction. This could theoretically happen, but it is generally assumed (unless otherwise stated) that there is steady-state flow in a circuit.

Insulators

Insulators are materials that prevent the flow of heat (thermal insulators) or electric charge (electrical insulators). The opposite of electrical insulators are conductors and semiconductors, which permit the flow of charge (a semiconductor, strictly speaking, is also an insulator, since it prevents the flow of electric charge at low temperatures, unless it is doped with atoms that release extra charges to carry the current). The term electrical insulator has the same meaning as the term dielectric, but the two terms are used in different contexts. A perfect insulator is impossible to achieve due to the second law of thermodynamics. However, some materials, such as silicon dioxide, are very nearly perfect electrical insulators, which allows for flash memory technology.

Coulomb's law

The formula for Coulomb's law is as follows:

$$F = \frac{kq_1q_2}{r^2}$$

Where:

F = The force on each charge ((+) indicates repulsion; (-) indicates attraction).

k = The electrostatic constant, $9 \times 10^9 \frac{Nm^2}{C^2}$.

q_1 = The quantity of charge 1, measured in coulombs.
q_2 = The quantity of charge 2, measured in coulombs.
r = The radius of separation from center of one charge to the center of the other.

A coulomb is an incredibly large unit of charge. 1 coulomb = 6.3×10^{18} elementary charges.

Equipotential lines

Once we envision what an electric field looks like using a field map, we know something about the direction of the field, and the strength of the field, but very little about the electric potential of the field at different points. For this information, we need to create a series of curves that represent the amount of the electric potential at a given region, known as equipotential lines. The work done per unit of charge (electric potential) can be calculated as follows:

$$V = \frac{W}{q_{moved}}$$

Gauss's law

1. The total of the electric flux out of a closed surface is equal to the charge enclosed divided by the permittivity.
2. The electric flux through an area is defined as the electric field multiplied by the area of the surface projected in a plane perpendicular to the field.

Gauss's law is a general law applying to any closed surface. It is an important tool since it permits the assessment of the amount of enclosed charge by mapping the field on a surface outside of the charge distribution. For geometries of sufficient symmetry, it simplifies the calculation of the electric field.

Key magnetic principles

A current-carrying wire creates a magnetic field that circles around the wire. The strength of the field decreases as you move farther from the wire, and increases as the current increases. The direction of the field lines is given by the right-hand rule: your thumb points in the direction of the current, and your fingers wrap around the wire in the direction of the field lines. When two current-carrying wires are placed parallel to each other, the magnetic field of each wire affects the other. When the currents in the wires are in the same direction, the wires attract. Conversely, when the currents are running in opposite directions, the wires repel each other. The Biot-Savart law is used to calculate the magnetic field at a point near a given current configuration. Ampère's law can provide a faster way to calculate the magnetic field strength in certain situations that have some symmetry. It says that the total of the magnetic field that is parallel to the tiny segments around an Amperian loop (any closed path) is proportional to the net current through the loop. It is sometimes necessary to use a line integral in Ampère's law.

Toroids

A toroid is a solenoid that is bent into a circular "donut" shape. Its magnetic field reflects its solenoid origins. A solenoid creates a uniform magnetic field that runs along its axis. A toroid is a solenoid that is wrapped into a circle, creating a field that circles inside the coil. As with an ideal solenoid, there is no magnetic field outside of an ideal toroid. Ampère's law provides the tools to derive the equation for the magnetic field inside the coil of the toroid. To determine the magnitude of that field, we use a circle of radius r as our Amperian loop, and draw it so that it has the same center as the toroid and is enclosed by its coils. The radius, r, is greater than the radius, a, of the "donut hole" of the toroid, and less than the outer radius, b, of the toroid.

Hall effect

The Hall effect occurs where a magnetic field deflects electrons in a current-carrying strip. This effect reveals the sign of the charge carriers in conductors, such as gold and copper.

For over a century, scientists studied currents in wires, and their effects, but did not know whether a current was the result of positive or negative charges in motion. All they could conclude during this time was that a current in a conductor, such as gold or copper, was the result of either positive charge carriers moving in one direction, or negative charge carriers moving in the opposite direction. As you may know, the scientists initially established the wrong convention for ordinary wire; and, to this day, physicists and physics students draw conventional current as though the movement of positive charges, rather than electrons, make up an electrical current.

Properties of x-rays

The properties of x-rays are as follows:
- X-rays are invisible electromagnetic radiations. Their wavelength is less than that of the visible-light photons, and is larger than the γ-ray photons. They are generally on the order of a few 10s of nanometers.
- X-rays possess all properties of visible-light photons, such as reflection, diffraction, rectilinear propagation, etc. Refraction of X-rays has not yet been seen.
- Being electromagnetic waves, they travel at the speed of light: 3×10^8 m/s.
- Since they are not charged particles, they are not affected by either electric or magnetic fields.
- X-rays can ionize materials through which they pass, such as gases. X-rays, like γ-rays, produce fluorescence, and affect photographic plates.
- X-rays are highly penetrating. They can easily pass through thin sheets of paper, metal foils, tissues, etc.
- X-rays are stopped by high-density materials, such as lead, bones, etc.

Cathode rays

Cathode rays are capable of ionizing gas atoms if the potential difference is large, and the gas pressure is not high. Cathode rays also produce fluorescence in some materials. As they are energetic electrons, when they strike a certain substance, the substance starts to glow. Depending on the energy of the cathode rays, they can penetrate thin sheets of paper or metal foils. When cathode rays are stopped, they produce X-rays. X-rays are very small wavelength rays that find many practical applications. Cathode rays also affect photographic plates when they strike them. A cathode ray tube (CRT) is widely used in research laboratories to convert any signal (e.g., electrical, sound, etc.) into visual signals. These are called CRTs or oscilloscopes.

Similarities and differences between x-rays and cathode rays

Both X-rays and cathode rays were discovered when discharges from a discharge tube were studied in detail. However, the rays are completely different from one another.

Similarities
- Both rays are capable of ionizing materials though which they pass, especially gases.
- Both rays cause fluorescence when they strike any fluorescent material, such as zinc sulphide.
- Both rays affect photographic plates.

Differences
- Cathode rays are charged particles: they are negatively charged electrons. X-rays, on the other hand, are electromagnetic radiations: X-rays have no charges.
- Cathode rays emanate from the cathode itself. X-rays are emitted when high-energy electrons are stopped.
- Cathode rays have low penetrating powers. X-rays have high penetrating powers, although γ-rays are more penetrating than X-rays.

- Cathode rays travel at the speed given by the potential difference between the anode and cathode. X-rays always travel at the speed of light.
- Cathode rays are deflected by electric and magnetic fields. X-rays are unaffected by both electric and magnetic fields.

Photoelectric effect

The photoelectric effect provides evidence for the particle nature of light. It also provides evidence for quantization. If light shines on the surface of a metal, then there is a point at which electrons are ejected from the metal. The electrons will only be ejected once the threshold frequency is reached. Below the threshold frequency, no electrons are ejected. Above the threshold frequency, the number of electrons ejected depends upon the intensity of the light. Einstein assumed that light traveled in energy packets called photons. The energy of one photon can be calculated as follows:

$$E = h \times v$$

Where:
h = The Planck constant, 6.626 x 10^{-34} J·s.
v = The frequency of the electromagnetic wave.

Current

In electricity, current refers to electric current, which is the flow of electric charge. Lightning is an example of an electric current, as is the solar wind, which is the source of the polar aurorae (aurora australis and borealis). Probably the most familiar form of electric current is the flow of conduction electrons in a metallic wire. This is how the electric company delivers electricity. In electronics, electric current is most often the flow of electrons through conductors and devices, such as resistors, but it is also the flow of ions inside of a battery, or the flow of holes within a semiconductor. The symbol that is typically used for the amount of current, or the amount of charge flowing per unit of time, is I, which means 'intensity'. The SI unit of electrical current is the ampere (amp or A). Electric current is therefore, sometimes, informally referred to as amperage, by analogy with the term voltage. The formula for current is as follows:

$$I = \frac{dQ}{dt}$$

Where:
dQ = The amount of charge flowing through a material or circuit.
dt = The time interval being measured.

One amp of electric current is generated when a charge of 1 coulomb (C) flows across a point in a circuit in 1 sec. If the charge flowing in 1 sec is more than 1 C, say 5 C, then we say that there is a current of 5 A flowing through the circuit.

Current is measured using an ammeter. An ammeter has to be connected within the circuit to measure the current flowing within the circuit.

Current density

Current density is the current per unit (cross-sectional) area. Current density is an important consideration in the design of electrical and electronic systems. Most electrical conductors have a finite, positive resistance, making them dissipate power in the form of heat. Mathematically, current, φ, is defined as the net flux through an area, as follows:

$$\varphi = j \cdot A$$

Where:

j = The "current density", measured in amps per square meter (A/m^2).
A = The area through which the current is flowing, measured in square meters (m^2).

The current density is defined as follows:

$$j = \int_i n_i \cdot x_i \cdot u_i$$

Where:

n = The particle density (number of particles per unit volume).
x = The mass, charge, or any other characteristic whose flow one would like to measure.
u = The average velocity of the particles in each volume.

Speed of an electric current

The charged particles whose movement causes an electric current do not always move in straight lines. In metals, for example, they follow an erratic path, bouncing from atom to atom, but generally drifting in the direction of the electric field. The speed of an electric current, or drift velocity, can be calculated using the following equation:

$$I = nAvQ$$

Where:

I = The electric current.
n = The number of charged particles per unit volume.
A = The cross-sectional area of the conductor.
v = The drift velocity.
Q = The charge on each particle.

For example, in a copper wire with a cross-sectional area of 0.5 mm^2, carrying a current of 5 A, the drift velocity of the electrons is on the order of a millimeter per second. To take a different example, in the near-vacuum inside of a cathode ray tube (CRT), the electrons travel in near-straight lines ("ballistically") at about a tenth of the speed of light. However, we know that an electric signal travels much faster than this; usually close to the speed of light. These results show that the speed of the charged particles is not necessarily related to the speed of the electric signal.

Drift velocity

The basics of drift velocity are as follows:
- When a voltage is applied across the ends of a wire, an electric field is created inside of the wire: $E = V/L$, where L is the length of the wire.
- In a vacuum, the electric field would cause a charge to accelerate. In a wire, collisions of the conduction charges with impurities, imperfections, and vibrations of the atomic lattice cause the motion of the conduction charges to be slowed down. This represents a loss of energy, which is dissipated as heat. Over a wide range of conditions, the flow of the charges quickly achieves a steady-state value, and remains constant. The "average speed" at which the "free" charges are moving in the wire is called the drift velocity, v_d.
- The charge carriers in a wire are normally electrons. The number of conduction electrons that are "free" to participate in the current flow depends upon the atomic structure of material making up the wire. Conductors have many electrons that are able to participate, whereas insulators have few free electrons. Semiconductors are materials that lie somewhere between these two extremes.
- The current in a wire can be expressed as a function of the number of charge carriers per volume, the magnitude of the charge carriers, the drift velocity of the charge carriers, and the cross-sectional area of the wire.

Law of conservation of energy

The law of conservation of energy (voltage rule) states that, for any closed loop that you can trace in a circuit, the total potential energy (voltage) that is gained through emf sources must be equal to the total voltage drops due to the presence of resistors, capacitors, or inductors in the closed loop. This rule is a consequence of fact that work is path-independent. The work that is required to move a charge around a closed path in an electric field is always zero. In a circuit, the electric field is inside of the wires through which the charges are moving. The voltage across a resistor could be either a drop or a gain depending on the direction of the current and the direction of the loop that you choose. If the direction of the loop is opposite to the flow of current, then the voltage across a resistor is a gain rather than a drop, as it is when the loop and current direction are the same.

Internal resistance of a battery

When we measure the voltage of a battery, we say that we are measuring the terminal potential difference of the battery. The terminal potential difference that is measured under these circumstances is called the emf, E, of the battery (cell). The internal resistance of a battery is not constant but increases as the battery is used.

Resistors

An ideal resistor is a component with an electrical resistance that remains constant regardless of the applied voltage or current flowing through the device, or the rate of change of the current. Resistors may be fixed or variable. Variable resistors are also called potentiometers, or rheostats, and allow the resistance of the device to be altered by turning a shaft or sliding a control. Some resistors are long and thin, with the actual resisting material in the center, and a conducting metal leg on each end. This is called an axial package. Resistors used in computers and other devices are typically much smaller, often in surface-mount packages without leads. Larger power resistors come in more sturdy packages that are designed to dissipate heat efficiently, but they are all basically the same structure. Resistors are used as part of electrical networks, and are incorporated into microelectronic semiconductor devices. The critical measurement of a resistor is its resistance, which serves as a ratio of voltage to current, and is measured in ohms. A component has a resistance of 1 ohm if a voltage of 1 volt results in a current of 1 amp, which is equivalent to a flow of one coulomb of electrical charge (approximately 6.241506×10^{18} electrons) per second in the opposite direction.

Ohm's law

Ohm's law states that the direct current that flows in a conductor is directly proportional to the potential difference between its ends. It is usually formulated as follows:
$V = IR$
Where:
V = The potential difference, voltage, or energy (E) in volts.
I = The current in amperes.
R = The resistance of the conductor in ohms.
Other derivations of Ohm's law are as follows:
$E = IR$
$I = V/R = E/R$
$R = V/I = E/I$

Resistance in series

The accompanying circuit diagram shows two resistances, R_1 and R_2, connected in series. The total voltage drop across $(R_1 + R_2)$ is V, while the voltage drop across R_1 is V_1, and the voltage drop across R_2 is V_2.

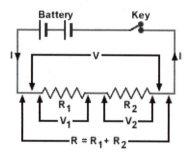

Since the same current, I, is flowing through both of the resistances, we know from Ohm's law that
$V_1 = I \times R_1$ and $V_2 = I \times R_2$
Also, $V = (V_1 + V_2) = I \times R_{total}$
Thus, we can see that $R_{total} = (R_1 + R_2)$

Resistance in parallel

The voltage drop across both of the resistances is V. The current flowing through the circuit is I. But, the current gets divided into two branches, I_1 and I_2, flowing through R_1 and R_2, respectively.

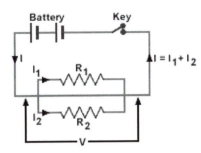

$I = I_1 + I_2$

But, from Ohm's law, $V = I_1 \times R_1$, and $V = I_2 \times R_2$

Also, $V = I \times R_{total}$

Hence, $\dfrac{1}{R_{total}} = \dfrac{1}{R_1} + \dfrac{1}{R_2}$

Thus, for resistances that are arranged in parallel, the reciprocal of total resistance is the sum of reciprocals of the individual resistances.

Resistance of a material

An ideal resistor has a fixed resistance across all frequencies and amplitudes of voltage or current. The equation to determine resistance of a section of material is as follows:

$R = \dfrac{\rho \cdot L}{A}$

Where:

ρ = The resistivity of the material.

L = The length of the material.

A = The cross-sectional area.

This can be extended to form an integral for more complex shapes, but this simple formula is applicable to cylindrical wires, and most common conductors. This value is subject to change at high frequencies due to the skin effect, which decreases the available surface area.

Electrical resistivity

The formula for the electrical resistivity, ρ, of a material can be obtained by rearranging the formula for the resistance, as follows:

$$\rho = \frac{RA}{L}$$

Where:
R = The resistance of a uniform specimen of the material, measured in ohms (Ω).
A = The cross-sectional area of the specimen, measured in square meters (m^2).
L = The length of the specimen, measured in meters (m).

The unit of measurement for ρ is ohm-meters (Ω-m).

Electrical resistivity can also be defined as follows:

$$\rho = \frac{E}{J}$$

Where:
E = The magnitude of the electric field, measured in volts per meter (V/m).
J = The magnitude of the current density, measured in amperes per square meter (A/m^2).

Finally, electrical resistivity can be defined as the inverse of the conductivity of the metal:

$$\rho = \frac{1}{\sigma}$$

Where:
σ = The conductivity of the substance, measured in siemens per meter (S/m).

Capacitors

A capacitor is a device that stores electric charge and electrical potential energy. Capacitance, C, is a measure of the ability of a device to store charge per unit of voltage applied across the device. Capacitance can be calculated as follows:

$$C = \frac{Q}{V}$$

Where:
Q = The charge stored in the capacitor, measured in coulombs (C).
V = The voltage drop across the capacitor, measured in volts (V).

The SI unit for capacitance is the farad, F, which is equivalent to C/V (coulombs per volt).

Alternating current

An alternating current (AC) is an electrical current where the magnitude and direction of the current varies cyclically, as opposed to direct current (DC), where the direction of the current stays constant. The usual waveform of an AC power circuit is a sine wave, as this results in the most efficient transmission of energy. However, in certain applications, different waveforms are used, such as triangular or square waves.

Used generically, AC refers to the form of electrical current that is used to deliver electricity to businesses and residences. However, audio and radio signals that are carried on electrical wire are also examples of alternating current. In these applications, an important goal is often the recovery of information that is encoded (or modulated) onto the AC signal. Alternating currents are usually associated with alternating voltages. An AC voltage, v, can be described mathematically as a function of time using the following equation:

$$v(t) = A \times \sin(\omega t)$$

Where:

A = The amplitude in volts (also called the peak voltage).

ω = The angular frequency in radians per second (rad/s)

t = The time in seconds.

Direct current

Direct current (DC), or "continuous current", is the continuous flow of electricity through a conductor, such as a wire, from high to low potential. In direct current, the electric charges always flow in the same direction, which distinguishes it from alternating current (AC). Direct current was originally used for electric power transmission after the development, by Thomas Edison, of the commercial generation of electricity in the late nineteenth century. High voltage direct current is used for long-distance, point-to-point power transmission, and for submarine cables, with voltages from a few kilovolts to approximately one megavolt. Within electrical engineering, the term DC is also a synonym for constant. For example, the voltage across a DC voltage source is constant, as is the current through a DC current source. The DC solution of an electric circuit is the solution where all voltages and currents are constant. In this context, a voltage (current) that is changing with time cannot be a DC voltage (current) even if the polarity (direction) does not change. However, it can be shown that such a changing voltage or current can be decomposed into the sum of a DC component and an AC component. The DC component is defined to be the average value of the voltage, or current, over all time. The average value of the AC component is exactly zero, as with, for example, a sine wave.

Rectifiers

A rectifier is a device, also known as a diode, that allows electric current to flow in only one direction. Rectification of the alternating high-voltage current from the transformer in an X-ray generator is essential to provide an X-ray tube with a high-voltage direct current. High-voltage rectifiers are, therefore, always incorporated into the high-voltage circuit in series with the X-ray tube. Previously, high-voltage rectifiers were vacuum tubes ("thermionic diode tubes"), but today they are all solid-state rectifiers. Selenium was the first material to be used in these rectifiers, but most X-ray generators today use silicon rectifiers. Silicon rectifiers are physically small, do not require a heated filament, and have a long lifetime. The silicon rectifier has a cathode made from a so-called N-type semiconductor (N for negative charge) that has a surplus of electrons, and an anode made from a P-type semiconductor (P for positive charge) that has a shortage of electrons (surplus of electron holes). A single silicon rectifier (a silicon cell) will resist a reverse voltage of about 1 kV. High-voltage silicon rectifiers are composed of a stack of single cells to withstand reverse voltages up to 150 kVp.

Diffraction gratings

In optics, a diffraction grating is an array of fine, parallel, equally spaced grooves ("rulings") on a reflecting or transparent substrate. When photons (electromagnetic energy) encounter a diffraction grating, diffractive and mutual-interference effects occur. Photons are reflected or transmitted in discrete directions, called "orders" or "spectral orders". Because the angle of deviation of the diffracted beam is wavelength dependent, a diffraction grating separates the incident beam spatially into its constituent wavelength components; i.e., it is dispersive. Each component of the electromagnetic spectrum is sent into a different direction, producing a rainbow of colors. This is visually similar to that produced by a prism, though the mechanism is very different. The groove dimensions and spacings are on the order of the wavelength in question. In the optical regime, in which the use of diffraction gratings is most common, there are many hundreds, or thousands, of grooves per millimeter.

Polarization

In electrodynamics, polarization is a property of waves, such as light and other electromagnetic radiation. Unlike more familiar wave phenomena, such as waves on water or sound waves, electromagnetic waves are three-dimensional, and it is their vector nature that gives rise to the phenomenon of polarization. The simplest manifestation of polarization to visualize is that of a plane wave, which is a good approximation to most light waves. A plane wave is one where the direction of the magnetic and electric fields are confined to a plane perpendicular to the direction of propagation. Simply because the plane is two-dimensional, the electric vector in the plane at a point in space can be decomposed into two orthogonal components. By considering the shape that is traced out in a fixed plane by the electric vector, such as when a plane wave passes over it, we obtain a description of the polarization state. In cases where the two components rotate, we call this circular polarization. The direction of rotation will depend on which of the two phase relationships exist. We call these cases right-hand circular polarization and left-hand circular polarization, depending on which way the electric vector rotates.

Reflection

The reflection of a ray of light involves a change in the direction of waves when they bounce off a surface or barrier. The rules of reflection are as follows:
- The angle of incidence is equal to the angle of reflection: $\angle i = \angle r$
- A ray that is traveling along the normal, NO, is reflected back along NO itself.
- The incident ray, the reflected ray, and the normal all lie in the same plane, or are co-planar.
- The image is as far back from the mirror as the object is in front of the mirror.
- If a plane mirror is rotated by angle ϑ, then for a given incident ray, AO, the reflected ray is rotated by 2ϑ.

Refraction

The path of a light ray is always a straight line in a given medium. If the density of the medium changes, the path of light will bend. This bending of light as it travels from a denser medium to a rarer medium, or vice-versa, is known as refraction. The rules of refraction are as follows:
- When a light ray travels from a rarer medium to a denser medium, the light ray bends toward the normal.
- When a light ray travels from a denser medium to a rarer medium, the light ray bends away from the normal.
- The incident ray, the refracted ray, and the normal are co-planar.

- A light ray traveling along the normal will not get refracted, and will pass undeviated.
- The ratio of the sine of the angle of incidence to that of the sine of the angle of refraction is constant for a given medium, called the refractive index, or *n*. This is called Snell's law:
- $n = \dfrac{\sin\theta_1}{\sin\theta_2}$

Critical angle

The critical angle is defined as the angle of incidence that provides an angle of refraction of 90 degrees. Make particular note that the critical angle is an angle of incidence value.

$$\text{Critical Angle} = \sin^{-1}\left(\dfrac{n_2}{n_1}\right) = \arcsin\left(\dfrac{n_2}{n_1}\right)$$

Where:
n_1 = Higher refractive index.
n_2 = Lower refractive index.

Dispersion of light with a prism

Newton had shown that light rays that we obtain from the sun consist of seven different colors: red, orange, yellow, green, blue, indigo, and violet. When rays of the sun are made to pass through a glass prism, we will see the seven different colors.

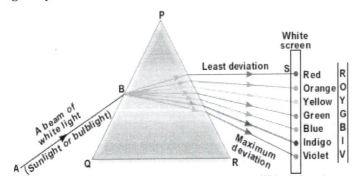

The splitting of a ray into its component colors is known as dispersion of light, and the band of colors is known as a spectrum. A spectrum of yellow light from a sodium lamp will remain yellow itself.

Total internal reflection

Total internal reflection, or TIR as it is intimately called, is the reflection of the total amount of incident light at the boundary between two media. TIR only takes place when both of the following two conditions are met:
- The light is in the denser medium, and approaching the less dense medium.
- The angle of incidence is greater than the so-called critical angle.

Note: Total internal reflection will not take place unless the incident light is traveling within the more optically dense medium towards the less optically dense medium.

Convex mirrors

In case of convex mirrors, the parallel rays, on reflection, appear to diverge from a point, F. This point is called the focal point of the convex mirrors, and the distance, PF, is called the focal length. The focus, in this case, is behind the mirror. If R is the radius of curvature of a spherical mirror, then the focal length, f, is R/2. f = (distance PF) = R/2

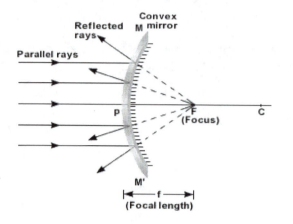

Concave mirror

In a concave mirror, they appear to converge at a point, F. The distance, PF, is called the focal length, and F is called the focal point. The focus is in front of the mirror.

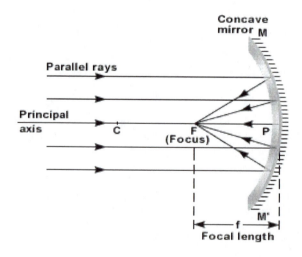

Center and radius of curvature

The center of curvature of a mirror is defined as the center of the hollow sphere from which the mirror has been cut. It is represented by the letter C in the figures above. It can be observed that the C of a convex mirror is behind the mirrored surface, while the C for a concave mirror is in front of the mirror. The radius of curvature is the radius of the sphere from which the mirrors (either convex or concave) are made. It is represented by the letter R. In the figures above, the distance CP is the R of the two mirrors.

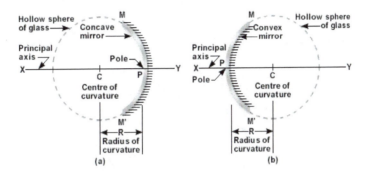

Aperture and focal length of a mirror

The aperture of a mirror is the portion of the hollow spherical surface from which the mirror reflections take place. The distance MM' is the aperture of the mirrors above. When parallel rays of light, coming from an infinite distance, fall on either a concave or a convex mirror, they are reflected back to a point on the principal axis, XY. The focus is where the image is formed of an object placed at a far distance. The focal length of a mirror is the distance between the focal point and the vertex of the first optical surface. In the figures above, if the focal point is C, then the focal length is the length of CP.

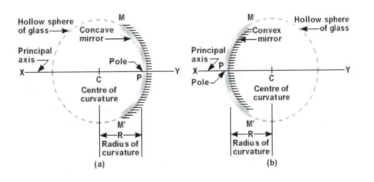

Pole and principal axis of a mirror

The pole of the mirror is the central point on the surface of the mirrors, represented by the letter P. A pole of the mirror can be found by drawing a straight line from the center, C, to the largest distance on the surface from C. Where the line cuts the mirror, you will find the pole, P. The principal axis of the mirror is a straight line that passes through the center of curvature, C, and the pole of the mirror, P. In the figures above, line XY is the principal axis of the mirrors. The principal axis of a spherical mirror functions similar to the normal of the plane mirror. A ray of light passing along the principal axis will be reflected back along the same path.

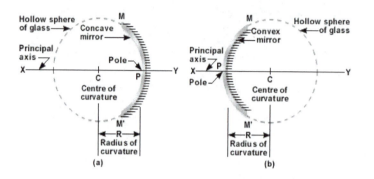

(a)   (b)

Real and virtual images

In a convex mirror, the object and its image lie on the opposite sides of the mirrored surface. The image, therefore, is a virtual image. It cannot be captured on a screen. In a concave mirror, on the other hand, the focus is real. The object and the image lie on the same side of the mirrored surface. A real image is called so because it can be caught on a screen. In a plane mirror, the image is also a virtual one because it does not form an image on the same side as that of the object.

Images by concave mirrors

1. A ray of light that is parallel to the principal axis, XP, passes through the focal point, F, after reflection.
2. A ray of light passing through the center of curvature, C, is reflected back, undeviated, along the same path.
3. The 3rd rule is the inverse of the 1st rule: When a ray of light passes through the focus, F, and strikes the mirror, MM', the reflected ray is parallel to the principal axis, XP. The following image is an example:

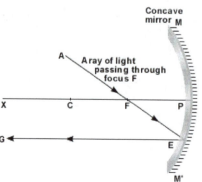

- 324 -

Convex and concave lenses

A convex lens focuses light rays, coming from an infinite distance, at its focal point. The lens is thicker in the middle. A concave lens defocuses light rays coming from infinite distance. The parallel light rays appear to diverge from the focal point of the lens. The lens is thinner in the middle.

Aperture, principal axis, and optical center of lenses

The maximum portion of the spherical surfaces from which the lens actions take place is called the aperture of the lens. The line joining the centers of curvature is known as the principal axis of the lens. The principal axis of a spherical lens functions similar to the normal of the plane mirror. A light ray passing along the principle axis will not be refracted. The intersection of the line joining the lens aperture and the principal axis is called the optical center of the lens. Any light ray passing through the optical center emerges parallel to the direction of the incident ray. The optical center is denoted by O.

Vision and the eye

The convex lens on the retina focuses light rays that are reflected from objects that are kept in front of the pupil. The amount of light entering the eye can be adjusted by the size of the pupil. In too bright of light, the iris adjusts so that the pupil narrows. In the dark, the pupil expands in order to take in more light. All of us have experienced this. For example, if there is a sudden electricity failure at night, then instantly we cannot see anything; but, after a short while we are able to see even in the darkness. The reason for this is that the iris takes a little time to expand the pupil to accommodate more light. Once more light enters the eye, we can somewhat see even in the dark. In pitch darkness, where there is no light reflected from anywhere, we would be unable to see anything. When the eye is focusing distant objects, the ciliary muscles are relaxed, and the lens of the eye is less convex. The ciliary muscles adjust in such a manner that the size of the eye is the focal length of the convex lens. If the ciliary muscles contract, then this makes the central portion of the convex lens bulge, and the focal length of the convex lens decreases. The rays from the object, after passing through the lens, converge at the focal plane, which is the retina. Thus, our eyes can see both distant and nearby objects by changing the shape of the lens. This ability to focus objects at various distances is called accommodation of the eye.

Lens equation

The lens equation defines the focal length based upon its relation to the object distance and the image distance, according to the following formula:

$$f = \left(p^{-1} + q^{-1} \right)^{-1}$$

Where:
f = The focal length.
p = The object distance.
q = The image distance.

Power of a lens

The power of a lens, P, is given as the inverse of its focal length measured in meters. The standard unit for measuring P is a dioptre, and is denoted by D. If the D for a lens equals 1, then it means that the lens has a focal length of 1 meter. The power of a convex lens is positive (+), while the power of a concave lens is negative (-).

Magnification

The ratio of the height of the image to the height of the object is known as the magnification, M:

$$M = \frac{H_2}{H_1}$$

Where:
H_1 = The height of the object.
H_2 = The height of the image.

Ray tracing

Ray tracing is a realistic method for rendering images (or frames) constructed in 3D computer graphics environments. It works by tracing the path that is taken by a ray of light through the scene, and calculating the reflection, refraction, or absorption of the ray whenever it intersects an object in the world—hence the name. Ray tracing's popularity stems from its realism over other rendering methods, such as scanline algorithms; effects, such as reflections and shadows, which are difficult to simulate in other algorithms, follow naturally from the ray-tracing algorithm. The popularity of the ray-tracing method also benefits from the fact that it is relatively simple to implement, and yet yields impressive graphical results; thus, it often represents a first entry into graphics programming for many individuals.

Hydrogen structure and spectra

A hydrogen atom is an atom of the element hydrogen. It is composed of a single negatively charged electron, attending a single positively charged proton, which composes the nucleus of the hydrogen atom. The electron is bound to the proton by the Coulomb force. The hydrogen atom has special significance in quantum mechanics as a simple physical system for which an exact solution to the Schrödinger equation exists, from which the experimentally observed frequencies and intensities of the hydrogen spectral lines can be calculated.

Atomic energy levels

The principle quantum number, n, is an integer value (1,2,3...) that is used to describe the quantum level, or shell, in which an electron resides. The principle quantum number is the primary number that is used to determine the amount of energy in an atom. Using one of the first important equations in atomic structure (developed by Niels Bohr), we can calculate the amount of energy in an atom with an electron at some value of n:

$$E_n = -\frac{Rhc}{n^2}$$

Where:
R = Rydberg constant, a value of 1.097×10^7 per meter (m^{-1}).
c = Speed of light, 3.0×10^8 meters per second (m/s).
h = Planck's constant, 6.63×10^{-34} Joule-seconds (J-s).
n = Principal quantum number, without units.

Components of the atomic nucleus

The atomic nucleus is the center of an atom. Nuclei are composed of protons and neutrons. The number of protons in an atomic nucleus is called the atomic number, and determines which element the atom is. For example, a nucleus with one proton (which is the only nucleus that may have no neutrons) constitutes an atom of hydrogen; a nucleus with six protons constitutes carbon; and a nucleus with eight protons constitutes oxygen. The number of neutrons determines the isotope of the element. In addition, the number of protons and neutrons in a nucleus are correlated: in lighter nuclei they are approximately equal, while heavier nuclei have a larger number of neutrons. The two numbers together determine the nuclide (type of nucleus). The masses of protons, neutrons, and electrons are very small. Protons and neutrons have nearly equal masses: a proton is 1.6726×10^{-27} kg, while a neutron is 1.6749×10^{-27} kg. Their combined number, the mass number, is approximately equal to the atomic mass of an atom. The mass of the electrons is small in comparison to the mass of the nucleus: an electron weighs 9.1094×10^{-31} kg. Thus, the mass of an electron is about 1830 times smaller than a proton. The dimension of an atom is of the order of 10^{-10} m. This unit of measurement is called an Angstrom, and is written as A°. That is, 10^{-10} m = 1 A°.

Isotopes

1. Isotopes are nuclides that have the same atomic number, but different mass numbers.
2. Isotopes of a given element are chemically identical.

Nuclear reactions

In a nuclear reaction, the parent nuclei undergo changes, and the products are new nuclei. In a nuclear reaction, the identity of the element changes because the nuclei undergo changes. This means that a new element with different proton and neutron numbers is formed. However, the total number of nucleons is conserved. In a nuclear reaction, a very large amount of energy is liberated.

Sometimes, to start a nuclear reaction, the reacting nuclei have to be bombarded at very high energies. This is necessary because the nuclei have to overcome the positive electrostatic repulsion between each other. However, endothermic nuclear reactions are not seen. All nuclear reactions are accompanied by strong radioactive emissions. Each isotope can have its own reactions. Nuclear reactions are not affected by the temperature or pressure applied on reacting nuclei. Nuclear reactions cannot be reversed. In some rare cases, the reactions can be reversed under very hard experimental conditions.

Radioactive decay

Radioactive decay is the set of various processes by which unstable atomic nuclei (nuclides) emit subatomic particles. Decay is said to occur in the parent nucleus, and to produce a daughter nucleus. The SI unit for measuring radioactive decay is the becquerel (Bq). If a quantity of radioactive material produces one decay event per second, then it has an activity of one Bq. Since any reasonably sized sample of radioactive material contains very many atoms, a becquerel is a tiny level of activity: numbers on the order of gigabecquerels are more common. The old standard unit for measuring the activity of a given radioactive sample is the curie. One curie is equivalent to the activity of 1 gram of radium, and is formally defined as the amount of material that will produce 3.7 x 10^{10} nuclear decays per second. Since 1 Bq is the amount of material that produces 1 nuclear decay per second, 1 curie is also equivalent to 3.7 x 10^{10} Bq.

Exponential decay

Exponential decay occurs when a quantity decreases at a rate proportional to its value. This can be expressed as follows:
$$\frac{dN}{dt} = -\lambda N$$
Where:
N = The quantity.
λ = The decay constant (a positive number).

This equation can be solved as follows:
$$N = Ce^{-\lambda t}$$
Where:
C = The constant of integration.

Note: The constant of integration, C, is often written as N_0 since it denotes the original quantity.

Radioactive decay

The types of radioactive decay are:
- Alpha – Radioactive decay in which an α-particle is emitted.
- Beta – Radioactive decay in which a β-particle is emitted. There are two types of β-decay: β⁻-decay and β⁺-decay.
- Gamma – Radioactive decay in which a γ-ray is emitted.

α-particles

The properties of α-particles are as follows:
- α-particles are nuclei of He. Emission of α-particles reduces the mass number of the emitting parent nucleus by 4, and reduces the atomic number by 2.
- α-particles are positively charged particles. Their charge is 2e.
- They are ejected with high kinetic energy, although relatively low velocity.
- They produce intense ionization of the surrounding material through which they pass.
- They are not very penetrating, as their mass is high.
- Being charged particles, they are deflected by both electric and magnetic fields.

Beta radiations

There are two types of beta radiations: electrons, denoted as β^-; and positrons, denoted as β^+. Although β^+- and α-particles are positively charged radiations, their deflection in an electric field is different: α-particles are about 7300 times more massive than the β^+-particles, and are therefore deflected much less.

γ-rays

The properties of γ-rays are as follows:
- γ-rays are photons or electromagnetic waves. Their wavelength is very small: $\sim 10^{-10}$ m.
- The emission of a γ-ray does not change any of the A, Z, or N numbers.
- γ-rays are uncharged and have high energies.
- γ-rays have very high penetrating power, higher than both the α- and β-rays.
- γ-rays have very low ionization power.
- Since they are uncharged, γ-rays cannot be deflected by either electric or magnetic fields.

Radiation

Types
The following are types of radiation:
- Alpha (α) – α-radiation consists of charged particles that are composed of 2 protons and 2 neutrons; their large relative size and charge gives them a low penetrating ability: skin, paper, or cloth can stop them. They are very damaging to live human tissue inside of the body.
- Beta (β) – β-radiation consists of fast-moving electrons or positrons; their small size and charge combine to give them a penetrating ability that is greater than alpha but less than gamma: a few mm of aluminum will stop them.
- Gamma (γ) – γ-radiation consists of photons or electromagnetic waves of very short wavelength, high energy, and high penetrating ability: several cm of lead is required to stop them.
- Neutron (n) – Neutron radiation consists of fast-moving, free neutrons. Their penetrating ability and damaging effects depend upon the neutron's energy.

<u>Sources</u>

Sources of radiation are as follows:

- Natural radiation:
  - o Cosmic Rays – From the sun, stars, etc.
  - o Certain Foods – Foods rich in potassium, such as bananas, salt-substitutes, and some salad dressings.
  - o Terrestrial – Radioactive isotopes are present in the crust of the earth, building materials, etc.
- Man-made radiation:
  - o Nuclear Reactors – Radiation is emitted from fission reactions, as well as from radioactive waste.
  - o Nuclear Bombs/Fallout – Bomb testing from the 1950s and 1960s.
  - o Medical – X-rays, cancer treatment, tracers, etc.
  - o Household Items – Glow-in-the-dark watches, smoke detectors, etc.

Units of radiation

The roentgen (R) is a measure of radiation intensity of X-rays or gamma-rays. It is formally defined as the radiation intensity that is required to produce an ionization charge of 2.58×10^{-4} coulombs per kilogram of air. It is one of the standard units for radiation dosimetry, but is not applicable to alpha-, beta-, or other particle emission, and does not accurately predict the tissue effects of gamma-rays of extremely high energies. The roentgen has mainly been used for calibration of X-ray machines. The rad is a unit of absorbed radiation dose in terms of the energy actually deposited in the tissue. The rad is defined as an absorbed dose of 0.01 joules of energy per kilogram of tissue. The more recent SI unit is the gray (Gy), which is defined as 1 joule of deposited energy per kilogram of tissue. To assess the risk of radiation, the absorbed dose is multiplied by the relative biological effectiveness of the radiation to get the biological dose equivalent in rems or sieverts.

Fusion reactions

In nuclear-fusion reactions, two light nuclei combine to form a heavy nucleus, with additional particles thrown off to conserve momentum (usually protons or neutrons). Fusion reactions can never be spontaneous. No chain reaction is present. Fusion reactions can be started by increasing the temperature of the nuclei to be fused. The temperature that is required is very high. Nuclear fusion has not yet been sustained in laboratory conditions. So far, nuclear fusion has only been used for making hydrogen bombs.

Fission reactions

In nuclear-fission reactions, a heavy nucleus breaks up to form light nuclei (usually neutrons), and splits into two roughly equally sized pieces. Fission reactions can be spontaneous. A chain reaction can sustain the reaction once started. Fission reactions can be started by bombarding one nucleus with high energy upon the other nuclei. Nuclear fission can be sustained and controlled in practical situations. Nuclear fission has been used for bombs, as well as for power generation.

Other nuclear reactions

Other types of nuclear reactions are as follows:
- Spallation – A nucleus is hit by a very-high-energy particle, and is smashed into many fragments.
- (d,n) and (d,p) Reactions – A deuteron beam impinges on a target, and the target nuclei absorb either the neutron or proton from the deuteron.
- (α,n) and (α,p) Reactions – Some of the earliest nuclear reactions that were studied involved an α-particle produced by α-decay, knocking a nucleon from a target nucleus.

Binding energy

Binding energy is the energy that is required to disassemble a whole into separate parts. A bound system has a lower potential energy than its constituent parts, which is what keeps the system together: it corresponds to a positive binding energy. At the nuclear level, binding energy is derived from the strong nuclear force, and is the energy that is required to disassemble a nucleus into neutrons and protons. At the atomic level, binding energy is derived from electromagnetic interaction, and is the energy that is required to disassemble an atom into electrons and a nucleus. In astrophysics, the gravitational binding energy of a celestial body is the energy that is required to disassemble it into space debris, which is not to be confused with the gravitational potential energy to separate a celestial body and a satellite to infinite distance, keeping each intact. Because a bound system is at a lower energy level, its mass must be less than its unbound constituents. Nuclear binding energy can be computed from the difference in the mass of a nucleus, and the sum of the mass of the neutrons and protons that make up the nucleus. Once this mass difference (also called the mass defect) is known, Einstein's formula, $E = mc^2$, can then be used to compute the binding energy of any nucleus.

Electron volts

An electron volt (eV) is a unit of energy defined as the work done to take a charge of 1 electron through a voltage difference of 1 volt. 1 eV = 1.6 x 10^{-19} joules. One million electron volts is written as 1 MeV. Thus, 1 MeV = 10^6 eV = 1.6 x 10^{-13} joules.

Energy release from a nuclear reaction

Three ways that energy can be released from a nuclear reaction are as follows:
- Kinetic energy of the product particles.
- Emission of very high energy ▯-rays.
- Some energy may remain in the nucleus as a metastable energy level.

When the product nucleus is metastable, this is indicated by placing an asterisk (*) next to its atomic number. This energy is eventually released through nuclear decay. A small amount of energy may also emerge in the form of X-rays. Generally, the product nucleus has a different atomic number, and thus the configuration of its electron shells is wrong. As the electrons rearrange themselves and drop to lower energy levels, internal transition X-rays (X-rays with precisely defined emission lines) may be emitted.

Appendix: Area, Volume, Surface Area Formulas

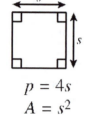

$$A = \tfrac{1}{2}\,bh$$

$$A = bh$$

$$A = \tfrac{1}{2}\,h(b_1 + b_2)$$

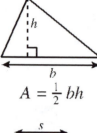

$$p = 4s$$
$$A = s^2$$

$$p = 2l + 2w$$
$$A = lw$$

$$c^2 = a^2 + b^2$$

$$C = 2\pi r$$
$$A = \pi r^2$$

$$V = \pi r^2 h$$
$$S.A. = 2\pi rh + 2\pi r^2$$

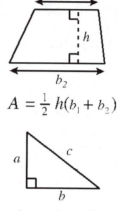

$$V = \tfrac{1}{3}\,\pi r^2 h$$
$$S.A. = \pi rl + \pi r^2$$

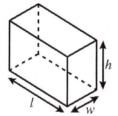

$$V = lwh$$
$$S.A. = 2lw + 2lh + 2wh$$

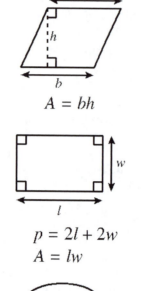

$$V = \tfrac{1}{3}\,Bh$$
$$S.A. = \tfrac{1}{2}\,lp + B$$

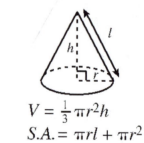

Pi

$$\pi \approx 3.14$$

Practice Test

Natural Science

Biology

1. The hydrogen bonds in a water molecule make water a good
    A. Solvent for lipids
    B. Participant in replacement reactions
    C. Surface for small particles and living organisms to move across
    D. Solvent for polysaccharides such as cellulose
    E. Example of an acid

2. When an animal takes in more energy that it uses over an extended time, the extra chemical energy is stored as:
    A. Fat
    B. Starch
    C. Protein
    D. Enzymes
    E. Cholesterol

3. Which of the following is an example of a cofactor?
    A. Zinc
    B. Actin
    C. Cholesterol
    D. GTP
    E. Chlorophyll

4. Which of the following statements regarding chemiosmosis in mitochondria is not correct?
    A. ATP synthase is powered by protons flowing through membrane channels
    B. Energy from ATP is used to transport protons to the intermembrane space
    C. Energy from the electron transport chain is used to transport protons to the intermembrane space
    D. An electrical gradient and a pH gradient both exist across the inner membrane
    E. The waste product of chemiosmosis is water

5. DNA replication occurs during which of the following phases?
    A. Prophase I
    B. Prophase II
    C. Interphase I
    D. Interphase II
    E. Telophase I

6. Which of the following parts of an angiosperm give rise to the fruit?
   A. Pedicel
   B. Filament
   C. Sepal
   D. Ovary
   E. Meristem

Questions 7 and 8 pertains to the following diagram representing a cross section of a tree trunk

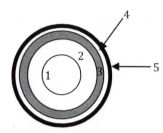

7. Which structure contains tissue that is dead at maturity?
   A. 1
   B. 2
   C. 3
   D. 4
   E. 5

8. Which structure transports carbohydrates to the roots?
   A. 1
   B. 2
   C. 3
   D. 4
   E. 5

9. When Ca^{2+} channels open in a presynaptic cell (doesn't the cell also depolarize?)
   A. The cell depolarizes
   B. The cell hyperpolarizes
   C. An action potential is propagated
   D. Synaptic vesicles release neurotransmitter
   E. The nerve signal is propagated by salutatory conduction

10. Which hormone is secreted by the placenta throughout pregnancy?
    A. Human chorionic gonadotropin (HCG)
    B. Gonadotropin releasing hormone (GnRH)
    C. Luteinizing hormone (LH)
    D. Follicle stimulating hormone (FSH)
    E. None of these

11. On a standard biomass pyramid, level 3 corresponds to which trophic level?
    A. Producers
    B. Decomposers
    C. Primary consumers
    D. Primary carnivores
    E. Secondary carnivores

12. The diagram below represents the three types of survivorship curves, describing how mortality varies as species age. Which of the following species is most likely to exhibit Type I survivorship?

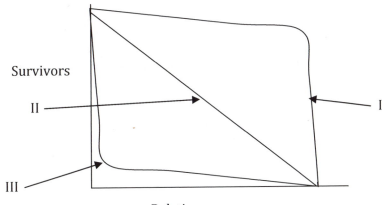

    A. Frogs
    B. Oysters
    C. Salmon
    D. Dolphins
    E. Shrimp

13. Which of the following is NOT a natural dispersal process that would lead to species colonization on an island?
    A. Mussels carried into a lake on the hull of a ship
    B. Drought connecting an island to other land
    C. Floating seeds
    D. Animals swimming long distances
    E. Birds adapted to flying long distances

14. A population of pea plants has 25% dwarf plants and 75% tall. The tall allele, T is dominant to dwarf (t). What is the frequency of the T allele?
    A. 0.75
    B. 0.67
    C. 0.5
    D. 0.25
    E. 0.16

- 335 -

15. All of the following are homologous structures EXCEPT
    A. Bird feathers
    B. Elephant eyelashes
    C. Human fingernails
    D. Dog fur
    E. Insect exoskeleton

16. The chemical bonds between hydrogen and oxygen in an H_2O molecule are an example of?
    A. Nonpolar covalent bonds
    B. Polar covalent bonds
    C. Ionic bonds
    D. Hydrogen bonds
    E. Van der Waals bonds

17. Phosphate, PO3-, is a chemical moiety found in all but which of the following metabolic compounds?
    A. Amino acids
    B. DNA
    C. RNA
    D. Phospholipids
    E. Nucleotides

18. An example of a coenzyme is:
    A. Iron
    B. Catalase
    C. Vitamin B1
    D. Glucose
    E. ATP

19.

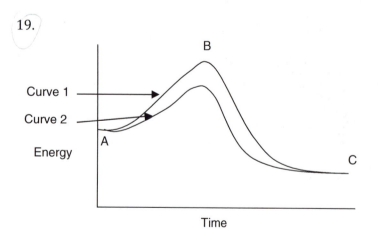

The graph above shows the potential energy of molecules during a chemical reaction. Which of the following statements about the reaction is true?
    A. An enzyme could have increased the potential energy at point C
    B. An enzyme was probably present in curve 2
    C. This is an exergonic reaction
    D. The curves show the potential energy of the enzyme
    E. The energy of the substrate is less than the energy of the products

20. In oxidative phosphorylation, high-energy electrons are passed from NAD and $FADH_2$ down the electron transport chain to a final electron acceptor. Which of the following is that electron acceptor?
   A. CO_2
   B. NAD+
   C. Pyruvate
   D. O_2
   E. ATP

21. Plant shoots demonstrate negative gravitropism, whereas roots demonstrate positive gravitropism. Which of the following plant hormones mediates this response?
   A. Ethylene
   B. Abscisic acid
   C. Jasmonic acid
   D. Gibberellins
   E. Auxin

22. Most of the CO_2 in blood is converted to carbonic acid in red blood cells. When a body is active, CO_2 production increases. Which of the following changes in pH would stimulate increased respiratory rate?
   A. A drop in pH
   B. A return to normal pH after a drop in pH
   C. A rise in pH
   D. A return to normal pH after a rise in pH
   E. No change in pH is needed to stimulate increased respiratory rate

23. The major inhibitory neurotransmitter in the central nervous system is:
   A. Acetylcholine
   B. Epinephrine
   C. GABA
   D. Dopamine
   E. Serotonin

24. A pea plant with purple flowers is crossed with a pea plant with white flowers. Half the progeny have purple flowers and half have white flowers. The allele for purple flowers is _____ to the allele for white flowers.
   A. Dominant
   B. Co-dominant
   C. Recessive
   D. Incompletely dominant
   E. Impossible to determine from the information provided

- 337 -

25. In a dihybrid cross between bean plants with red (R) wrinkled (w) seeds and white (r) smooth (W) seeds, the F1 progeny is all red and smooth. F1 plants are selfed, and the progeny are 1/2 red and smooth, 1/4 red and wrinkled, and 1/4 white and smooth. Red is dominant to white and smooth is dominant to wrinkled. Which is true of the R and W genes?
  - A. They are linked
  - B. They are unlinked
  - C. They are sex-linked
  - D. They are on different chromosomes
  - E. They cause abnormal chromosome segregation

26. What is the largest reservoir of phosphorous on the planet?
  - A. The ocean
  - B. Plants
  - C. Soil
  - D. The atmosphere
  - E. Rocks and ocean sediments

27. Species that inhabit an island because they were transported there by humans are called
  - A. Invasive species
  - B. Introduced species
  - C. Dispersed species
  - D. Native species
  - E. Mutualistic species

28. The combination of natural selection and Mendelian genetics is known as:
  - A. Inheritance of acquired characters
  - B. Microevolution
  - C. Macroevolution
  - D. The modern synthesis
  - E. Natural transformation of species

29. New mutations
  - A. Are rare
  - B. Are usually beneficial
  - C. Result from sexual reproduction
  - D. Result from reproductive isolation
  - E. Are the raw material for natural selection

30. In the absence of selective pressure, but in a small population, allele frequencies will likely change because of:
  - A. Genetic drift
  - B. Gene flow
  - C. The founder effect
  - D. Nonrandom mating

31. All but which of the following processes are ways of moving solutes across a plasma membrane?
    A. Osmosis
    B. Passive transport
    C. Active transport
    D. Facilitated diffusion
    E. Endocytosis

32. Prokaryotic and eukaryotic cells are similar in having which of the following?
    A. Membrane-bound organelles
    B. Protein-studded DNA
    C. Presence of a nucleus
    D. Integral membrane proteins in the plasma membrane
    E. Flagella composed of microtubules

33. Enzymes catalyze biochemical reactions by
    A. Lowering the potential energy of the products
    B. Separating inhibitors from products
    C. Forming a complex with the products
    D. Lowering the activation energy of the reaction
    E. Providing energy to the reaction

34. In a strenuously exercising muscle, NADH begins to accumulate in high concentration. Which of the following metabolic process will be activated to reduce the concentration of NADH?
    A. Glycolysis
    B. The Krebs cycle
    C. Lactic acid fermentation
    D. Oxidative phosphorylation
    E. Acetyl CoA synthesis

35. The combination of DNA with histones is called
    A. A centromere
    B. Chromatin
    C. A chromatid
    D. Nucleoli
    E. A plasmid

36. Which of the following is true of the enzyme telomerase?
    A. It is active on the leading strand during DNA synthesis
    B. It requires a chromosomal DNA template
    C. It acts in the $3' \rightarrow 5'$ direction
    D. It adds a repetitive DNA sequence to the end of chromosomes
    E. It takes the place of primase at the ends of chromosomes

37. Which section of the digestive system is responsible for water reabsorption?
    A. The large intestine
    B. The duodenum
    C. The small intestine
    D. The gallbladder
    E. The stomach

- 339 -

38. Which of the following hormones triggers ovulation in females?
    A. Estrogen
    B. Progesterone
    C. Serotonin
    D. Luteinizing hormone
    E. Testosterone

39. Which of the following is not a mechanism that contributes to cell differentiation and development in embryos?
    A. Asymmetrical cell division
    B. Asymmetrical cytoplasm distribution
    C. Organizer cells
    D. Location of cells on the lineage map
    E. Homeotic genes

40. An individual with an AB blood type needs a blood transfusion. Which of the following types could NOT be a donor?
    A. O
    B. AB
    C. A
    D. B
    E. All can be donors.

General Chemistry

1. Which substance is most likely to be a solid at STP?
   A. Kr
   B. Na
   C. NH_3
   D. Xe

2. A weather balloon is filled with 1000 mol of He gas at 25 °C and 101 kPa of pressure. What is the volume of the weather balloon?
   A. 24518 m3
   B. 24.5 m3
   C. 2 m3
   D. 245 m³

3. Which is the correct order of increasing intermolecular attractive forces?
   A. Dipole-dipole<ionic<hydrogen bonding<London dispersion
   B. Ionic<dipole-dipole<London dispersion<hydrogen bonding
   C. Hydrogen bonding<London dispersion<ionic<dipole-dipole
   D. London dispersion<dipole-dipole<hydrogen bonding<ionic

4. Three liquids, X, Y and Z are placed in separate flasks, each of which is suspended in a water bath at 75 °C. The boiling points of each liquid are
   > X, 273 K
   > Y, 340 K
   > Z, 360 K
   Which of the three liquids will begin to boil after warming to 75 °C?
   A. X, Y, and Z
   B. X and Z
   C. X and Y
   D. Y and Z

5. Gas X is in a cylinder at 1 atm of pressure and has a volume of 10 L at 0° C. Gas X spontaneously decomposes to gas Y, according to the equation

   $$X \longrightarrow 3Y$$

   The temperature in the cylinder remains the same during the reaction. What is the pressure in the cylinder now?
   A. 1 atm
   B. 3 atm
   C. 4 atm
   D. Cannot be determined

6. 100 g of H_3PO_4 is dissolved in water, producing 400 mL of solution. What is the normality of the solution?
   A. 2.55 N
   B. 1.02 N
   C. 7.65 N
   D. 0.25 N

7. 100 mL of a 0.1 M solution of NaOH is neutralized to pH 7 with H_2SO_4. How many grams of H_2SO_4 are required to achieve this neutralization?
    A. 4.9 g
    B. 0.98 g
    C. 9.8 g
    D. 0.49 g

8. Place the following in the correct order of increasing solubility in water.
    A. Butanol<ethanol<octane<NaCl
    B. Ethanol<NaCl<octane<butanol
    C. NaCl<octane<butanol<ethanol
    D. Octane<butanol<ethanol<NaCl

9. Which of the following represents the correct increasing order of acidity?
    A. CH_3COOH<CH_3OH<CH_3CH_3<HCl
    B. CH_3CH_3<CH_3OH<CH_3COOH<HCl
    C. CH_3CH_3<CH_3COOH<CH_3OH<HCl
    D. CH_3OH<CH_3CH_3<HCl<CH_3COOH

10. Which of the following radioactive emissions results in an increase in atomic number?
    A. Alpha
    B. Beta
    C. Gamma
    D. Neutron

11. The best way to separate isotopes of the same element is to exploit:
    A. Differences in chemical reactivity
    B. Differences in reduction potential
    C. Differences in toxicity
    D. Differences in mass

12. Describe the correct outer shell electronic arrangement of phosphorous.
    A. $4s^2 4p^3$
    B. $3s^2 3p^3$
    C. $2s^2 3p^3$
    D. $2s^2 2p^3$

13. Place the following elements in order of decreasing electronegativity: N, As, Bi, P, Sb

    A. As>Bi>N>P>Sb
    B. N>P>As>Sb>Bi
    C. Bi>Sb>As>P>N
    D. P>N>As>Sb>Bi

14. Atoms that are sp^2 hybridized will have what sort of hybrid orbital geometry around them?
    A. Tetrahedral
    B. Trigonal planar
    C. Linear
    D. Angled

15. Balance the following reaction between sulfuric acid and aluminum hydroxide by filling in the correct stoichiometric values for each chemical.

$$\_ H_2SO_4 + \_ Al(OH)_3 \rightarrow \_ Al_2(SO_4)_3 + \_ H_2O$$

A. 3, 2, 1, 6
B. 2, 3, 1, 3
C. 3, 3, 2, 6
D. 1, 2, 1, 4

16. Methane gas is burned in pure oxygen at 200 °C and 1 atm of pressure to produce CO_2 and H_2O according to the equation

$$CH_4 + 2O_2 \rightarrow CO_2 + 2H_2O$$

If 10 L of methane gas were burned, and the final temperature and pressure remained the same, how many liters of gaseous products are produced by the reaction?

A. 10 L
B. 20 L
C. 30 L
D. 40 L

17. 10 g of salt XY (MW = 100 g/mol) is added to 1 liter of water with stirring. The salt dissociates into ions X^+ and Y^-. After equilibrium is established, the undissolved portion of the salt was removed by filtration, weighed, and found to be 9.5 g. What is the K_{sp} for this salt?

A. 5 x 10-2
B. 5 x 10-3
C. 1 x10-2
D. 2.5 x 10-5

18. What will be the pH of 2 L of a 0.1 M aqueous solution of HCl?

A. 2
B. -1
C. 1
D. 0.05

19. For the conversion of water into steam, which of the following is true?

A. $\Delta T=0, \Delta S>0$
B. $\Delta T>0, \Delta S = 0$
C. $\Delta T =0, \Delta S <0$
D. $\Delta T >0, \Delta S >0$

- 343 -

20. What would be the correct IUPAC name for the following compound?

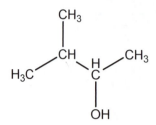

A. 3-methyl-2-butanol
B. 2-methyl-3-butanol
C. 3,3-dimethyl-2-propanol
D. 2-Hydroxy-3-methyl butane

21. Which of the following molecules are cis alkenes?

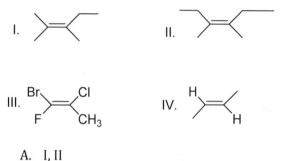

A. I, II
B. II, III
C. III, IV
D. I, IV

22. A liquid is held at its freezing point and slowly allowed to solidify. Which of the following statements about this event are true?
A. During freezing, the temperature of the material decreases
B. While freezing, heat is given off by the material
C. During freezing, heat is absorbed by the material
D. During freezing, the temperature of the material increases

23. Nuclear chain reactions, such as the one that is exploited in nuclear power plants, are propagated by what subatomic particle(s)?
A. Protons
B. Neutrons
C. Electrons
D. Neutrons and protons

24. An alpha particle consists of
A. Two electrons and two protons
B. Two electrons and two neutrons
C. Four neutrons
D. Two protons and two neutrons

25. Arrange the following elements in order of increasing atomic radius:
    A. K<Zn<Fe<As<Kr
    B. K<Fe<Zn<Kr<As
    C. Kr<As<Fe<K<Zn
    D. Kr<As<Zn<Fe<K

26. When a solid is heated and transforms directly to the gaseous phases, this process is called:
    A. sublimation
    B. fusion
    C. diffusion
    D. condensation

27. Which bond has the shortest length?
    A. sp^2
    B. sp^3
    C. sp
    D. pi

28. Resonance structures can be defined as:
    A. Two or more structures that have different atoms bound to different atoms
    B. Two structures that have a similar structure but different formula
    C. Two or more structures that have the same formula, but are different in shape
    D. Two or more structures that differ only in the arrangement of electrons in the structures

29. How many electrons are in the atom $\frac{45}{20}$Ca ?
    A. 20
    B. 45
    C. 65
    D. 25

30. For the reaction $CO_2(g) + H_2(g) \rightarrow CO(g) + H_2O(l)$, which of the following will occur if the pressure of the reaction is increased?
    A. The reaction rate will increase
    B. The reaction rate will decrease
    C. The reaction equilibrium will shift to the right
    D. The reaction equilibrium will shift to the left

Organic Chemistry

1. Alkanes increase in molecular weight
   A. by 14 units per mole per carbon atom
   B. by 15 units per mole per carbon atom
   C. by 14 grams per mole per carbon atom
   D. by 12 grams per mole per carbon atom

2. A specific combination of atoms that imparts common properties to a series of compounds is
   A. a functional group
   B. a substituent
   C. a diluent
   D. an eluent

3. Benzene, C_6H_6,
   A. has three sites of unsaturation
   B. is aromatic
   C. is non-flammable
   D. is a waxy solid at room temperature

4. Ethanol, C_2H_5OH, and propanol, C_3H_7OH, are
   A. homologous alcohols
   B. isomers
   C. not water soluble
   D. gases at room temperature

5. The structural formulas CH_3CH_2OH and CH_3OCH_3 are
   A. the same
   B. non-isomeric
   C. ethanol and methanol
   D. ethanol and dimethyl ether

6. Water adds to the carbonyl group to form
   A. acetals and ketals
   B. hydroxy ketones
   C. saccharides
   D. esters

7. An sp^3 carbon atom that has a completely asymmetric arrangement of four substituent groups is called
   A. a conformer
   B. a chiral center
   C. a reactive center
   D. a stereoisomer

8. Enantiomers
   A. have identical physical properties
   B. rotate plane polarized light in equal but opposite directions
   C. can be separated from each other by various methods
   D. all of the above

9. Triple bonds to carbon atoms are found in
   A. alkynes and cycloalkenes
   B. alkynes and alkenones
   C. nitriles and alkynes
   D. aromatic compounds

10. Aldehydes react with Tollens' reagent to produce
   A. ketones and silver ions
   B. carboxylic acids and silver atoms
   C. carboxylic acids and silver ions
   D. no reaction

11. Jones oxidation of alcohols and aldehydes is used to produce carboxylic acids by reaction with
   A. $K_2Cr_2O_7$ in concentrated H_2SO_4
   B. CrO_3 in sulfuric acid
   C. $KMnO_4$ in sulfuric acid
   D. MnO_2 in hydrochloric acid

12. High-boiling liquids should be distilled under reduced pressure because
   A. they have high vapor pressures
   B. they have low melting points
   C. they can decompose at temperatures below their boiling points
   D. they do not boil at normal pressure

13. A monosaccharide is
   A. a cyclic ketone
   B. a branched chain aldehyde
   C. a simple sugar
   D. an α-hydroxycarboxylic acid

14. Removal of an α hydrogen atom from a carbonyl compound is favored by
   A. delocalization of the remaining negative charge
   B. enolate formation
   C. 3° amines
   D. none of the above

15. Substituent groups can be added to benzene rings by a
   A. Claisen condensation reaction
   B. Wittig reaction
   C. Friedel-Crafts reaction
   D. bicycloannulation reaction

16. Reaction of benzaldehyde with diborane and mild acid produces
    A. benzoic acid
    B. benzyl alcohol
    C. 9-borabicyclononane (9-BBN)
    D. dibenzoyl

17. Reaction between alkyl halides and primary amines
    A. produce 2° amines
    B. produce 2° and 3° amines
    C. produce 2° and 3° amines and quaternary ammonium salts
    D. do not occur

18. The reaction of P_2O_5 with water to produce phosphoric acid is
    A. $P_2O_5 + 2\,H_2O \rightarrow 2\,H_2PO_3$
    B. $P_2O_5 + 3\,H_2O \rightarrow 2\,H_3PO_4$
    C. $2\,P_2O_5 + 5\,H_2O \rightarrow 4\,H_3PO_5$
    D. $2\,P_2O_5 + 6\,H_2O \rightarrow 4\,H_3PO_4$

19. In a redox reaction
    A. the reducing agent gains electrons
    B. the oxidizing agent loses electrons
    C. the oxidizing agent is reduced as the reducing agent is oxidized
    D. oxidation occurs first followed by reduction

20. The following molecule is

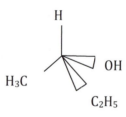

    A. S-2-butanol
    B. R-2-butanol
    C. D- butyl alcohol
    D. L- butyl alcohol

21. The addition of an anionic species to the β position of an α, β-unsaturated ketone is called a
    A. Michaelson-Morley experiment
    B. Michaelson reaction
    C. Michael addition
    D. Mitchell addition

22. Anthracene, phenanthrene and other similar compounds are known as
    A. simple hydrocarbons
    B. diketo carbonyl compounds
    C. polycyclic aromatic hydrocarbons
    D. dioxins

23. Carbon and nitrogen
    A. only bond to each other in primary amines
    B. form a double bond to each other in imines
    C. cannot bond to each other
    D. cannot form a triple bond to each other

24. Lactones and lactams are
    A. cyclic esters and amides
    B. cyclic ketones and amines
    C. hydroxy ketones and hydroxy aldehydes
    D. cyclic ketones and ethers

25. Molecules of compounds such as ☐-carotene have alternating C=C and C-C bonds. Such double bonds are known as
    A. repeating
    B. segregated
    C. conjugated
    D. non-alternant

26. Side-by-side overlap of p orbitals in a molecular structure results in
    A. π bonding and delocalization of the p orbital electrons
    B. resonance destabilization
    C. non-aromaticity
    D. steric strain

27. A mixture of equal quantities of enantiomers is called
    A. a diastereomeric mixture
    B. a *meso*- structure
    C. a racemic mixture
    D. a eutectic mixture

28. When drops of a solution of Br_2 in CCl_4 are added to a similar solution of an unknown compound, the color due to Br_2 disappears. This indicates that
    A. a carbonyl group is present in the unknown molecule
    B. the unknown compound is a carboxylic acid
    C. the unknown compound has C=C or C≡C bonds
    D. an amide has been formed

29. Ketones and aldehydes
    A. form a colorless adduct with 2,4-DNP
    B. form a colored iminium salt with 2,4-DNP
    C. form a highly colored solid adduct with 2,4-DNP
    D. do not react with 2,4-DNP

30. In a haloform test, a positive result indicates
    A. a methyl group adjacent to a carbonyl group
    B. a cyclic ketone
    C. a cyclic aldehyde
    D. an α-methylene ester

- 349 -

Reading Comprehension

Questions 1 – 10 are based on the following passage:

Cilia and flagella are tubular structures found on the surfaces of many animal cells. They are examples of organelles, sub-cellular structures that perform a particular function. By beating against the surrounding medium in a swimming motion, they may endow cells with motility or induce the medium to circulate, as in the case of gills. Ciliated cells typically each contain large numbers of cilia 2 -10 μm (micrometer) long. In contrast, flagellated cells usually have one or two flagella, and the structures can be as long as 200 μm. For both types of structure, the diameters are less than 0.5 μm.

Although they share similar structures, the motion of the two organelles is somewhat different. Flagella beat in a circular, undulating motion that is continuous. The effective stroke of a cilium's beat, which generates the power, is followed by a more languid recovery to the original position. During the recovery stroke, they are brought in close to the membrane of the cell. Cilia usually beat in coordinated waves, so that at any given moment some are in the midst of their power stroke while others are recovering. This provides for a steady flow of fluid past gill surfaces or the epithelia lining the lungs or digestive tract.

The construction of both organelles is very similar. A portion of the cell membrane appears to be stretched over a framework made of tubulin polymers. A polymer is a long, chain-like molecule made of smaller units that are strung together. In this case, the subunits are molecules of the protein tubulin. The framework, or skeleton, of a cilium or flagellum consists of 9 pairs of tubulin polymers spaced around the periphery, and two more single polymers of tubulin that run along the center of the shaft. This is called a 9+2 pattern.

The motion of the organelles results from chemical reactions that cause the outer polymers to slide past one another. By doing so, they force the overall structure to bend. This is similar to the mechanism of contraction of skeletal muscle. In cilia and flagella, the nine outer polymer pairs of the skeleton have along their lengths molecules of a rod-shaped protein called dynein. The dynein rods can grasp, or bind to, the neighboring tubulin polymer. Energy is then used to drive a chemical reaction that causes the dynein arms to bend, causing one tubulin polymer to move along the length of the other. Through a coordinated series of thousands of such reactions, the cilium or flagellum will beat.

Cilia have also provided some of the best evidence for the inheritance of traits by a mechanism that does not involve DNA. *Paramecium* is a single-celled ciliated protist that lives in ponds. In one variety, the stroke cycle of the cilia is clockwise (right-handed). In another variety, it is counter-clockwise (left-handed). When the cells divide, left-handed cells give rise to more left-handed cells, and *vice versa*. T.M. Sonneborn of Indiana University managed to cut tiny pieces of cell membrane from a left-handed *Paramecium* and graft them onto a right-handed one. The cell survived, and the direction of the stroke did not change, despite the fact that cilia

- 350 -

were now in a cell with a right-handed nucleus and surrounded by right-handed cilia, they continued to rotate to the left. A *paramecium* reproduces by dividing, and Sonneborn followed the transplanted patch for several generations, but it did not change direction. This suggested that the direction of rotation is a property of the cilium itself, and is not influenced by the DNA in the nucleus. In another experiment, Sonneborn transplanted the nucleus of a right-handed cell into a left-handed cell from which the original nucleus had been removed. The cell's cilia kept their counter-clockwise direction of rotation. Further, when this cell divided, all subsequent generations maintained it as well. This proved that the direction of rotation could be inherited in a manner completely independent of the chromosomal DNA.

One theory to explain this is the concept of *nucleation*. According to this idea, the tubulin proteins in left- and right-handed *Paramecia* are the same, so that the genes that give rise to them are also identical. However, once they begin to chain together in a left- or right-handed manner, they continue to do so. Therefore the direction of rotation does not depend upon the genes, but rather on some basal structure that is passed on to the cell's offspring when it divides.

1. Cilia and flagella are both
    A. Proteins.
    B. Sub-cellular structures that perform a particular function.
    C. Organelles that beat in a continuous undulating motion.
    D. Single-celled protists

2. According to the passage, where would you expect to find cilia?
    A. Stomach lining
    B. Back of the hand
    C. Lining of the heart
    D. Circulatory system

3. According to the passage, how many tubulin polymers make up the entire 9+2 pattern seen in cilia and flagella?
    A. 11
    B. 9
    C. 20
    D. Passage doesn't say

4. Two proteins mentioned in this passage are
    A. Tubulin and Paramecium.
    B. Tubulin and dynein.
    C. Tubulin and flagellin.
    D. Tubulin and Sonneborn.

5. Which of the following describes how the beating motion of flagella is caused?
    A. The two central polymers slide past one another.
    B. Dynein causes the outer polymer pairs to slide past one another.
    C. Dynein causes each of the outer polymers to bend.
    D. The organelle increases in diameter.

6. Polymers are always
    A. Made of protein.
    B. Made of tubulin.
    C. Made of subunits.
    D. Arranged in a 9+2 array.

7. The passage implies that T.M. Sonneborn was
    A. A zookeeper.
    B. A scientist at Indiana University.
    C. A chemist.
    D. A medical practitioner.

8. It was shown that, if cilia with a counterclockwise rotation are grafted onto a cell whose native cilia beat clockwise, the transplants will
    A. Beat clockwise.
    B. Stop beating.
    C. Beat randomly.
    D. Beat counterclockwise.

9. The passage describes cilia and flagella and tells us that
    A. Cilia may be 200 μm long.
    B. Flagella are less than 0.5 μm long.
    C. Cells can have more than two flagella.
    D. Flagella are less than 0.5 μm in diameter.

10. Sonneborn's experiments showed that
    A. Chromosomes influence the inheritance of rotational direction in cilia.
    B. Rotational direction in cilia is inherited by a mechanism that does not involve DNA.
    C. Chromosomes do not influence the inheritance of rotational direction in flagella.
    D. Rotational direction in cilia is random.

Questions 11 – 22 are based on the following passage:

Annelids

The phylum Annelida, named for the Latin word *anellus*, meaning "ring", includes earthworms, leeches, and other similar organisms. In their typical form, these animals exhibit bilateral symmetry, a cylindrical cross section, and an elongate body divided externally into segments (*metameres*) by a series of rings (*annuli*). They are segmented internally as well, with most of the internal organs repeated in series in each segment. This organization is termed *metamerism*. Metameric segmentation is the distinguishing feature of this phylum, and provides it with a degree of evolutionary plasticity in that certain segments can be modified and specialized to perform specific functions. For example, in some species certain of the locomotor *parapodia*, or feet, may be modified for grasping, and some portions of the gut may evolve digestive specializations.

The gut is a straight, muscular tube that functions independently of the muscular activity in the body wall. The Annelida resemble the nematodes, another worm phylum, in possessing a fluid-filled internal cavity separating the gut from the body wall. In both phyla, this cavity is involved in locomotion. However, in the annelids this space is formed at a much later time during the development of the embryo, and presumably evolved much later as well. This fluid-filled internal space is called a true *coelum*.

The annelid excretory and circulatory systems are well developed, and some members of the phylum have evolved respiratory organs. The nervous system offers a particular example of metameric specialization. It is concentrated anteriorly into enlarged cerebral ganglia connected to a ventral nerve cord that extends posteriorly and is organized into repeating segmental ganglia.

This phylum includes members bearing adaptations required for aquatic (marine or freshwater) or terrestrial habitats. They may be free-living entities or exist as parasites. Among the best known are the earthworm *Lumbricus*, the water leech *Hirudo*, and the marine worm *Nereis*.

11. What is the purpose of this passage?
    A. To describe the annelid nervous system.
    B. To describe the annelid digestive system.
    C. To introduce distinctive features of annelid anatomy.
    D. To define metamerism.
    E. To tell readers about earthworms.

12. What is meant by the term *metamerism*?
    A. Segmentation of the anatomy
    B. A series of rings
    C. Bilateral symmetry
    D. Evolutionary plasticity
    E. Specialization

13. What is meant by the term *parapodia*?
    A. Specialization
    B. Grasping appendages
    C. Locomotion
    D. Metameres
    E. Feet

14. One evolutionary advantage of segmentation is that
    A. Segmented animals have many feet.
    B. Segmented animals have a fluid-filled coelum.
    C. Parts of some segments can become specialized to perform certain functions.
    D. Segments can evolve.
    E. Segments are separated by rings.

15. A group of worms other than the Annelida are called
    A. Lumbricus
    B. Nematodes
    C. Leeches
    D. Parapodia
    E. Metameres

16. Some annelid feet may be specialized in order to
    A. be used for locomotion.
    B. be segmented.
    C. be fluid-filled.
    D. evolve.
    E. grasp things.

17. A difference between the annelid coelum and the fluid-filled cavity of other worms is that
    A. the annelid coelum is involved in locomotion.
    B. the annelid coelum is formed later.
    C. the annelid coelum is formed during embryology.
    D. the annelid coelum is cylindrical in cross section.
    E. the annelid coelum separates the gut from the body wall.

18. An example of metameric specialization in the nervous system is
    A. segmental ganglia.
    B. the ventral nerve cord.
    C. respiratory organs.
    D. parpapodia
    E. cerebral ganglia

19. The main difference between the Annelida and all other animal phyla is that
    A. the Annelida are worms.
    B. the Annelida include the leeches.
    C. the Annelida are metameric.
    D. the Annelida are aquatic.
    E. the Annelida are specialized.

20. The purpose of the last paragraph in the passage is to
    A. give familiar examples of members of the annelid phylum.
    B. show that annelids may be parasites.
    C. tell the reader that annelids may be adapted to aquatic environments.
    D. show that there are many annelids in nature and that they are adapted to a wide variety of habitats.
    E. tell the reader that earthworms are annelids.

21. The fluid-filled cavity in the nematodes is used for
    A. defense.
    B. reproduction.
    C. feeding.
    D. the gut.
    E. movement.

22. Members of the Annelida are
    A. free-living animals.
    B. parasites.
    C. aquatic.
    D. terrestrial.
    E. all the above

VISUAL PERCEPTION

It is tempting to think that your eyes are simply mirrors that reflect whatever is in front of them. Researchers, however, have shown that your brain is constantly working to create the impression of a continuous, uninterrupted world.

For instance, in the last ten minutes, you have blinked your eyes around 200 times. You have probably not been aware of any of these interruptions in your visual world. Something you probably have not seen in a long time without the aid of a mirror is your nose. It is always right there, down in the bottom corner of your vision, but your brain filters it out so that you are not aware of your nose unless you purposefully look at it.

Nor are you aware of the artery that runs right down the middle of your retina. It creates a large blind spot in your visual field, but you never notice the hole it leaves. To see this blind spot, try the following: Cover your left eye with your hand. With your right eye, look at the O on the left. As you move your head closer to the O, the X will disappear as it enters the blind spot caused by your optical nerve.

O   X

Your brain works hard to make the world look continuous!

23. The word <u>filters</u>, as used in this passage, most nearly means:
    A. Alternates
    B. Reverses
    C. Ignores
    D. Depends

24. The word <u>retina</u>, as used in this passage, most nearly means:
    A. Optical illusion
    B. Part of the eye
    C. Pattern
    D. Blindness

25. Which of the following statements can be inferred from this passage?
    A. Not all animals' brains filter out information.
    B. Visual perception is not a passive process.
    C. Blind spots cause accidents.
    D. The eyes never reflect reality.

26. What is the author's purpose for including the two letters in the middle of the passage?
    A. To demonstrate the blind spot in the visual field.
    B. To organize the passage.
    C. To transition between the last two paragraphs of the passage.
    D. To prove that the blind spot is not real.

27. What is the main purpose of this passage?
   A. To persuade the reader to pay close attention to blind spots.
   B. To explain the way visual perception works.
   C. To persuade the reader to consult an optometrist if the O and X disappear.
   D. To prove that vision is a passive process.

28. Based on the passage, which of the following statements is true?
   A. The brain cannot accurately reflect reality.
   B. Glasses correct the blind spot caused by the optical nerve.
   C. Vision is the least important sense.
   D. The brain fills in gaps in the visual field.

29. The author mentions the nose to illustrate what point?
   A. The brain filters out some visual information.
   B. Not all senses work the same way.
   C. Perception is a passive process.
   D. The sense of smell filters out information.

30. Which of the following statements can be inferred from the second paragraph?
   A. The brain filters out the sound created by the shape of the ears.
   B. The brain does not perceive all activity in the visual field.
   C. Closing one eye affects depth perception.
   D. The brain evolved as a result of environmental factors.

Questions 31 – 36 are based on the following passage:

The immune system is a network of cells, tissues, and organs that defends the body against attacks by foreign invaders. These invaders are primarily microbes—tiny organisms such as bacteria, parasites, and fungi—that can cause infections. Viruses also cause infections, but are too primitive to be classified as living organisms. The human body provides an ideal environment for many microbes. It is the immune system's job to keep the microbes out or destroy them.

The immune system is amazingly complex. It can recognize and remember millions of different enemies, and it can secrete fluids and cells to wipe out nearly all of them. The secret to its success is an elaborate and dynamic communications network. Millions of cells, organized into sets and subsets, gather and transfer information in response to an infection. Once immune cells receive the alarm, they produce powerful chemicals that help to regulate their own growth and behavior, enlist other immune cells, and direct the new recruits to trouble spots.

Although scientists have learned much about the immune system, they continue to puzzle over how the body destroys invading microbes, infected cells, and tumors without harming healthy tissues. New technologies for identifying individual immune cells are now allowing scientists to determine quickly which targets are triggering an immune response. Improvements in microscopy are permitting the first-ever observations of living B cells, T cells, and other cells as they interact within lymph nodes and other body tissues.

In addition, scientists are rapidly unraveling the genetic blueprints that direct the human immune response, as well as those that dictate the biology of bacteria, viruses, and parasites. The combination of new technology with expanded genetic information will no doubt reveal even more about how the body protects itself from disease.

31. What is the main idea of the passage?
    A. Scientists fully understand the immune system.
    B. The immune system triggers the production of fluids.
    C. The body is under constant invasion by malicious microbes.
    D. The immune system protects the body from infection.

32. Which statement is *not* a detail from the passage?
    A. Most invaders of the body are microbes.
    B. The immune system relies on excellent communication.
    C. Viruses are extremely sophisticated.
    D. The cells of the immune system are organized.

33 What is the meaning of the word *ideal* as it is used in the first paragraph?
    A. thoughtful
    B. confined
    C. hostile
    D. perfect

34. Which statement is *not* a detail from the passage?
    A. Scientists can now see T cells.
    B. The immune system ignores tumors.
    C. The ability of the immune system to fight disease without harming the body remains mysterious.
    D. The immune system remembers millions of different invaders.

35. What is the meaning of the word *enlist* as it is used in the second paragraph?
    A. call into service
    B. write down
    C. send away
    D. put across

36. What is the author's primary purpose in writing the essay?
    A. to persuade
    B. to analyze
    C. to inform
    D. to entertain

Questions 37 – 40 are based on the following passage:

It is most likely that you have never had diphtheria. You probably don't even know anyone who has suffered from this disease. In fact, you may not even know what diphtheria is. Similarly, diseases like whooping cough, measles, mumps, and rubella may all be unfamiliar to you. In the nineteenth and early twentieth centuries, these illnesses struck hundreds of thousands of people in the United States each year, mostly children, and tens of thousands of people died. The names of these diseases were frightening household words. Today, they are all but forgotten. That change happened largely because of vaccines.

You probably have been vaccinated against diphtheria. You may even have been exposed to the bacterium that causes it, but the vaccine prepared your body to fight off the disease so quickly that you were unaware of the infection. Vaccines take advantage of your body's natural ability to learn how to combat many disease-causing germs, or microbes. What's more, your body remembers how to protect itself from the microbes it has encountered before. Collectively, the parts of your body that remember and repel microbes are called the immune system. Without the proper functioning of the immune system, the simplest illness—even the common cold—could quickly turn deadly.

On average, your immune system needs more than a week to learn how to fight off an unfamiliar microbe. Sometimes, that isn't enough time. Strong microbes can spread through your body faster than the immune system can fend them off. Your body often gains the upper hand after a few weeks, but in the meantime you are sick. Certain microbes are so virulent that they can overwhelm or escape your natural defenses. In those situations, vaccines can make all the difference.

Traditional vaccines contain either parts of microbes or whole microbes that have been altered so that they don't cause disease. When your immune system confronts these harmless versions of the germs, it quickly clears them from your body. In other words, vaccines trick your immune system in order to teach your body important lessons about how to defeat its opponents.

37. What is the main idea of the passage?
    A. The nineteenth and early twentieth centuries were a dark period for medicine.
    B. You have probably never had diphtheria.
    C. Traditional vaccines contain altered microbes.
    D. Vaccines help the immune system function properly.

38. Which statement is *not* a detail from the passage?
    A. Vaccines contain microbe parts or altered microbes.
    B. The immune system typically needs a week to learn how to fight a new disease.
    C. The symptoms of disease do not emerge until the body has learned how to fight the microbe.
    D. A hundred years ago, children were at the greatest risk of dying from now-treatable diseases.

39. What is the meaning of the word *virulent* as it is used in the third paragraph?
    A. tiny
    B. malicious
    C. contagious
    D. annoying

40. What is the author's primary purpose in writing the essay?
    A. to entertain
    B. to persuade
    C. to inform
    D. to analyze

Physics

1. Which of the following measurements has the most significant digits?
   A. 0.2990
   B. 2.9900
   C. 2.997
   D. 0.00209

2. A person walks 4 meters in a single direction. He or she then changes directions and walks an additional 9 meters. What is the total magnitude of the displacement of the person?
   A. It is 13 meters.
   B. It is always larger than 9 meters but less than 13 meters.
   C. It is less than 13 meters and as small as 5 meters.
   D. It is less than 5 meters.

3. An automobile increased its speed uniformly from 20 m/s to 30 m/s at rate 5 m/s². During this time it traveled 50 meters. How long did it take the automobile to make this change?
   A. 5 seconds
   B. 2 seconds
   C. 10 seconds
   D. Can't be determined.

4. Which of the following demonstrations best illustrates Newton's first law?
   A. Giving a billiard ball at rest on a smooth level table a small push and letting it roll on the table.
   B. Dragging a box on a table at a constant speed by exerting a force just enough to overcome the force of friction.
   C. Trying without success to move a heavy bureau or filing cabinet on the floor.
   D. Running a current through two parallel wires.

5. A lead sphere 10 centimeters in diameter is attached to a 10-meter wire and suspended from a beam in a large warehouse. A lead sphere 1 meter in diameter is placed next to the smaller sphere, almost touching. Ignoring friction, which statement is true?
   A. The small sphere will move slightly towards the big sphere, but the big sphere will not move.
   B. The big sphere will move slightly toward the small sphere, but the small sphere will not move.
   C. Neither sphere will move.
   D. Both spheres will move slightly towards each other.

6. Two spring scales having negligible mass are connected together and used to weigh a 10 kg object, as shown below.

What will be the reading on the scales?
  A. Both scales will read 10 pounds.
  B. Each scale will read 49 newtons.
  C. The sum of the two readings will be 196 newtons.
  D. The bottom scale will read 98 newtons and the top scale will read 0 newtons.

7. The ideal mechanical advantage (IMA) of a pulley system indicates how much force is required to lift a mass. A fixed pulley has an IMA of 1 because all it only changes the direction of the force. A floating pulley has an IMA of 2. The total IMA is the product of the individual pulleys' IMAs. What is the ideal mechanical advantage of the pulley system below?

  A. 1
  B. 2
  C. 3
  D. 4

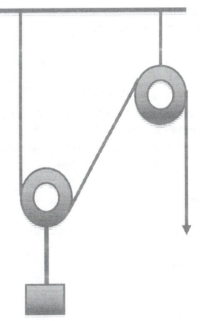

8. A piece of art of mass 200 kg is suspended from two nails so that the angle the hanging wires make is 40° with the horizontal. What is the tension in the hanging wires? (Note: Sin 40° = 0.64 and Cos 40° = 0.77).
   A.   1279 N
   B.   1524 N
   C.   1960 N
   D.   3048 N

9. Two cars driving in opposite directions collide. If you ignore friction and any other outside interactions, which of the following statements is always true?
   A.   The total momentum is conserved.
   B.   The sum of the potential and kinetic energy are conserved.
   C.   The total velocity of the cars is conserved.
   D.   The total impulse is conserved.

10. A bowling ball with a mass of 4 kilograms moving at a speed of 10 meters per second hits a stationary 1 kg bowling ball in a head-on elastic collision. What is the speed of the stationary ball after the collision?
   A.   0 m/s
   B.   10 m/s.
   C.   Less than 10 m/s, but not 0 m/s.
   D.   More than 10 m/s

11. Which statement best explains why the work done by a gravitational force on an object does not depend on the path the object takes?
   A.   Work depends on the path when there is friction. The longer the path the more energy is required to overcome friction.
   B.   Gravitational fields that arise from the interaction between point masses always produce elliptical paths of motion.
   C.   A falling object experiences a change in potential energy.
   D.   When an object falls down the work done by gravity is positive and when an object is thrown up the work done by gravity is negative.

12. A motorcycle weighs twice as much as a bicycle and is moving twice as fast. Which of the following statements is true?
   A.   The motor cycle has four times as much kinetic energy as the bicycle.
   B.   The motor cycle has eight times as much kinetic energy as the bicycle.
   C.   The bicycle and the motorcycle have the same kinetic energy.
   D.   The bicycle has four times as much kinetic energy as the motorcycle.

13. Two objects of masses m and M are a distance R apart. The force of their gravitational attraction is given by GmM/R^2. Their gravitational potential energy is given by $-GmM/R$. If the distance between these two objects doubles from 100 km to 200 km, what happens to the ratio of the gravitational force to the gravitational potential energy?
   A.   Doubled
   B.   Quadrupled
   C.   Halved
   D.   Quartered

14. How much does it cost to operate a 5 kilowatt electric motor for 12 hours if electricity is 6 cents per kilowatt-hour?
    A. $0.025
    B. $3.60
    C. $14.4
    D. $360

15. The equation for the amplitude of the motion of an object undergoing simple harmonic motion is A sin (5 t). Assuming the wave's phase is measured in radians, what is the period of the motion?
    A. Sin (5 t)
    B. 0.2 seconds
    C. 1.26 seconds
    D. A

16. What is the speed of a wave with a frequency of 12 Hz and a wavelength of 3 meters?
    A. 12 meters per second
    B. 36 meters per second
    C. 4 meters per second
    D. 0.25 meters per second

17. Transverse travelling waves propagate through a taut string of length 20 meters at a speed of 4 m/s. Standing waves are set up in this string which is fixed at both ends. What is the smallest frequency possible for the standing waves?
    A. 0.1 Hz
    B. 0.05 Hz
    C. 0.2 Hz
    D. 0.4 Hz

18. The speed of a travelling wave in a stretched string is given by $\sqrt{T/\mu}$, where T is the tension in the string and μ is the mass per unit length. A 2 meter long stretched string with a mass of 0.010 kilograms is made to resonate with standing waves at 50 Hz. What tension in the string is needed to produce the fourth harmonic? (Note: the fourth harmonic fits 2 full waves into the length of the string).
    A. 12.5 newtons
    B. 25 newtons
    C. 50 newtons
    D. 10,000 newtons

19. A hydraulic lift needs to raise a 3.5×10^3 newton truck. The input piston has a diameter of 2.0 cm and the output piston has a diameter of 24 cm. What minimum force must be applied to the input piston?
    A. 24 N
    B. 292 N
    C. 42,000 N
    D. 504,000 N

20. An incompressible ideal fluid is flowing through a pipe 5.0 cm in radius at a speed of 6.0 m/s. The pipe narrows to 3.0 cm. What is the speed of flow in the narrower section?
  A. 10 m/s
  B. 3.6 m/s
  C. 16.7 m/s
  D. Can't be determined from the given information.

21. Which statement correctly describes the elastic limit of a metal rod?
  A. The elastic limit occurs when a deformed object will no longer return to its original shape.
  B. The elastic limit occurs when the rod breaks.
  C. The elastic limit occurs when the stress stops producing a strain.
  D. The elastic limit assumes that the forces between molecules in a metal act like springs.

22. A charge +2q is placed at the origin of a coordinate system and a charge of -q is placed at a distance d from the origin. How far from the origin must a third charge +q be placed so that the net force on it is 0 newtons?
  A. Less than d/2
  B. Between d/2 and d
  C. Between d and 2d
  D. Greater than 2d

23. An electron moves in a uniform electric field in the same direction as the electric field from point A to point B. Which of the following statements is true?
  A. The potential energy of the electron decreased
  B. The potential energy of the electron
  C. The potential energy of the electron remained constant
  D. The potential energy of the electron was converted into kinetic energy

24. The charged particle moving through a magnetic field will be subject to a force of F = qvB Sinθ, where q is the charge, v is the particle's velocity, B is the magnetic field strength, and θ is the particle's angle between the magnetic field vector and the velocity vector. Charged particles from space enter the earth's atmosphere all the time. For example, the Aurora Borealis or Northern Lights are created by positive and negative charges passing through the Earth's magnetic field. Assume a proton with a speed of 8.0×10^6 meters per second enters the Earth's magnetic field at an angle of 45°, at a point where the magnetic field is 0.5 Teslas. What is the magnetic force acting on the proton? Note: the proton has a charge of 1.6×10^{-19} coulombs.
  A. 6.4×10^{-17} newtons
  B. 4.5×10^{-17} newtons
  C. 4.5×10^{-13} newtons
  D. 5.5×10^{-17} tesla

25. A solenoid is made of loops of wire, through which a current is run. What is the purpose of putting a lot of loops into a solenoid?
  A. To increase the magnetic field inside the solenoid.
  B. To increate the magnetic field outside the solenoid.
  C. To decrease the magnetic field inside the solenoid.
  D. To decrease the magnetic field outside the solenoid.

26. Which of the following gives the correct order of electromagnetic radiation from the lowest frequency to the highest frequency?
    A. microwaves, UHF radio waves, x-rays, visible light
    B. UHF radio waves, microwaves, visible light, x-rays
    C. UHF radio waves, microwaves, visible light, x-rays
    D. microwaves, x-rays, visible light, UHF radio waves

27. Which of the following statements about electricity flowing through a circuit can be correctly derived from Ohm's law?
    A. Increasing the voltage decreases the current if the resistance remains unchanged.
    B. Increasing the current and the resistance decreases the voltage.
    C. Increasing the current increases the voltage if the resistance is unchanged.
    D. Decreasing the resistance increases the current if the voltage remains unchanged.

28. Consider one tungsten wire of length L and cross-sectional area A and another tungsten wire of length $2L$ and area $2A$. Assuming both wires are the same temperature, which of the following statements is true?
    A. The resistance of the two wires is the same.
    B. The resistance of the longer wire is twice the resistance of the shorter wire.
    C. The resistance of the longer wire is half the resistance of the shorter wire.
    D. The resistance of the longer wire is four times the resistance of the shorter wire.

29. Adding multiple capacitors to a circuit is much the opposite as adding multiple resistors. Adding resistors in series, for example, creates an effective resistance equal to their sum. To add resistors in parallel, you must add the reciprocals of their resistance. With capacitors, however, you use reciprocals when adding them in series and you sum the capacitance when adding in parallel. Given the following diagram, what is the total capacitance of the circuit?

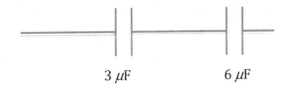

3 μF   6 μF

    A. 2-microfarads
    B. 9-microfarads
    C. 0.5-microfarads
    D. 4.5 microfarads

30. A miniature heater has a power rating of 50 watts and is connected to a battery with an electromotive force of 10 volts. What current flows through the heater?
    A. 500 amperes
    B. 5 amperes
    C. 200 milliamperes
    D. 3.1×10^{19} electrons per second

31. A lens forms an upright image 19 cm from a lens of an object 49 cm from the lens. The object and image are on the same side of the lens. What is the magnification of the image?
   A. 0.39
   B. 2.6
   C. 13.7
   D. 31.2

32. Which of the forces depicted below produces a counter-clockwise torque around the pivot point?

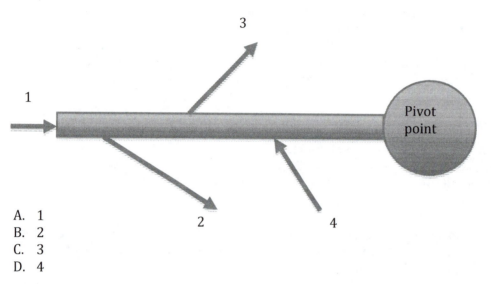

   A. 1
   B. 2
   C. 3
   D. 4

33. You blow up a rubber balloon and hold the opening tight with your fingers. You then release your fingers, causing air to blow out of the balloon. This pushes the balloon forward, causing the balloon shoots across the room. Which of Newton's laws best explains the cause of this motion?
   A. First law
   B. Second law
   C. Third law
   D. Law of gravity

34. Which has a greater moment of inertia about an axis through its center: a solid cylinder or a hollow cylinder? Both cylinders have the same mass and radius.
   A. Solid cylinder
   B. Hollow cylinder
   C. Both have same moment of inertia.
   D. It depends on how quickly the cylinders are rolling.

35. Astronauts in orbit are sometimes considered to be "weightless." Consider the four propositions about *weightlessness* and determine which ones are true.
I. Weightlessness occurs in outer space because the force of gravity becomes negligible.
II. Weightlessness occurs when a ski jumper makes a jump.
III. Weightlessness occurs when you roll a baseball on the ground.
   A. I only.
   B. II only.
   C. I and II.
   D. I, II and III.

36. The potential energy of a spring is represented as $\frac{1}{2}kx^2$, where k represents the spring constant and x is the displacement of the spring from its position when it is not stretched. A massless spring is suspended from a support and a 100-g mass is attached, stretching it 2 centimeters. If another 100-g mass is attached, what is the new potential energy of the spring?
    A. Half as much as with one 100-g mass attached.
    B. One-forth as much as with one 100-g mass attached.
    C. Twice as much as with one 100-g mass attached.
    D. Four times as much as with one 100-g mass attached.

37. Which of the following statement about refraction is true.
    A. Refraction means a change in direction of the wave.
    B. The angle of reflection equals the angle of refraction.
    C. The frequency in a refracted wave changes.
    D. The phase of a refracted wave changes.

38. What corresponds to the amplitude of a sound wave?
    A. loudness
    B. pressure differential of fluctuations
    C. magnitude of motion of air molecules
    D. power

39. The density of helium is much lower than that of air. How does the speed of sound traveling through helium gas compare to the speed of sound in air?
    A. It is faster
    B. It is slower
    C. It is the same speed
    D. It cannot be determined without knowing their atomic masses

40. What property of a sound wave in air corresponds to the frequency of the sound?
    A. pitch
    B. high and low
    C. timbre
    D. overtones

Quantitative Reasoning

1. A man decided to buy new furniture from Futuristic Furniture for $2600. Futuristic Furniture gave the man two choices: pay the entire amount in one payment with cash, or pay $1000 as a down payment and $120 per month for two full years in the financial plan. If the man chooses the financial plan, how much more would he pay?
   A. $1480 more
   B. $1280 more
   C. $1600 more
   D. $2480 more

2. What is the value of r in the following equation?
$29 + r = 420$
   A. $r = 29/420$
   B. $r = 420/29$
   C. $r = 391$
   D. $r = 449$

3. If 35% of a paycheck was deducted for taxes and 4% for insurance, what is the total percent taken out of the paycheck?
   A. 20%
   B. 31%
   C. 39%
   D. 42%

4. In the year 2000, 35% of the company sales were in electronics. The table below shows how electronic sales have changed for the company over the years. Find the percent of electronics sold in 2005.

Years	Change
2000 - 2001	-2
2001 - 2002	-1
2002 - 2003	+6
2003 - 2004	-1
2004 - 2005	+2

   A. 2%
   B. 11%
   C. 39%
   D. 42%

5. A woman wants to stack two small bookcases beneath a window that is $26\frac{1}{2}$ inches from the floor. The larger bookcase is $14\frac{1}{2}$ inches tall. The other bookcase is $8\frac{3}{4}$ inches tall. How tall with the two bookcases be when they are stacked together?
   A. 12 inches tall
   B. $23\frac{1}{4}$ inches tall
   C. $35\frac{1}{4}$ inches tall
   D. 41 inches tall

- 368 -

6. Solve for y in the following equation if $x = -3$

$y = x + 5$

    A. $y = -2$
    B. $y = 2$
    C. $y = 3$
    D. $y = 8$

7. Put the following integers in order from greatest to least:

-52, 16, -12, 14, 8, -5, 0

    A. -52, 16, -12, 14, 8, -5, 0
    B. 0, -5, 8, -12, 14, 16, -52
    C. -5, -12, -52, 0, 8, 14, 16
    D. 16, 14, 8, 0, -5, -12, -52

8. If number x is subtracted from 27, the result is -5. What is number x?

    A. 22
    B. 25
    C. 32
    D. 35

9. What is the simplest way to write the following expression?

$5x - 2y + 4x + y$

    A. $9x - y$
    B. $9x - 3y$
    C. $9x + 3y$
    D. $x ; y$

10. Find the sum.

$(3x^2 + x + 3) + 8x^2 + 5x + 16$

    A. $7x^2 + 29 x^2$
    B. $11x^2 + 6x + 19$
    C. $30x + 19$
    D. $(3x^2 + 3x) + 13x^2 + 16$

11. What is the perimeter of the following figure?

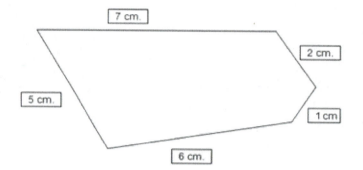

A. 15cm
B. 18cm
C. 21 cm
D. 36cm

12. To begin making her soup, Jennifer added four containers of chicken broth with 1 liter of water into the pot. Each container of chicken broth contains 410 milliliters. How much liquid is in the pot?

A. 1.64 liters
B. 2.64 liters
C. 5.44 liters
D. 6.12 liters

13. According to the table below, which snack is made with no more than 4 grams of sugar and between 4-6 grams of carbohydrates?

Snack (amount per serving)	Grams of Sugar per Serving	Grams of Carbohydrates per Serving
Snappy Cookies (3)	6	8
Snappy Crackers (8)	6	4
Snappy Cheese (2)	0	0
Snappy Twisters (4)	4	5
Snappy Chews (20)	0	8

A. Snappy Cookies
B. Snappy Crackers
C. Snappy Cheese
D. Snappy Twisters

14. Which of the following fractions is halfway between 2/5 and 4/9?

A. 2/3
B. 2/20
C. 17/40
D. 19/45

- 370 -

15. Which of the following is the largest number?
   A. 1/2
   B. 3/8
   C. 7/16
   D. 13/54

16. Of the following expressions, which is equal to $6\sqrt{10}$?
   A. 36
   B. $\sqrt{600}$
   C. $\sqrt{360}$
   D. $\sqrt{6}$

17. Which number equals 2^{-3}?
   A. 1/2
   B. 1/4
   C. 1/8
   D. 1/16

18. What is the average of $\dfrac{7}{5}$ and 1.4 ?

   A. 5.4
   B. 1.4
   C. 2.4
   D. 7.4

19. Two numbers are said to be reciprocal if their product equals 1. Which of the following represents the reciprocal of the variable x ?
   A. $x - 1$
   B. $\dfrac{1}{x}$
   C. x^{-1}
   D. Both B and C.

20. A taxi service charges $5.50 for the first 1/5 of a mile, $1.50 for each additional 1/5 of a mile, and 20¢ per minute of waiting time. Joan took a cab from her place to a flower shop 8 miles away, where she bought a bouquet, then another 3.6 miles to her mother's place. The driver had to wait 9 minutes while she bought the bouquet. What was the fare?
   A. $20
   B. $120.20
   C. $92.80
   D. $91

21. Which of the following expressions is equivalent to the equation $3x^2 + 4x - 15$?
   A. $(x - 3)(x + 5)$
   B. $(x + 5)(3 + x^2)$
   C. $x(3x + 4 - 15)$
   D. $(x + 3)(3x - 5)$

- 371 -

22. Prizes are to be awarded to the best pupils in each class of an elementary school. The number of students in each grade is shown in the table, and the school principal wants the number of prizes awarded in each grade to be proportional to the number of students. If there are twenty prizes, how many should go to fifth grade students?

Grade	1	2	3	4	5
Students	35	38	38	33	36

   A. 5
   B. 4
   C. 7
   D. 3

23. Which of the following numbers is a prime number?
   A. 15
   B. 11
   C. 33
   D. 4

24. Which of the following expressions is equivalent to $3(\frac{6x-3}{3}) - 3(9x+9)$?
   A. $-3(7x+10)$
   B. $-3x+6$
   C. $(x+3)(x-3)$
   D. $3x^2-9$

25. Evaluate the expression $(x-2y)^2$ where x = 3 and y = 2.
   A. -1
   B. +1
   C. +4
   D. -2

26. Bob decides to go into business selling lemonade. He buys a wooden stand for $45 and sets it up outside his house. He figures that the cost of lemons, sugar, and paper cups for each glass of lemonade sold will be 10¢. Which of these expressions describes his cost for making *g* glasses of lemonade?
   A. $\$45 + \$0.1 \times g$
   B. $\$44.90 \times g$
   C. $\$44.90 \times g + 10$¢
   D. 90

27. Which of the following expressions is equivalent to $(3x^{-2})^3$?
   A. $9x^{-6}$
   B. $9x^{-8}$
   C. $27x^{-8}$
   D. $27x^{-4}$

28. Sally wants to buy a used truck for her delivery business. Truck A is priced at $450 and gets 25 miles per gallon. Truck B costs $650 and gets 35 miles per gallon. If gasoline costs $4 per gallon, how many miles must Sally drive to make truck B the better buy?
  A. 600
  B. 7500
  C. 340
  D. 740

29. Given the equation $\dfrac{3}{y-5} = \dfrac{15}{y+4}$, what is the value of y?
  A. 45
  B. 54
  C. $\dfrac{29}{4}$
  D. $\dfrac{4}{29}$

30. Which of the following expressions is equivalent to $(a)(a)(a)(a)(a)$ for all values of a, positive or negative?
  A. $5a$
  B. a^{-5}
  C. $a^{-\frac{1}{5}}$
  D. a^5

31.

English-Metric Equivalents	
1 meter	1.094 yard
2.54 centimeter	1 inch
1 kilogram	2.205 pound
1 liter	1.06 quart

A sailboat is 19 meters long. What is its length in inches?
  A. 254
  B. 1094
  C. 4826
  D. 748

- 373 -

Questions 32 and 33 are based upon the following table:

Kyle bats third in the batting order for the Badgers baseball team. The table shows the number of hits that Kyle had in each of 7 consecutive games played during one week in July.

Day of Week	Number of Hits
Monday	1
Tuesday	2
Wednesday	3
Thursday	1
Friday	1
Saturday	4
Sunday	2

32. What is the mode of the numbers in the distribution shown in the table?
   A. 1
   B. 2
   C. 3
   D. 4

33. What is the mean of the numbers in the distribution shown in the table?
   A. 1
   B. 2
   C. 3
   D. 4

34. $(2a^2b - 3c^3)(3a^3b + 4c) =$
   A. $5a^6b^2 + 12c^4 - 9a^3bc^3 - 12c^4$
   B. $5a^5b^2 + 8a^2bc - 9a^3bc^3 + 12c^4$
   C. $6a^5b^2 + 8a^2bc - 9a^3bc^3 + 12c^4$
   D. $6a^5b^2 + 8a^2bc - 9a^3bc^3 - 12c^4$

35. In the following inequality, solve for x.
$-4x + 8 \geq 48$
   A. $x \geq 10$
   B. $x \geq -10$
   C. $x \leq 10$
   D. $x \leq -10$

36. Two even integers and one odd integer are multiplied together. Which of the following could be their product?
   A. 3.75
   B. 9
   C. 16.2
   D. 24

37. There are 80 mg / 0.8 ml in Acetaminophen Concentrated Infant Drops. If the proper dosage for a four year old child is 240 mg, how many milliliters should the child receive?
    A. 0.8 ml
    B. 1.6 ml
    C. 2.4 ml
    D. 3.2 ml

38. Using the chart below, which equation describes the relationship between x and y?

    A. x = 3y
    B. y = 3x
    C. y = 1/3x
    D. x/y = 3

x	y
2	6
3	9
4	12
5	15

39. On a highway map, the scale indicates that 1 inch represents 45 miles. If the distance on the map is 3.2 inches, how far is the actual distance?
    A. 45 miles
    B. 54 miles
    C. 112 miles
    D. 144 miles

40. What fractional part of an hour is 400 seconds?
    A. 1/5
    B. 1/6
    C. 1/7
    D. 1/9

- 375 -

Answers and Explanations

Natural Science

Biology

1. C: The hydrogen bonds between water molecules cause water molecules to attract each other (negative pole to positive pole. and "stick" together. This gives water a high surface tension, which allows small living organisms, such as water striders, to move across its surface. Since water is a polar molecule, it readily dissolves other polar and ionic molecules such as carbohydrates and amino acids. Polarity alone is not sufficient to make something soluble in water, however; for example, cellulose is polar but its molecular weight is so large that it is not soluble in water.

2. A: Long term energy storage in animals takes the form of fat. Animals also store energy as glycogen, and plants store energy as starch. , but these substances are for shorter-term use. Fats are a good storage form for chemical energy because fatty acids bond to glycerol in a condensation reaction to form fats (triglycerides). This reaction, which releases water, allows for the compacting of high-energy fatty acids in a concentrated form.

3. A: A cofactor is an inorganic substance that is required for an enzymatic reaction to occur. Cofactors bind to the active site of the enzyme and enable the substrate to fit properly. Many cofactors are metal ions, such as zinc, iron, and copper.

4. B: Proteins in the inner membrane of the mitochondrion accept high-energy electrons from NAD and $FADH_2$, and in turn transport protons from the matrix to the intermembrane space. The high proton concentration in the intermembrane space creates a gradient which is harnessed by ATP synthase to produce ATP.

5. C: Although there are two cell divisions in meiosis, DNA replication occurs only once. It occurs in interphase I, before M phase begins.

6. D: The ovary houses the ovules in a flower. Pollen grains fertilize ovules to create seeds, and the ovary matures into a fruit.

7. A: The actual wood of a tree trunk is made of dead xylem tissue. It does not function in the transport of water, but rather functions only in support.

8. C: The phloem transports carbohydrates from the shoot to the roots. Phloem tissue is living and is located outside the xylem.

9. D: When Ca^{2+} channels open, calcium enters the axon terminal and causes synaptic vesicles to release neurotransmitter into the synaptic cleft.

10. E: The placenta secretes progesterone and estrogen once a pregnancy is established. Early in pregnancy, the placenta secretes hCG.

11. D: At the lowest trophic level are the producers, followed by primary consumers. Primary carnivores follow consumers, followed by secondary carnivores.

12. D: Type I curves describe species in which most individuals survive to middle age, after which deaths increase. Dolphins have few offspring, provide extended care to the young, and live a long time.

13. A: Transportation by humans or human-associated means is not considered a natural dispersal process.

14. C: According to Hardy-Weinberg equilibrium, $p + q = 1$ and $p^2 + 2pq + q^2 = 1$. In this scenario, $q^2 = 0.25$, so $q = 0.5$. p must also be 0.5.

15. E: Structures are homologous because they derive from a common ancestor. Insects do not share a common ancestor with birds and mammals. Birds and mammals share a reptile ancestor.

16. B: The bonds between hydrogen and oxygen in water involve shared electrons and are therefore covalent. But the electrons are shared unequally because oxygen is more electronegative than hydrogen, so the shared electrons are more attracted to oxygen. Hydrogen – oxygen bonding *between* water molecules is an example of hydrogen bonding.

17. A: Amino acids contain carbon, oxygen, nitrogen, hydrogen, and sometimes sulfur. Polypeptides do not contain phosphate as an integral component. However, they may be phosphorylated by an enzyme following translation.

18. C: Coenzymes are organic cofactors that are necessary for certain enzymatic reactions. Cofactors bind to the active site and allow the substrate to fit properly. Many coenzymes are vitamins, some of which are not made by cells but must be obtained through the diet.

19. B: The activation energy, or peak, is lower in curve 2, which means that a catalyst was present. Enzymes work by lowering the activation energy of reactions.

20. D: Oxygen is the final electron acceptor, which is why oxygen is required for cellular respiration. Oxygen combines with two electrons and two protons to form water, one of the waste products of cellular respiration. The other waste product is carbon dioxide.

21. E: Auxin controls cell wall plasticity and is produced at root and shoot tips. It controls the responses of these structures to light and gravity.

22. A: When the CO_2 concentration is high, more carbonic acid is formed, and the body needs to increase respiration to remove it from the blood. Thus, a drop in pH causes an increase in the respiratory rate.

23. C: GABA is an inhibitory neurotransmitter in the brain, although it may occasionally function as an excitatory neurotransmitter.

24. E: Because we are not told whether the parent plants are homozygous or heterozygous, it is not possible to determine the dominance of one allele over another.

25. A: If the genes were unlinked, a 9:3:3:1 distribution of phenotypes would appear in the F2 generation because of independent segregation of the traits.

26. E: Phosphorus, like other minerals such as calcium and magnesium, is found in its largest quantities in rocks and other sediments. It is released into the environment through erosion. Synthetic fertilizer is the main source of phosphorous for crop plants.

27. B: Species that inhabit a particular ecosystem that were transported by humans to that location are called introduced species. They may or may not be invasive, depending on whether or not they displace native species.

28. D: Darwin and Mendel were contemporaries but were apparently not aware of each other's work. Around the beginning of the 20th century, Mendel's discoveries about genetics were incorporated into Darwinism, resulting in what is called the modern synthesis.

29. E: The variation caused by mutation is the raw material for natural selection.

30. A: Genetic drift is the random change in allele frequencies. In a small population, some alleles may increase or decrease for no other reason than by chance.

31. A: Osmosis is the movement of water molecules (not solutes) across a semi-permeable membrane. Water moves from a region of higher concentration to a region of lower concentration. Osmosis occurs when the concentrations of a solute differ on either side of a semi-permeable membrane. For example, a cell (containing a higher concentration of water) in a salty solution (containing a lower concentration of water) will lose water as water leaves the cell. This continues until the solution outside the cell has the same salt concentration as the cytoplasm.

32. D: Both prokaryotes and eukaryotes interact with the extracellular environment and use membrane-bound or membrane-associated proteins to achieve this. They both use diffusion and active transport to move materials in and out of their cells. Prokaryotes have very few proteins associated with their DNA, whereas eukaryotes' DNA is richly studded with proteins. Both types of living things can have flagella, although with different structural characteristics in the two groups. The most important differences between prokaryotes and eukaryotes are the lack of a nucleus and membrane-bound organelles in prokaryotes.

33. D: Enzymes act as catalysts for biochemical reactions. A catalyst is not consumed in a reaction, but, rather, lowers the activation energy for that reaction. The potential energy of the substrate and the product remain the same, but the activation energy—the energy needed to make the reaction progress—can be lowered with the help of an enzyme.

34. C: Lactic acid fermentation converts pyruvate into lactate using high-energy electrons from NADH. This process allows ATP production to continue in anaerobic conditions by providing NAD^+ so that ATP can be made in glycolysis.

35. B: DNA wrapped around histone proteins is called chromatin. In a eukaryotic cell, DNA is always associated with protein; it is not "naked" as with prokaryotic cells.

36. D: Each time a cell divides; a few base pairs of DNA at the end of each chromosome are lost. Telomerase is an enzyme that uses a built-in template to add a short sequence of DNA over and

over at the end of chromosomes—a sort of protective "cap". This prevents the loss of genetic material with each round of DNA replication.

37. A: The large intestine's main function is the reabsorption of water into the body to form solid waste. It also allows for the absorption of vitamin K produced by microbes living inside the large intestine.

38. D: Positive feedback from rising levels of estrogen in the menstrual cycle produces a sudden surge of luteinizing hormone (LH). This high level triggers ovulation.

39. D: A lineage map describes the fates of cells in the early embryo: in other words, it tells which germ layer different cells will occupy. In some small organisms such as the nematode *Caenorhabditis elegans*, all of the adult cells can be traced back to the egg. A lineage map is not a mechanism of embryo development, but rather a tool for describing it.

40. E: An individual with AB blood is tolerant to both the A carbohydrate on red blood cells and the B carbohydrate as "self" and can therefore accept any of the 4 different blood types.

General Chemistry

1. B: Na (sodium) is a solid at standard temperature and pressure, which is 0°C (273 K) and 100 kPa (0.986 atm), according to IUPAC. The stronger the intermolecular forces, the greater the likelihood of the material being a solid. Kr and Xe are noble gases and have negligible intermolecular attraction. NH_3 has some hydrogen bonding but is still a gas at STP. Sodium is an alkali metal whose atoms are bonded by metallic bonding and is therefore a solid at STP.

2. B: The ideal gas law PV=nRT is rearranged to solve for V, and we get V = nRT/P. R is the gas constant, 0.08206 L atm/mol K, and the Celsius temperature must be converted to Kelvin, by adding 273 to 25°C to obtain 298 K. The pressure must be converted to atmospheres, which 101 kPa is essentially 1 atm (0.9967 atm). Plugging the numbers into the equation we get V = 1000 mol (0.08206 L atm/mol K)(298 K)/1 atm, which gives V = 24,453 L. A liter is a cubic decimeter (dm^3) and when converted gives V = 24.5 m^3.

3. D: London dispersion forces are the weakest intermolecular forces. These interactions occur in all molecules due to unequal electron density around the nucleus, which results in a momentary dipole. Dipole-dipole interactions are those between two polar molecules. The more positive portion of one molecule is attracted to the negative portion of a different molecule. Hydrogen bonding is a stronger type of dipole-dipole interaction which occurs between a hydrogen in one molecule and a nitrogen, oxygen or fluorine atom in another molecule. Hydrogen bonding only occurs between molecules containing H-F, H-O or H-N bonds. Ionic bonds are the strongest intermolecular forces. In ionic molecules, a positive ion is attracted to a negative ion. NaCl is entirely ionic with full charge separation, and the ions are tightly bound to each other in an organized crystalline network.

4. C: To convert from degrees Celsius to Kelvin, add 273. 75° C is equivalent to 348 K. Both X and Y have lower boiling points, which means that they will each boil in the water bath. Z will never become warm enough to boil.

5. B: Since both the volume and the temperature remain fixed, the only variable that changes is the number of moles of particles. Because there are now 3 times the number of particles as there were originally, the pressure must increase proportionately and so the pressure must be 3 atm.

6. C: Normality refers to the concentration of acid equivalents (H^+ ions), not the concentration of the solute. 100 g of phosphoric acid has a MW of 98 g/mol. So, 100g/98 g/mol = 1.02 moles of phosphoric acid are in solution. The total volume of the solution is 0.4 L, so the molarity of the solution is 1.02 mol/0.4 L = 2.55 M. Since there are three acid equivalents for every mole of phosphoric acid, the normality is 3 x 2.55 = 7.65 N.

7. D: 100 mL of a 0.1 M solution of NaOH contains 0.01 moles of NaOH. That means 0.01 moles of acid are required to completely neutralize the solution. The MW of sulfuric acid is 98, so 0.98 g of sulfuric acid is 0.01 mole. But since sulfuric acid has two equivalents of acid per mole, only 0.005 mole of the acid is required or 0.49 g.

8. D: Octane is a nonpolar hydrocarbon with little or no water solubility. Butanol is an alcohol with a small amount of solubility due to its polar –OH group. Ethanol is a smaller, more polar alcohol that is very soluble in water. NaCl is an ionic salt that is highly soluble in water.

9. B: Ethane is an alkane and only very weakly acidic. Methanol, an alcohol, has a slightly acidic proton attached to the oxygen. Acetic acid is much more acidic than methanol with the acidic proton attached to the carboxyl group. Hydrochloric acid is highly acidic and completely dissociates in water.

10. B: Beta emission represents the spontaneous decay of a neutron into a proton with the release of an electron. Therefore the resulting nucleus will have one more proton than it did before the reaction, and protons represent the atomic number of an atom. Alpha decay results in the emission of a helium nucleus. The resulting nucleus of an alpha decay would lose two protons and two neutrons, causing a decrease in both the atomic number and the mass number. Gamma decay does not affect the numbers of protons or neutrons in the nucleus. It is an emission of a photon, or packet of energy.

11. D: Isotopes of the same element must have the same chemical behavior, so A, B, and C all represent, in one form or another, chemical behavior. Isotopes differ in mass, and this can be used to separate them by some appropriate physical property.

12. B: Phosphorus is in the third period, so the outermost levels must be 3s, 3p. Phosphorus is in Group 5A, which indicates that it has 5 valence electrons. To fill the 3s and 3p, 2 electrons first fill the s orbital, and then the remaining 3 electrons enter the p orbitals. So, $3s^2 3p^3$.

13. B: The trend within any column of the periodic table is that electronegativity decreases going down the column.

14. B: Hybrid orbitals arrange themselves to be as far from each other as possible. An sp^2 atom has three hybrid orbitals, so they arrange themselves to be trigonal planar, with 120 ° between the bonds.

15. A: By comparing the products to the reactants, there must be at least two Al atoms in the starting material, and at least three sulfate groups. Therefore, a coefficient of 2 must be placed in front of $Al(OH)_3$ and a coefficient of 3 must be placed in front of H_2SO_4. To make the number of

hydrogen and oxygen atoms equal on both sides of the equation, a coefficient of 6 must be placed in front of H_2O.

16. C: The equation shows that for every liter of methane reacted, one liter of CO_2 and 2 liters of water vapor will be produced. So a total of three liters of gaseous products will be formed for every liter of methane burned. Because the temperature of the reaction products is 200 °C, the water produced will be in vapor (gas) form and not in liquid form. Since 10L of methane were burned, 30 L of gaseous products were formed.

17. D: 0.5 g of the salt dissolved, which is 0.005 mol of the salt. Since the volume is 1 L, the molarity of the salt is 0.005 M. This means that both species X and Y are present at 0.005 M concentration. The K_{sp} = [X][Y], or [0.005][0.005] which equals 2.5×10^{-5}.

18. C: HCl is a strong acid that will completely dissociate. pH = $-\log_{10}[H^+]$, which for this problem is pH=$-\log_{10}(0.1)$ = 1. The volume of the solution has no bearing on the pH since we know the concentration.

19. A: When liquid water changes to steam, the temperature is constant, as in all phase changes. The entropy increases due to the increase in disorder from a liquid to a gas.

20. A: The longest straight chain of carbons is four, so the parent name is butane. The alcohol takes number precedence, so it is in the -2- position, placing the methyl in the -3- position. The suffix becomes –ol since it is an alcohol, so the name is 3-methyl-2-butanol.

21. B: Cis isomers have substituent groups that are on the same side of the molecule across the double bond. Trans isomers are those with substituent groups that are on opposite sides of the molecule across the double bond. I is neither cis nor trans, since both substituents on the same carbon are identical. IV is trans because the two methyl groups are on opposite sides of the molecule. II is cis due to both ethyl groups being on the same side of the molecule. III is also considered cis, although each substituent is different. The heaviest groups on each end of the double bond must be on the same side of the double bond to be cis.

22. B: Freezing is an exothermic event; therefore heat must be given off. The temperature of the material remains unchanged at the freezing point during the process.

23. B: Neutrons are neutral in charge, and can impact a nucleus in order to break it.

24. D: An alpha particle is a helium nucleus, which contains two protons and two neutrons.

25. D: All of the elements belong to the same row in the periodic table. Atomic radii increase going from right to left in any row of the periodic table. Although these elements belonged to the same row, it is important to also know that atomic radii increase from top to bottom in the groups of the periodic table.

26. A: Sublimation is the process of a solid changing directly into a gas without entering the liquid phase. Fusion refers to a liquid turning into a solid. Diffusion is the process of a material dispersing throughout another. Condensation is generally a gas turning into a liquid.

27. C: The more s character the bond has, the shorter it will be. A triple bond is stronger and shorter than a double bond, which is stronger and shorter than a single bond. An sp orbital is found in a triple bond. An sp^2 orbital is found in a double bond and sp^3 orbitals are found in single bonds.

28. D: Resonance structures have the same atoms connected to the same atoms, but differ only in electronic structure amongst the atoms. Isomers are molecules that have the same formula but differ in structure. Structural isomers differ in how the atoms are bonded to each other. Stereoisomers are isomers that have the same bonding structure but different arrangements, for example, cis- and trans- isomers.

29. A: Since the atomic number is 20, which represents the number of protons in the atom, there must be an equal number of electrons in a neutral atom. Protons have a positive charge and electrons are negative. Equal numbers of protons and electrons will result in a neutral atom, or zero charge.

30. C: A pressure increase will force the reaction to go further to the right, which lowers gas pressure to restore equilibrium. Since the water formed is in the liquid phase, it does not appear in the equilibrium equation, so only 1 mole of gas is produced and is part of the equation.

Organic Chemistry

1. C: Molecular weights are expressed as grams per mole. Each additional carbon atom to the alkane requires two additional hydrogen atoms. The molecular formula of the alkane will therefore increase by $-CH_2-$, which incrementally increases the molecular weight by 14 g per mole.

2. A: This is the definition of a functional group. "Substituent" refers to an atom or group of atoms attached to a specific carbon atom within a molecule and describes the structure of the molecule rather than its chemical behavior. A "diluent" is a solvent used to dilute the concentration of a solution. An "eluent" is a solvent used to elute materials in a chromatographic separation process.

3. B: The saturated hydrocarbon formula for a six-carbon molecule is C_6H_{14}. Two H atoms are lost for each site of unsaturation (a ring or a double bond to C). The difference of 8 H atoms in the two formulas means there are four sites of unsaturation, not three. Benzene is a highly flammable, sweet-smelling, oily liquid at room temperature. "Aromatic" refers to the electronic structure of the molecule, not to its odor.

4. A: Isomers must have the same molecular formula. Ethanol and propanol are both very soluble in water, and both are clear, colorless liquids at room temperature. The two formulas differ by one $-CH_2-$ unit, and are therefore two members of the homologous series of alcohols.

5. D: The two standard formulas, as written, portray different molecular structures and are therefore not the same. They do represent the same molecular formula, C_2H_6O, though not the same molecular structure, and therefore are isomeric. The molecular formula of methanol is CH_3OH, or CH_4O.

6. A: The carbonyl group is somewhat polarized by the electronegativity of the O atom relative to that of the C atom. With a mild acid catalyst, the carbonyl O atom can be protonated to form a carbonium ion stabilized by two $-OH$ groups. Addition of a molecule of H_2O to the C atom, followed by the loss of H^+ produces an acetal from an aldehyde or a ketal from a ketone. With a mild base

catalyst, an OH⁻ first adds to the carbonyl C atom and the resulting alkoxy anion extracts a proton from a water molecule to form the acetal or ketal and regenerate the OH⁻ ion.

7. B: An asymmetrically substituted *sp³* carbon atom is optically active and rotates the plane of plane-polarized light either clockwise or counter-clockwise. The order of priority of substituents about the axis of one of the bonds is either clockwise or counter-clockwise. The atom is thus described as having "handedness" or "chirality", as in left-handed or right-handed. It is a chiral center.

A conformer is a conformational isomer, such as the *chair* and *boat* conformations of the cyclohexane ring. It is a reactive center only if it is the location in the molecule at which a particular reaction occurs, which is not always the case. Stereoisomer describes the relative configurations of two or more chiral centers in a molecule.

8. D: Enantiomers are left-handed and right-handed versions of the same chemical compound. They therefore have identical physical properties. As enantiomers, their only difference is that they rotate the plane of plane-polarized light in opposite direction by an equal amount. Numerous methods have been developed by which enantiomers in a mixture can be separated from each other. When reacted with a compound having a single chiral center of known configuration, two new compounds are formed that have different molecular structures. These new compounds have different chemical and physical properties that permit their separation by normal methods. After being separated in this way, reversing or undoing the addition reaction releases the original enantiomers as a single pure isomer. Chromatographic methods that employ a chiral adsorbent also have the ability to separate enantiomers in a mixture.

9. C: Nitriles are characterized by the –CN functional group, in which the carbon atom is triply bonded to the nitrogen atom. Alkynes are characterized by a triple bond between two carbon atoms. Cycloalkenes are ringed structures which have a double bond between two carbon atoms. Alkenones contain both carbon-carbon double bonds and ketone carbonyl groups. "Aromatic" refers to the electronic structure of certain molecules, such as benzene, and describes the greater stability of the molecule due to the delocalization of electrons between adjacent and overlapping p-orbitals.

10. B: The oxidizing agent in Tollens' reagent is silver ion from silver oxide, Ag_2O. It will oxidize an aldehyde to a carboxylic acid. In this redox reaction, the silver ion is reduced from Ag^+ to Ag^o, or neutral silver atoms. This is a classic characterization test in which a positive result is indicated by the formation of a silver 'mirror' coating in the test tube.

11. B: Jones oxidations are carried out by the treatment of an alcohol or an aldehyde with a solution of CrO_3 in mild sulfuric acid solution. A solution of $K_2Cr_2O_7$ in concentrated sulfuric acid produces "chromic acid", a very strongly oxidizing solution sometimes used as a 'last resort' to clean chemical residues from laboratory glassware. Chromic acid oxidizes organic compounds completely to CO_2 and H_2O, and does not stop at the carboxylic acid stage of the process. Potassium permanganate, $KMnO_4$, and manganese dioxide, MnO_2, are also used as oxidizing agents, but neither of these is the Jones' reagent.

12. C: It is entirely possible that the molecules of the compound can decompose at the elevated temperatures before the boiling point of the material is attained. Reducing the pressure lowers the temperature at which materials boil, so distillation can occur before the material ever becomes hot enough to decompose. High-boiling materials do boil at normal pressure, but at temperatures that are high enough to be a concern in regard to safety, energy use, etc. Boiling point and vapor pressure are inversely related; higher vapor pressure means lower boiling point. The melting point of a compound is not related to its boiling point.

13. C: Monosaccharides are simple sugar molecules, or single carbohydrate molecules, such as glucose and fructose. They are cyclic compounds but do not have a carbonyl group when they are in that form, so they cannot be classified as either ketones or aldehydes. They have several –OH groups, as carbohydrates do, but they are not carboxylic acids.

14. A: The electron-withdrawing power of the carbonyl O atom draws electron density through the C=O π bond away from the α C-H bonds. This makes it easier for the sp^3 α carbon atom to hybridize to $sp^2 + p$ and form an extended π system. This renders the α position sufficiently acidic that a proton can be extracted by a strong base. The extra electron of the negative charge in the free p orbital is stabilized by delocalization into the carbonyl π orbital system. The negatively-charged ion formed by the extraction of an α proton is called an enolate ion because its structure is similar to the enol form of a carbonyl compound. Tertiary amines are generally not sufficiently strong bases to extract an α proton.

15. C: Friedel-Crafts reactions use strong Lewis acids to activate the benzene ring to the replacement of H atoms by alkyl or aryl substituent groups. The Lewis acid catalyst coordinates the π system of the benzene ring and the halide of the alkyl or aryl halide. This produces a good electrophile that can add to the benzene ring and displace a proton. The reaction can also be used for halogenation and acylation of benzene ring structures. Claisen condensation involves the addition of an enolate ion to an ester with loss of H_2O from the initial product to form an enone structure. Wittig reactions add a phosphine to a carbonyl group. Bicycloannulation reactions add two new ring structures to a substrate molecule in one step.

16. B: Diborane (B_2H_6) is a reducing agent used to convert aldehydes and ketones to alcohols. Therefore, the reaction of benzaldehyde with diborane produces benzyl alcohol. Benzoic acid is produced by oxidation of benzaldehyde. 9-BBN is a bulky, sterically hindered borane compound used to reduce aldehydes, ketones and other compounds in specific ways. Dibenzoyl has the structure indicated as C_6H_5-(C=O)-(C=O)-C_6H_5 and is not formed in the reaction.

17. C: The amine N atom coordinates one alkyl halide molecule to form a dialkylammonium halide species, which then loses HX to form a secondary amine. The secondary amine undergoes the same coordination–elimination sequence to form a tertiary amine from the intermediate trialkylammonium halide species. The tertiary amine coordinates the alkyl halide to form a tetraalkylammonium halide, but cannot eliminate HX. All three secondary and tertiary amines and quaternary ammonium salts are produced in the reaction.

18. B: This is the balanced equation. The other three are not balanced.

19. C: In simple terms, the loss of electrons is oxidation, and the gain of electrons is reduction. In a redox reaction, one species is reduced and another is oxidized. There must always be one of each for a redox reaction to occur. One species will be the reducing agent and the other will be the oxidizing agent. They have an equal but opposite effect on each other in that the reducing agent

gives up the same number of electrons as the oxidizing agent accepts. Since the reducing agent gives up electrons, it is oxidized, and similarly since the oxidizing agent accepts electrons, it is reduced.

20. A: The R- and S- designations of stereochemistry refer to the absolute order of substituents about an asymmetric center. To determine the order, one visualizes the molecule as seen in the direction of the bond to the lowest priority substituent, which in this case was the C-H bond. The priorities of the remaining three substituents are assigned from highest to lowest using the same rules as for E- and Z- designations. Their order then determines the designation as R- for clockwise order and S- for counterclockwise order. The D- and L- designations refer to the direction in which the compound rotates the plane of plane-polarized light passing through the molecules, D- for dextrorotatory, or to the right, and L- for levorotatory, or to the left.

21. C: The α,β-unsaturated ketone system is polarized by the carbonyl group through its extended π bond system. The carbonyl C atom and the β C atom are both subject to attack by a nucleophile. The Michael addition takes advantage of this to add a carbon nucleophile at the β position. This forms a new C-C bond and is irreversible because of that. The actual product of the reaction upon completion is an enol, but this immediately rearranges to the ketone form. The "Michelson-Morley experiment" was an exercise to measure the speed of light. "Michaelson reaction" and "Mitchell addition" are made-up terms and have no meaning.

22. C: The benzene ring is described as "aromatic" because of the extra stability imparted by the geometry of the molecule, the continuous overlap of the p orbitals in its π bond system, and the number of π electrons. The naphthalene molecule has the structure of two benzene rings fused together. That is, one of the C-C bonds is common to both rings. A vast array of molecules up to and including graphene can be constructed from fused benzene rings. This includes the compounds anthracene and phenanthrene. Compounds of three or more fused benzene rings are referred to as polyaromatic hydrocarbons, or PAHs. Simple hydrocarbons are the alkanes and other such compounds. PAHs do not contain carbonyl groups at all and therefore are not "diketo carbonyl compounds". Nor do they contain O atoms in a heterocyclic structure and so are not dioxins. PAHs are known to produce dioxins through incomplete combustion and reactions with molecular oxygen.

23. B: Carbon and nitrogen atoms are found bonded to each other in many types of compounds, not just in 1° amines. Thus they obviously do bond to each other, and the nitrile group, -CN, is characterized by the triple bond between the C and N atoms. An imine is characterized by the double bond between the C and N atoms, analogous to the double bond between C and O in the carbonyl group.

24. A: Lactones are formed by molecules that have both an –OH group and a –COOH group in their molecular structures. Lactams are formed by molecules that have both an –NH$_2$ or –NHR group and a –COOH group in their molecular structures. Intramolecular condensation reactions form a cyclic structure through formation of an ester or amide linkage.

25. C: The correct term is "conjugated", which refers to an alternating arrangement of single bonds and multiple bonds. Their relationship is alternant in some conjugated systems and non-alternant in other conjugated systems, such as in an amide. Conjugated bonds are not segregated, or isolated from each other, within the molecule.

26. A: The main bond between two *sp* or *sp²* hybridized atoms is the σ (sigma) bond directly between them. A second bond is formed between the two atoms by the sideways overlap of the adjacent *p* orbitals. This is called a π (pi) bond. Electrons in the adjacent *p* orbitals are able to move freely, or delocalize, through the π bond system.

27. C: A racemic mixture contains exactly equal quantities of the two enantiomers of a chiral compound, and is therefore not optically active itself. A eutectic mixture consists of two or more different compounds in which the mixture has a lower melting point than the individual compounds. A diastereomeric mixture is a mixture of diastereomeric compounds, each having two or more chiral centers. A *meso-* structure is a molecule that contains two chiral centers in which the orientation of substituents about one of the centers is the mirror image of the orientation of substituents about the other center.

28. C: The Br_2/CCl_4 test is the characteristic test for the presence of C=C and C≡C bonds in an organic compound. The color due to Br_2 disappears as the Br_2 adds across the double or triple bond to form the corresponding dibromo compound. For example, cyclohexene would react with Br_2/CCl_4 to produce colorless 1,2-dibromocyclohexane.

29. C: 2,4-Dinitrophenylhydrazine adds as a nucleophile to the carbonyl carbon atom of aldehydes and ketones. Rearrangement and elimination of H_2O results in the formation of a 2,4-dintrophenylhydrazone, which is usually a highly-colored crystalline solid. This is a classic derivatization test used to identify and characterize aldehydes and ketones.

30. D: Proton signals in NMR exhibit "spin splitting" according to the number of different protons on adjacent carbon atoms. Protons experiencing identical magnetic environments produce identical signals, so the three protons of a single methyl group produce just one peak at about ⬚1.0. In an ethyl group, $-CH_2CH_3$, the three methyl protons are affected by the two $-CH_2-$ protons and their signal is split into three slightly different peaks called a "triplet". The $-CH_2-$ proton signal is split by the three $-CH_3$ protons into four slightly different peaks called a quartet. Integration of the quartet and the triplet sets of peaks is in the ratio of 2:3 respectively, according to the number of each different type of proton. There is certainly one ethyl group present indicated by this pattern, but it does not preclude the possibility that there may be two or more identical ethyl groups in the molecule. They would still have a 2:3 integration ratio, so in this case the correct answer is (D).

Reading Comprehension

1. B: Cilia and flagella are both organelles, which are defined in the first paragraph as sub-cellular structures that perform a particular function.

2. A: The second paragraph describes the function of cilia as providing fluid flow across the gills or the epithelia lining the digestive tract. The stomach is part of the digestive tract.

3. C: The third paragraph of the text describes 9 peripheral pairs of polymers, and 2 central ones, or 20 in all.

4. B: Tubulin and dynein are both defined as proteins in the text. Flagellin is a protein, but it is not mentioned in the text. Sonneborn is not a protein; he was a scientist.

5. B: The mechanism is described in detail in the fourth paragraph. Dynein causes the outer polymer pairs to slide past each other, not to bend. The inner polymers do not have dynein associated with them, so they are not involved in the bending. And the passage cites no evidence to suggest that the organelles contract.

6. C: Although the polymers in this passage are made of protein subunits, the definition is more general. The third paragraph tells us that in this case the subunits are tubulin proteins.

7. B: The fifth paragraph describes Sonneborn as "of Indiana University" and doing scientific research.

8. D: The experiment described in the fifth paragraph showed that the cilia always retained their original direction of rotation.

9. D: This is mentioned in the first paragraph.

10. B: The experiment demonstrated that the cilia's rotational direction was not dependent upon the DNA in their nuclei. Sonneborn performed his experiment with cilia, not with flagella.

11. C: The passage describes several distinctive features of annelid anatomy and tells how some of them differ from other worms.

12. A: The term is defined in the text as an organization of the anatomy into segments.

13. D: The term is defined in the text between commas.

14. C: The text gives the example of feet specializing into grasping organs to illustrate this evolutionary advantage of segmental plasticity.

15. B: *Nematodes* differ from the annelids in the structure of the coelum. *Lumbricus* and leeches are both members of the Annelida.

16. E: The text gives the example of parapodia modified for grasping to illustrate evolutionary plasticity among metameres.

17. B: The text states that the annelid coelum is formed later during embryology and probably evolved at a later time, as well.

18. E: The text indicates that the cerebral ganglia are enlarged, whereas the remaining ganglia in the nerve cord are merely repeating (unspecialized) units.

19. C: The text defines metemeres as segments, and discusses segmentation as the distinguishing feature of the phylum.

20. D: The paragraph tells us that annelids can live in salt or fresh water and on land, and then gives examples.

21. E: The text indicates that both nematodes and annelids possess a fluid-filled cavity which is involved in locomotion, or movement.

22. E: The last paragraph indicates that annelids occupy all the habitats listed and gives examples.

23. C: Sentence reads, "Your brain <u>filters</u> [your nose] out," which means your brain ignores it.

24. B: Only choice B reflects the meaning of the term "retina," which is a part of the eye's anatomy.

25. B: The final sentence reads, "Your brain works hard to make the world look continuous." It follows that visual perception is an active process, not a passive one, making choice B the best answer.

26. A: If the reader follows the instructions given in the paragraph, the O and X in the middle of the passage can be used to demonstrate the blind spot in the visual field. Choice A is the best answer.

27. B: The passage explains the way that visual perception works. Choice B is the best answer.

28. D: Much of the information in the passage is provided to show examples of how the brain fills in gaps in the visual field. Choice D is the best answer.

29. A: The author of the passage mentions the nose to demonstrate how the brain filters information out of the visual field. Choice A is the best answer.

30. B: Choice B can be inferred from the second paragraph. The paragraph states that the brain filters out information, which means that the brain does not perceive all activity in the visual field.

31. D: The main idea of the passage is that the immune system protects the body from infection. The author repeatedly alludes to the complexity and mystery of the immune system, so it cannot be true that scientists fully understand this part of the body. It is true that the immune system triggers the production of fluids, but this description misses the point. Similarly, it is true that the body is under constant invasion by malicious microbes; however, the author is much more interested in the body's response to these microbes. For this reason, the best answer choice is D.

32. C: The passage never states that viruses are extremely sophisticated. In fact, the passage explicitly states the opposite. The passage says that viruses are too primitive, or early in their development, to be classified as living organisms.

33. D: In the first paragraph, the word *ideal* means "perfect." Take a look at the context in which the word is used. The author is describing how many millions of microbes can live inside the human body. It would not make sense, then, for the author to be describing the body as a *hostile* environment for microbes. Moreover, whether or not the body is a confined environment would not seem to have much bearing on whether it is good for microbes. Rather, the paragraph suggests that the human body is a perfect environment for microbes.

34. B: The passage never states that the immune system ignores tumors. Indeed, at the beginning of the third paragraph, the author states that scientists remain puzzled by the body's ability to fight tumors. This question is a little tricky, because it is common knowledge that many tumors prove fatal to the human body. However, you should not take this to mean that the body does not at least try to fight tumors.

35. A: In the second paragraph, the word *enlist* means "call into service." The use of this word is an example of figurative language. In this case, the author is describing the efforts of the immune system as if they were a military campaign. The immune system *enlists* other cells, and then directs these *recruits* to areas where they are needed.

36. C: The author's primary purpose in writing this essay is to inform. The passage is written in a clear, declarative style with no obvious prejudice on the part of the author. The primary intention of the passage seems to be providing information about the immune system to a general audience.

37. D: The main idea of this passage is that vaccines help the immune system function properly. Answer choices A, B, and C express details from the passage, but only answer choice D is a comprehensive summary of the author's message.

38. C: This passage does not state that the symptoms of disease will not emerge until the body has learned to fight the disease. On the contrary, the passage implies that a person may become quite sick and even die before the body learns to effectively fight the disease.

39. B: In the third paragraph, the word *virulent* means "malicious." The word *virulent* could in some circumstances mean contagious or annoying. However, since the passage is not talking about transfer of the disease and is referring to a serious illness, malicious is the more appropriate answer.

40. C: The author's primary purpose in writing this essay is to inform. If the above passage took an objective look at the pros and cons of various approaches to fighting disease, we would say that the passage was a piece of analysis. Because the purpose of this passage is to present new information to the reader in an objective manner, however, it is clear that the author's intention is to inform.

Physics

1. B: Significant digits indicate the precision of the measurement. Answer B has 5 significant figures. A and C each have 4. D has 3. The leading zeros in Answers A and D and are not counted as significant digits, but zeros at the end of the number (as in Answers A and B) do count. In answer D, the zero in between 2 and 9 is significant.

2. C: Displacement is a vector that indicates the change in the location of an object. Answer A would be correct if the question asked for the total distance the person walked or if the person didn't change direction. If the person turned around 180°, the displacement could be as small as 5 meters. If the person changed directions only a fraction of a degree, its magnitude would be *less* than 13 meters, not as *large* as 13 meters.

3. B: The answer can be determined because the rate of acceleration is uniform. Since the acceleration is 5 m/s², the velocity increases by 5 m/s every second. If it starts at 20 m/s, after 1 second it will be going 25 m/s. After another second it will be going 30 m/s, so the total time is 2 seconds. You can also calculate this time by using the average speed. Since the object undergoes uniform acceleration, the average speed is 25 m/s. Using the distance traveled, the same result is obtained. $t = d / v = 50$ meters $/ 25$ m/s $= 2$ seconds.

4. A: Newton's first law (inertia) says an object in motion stays in motion, and an object at rest stays at rest, unless external forces act on them. I is an excellent demonstration because it shows the ball at rest and in motion. At rest, the ball stays at rest until a force acts on it. When the ball is moving, there is no force acting on the ball in the direction of motion. Thus, the natural state of the ball is to be at rest or moving with a constant speed. Ans. C is not a good demonstration because the force of friction is what makes it hard to move the heavy object. Ans B is a good demonstration of equilibrium and friction. Ans D, running a current through wires, has nothing to do with Newton's first law.

5. D: There will be a gravitational force of attraction between the two spheres determined by the universal constant of gravity, the distance between the spheres, and the mass of the spheres. Since both objects are affected by this force (remember, Newton's 3rd law says the force needs to be equal and opposite), both objects will experience a slight acceleration and start moving towards each other a tiny amount (when we ignore friction). Using $F = ma$, you know that the less massive sphere will experience a larger acceleration than the more massive one.

6. C: The weight of an object near Earth's surface is given by $W = mg$, where $g = 9.8$ m/s². The Earth exerts a force on the 10 kg object equal 10 kg x 9.8 m/s²= 98 N. This weight pulls on the lower spring, stretching it until it reads 98 N. The lower spring then exerts a force of 98 N on the upper spring, causing it to read 98 N.

7. B: The ideal mechanical advantage (IMA) of a simple machine ignores friction. It is the effort force divided into the resultant force. It is also the distance the effort force moves divided by the distance the resultant force moves. The IMA of a fixed pulley is 1 because all a fixed pulley does is change the direction of the effort force. A moveable pulley, however, doubles the force by increasing the distance by two. In this case, there is one fixed pulley and one floating pulley. Since the IMA of the fixed pulley is 1, and the floating pulley doubles this, the total IMA is 2.

8. D: The weight of the art is 200 kg x 9.8 m/s² = 1960 N. This is the total force pulling DOWN on the wires. However, the tension acts along a 40° angle, and the vertical force is T sinθ. However there are two ends to the wire, which splits the tension, meaning the weight is spread across 2T sinθ. So 2T sinθ = w. Therefore, T = ½ x 1960 N / sin(40) = 1524 N. Note: There's also a horizontal component to the tension forces, each expressed as T cosθ. The net force of the left and right tensions is zero. Answer A is calculated using the Cos(40) instead of Sin(40).

9. A: In a closed system (when you ignore outside interactions), the total momentum is constant and conserved. The total energy would also be conserved, although not the sum of the potential and kinetic energy. Some of the energy from the collision would be turned into thermal energy (heat) for example. Nor is the total velocity conserved, even though the velocity is a component of the momentum, since the momentum also depends on the mass of the cars. The impulse is a force over time that causes the momentum of a body to change. It doesn't make sense to think of impulse as conserved, since it's not necessarily constant throughout a collision.

10. D: Since this is a head-on elastic collision, you could use conservation of kinetic energy and momentum to actually solve this problem. However, in this case, you only need to think through the answers to arrive at a correct conclusion. Clearly the ball after it's struck won't be going 0 m/s. And since this is an elastic collision, and it is hit by a much larger ball, it must be going faster than the larger ball was originally moving. Therefore, the ball will be moving at more than 10 m/s. If this were an inelastic collision where the balls stuck together, the ball would final velocity would be less than 10 m/s.

11. C: To determine how much work is done by a gravitational force, you should calculate the change in that object's potential energy = mgh, where m = mass, g = the gravitational acceleration 9.8 m/s² and h = height. Therefore, the work done only depends on the change in height and not on the path taken. In Answer A, the work done by gravity doesn't have anything to do with friction, so this is not a good explanation. Friction is a separate force. Answer D, although true, doesn't explain why the work doesn't depend on the path.

12. B: Kinetic energy is the energy of motion and is defined as 1/2mv². Using this equation, if you double the mass and the velocity of an object, you find KE = 1/2(2m')(2v')² or 8 times the original KE. Therefore, the motorcycle has 8 times as much kinetic energy as the bicycle.

13. C: From the question, doubling distance would lower the gravitational force by a factor of 1/4, since the force is proportional to 1/R². The gravitational potential would be 1/2 of the original because it is proportional to 1/R. Therefore, the ratio of the new force to the new potential would be 1/4 ÷ 1/2, or 1/2 of the original ratio.

14. B: Power is the amount of work done divided by the time it took to do the work. A kilowatt-hour is a unit of work. A 5 KW engine running for 12 hours produces 5 x 12 = 60 kilowatt-hours of work. At $0.06 per Kw-h, this is 60 x 0.06 = $3.60. The other answers all occur from simple math mistakes.

15. C: The phase will cycle through 2π radians. Therefore, 5t = 2π and t = 2π/5 = 1.26 seconds.

16. B: The speed of a wave is the product of its wavelength and frequency. V = νf. Here, ν = 12 x 3 = 36 m/s.

17. A: A standing wave remains stationary, and the fixed points at both ends are the wave's nodes. Nevertheless, a standing waves with nodes at both ends of the string can have several forms. It may

have one anti-node (i.e., it will arc across), two anti-nodes (this looks like a sine wave), three anti-nodes (with 1.5 sine waves), etc. However, waves with just one anti-node will the longest wavelength and thus the smallest frequency. For a wave with one anti-node, the string will have only 1/2 of a wave, so 20 m represents a half-wavelength and the full wavelength is 40 m. Using the wave equation ($v = \lambda f$) gives the correct answer. f = v/λ = 4 m/s / 40 m = 0.1 Hz.

18. A: For standing waves, the string must be fixed at both ends. The wavelength at the fundamental frequency is 4 meters and the wavelength when the string resonates at the fourth harmonic is 1 meter. Using the wave equation $v = \lambda f$, the frequency at the fourth harmonic is v/1 m = 50 Hz. Hence the necessary speed is 50 m/s. Furthermore, the mass per unit length is 0.01 kg / 2 meters = 0.005 kg/m. Thus the tension is the string is $v^2 \times \mu = 50^2$ x 0.005 = 12.5 newtons.

19. A: Pascal's law is that the pressure on the input piston is equal to the pressure on the output piston. (To move the truck, of course, the input piston moves a much greater distance than the output piston.) Since the pressure depends on the area of the pistons, and the area = πr^2, you need only find the ratio of the two areas to find the necessary force. Since the diameter is twice the radius, you can simplify this step by taking the ratio of the square of the diameters. $2^2 / 24^2 = 0.007$. Multiplying this by the weight of the car gets 0.007 x 3500 N = 24 N. Remember also that the point of a hydraulic lift is to reduce the force, not increase it.

20. C: In an ideal fluid, from the conservation of mass, ρvA is constant. Since the area (A) decreases by a factor $3^2/5^2 = 0.36$, the speed increases by $5^2/3^2$. So 6 m/s x $5^2/3^2$ = 16.7 m/s. Incompressible means the density (ρ) is a constant. An ideal fluid has no viscosity, there is no rotational flow, and the flow is the same throughout the liquid, so answer D is not correct.
Concept of turbulence at high velocities

21. A: When an external force deforms a solid material, it will return to its initial position when the force is removed. This is called elasticity and is exhibited by springs. If too much force is applied and the elastic limit is exceeded, the rod won't return to its original shape any longer. As with springs, the deformation is directly proportional to the stress. The elastic limit occurs in rods subjected to a tensile force when the strain stops being directly proportional to the stress. The typical pattern when the force increases is that the strain increases linearly, then it doesn't increase as much, and then it breaks.

22. D: The third charge, which is positive, will be repelled by the charge of +2q and attracted to the charge of -q. For this reason, the third charge can't be between the two other charges and have a net force of 0, since it would always jointly be pushed and pulled towards the negative charge. It must be past the more distant negative charge. If the charge were situated at a distance of 2d from the origin, which is distance d from the negative charge, it would have a repulsive force of F = k (q)(2q) / (2d)^2 and an attractive force of F = k (q)(q) / (d)^2, meaning the attractive force is still too small by 1/2 the repulsive force. Thus the particle must be past the distance of 2d, or Answer D. If you solve this distance quadratically, the particle is at 3.41 d.

23. B: The direction of the electric field is the same as the direction of the force on a positive test charge. Moving a negative charge in the direction of the electric field requires an external force to oppose the electric field. This would increase the electron's potential energy.

24. C: The force F = qvB Sinθ = $(1.6 \times 10^{-19}$ coulombs$)(8.0 \times 10^6$ m/s$)(0.5$ T$)$ Sin (45) = 4.5 x 10^{-13} N.

25. A: Solenoids create a magnetic field inside the coils. Outside the solenoid, the magnetic field is practically zero, so increasing the number of coils won't have much effect on the exterior field strength. Inside the coils, increasing the number and density of coils increases the field strength.

26. C: Radio waves have the lowest frequency and the longest wavelength. Microwaves also have low frequencies and long wavelengths compared to visible light. X-rays are highly energetic and have higher frequencies and smaller wavelengths than visible light.

27. C: Ohm's law is that $V = IR$. Answer C is the only relation that holds true using this equation. If the resistance doesn't change, increasing the current on the right side must cause the voltage to also increase on the left side.

28. A: Answer A would be correct if the temperature of the two wires was the same. Wires have the least resistance when they are short and fat. This is expressed as $R = \rho L / A$, where ρ is the resistivity of the substance, L is the length and A is the area. Since both wires are tungsten, they must have the same resistivity. So doubling the length and area adds a factor of 2 to both the top and bottom of the equation, giving no change in overall resistance.

29. A: Since these capacitors are connected in series you must add the reciprocals of their capacitance. $1/C_{total} = 1/C_1 + 1/C_2$. So $1/C_{total} = 1/3 + 1/6 = 1/2$. Thus $C_{total} = 2$ microfarads.

30. B: Power is the rate at which work is done. It can be expressed as $P = VI$ or $P = IR^2$. With 10 volts and 50 watts, the current is $I = P/V = 50w / 10v = 5$ amps. Current is measured in coulombs/second, watts in joules/second, and volts in joules/coulomb. Answer D is equivalent to 5 amps since the charge on an electron is 1.6×10^{-19} coulombs.

31. A: The magnification of a lens can be calculated from its image distance, i, and its object distance, o. $M = i/o$. Here $M = 19/49 = 0.39$.

32. B: Clockwise is the direction the hands of a clock rotate when looking at the clock, so a counterclockwise torque would require a force that pushes or pulls down on the lever. The pivot point is the axis of rotation. We don't care about the components of these forces that push either to the left or right, since these components do not produce any torque. Force 1 is directed into the axis, so it produces no torque. Forces 3 and 4 both push up on the lever. The only force producing a counter-clockwise rotation is Force 2.

33. C: All three laws are operating, but the third law (forces come in equal and opposite pairs) best explains the motion. The first law (inertia) is shown from the fact that the balloon doesn't move until a force acts upon it. The second law ($F = ma$) is shown because you can see the force and the acceleration. The force comes from the contraction of the rubber balloon. The stretched rubber exerts a force on the air inside the balloon. This causes the air to accelerate in accordance with the second law. You can't see this acceleration because the air is invisible and because it is all the air in the room that the balloon is exerting a force on. However, the air in the room exerts and equal and opposite force on the balloon (this is Newton's third law), which causes the balloon to accelerate in the direction it did.

34. B: The moment of inertia of a point mass about any axis is given by mR^2, where R is the distance from the axis. The moment of inertia of a solid object is calculated by imagining that the object is made up of point masses and adding the moments of inertia of the point masses. The average radius of the particles in a hollow cylinder will be R (all the mass is at radius R). For a solid cylinder,

- 393 -

however, the average radius is less than R, meaning the overall moment of inertia will be smaller, which means Answer B is correct. To actually calculate the moment of inertia of a cylinder of thickness $R_2 - R_1$ is $\frac{1}{2}m(R_1^2 + R_2^2)$. For a solid cylinder, $R_1 = 0$ meters. For a hollow cylinder, $R_1 = R_2$.

35. B: The phenomenon known as weightlessness is caused by an object being in free fall. An object in space still experiences a gravitational force due to the earth, but if that object is in orbit, it's effectively free falling around the earth, which causes it to experience weightlessness. Here, proposition I is wrong because you have to be pretty far away from a star for gravity to become negligible. In fact, objects only stay in orbit because the earth's gravity pulls on them and causes them to change direction. This means the usual experience of weight is lost, as you can see by the floating objects and people inside an orbiting spaceship. The same thing happens to a ski jumper, who is in free fall after he or she jumps. If the jumper is carrying a rock, for example, that rock will feel weightless while the jumper is in the air. A rolled baseball is not in freefall and does not experience weightlessness.

36. D: The formula for the potential energy of a spring comes from calculating how much work is required to stretch a spring an amount x. Hooke's law applies so the force increases uniformly from 0 N to kx, where k is the spring constant. Hence, $PE = \frac{1}{2}kx^2$. There are two ways to solve this problem. If you recognize that doubling the mass will double how much the spring is stretched, you can easily see that $(2x)^2$ shows the potential energy of the spring quadruples. If you don't realize that the displacement doubles, you can easily prove it, since $F = ma = -kx$ for a spring. Doubling the mass would double the force, and thereby double the displacement x. The spring constant is just that, a constant, and will not change unless you use a different type of spring.
$PE = -GmM/r$ (gravitational, general)

37. A: Refraction occurs when a wave enters a new medium. The boundary between the old medium and the new medium produces a reflected wave and a refracted wave. Since the medium is different, the speed and direction of the refracted wave changes. This changes the wavelength, but the frequency remains the same. The angle of reflection depends on the angle of incidence of the wave that strikes the boundary. The angle of refraction depends partly on this angle of incidence, but also on the indices of refraction of the two substances. Although refraction is defined as a wave changing direction when it enters a new substance, a wave will not change direction if it enters this new medium exactly perpendicular to the surface.

38. B: When a tuning fork vibrates it creates areas of condensation (higher pressure) and rarefactions (lower pressure) that propagate through the air because of the air's elasticity. The distance between the condensations or rarefactions is the wavelength of the sound. The amplitude of the sound is half the difference between the pressure of the condensation and the pressure of the rarefaction. Loudness and power are both logarithmic measures that depend on the amplitude, but are not directly proportional to it. For example, doubling the amplitude will not double the loudness or power; those quantities will increase just slightly.

39. A: Sound travels much faster through helium than through air. Generally, the speed of sound can be calculated by speed = $\sqrt{(k \times P / \rho)}$, where k is the index of specific heats, P is pressure and ρ is density. Since helium has a much lower density, it would have a higher speed.

40. A: The frequency of a sound wave directly determines its pitch. We say the pitch of 480 Hz is higher than the pitch of 440 Hz. High and low are the words we use to describe pitch. Overtones refer to the frequencies above the fundamental frequency in a musical instrument. Two singers

singing the same note at the same loudness will sound differently because their voices have different timbres.

Quantitative Reasoning

1. B: Multiply $120 by 24 months (a full two years) to get $2880. Add the thousand dollars for the down payment to get $3880. Find the difference between the entire amount all at once ($2600) and the amount pain in the plan ($3800). To find the difference, you subtract. The difference shows that $1280 more is paid with the installment plan.

2. C:
$29 + r = 420$
$29 + r - 29 = 420 - 29$
$r = 391$

3. C: To solve, find the sum. 35% + 4% = 39%

4. C: Electronics sales $= x$
$x = 35 + (-2) + (-1) + (+6) + (-1) + (+2)$
$x = (35 + 6 + 2) + (-2 + (-1) + (-1))$
$x = (43) + (-4)$
$x = 39$

5. B: Add to solve. The height of the window from the floor is not needed in this equation. It is extra information. You only need to add the heights of the two bookcases. Change the fractions so that they have a common denominator. After you add, simplify the fraction.
$14\frac{1}{2} + 8\frac{3}{4}$
$= 14\frac{2}{4} + 8\frac{3}{4}$
$= 22\frac{5}{4}$
$= 23\frac{1}{4}$

6. B: $y = x + 5$, and you were told that $x = -3$. Fill in the missing information for x, then solve.
$y = (-3) + 5$
$y = 2$

7. D: Think of the numbers as they would be on a number line to place them in the correct order.

8. C: In this problem, if you do not know how to solve, try filling in the answer choices to see which one checks out. Many math problems may be solved by a guess and check method when you have a selection of answer choices.
$27 - x = -5$
$x = 32$

9. A: Add the numbers with x together, as follows: 5x + 4x = 9x
Add the y numbers, as follows: -2y + y = -y
Put the x and y numbers back into the same equation: 9x – y.

10. B: To solve, line up the like terms, as follows:

$$
\begin{array}{r}
3x^2 + x + 3 \\
+ 8x^2 + 5x + 16 \\
\hline
11x^2 + 6x + 19
\end{array}
$$

11. C: To find perimeter, add the sides.

12. B: 410 ml x 4 containers = 1640 ml
Change to liters: 1640 ÷ 1000 = 1.64
Add the liter that was already in the pot: 1.64 + 1 = 2.64 liters

13. D: Snappy Twisters are the only ones that fall into the criteria listed in the question. The use of the words "no more than" is important to notice.

14. D: Find the common denominator for the two fractions so that you can compare them. You can use the common denominator of 45, as follows:
2/5 = 18/45
4/9 = 20/45
Look at the numerators: 18 and 20. The number halfway between them is 19, so the answer is 19/45

15. A: The fraction of 1/2 is the same as 50%. None of the other fractions are equal to that.

16. C:
$$10\sqrt{6} \neq 6\sqrt{10}.$$
$$36 = 6^2 \neq 6\sqrt{10}$$
$$\sqrt{600} = \sqrt{6 \cdot 100} = 10\sqrt{6} \neq 6\sqrt{10}$$
$$\sqrt{6} \neq 6\sqrt{10}$$
$$10\sqrt{6} \neq 6\sqrt{10}$$

17. C: The expression 2^{-3} is equivalent to $\dfrac{1}{2^3}$, and since $2^3 = 8$, it is equivalent to 1/8.

A. $\dfrac{1}{4} = 2^{-2}$

B. $\dfrac{1}{12} \neq \dfrac{1}{8}$

D. $\dfrac{1}{16} = 2^{-4}$

18. B: The value of the fraction $\dfrac{7}{5}$ can be evaluated by dividing 7 by 5, which yields 1.4. The average of 1.4 and 1.4 is $\dfrac{1.4 + 1.4}{2} = 1.4$.

19. D: The product of x and $\dfrac{1}{x}$ is $\dfrac{1}{x} \times x = \dfrac{x}{x} = 1$. The expression x^{-1} is equivalent to $\dfrac{1}{x}$. Thus, both B and C are correct.

A. $(x-1) \times x = x^2 - x \neq 1$

D. $x^2 \times x = x^3$, which is only equal to 1 if $x = 1$.

20. C: The total distance traveled was $8 + 3.6 = 11.6$ miles. The first 1/5 of a mile is charged at the higher rate. Since $1/5 = 0.2$, the remainder of the trip is 11.4 miles. Thus the fare for the distance traveled is computed as $\$5.50 + 5 \times 11.4 \times \$1.50 = \$91$. To this the charge for waiting time must be added, which is simply 9 x 20¢ = 180¢ = \$1.80. Finally, add the two charges, \$91 + \$1.80 = \$92.80.

21. D: Each term of each expression in parentheses must be multiplied by each term in the other. Thus for D, $(x+3)(3x-5) = 3x^2 + 9x - 5x - 15 = 3x^2 + 4x - 15$

A. $(x-3)(x+5) = x^2 - 3x + 5x - 15 = x^2 + 2x - 15 \neq 3x^2 + 4x - 15$

B. $(x+5)(3+x^2) = 3x + 15 + x^3 + 5x^2 \neq 3x^2 + 4x - 15$

C. $x(3x+4-15) = 3x^2 + 4x - 15x = 3x^2 - 11x \neq 3x^2 + 4x - 15$

22. B: First determine the proportion of students in Grade 5. Since the total number of students is 180, this proportion is $\dfrac{36}{180} = 0.2$, or 20%. Then determine the same proportion of the total prizes, which is 20% of twenty, or $0.2 \times 20 = 4$.

A. $5 \neq 0.2 \times 20$

C. $7 \neq 0.2 \times 20$

D. $3 \neq 0.2 \times 20$

23. B: A prime number is a natural, positive, non-zero number which can be factored only by itself and by 1. This is the case for 11.

A. 15 = 5 x 3, and thus is not a prime number.

C. 33 = 11 x 3, and thus is not a prime number.

D. 4 = 2 x 2, and thus is not a prime number.

24. A: From the starting expression, compute:

$3(\dfrac{6x-3}{3}) - 3(9x+9) = 3(2x-1) - 27x - 27 = 6x - 3 - 27x - 27 = -21x - 30 = -3(7x+10)$

B. $-3x + 6 \neq 3(\dfrac{6x-3}{3}) - 3(9x+9)$

C. $(x+3)(x-3) = x^2 + 3x - 3x - 9 = x^2 - 9 \neq 3(\dfrac{6x-3}{3}) - 3(9x+9)$

D. $3x^2 - 9 \neq 3(\dfrac{6x-3}{3}) - 3(9x+9)$

25. B: Compute as follows: $(3 - 2 \times 2)^2 = (3-4)^2 = (-1)^2 = 1$.

26. A: Each glass of lemonade costs 10¢, or $0.10, so that g glasses will cost $g \times \$0.10$. To this, add Bob's fixed cost of $45, giving the expression in A.

27. C: Evaluate as follows:
$$(3x^{-2})^3 = 3^3 \times (x^{-2})^3 = 27 \times (\frac{1}{x^2})^3 = 27 \times \frac{1}{x^8} = 27x^{-8}$$

28. D: Let P_A = the price of truck A and P_B that of truck B. Similarly let M_A and M_B represent the gas mileage obtained by each truck. The total cost of driving a truck n miles is
$$C = P + n \times \frac{\$4}{M}$$
To determine the break-even mileage, set the two cost equations equal to one another and solve for n:
$$P_A + n \times \frac{\$4}{M_A} = P_B + n \times \frac{\$4}{M_B}$$
$$n \times (\frac{\$4}{M_A} - \frac{\$4}{M_B}) = P_B - P_A$$
$$n = \frac{P_B - P_A}{(\frac{\$4}{M_A} - \frac{\$4}{M_B})}$$
Plugging in the given values:
$$n = \frac{650 - 450}{(\frac{4}{25} - \frac{4}{35})} = \frac{200}{(0.16 - 0.11)} = 740 \text{ miles.}$$

29. C: Rearranging the equation gives
$3(x+4) = 15(x-5)$, which is equivalent to
$15x - 3x = 12 + 75$, or
$12x = 87$, and solving for x,
$x = \frac{87}{12} = \frac{29}{4}$.

30. D: The product $(a)(a)(a)(a)(a)$ is defined as a to the fifth power.

31. D: There are two ways to solve this problem: either convert meters to centimeters and then use the conversion factor in the table to convert centimeters to inches, or else use the table to convert meters to yards, and then convert to inches.
In the first instance, recall that there are 100 centimeters in a meter (*centi* means "hundredth").
Therefore $19m = 1900cm = (\frac{1900}{2.54}) = 748$ inches.
In the second instance, recall that there are 36 inches in a yard, therefore
$19m = 19 \times 1.094 = 20.786 yd = 20.786 \times 36 = 748$ inches.

Proportions are commonly used for conversions. After converting meters to centimeters set up proportions to solve for an unknown variable, x.

$$\frac{1990 \text{ cm}}{x \text{ in}} = \frac{2.54 \text{ cm}}{1 \text{ in.}}$$ Cross multiply.

$1900 = 2.54x$ Divide each side by 2.54 to solve for x. $x = 748$

32. A: The mode is the number that appears most often in a set of data. If no item appears most often, then the data set has no mode. In this case, Kyle achieved one hit a total of three times, two hits twice, three hits once, and four hits once. One hit occurred the most times, therefore the mode of the data set is 1.

33. B: The mean, or average, is the sum of the numbers in a data set divided by the total number of items. This data set contains seven items, one for each day of the week. The total number of hits that Kyle had during the week is the sum of the numbers in the right-hand column, or 14. This gives: $Mean = \dfrac{14}{7} = 2$.

34. D: To multiply two binomials, use the FOIL method. FOIL stands for First, Outside, Inside, Last. When multiplying each pair of terms, remember to multiply the coefficients, then add the exponents of each separate variable. So the product of the First terms is $2a^2b \cdot 3a^3b = 6a^5b^2$. The product of the Outside terms is $2a^2b \cdot 4c = 8a^2bc$. The product of the Inside terms is $-3c^3 \cdot 3a^3b = -9a^3bc^3$. The product of the Last terms is $-3c^3 \cdot 4c = -12c^4$. The final answer is simply the sum of these four products.

35. D:
$-4x + 8 \geq 48$
To solve for x, first isolate the variable.
$-4x \geq 48 - 8$
$-4x \geq 40$
Then, divide both sides by -4 to solve for x.
When an inequality is divided by a negative number, the sign must change directions.
$-4x/-4 \geq 40/-4$
$x \leq -10$

36. D: Integers include all positive and negative whole numbers and the number zero. The product of three integers must be an integer, so you can eliminate any answer choice that is not a whole number: choices (A) and (C). The product of two even integers is even. The product of even and odd integers is even. The only even choice is 24.

37. C: Divide the mg the child should receive by the number of mg in 0.8 ml to determine how many 0.8 ml doses the child should receive: $240 \div 80 = 3$. Multiply the number of doses by 0.8 to determine how many ml the child should receive: $3 \times 0.8 = 2.4$ ml

38. B: The chart indicates that each x value must be tripled to equal the corresponding y value, so $y = 3x$. One way you can determine this is by plugging corresponding pairs of x and y into the answer choices.

39. D: Use the following proportion: $\dfrac{1\ \text{in.}}{45\ \text{miles}} = \dfrac{3.2\ \text{inches}}{x\ \text{miles}}$

Cross multiply: $x = (45)(3.2) = 144$

40. D: Each hour has 60 minutes, and each of those minutes has 60 seconds. Expressed in seconds, then, an hour is 60 x 60 = 3600. 400/3600 = 1/9.

Secret Key #1 - Time is Your Greatest Enemy

Pace Yourself

Wear a watch. At the beginning of the test, check the time (or start a chronometer on your watch to count the minutes), and check the time after every few questions to make sure you are "on schedule."

If you are forced to speed up, do it efficiently. Usually one or more answer choices can be eliminated without too much difficulty. Above all, don't panic. Don't speed up and just begin guessing at random choices. By pacing yourself, and continually monitoring your progress against your watch, you will always know exactly how far ahead or behind you are with your available time. If you find that you are one minute behind on the test, don't skip one question without spending any time on it, just to catch back up. Take 15 fewer seconds on the next four questions, and after four questions you'll have caught back up. Once you catch back up, you can continue working each problem at your normal pace.

Furthermore, don't dwell on the problems that you were rushed on. If a problem was taking up too much time and you made a hurried guess, it must be difficult. The difficult questions are the ones you are most likely to miss anyway, so it isn't a big loss. It is better to end with more time than you need than to run out of time.

Lastly, sometimes it is beneficial to slow down if you are constantly getting ahead of time. You are always more likely to catch a careless mistake by working more slowly than quickly, and among very high-scoring test takers (those who are likely to have lots of time left over), careless errors affect the score more than mastery of material.

Secret Key #2 - Guessing is not Guesswork

You probably know that guessing is a good idea. Unlike other standardized tests, there is no penalty for getting a wrong answer. Even if you have no idea about a question, you still have a 20-25% chance of getting it right.

Most test takers do not understand the impact that proper guessing can have on their score. Unless you score extremely high, guessing will significantly contribute to your final score.

Monkeys Take the Test

What most test takers don't realize is that to insure that 20-25% chance, you have to guess randomly. If you put 20 monkeys in a room to take this test, assuming they answered once per question and behaved themselves, on average they would get 20-25% of the questions correct. Put 20 test takers in the room, and the average will be much lower among guessed questions. Why?

1. The test writers intentionally write deceptive answer choices that "look" right. A test taker has no idea about a question, so he picks the "best looking" answer, which is often wrong. The monkey has no idea what looks good and what doesn't, so it will consistently be right about 20-25% of the time.
2. Test takers will eliminate answer choices from the guessing pool based on a hunch or intuition. Simple but correct answers often get excluded, leaving a 0% chance of being correct. The monkey has no clue, and often gets lucky with the best choice.

This is why the process of elimination endorsed by most test courses is flawed and detrimental to your performance. Test takers don't guess; they make an ignorant stab in the dark that is usually worse than random.

$5 Challenge

Let me introduce one of the most valuable ideas of this course—the $5 challenge:

You only mark your "best guess" if you are willing to bet $5 on it.
You only eliminate choices from guessing if you are willing to bet $5 on it.

Why $5? Five dollars is an amount of money that is small yet not insignificant, and can really add up fast (20 questions could cost you $100). Likewise, each answer choice on one question of the test will have a small impact on your overall score, but it can really add up to a lot of points in the end.

The process of elimination IS valuable. The following shows your chance of guessing it right:

If you eliminate wrong answer choices until only this many remain:	Chance of getting it correct:
1	100%
2	50%
3	33%

However, if you accidentally eliminate the right answer or go on a hunch for an incorrect answer, your chances drop dramatically—to 0%. By guessing among all the answer choices, you are GUARANTEED to have a shot at the right answer.

That's why the $5 test is so valuable. If you give up the advantage and safety of a pure guess, it had better be worth the risk.

What we still haven't covered is how to be sure that whatever guess you make is truly random. Here's the easiest way:

Always pick the first answer choice among those remaining.

Such a technique means that you have decided, **before you see a single test question**, exactly how you are going to guess, and since the order of choices tells you nothing about which one is correct, this guessing technique is perfectly random.

This section is not meant to scare you away from making educated guesses or eliminating choices; you just need to define when a choice is worth eliminating. The $5 test, along with a pre-defined random guessing strategy, is the best way to make sure you reap all of the benefits of guessing.

Secret Key #3 - Practice Smarter, Not Harder

Many test takers delay the test preparation process because they dread the awful amounts of practice time they think necessary to succeed on the test. We have refined an effective method that will take you only a fraction of the time.

There are a number of "obstacles" in the path to success. Among these are answering questions, finishing in time, and mastering test-taking strategies. All must be executed on the day of the test at peak performance, or your score will suffer. The test is a mental marathon that has a large impact on your future.

Just like a marathon runner, it is important to work your way up to the full challenge. So first you just worry about questions, and then time, and finally strategy:

Success Strategy

1. Find a good source for practice tests.
2. If you are willing to make a larger time investment, consider using more than one study guide. Often the different approaches of multiple authors will help you "get" difficult concepts.
3. Take a practice test with no time constraints, with all study helps, "open book." Take your time with questions and focus on applying strategies.
4. Take a practice test with time constraints, with all guides, "open book."
5. Take a final practice test without open material and with time limits.

If you have time to take more practice tests, just repeat step 5. By gradually exposing yourself to the full rigors of the test environment, you will condition your mind to the stress of test day and maximize your success.

Secret Key #4 - Prepare, Don't Procrastinate

Let me state an obvious fact: if you take the test three times, you will probably get three different scores. This is due to the way you feel on test day, the level of preparedness you have, and the version of the test you see. Despite the test writers' claims to the contrary, some versions of the test WILL be easier for you than others.

Since your future depends so much on your score, you should maximize your chances of success. In order to maximize the likelihood of success, you've got to prepare in advance. This means taking practice tests and spending time learning the information and test taking strategies you will need to succeed.

Never go take the actual test as a "practice" test, expecting that you can just take it again if you need to. Take all the practice tests you can on your own, but when you go to take the official test, be prepared, be focused, and do your best the first time!

Secret Key #5 - Test Yourself

Everyone knows that time is money. There is no need to spend too much of your time or too little of your time preparing for the test. You should only spend as much of your precious time preparing as is necessary for you to get the score you need.

Once you have taken a practice test under real conditions of time constraints, then you will know if you are ready for the test or not.

If you have scored extremely high the first time that you take the practice test, then there is not much point in spending countless hours studying. You are already there.
Benchmark your abilities by retaking practice tests and seeing how much you have improved. Once you consistently score high enough to guarantee success, then you are ready.

If you have scored well below where you need, then knuckle down and begin studying in earnest. Check your improvement regularly through the use of practice tests under real conditions. Above all, don't worry, panic, or give up. The key is perseverance!

Then, when you go to take the test, remain confident and remember how well you did on the practice tests. If you can score high enough on a practice test, then you can do the same on the real thing.

General Strategies

The most important thing you can do is to ignore your fears and jump into the test immediately- do not be overwhelmed by any strange-sounding terms. You have to jump into the test like jumping into a pool- all at once is the easiest way.

Make Predictions

As you read and understand the question, try to guess what the answer will be. Remember that several of the answer choices are wrong, and once you begin reading them, your mind will immediately become cluttered with answer choices designed to throw you off. Your mind is typically the most focused immediately after you have read the question and digested its contents. If you can, try to predict what the correct answer will be. You may be surprised at what you can predict.

Quickly scan the choices and see if your prediction is in the listed answer choices. If it is, then you can be quite confident that you have the right answer. It still won't hurt to check the other answer choices, but most of the time, you've got it!

Answer the Question

It may seem obvious to only pick answer choices that answer the question, but the test writers can create some excellent answer choices that are wrong. Don't pick an answer just because it sounds right, or you believe it to be true. It MUST answer the question. Once you've made your selection, always go back and check it against the question and make sure that you didn't misread the question, and the answer choice does answer the question posed.

Benchmark

After you read the first answer choice, decide if you think it sounds correct or not. If it doesn't, move on to the next answer choice. If it does, mentally mark that answer choice. This doesn't mean that you've definitely selected it as your answer choice, it just means that it's the best you've seen thus far. Go ahead and read the next choice. If the next choice is worse than the one you've already selected, keep going to the next answer choice. If the next choice is better than the choice you've already selected, mentally mark the new answer choice as your best guess.

The first answer choice that you select becomes your standard. Every other answer choice must be benchmarked against that standard. That choice is correct until proven otherwise by another answer choice beating it out. Once you've decided that no other answer choice seems as good, do one final check to ensure that your answer choice answers the question posed.

Valid Information

Don't discount any of the information provided in the question. Every piece of information may be necessary to determine the correct answer. None of the information in the question is there to throw you off (while the answer choices will certainly have information to throw you off). If two seemingly unrelated topics are discussed, don't ignore either. You can be confident there is a relationship, or it wouldn't be included in the question, and you are probably going to have to determine what is that relationship to find the answer.

Avoid "Fact Traps"

Don't get distracted by a choice that is factually true. Your search is for the answer that answers the question. Stay focused and don't fall for an answer that is true but incorrect. Always go back to the question and make sure you're choosing an answer that actually answers the question and is not just a true statement. An answer can be factually correct, but it MUST answer the question asked. Additionally, two answers can both be seemingly correct, so be sure to read all of the answer choices, and make sure that you get the one that BEST answers the question.

Milk the Question

Some of the questions may throw you completely off. They might deal with a subject you have not been exposed to, or one that you haven't reviewed in years. While your lack of knowledge about the subject will be a hindrance, the question itself can give you many clues that will help you find the correct answer. Read the question carefully and look for clues. Watch particularly for adjectives and nouns describing difficult terms or words that you don't recognize. Regardless of if you completely understand a word or not, replacing it with a synonym either provided or one you more familiar with may help you to understand what the questions are asking. Rather than wracking your mind about specific detailed information concerning a difficult term or word, try to use mental substitutes that are easier to understand.

The Trap of Familiarity

Don't just choose a word because you recognize it. On difficult questions, you may not recognize a number of words in the answer choices. The test writers don't put "make-believe" words on the test; so don't think that just because you only recognize all the words in one answer choice means that answer choice must be correct. If you only recognize words in one answer choice, then focus on that one. Is it correct? Try your best to determine if it is correct. If it is, that is great, but if it doesn't, eliminate it. Each word and answer choice you eliminate increases your chances of getting the question correct, even if you then have to guess among the unfamiliar choices.

Eliminate Answers

Eliminate choices as soon as you realize they are wrong. But be careful! Make sure you consider all of the possible answer choices. Just because one appears right, doesn't mean that the next one won't be even better! The test writers will usually put more than one good answer choice for every question, so read all of them. Don't worry if you are stuck between two that seem right. By getting down to just two remaining possible choices, your odds are now 50/50. Rather than wasting too much time, play the odds. You are guessing, but guessing wisely, because you've been able to knock out some of the answer choices that you know are wrong. If you are eliminating choices and realize that the last answer choice you are left with is also obviously wrong, don't panic. Start over and consider each choice again. There may easily be something that you missed the first time and will realize on the second pass.

Tough Questions

If you are stumped on a problem or it appears too hard or too difficult, don't waste time. Move on! Remember though, if you can quickly check for obviously incorrect answer choices, your chances of guessing correctly are greatly improved. Before you completely give up, at least try to knock out a couple of possible answers. Eliminate what you can and then guess at the remaining answer choices before moving on.

Brainstorm

If you get stuck on a difficult question, spend a few seconds quickly brainstorming. Run through the complete list of possible answer choices. Look at each choice and ask yourself, "Could this answer the question satisfactorily?" Go through each answer choice and consider it independently of the other. By systematically going through all possibilities, you may find something that you would otherwise overlook. Remember that when you get stuck, it's important to try to keep moving.

Read Carefully

Understand the problem. Read the question and answer choices carefully. Don't miss the question because you misread the terms. You have plenty of time to read each question thoroughly and make sure you understand what is being asked. Yet a happy medium must be attained, so don't waste too much time. You must read carefully, but efficiently.

Face Value

When in doubt, use common sense. Always accept the situation in the problem at face value. Don't read too much into it. These problems will not require you to make huge leaps of logic. The test writers aren't trying to throw you off with a cheap trick. If you have to go beyond creativity and make a leap of logic in order to have an answer choice answer the question, then you should look at the other answer choices. Don't overcomplicate the problem by creating theoretical relationships or explanations that will warp time or space. These are normal problems rooted in reality. It's just that the applicable relationship or explanation may not be readily apparent and you have to figure things out. Use your common sense to interpret anything that isn't clear.

Prefixes

If you're having trouble with a word in the question or answer choices, try dissecting it. Take advantage of every clue that the word might include. Prefixes and suffixes can be a huge help. Usually they allow you to determine a basic meaning. Pre- means before, post- means after, pro - is positive, de- is negative. From these prefixes and suffixes, you can get an idea of the general meaning of the word and try to put it into context. Beware though of any traps. Just because con is the opposite of pro, doesn't necessarily mean congress is the opposite of progress!

Hedge Phrases

Watch out for critical "hedge" phrases, such as likely, may, can, will often, sometimes, often, almost, mostly, usually, generally, rarely, sometimes. Question writers insert these hedge phrases to cover every possibility. Often an answer choice will be wrong simply because it leaves no room for exception. Avoid answer choices that have definitive words like "exactly," and "always".

Switchback Words

Stay alert for "switchbacks". These are the words and phrases frequently used to alert you to shifts in thought. The most common switchback word is "but". Others include although, however, nevertheless, on the other hand, even though, while, in spite of, despite, regardless of.

New Information

Correct answer choices will rarely have completely new information included. Answer choices typically are straightforward reflections of the material asked about and will directly relate to the question. If a new piece of information is included in an answer choice that doesn't even seem to relate to the topic being asked about, then that answer choice is likely incorrect. All of the information needed to answer the question is usually provided for you, and so you should not have to make guesses that are unsupported or choose answer choices that require unknown information that cannot be reasoned on its own.

Time Management

On technical questions, don't get lost on the technical terms. Don't spend too much time on any one question. If you don't know what a term means, then since you don't have a dictionary, odds are you aren't going to get much further. You should immediately recognize terms as whether or not you know them. If you don't, work with the other clues that you have, the other answer choices and terms provided, but don't waste too much time trying to figure out a difficult term.

Contextual Clues

Look for contextual clues. An answer can be right but not correct. The contextual clues will help you find the answer that is most right and is correct. Understand the context in which a phrase or statement is made. This will help you make important distinctions.

Don't Panic

Panicking will not answer any questions for you. Therefore, it isn't helpful. When you first see the question, if your mind goes blank, take a deep breath. Force yourself to mechanically go through the steps of solving the problem and using the strategies you've learned.

Pace Yourself

Don't get clock fever. It's easy to be overwhelmed when you're looking at a page full of questions, your mind is full of random thoughts and feeling confused, and the clock is ticking down faster than you would like. Calm down and maintain the pace that you have set for yourself. As long as you are on track by monitoring your pace, you are guaranteed to have enough time for yourself. When you get to the last few minutes of the test, it may seem like you won't have enough time left, but if you only have as many questions as you should have left at that point, then you're right on track!

Answer Selection

The best way to pick an answer choice is to eliminate all of those that are wrong, until only one is left and confirm that is the correct answer. Sometimes though, an answer choice may immediately look right. Be careful! Take a second to make sure that the other choices are not equally obvious. Don't make a hasty mistake. There are only two times that you should stop before checking other answers. First is when you are positive that the answer choice you have selected is correct. Second is when time is almost out and you have to make a quick guess!

Check Your Work

Since you will probably not know every term listed and the answer to every question, it is important that you get credit for the ones that you do know. Don't miss any questions through careless mistakes. If at all possible, try to take a second to look back over your answer selection and make sure you've selected the correct answer choice and haven't made a costly careless mistake (such as marking an answer choice that you didn't mean to mark). This quick double check should more than pay for itself in caught mistakes for the time it costs.

Beware of Directly Quoted Answers

Sometimes an answer choice will repeat word for word a portion of the question or reference section. However, beware of such exact duplication – it may be a trap! More than likely, the correct choice will paraphrase or summarize a point, rather than being exactly the same wording.

Slang

Scientific sounding answers are better than slang ones. An answer choice that begins "To compare the outcomes…" is much more likely to be correct than one that begins "Because some people insisted…"

Extreme Statements

Avoid wild answers that throw out highly controversial ideas that are proclaimed as established fact. An answer choice that states the "process should used in certain situations, if…" is much more likely to be correct than one that states the "process should be discontinued completely." The first is a calm rational statement and doesn't even make a definitive, uncompromising stance, using a hedge word "if" to provide wiggle room, whereas the second choice is a radical idea and far more extreme.

Answer Choice Families

When you have two or more answer choices that are direct opposites or parallels, one of them is usually the correct answer. For instance, if one answer choice states "x increases" and another answer choice states "x decreases" or "y increases," then those two or three answer choices are very similar in construction and fall into the same family of answer choices. A family of answer choices is when two or three answer choices are very similar in construction, and yet often have a directly opposite meaning. Usually the correct answer choice will be in that family of answer choices. The "odd man out" or answer choice that doesn't seem to fit the parallel construction of the other answer choices is more likely to be incorrect.

- 411 -

Copyright © Mometrix Media. You have been licensed one copy of this document for personal use only. Any other reproduction or redistribution is strictly prohibited. All rights reserved.

Additional Bonus Material

Due to our efforts to try to keep this book to a manageable length, we've created a link that will give you access to all of your additional bonus material.

Please visit http://www.mometrix.com/bonus948/oat to access the information.